Energy, Governance and Sustainability

THE IUCN ACADEMY OF ENVIRONMENTAL LAW SERIES

Series Editors: Kurt Deketelaere, *University of Leuven, Leuven, Belgium* and Zen Makuch, *Imperial College, London, UK*

As environmental law increases in importance as an area of legal research, this series brings together some of the most current research carried out by the IUCN Academy of Environmental Law, a global network of environmental law scholars. Each volume in the series addresses an important issue in the field and presents original research analysis and assessment, along with a much-needed synthesis of the state of environmental law. Directions as to the positive role that environmental law can play at a global level are also emphasized. This series provides essential reading for scholars throughout the world with an interest in cutting edge environment-related issues, and will no doubt play an important role in shaping future debate.

Titles in this series include:

Environmental Governance and Sustainability
Edited by Paul Martin, Li Zhiping, Qin Tianbao, Anel Du Plessis, Yves Le Bouthillier and Angela Williams

Poverty Alleviation and Environmental Law
Edited by Yves Le Bouthillier, Miriam Alfie Cohen, Jose Juan Gonzalez Marquez, Albert Mumma and Susan Smith

Local Climate Change Law
Environmental Regulation in Cities and Other Localities
Edited by Benjamin J. Richardson

Biodiversity and Climate Change
Linkages at International, National and Local Levels
Edited by Frank Maes, An Cliquet, Willemien du Plessis and Heather McLeod-Kilmurray

Global Environmental Law at a Crossroads
Edited by Robert V. Percival, Jolene Lin and William Piermattei

Water and the Law
Towards Sustainability
Edited by Michael Kidd, Loretta Feris, Tumai Murombo and Alejandro Iza

The Search for Environmental Justice
Edited by Paul Martin, Sadeq Z. Bigdeli, Trevor Daya-Winterbottom, Willemien du Plessis and Amanda Kennedy

Implementing Environmental Law
Edited by Paul Martin and Amanda Kennedy

Energy, Governance and Sustainability
Edited by Jordi Jaria i Manzano, Nathalie Chalifour and Louis J. Kotzé

Energy, Governance and Sustainability

Edited by

Jordi Jaria i Manzano

Serra Hunter Fellow, Universitat Rovira i Virgili, Catalonia, Spain

Nathalie Chalifour

Associate Professor, University of Ottawa, Canada

Louis J. Kotzé

Research Professor, North-West University, South Africa

THE IUCN ACADEMY OF ENVIRONMENTAL LAW SERIES

Edward Elgar
PUBLISHING

Cheltenham, UK • Northampton, MA, USA

Published by
Edward Elgar Publishing Limited
The Lypiatts
15 Lansdown Road
Cheltenham
Glos GL50 2JA
UK

Edward Elgar Publishing, Inc.
William Pratt House
9 Dewey Court
Northampton
Massachusetts 01060
USA

A catalogue record for this book
is available from the British Library

Library of Congress Control Number: 2015959658

This book is available electronically in the **Elgar**online
Law subject collection
DOI 10.4337/9781785368462

MIX
Paper from
responsible sources
FSC® C013056
FSC
www.fsc.org

ISBN 978 1 78536 811 0 (cased)
ISBN 978 1 78536 846 2 (eBook)

Typeset by Columns Design XML Ltd, Reading
Printed and bound in Great Britain by TJ International Ltd, Padstow

Contents

Contributors

EDITORS

Nathalie Chalifour is an Associate Professor at the Faculty of Law, University of Ottawa and Co-Director of the Centre for Environmental Law and Global Sustainability. Her main area of research is environmental law and policy, with a focus on the intersection between the environment, the economy and social justice. Her publications address a variety of topics, including climate change, carbon taxation, environmental justice, the green economy, brownfields, environmental assessment, sustainable food policy and environmental human rights. Prior to joining the Law Faculty, Prof. Chalifour was senior advisor to the President of the National Round Table on the Environment and the Economy; Policy Advisor to the World Wildlife Fund; founded TRAFFIC Canada; and taught at the University of Nairobi, Kenya. She obtained her Doctorate of Law at Stanford University, and holds a Master in Juridical Sciences which she obtained as a Stanford Fellow and Fulbright Scholar.

Jordi Jaria i Manzano, BA and LLB (Universitat de Barcelona), Ph.D, European Doctorate Mention (Universitat Rovira i Virgili), is Serra Húnter Fellow of Constitutional and Environmental Law at Universitat Rovira i Virgili (URV), in Tarragona (Catalonia). He is also Researcher at the Tarragona Centre for Environmental Law Studies, CEDAT, in the same University. Professor Jaria i Manzano is Executive Editor of the *Revista Catalana de Dret Ambiental* [*Catalan Journal of Environmental Law*] and was Director of the Masters Programme on Environmental Law in the URV. His research is focused on environmental justice, global constitutionalism, comparative law, federalism and cultural diversity. He has written a number of research works (books, book chapters and articles) in these fields, mostly in Spanish, such as *La cuestión ambiental y la transformación de lo público* (Tirant lo Blanch, 2011), and has taken part in different research projects, such as EJOLT (Environmental Justice Organizations, Liabilities and Trade), financed by the European Commission (2011–15).

Louis J. Kotzé, B Com., LLB, LLM, LLD, is Research Professor of Law at the Faculty of Law of the North-West University (Potchefstroom Campus), South Africa; and Visiting Professor of Environmental Law at the University of Lincoln, United Kingdom. His recent books include *Global Environmental Governance: Law and Regulation for the 21st Century* (Edward Elgar, 2012); *Research Handbook on Human Rights and the Environment* (with Anna Grear (eds), Edward Elgar, 2015); and *Transboundary Governance of Biodiversity* (with Thilo Marauhn (eds), Brill Nijhoff, 2014). His research focuses on environmental constitutionalism, the Anthropocene, human rights and the environment, and global environmental governance. He is Co-editor of the *Journal of Human Rights and the Environment* (Edward Elgar) and Deputy-Director of the Global Network for Human Rights and the Environment.

CONTRIBUTORS

Klaus Bosselmann is Professor of Law at the University of Auckland where he teaches global environmental law, environmental constitutionalism and legal theory. He previously taught at the Free University in Berlin and was a co-founder of Germany's first institute for environmental law in 1987. Since 1998 he is the founding director of the New Zealand Centre for Environmental Law. He has served as a consultant to the OECD, the EU and the governments of Germany and New Zealand, and has been a visiting professor at leading universities in Europe, Canada, United States, Brazil and Australia. Prof. Bosselmann is chair of the IUCN World Commission on Environmental Law Ethics Specialist Group, co-chair of the Global Ecological Integrity Group and executive member of other professional bodies. He has authored 14 books, most recently *Earth Governance* (2015), edited or co-edited a further 12 books and has written over 120 book chapters and articles. For his work he has received several awards, including the inaugural Senior Scholarship Prize of the IUCN Academy of Environmental Law (2009).

John Bowie is an Energy and Climate Law Advisor at the Pace Energy and Climate Center at Pace Law School. He joined the Energy and Climate Center in September 2014 after graduating *cum laude* from Pace Law School with his JD, earning the distinction of the Bohn Vergari Public Service Award for the Best Environmental Law Student. He has a BS in Biochemistry from Hobart and William Smith Colleges, and an MA in Depth Psychology from Pacifica Graduate Institute. He was a research fellow at the University of Malaysia Sarawak, examining integrated river basin management strategies in Malaysian Borneo. Upon returning to the United States, John Bowie worked with the environmental non-profit Wild Equity Institute in San Francisco, as part of a campaign to preserve endangered species and critical coastal habitat, and petitioned for environmentally and fiscally responsible amendments to the San Francisco budget. He has also worked as a LEED AP sustainable design coordinator at an architecture firm in Toronto, Ontario.

Erin Daly is Professor of Law at Widener Law Delaware. She served as Interim Dean and Vice Dean of the Law School in 2013–15. She received a BA from Wesleyan University, and her JD from the University of Michigan. Daly's fields include constitutional, First Amendment, administrative, human rights, comparative constitutional and environmental law. On sabbatical during 2015–16, Prof. Daly is serving as the Vice President for Institutional Development at the Université de la Fondation Aristide, in Port-au-Prince, Haiti. Prof. Daly has written extensively on comparative constitutional law and transitional justice issues throughout the world. Most recently, she and Prof. James R. May published *Global Environmental Constitutionalism* (Cambridge, 2015). Her previous books include *Dignity Rights: Courts, Constitutions and the Worth of the Human Person* (U. Penn, 2012), and *Reconciliation in Divided Societies* (with Jeremy Sarkin, U. Penn, 2006). Her forthcoming works include *Environmental Constitutionalism in Context* (with James R. May, Edward Elgar, 2016).

Trevor Daya-Winterbottom combines research and teaching at the Faculty of Law, University of Waikato, with legal consultancy and practice as a Barrister sole. He holds a BA (Hons) in Law from the Liverpool John Moores University, where highlights of the degree course included studying public international law with Prof. Malcolm Shaw QC and Prof. Patrick Thornberry CMG, and studying jurisprudence with the renowned Jewish legal scholar, Prof. Bernard Jackson. He also holds a Diplôme in human rights law from the Institut International des Droits de l'Homme (Strasbourg), and was a member of the very first cohort to graduate with an MA in Environmental Law from De Montfort University, Leicester. He is a Fellow of the Royal Society of Arts; a Fellow of the Royal Geographic Society; a Member of the Royal Society of New Zealand; a Legal Associate of the Royal Town Planning Institute; and a Member of the New Zealand Centre for Environmental Law. His teaching, research and consultancy focus on administrative law and aspects of international, comparative and domestic environmental law.

Cristiane Derani is Professor at Federal University of Santa Catarina since 2010. She was a Ph.D student at J.W. Goethe Universität, Frankfurt

a. M. (1991–93), and made a postdoctoral stage at the École des Hautes Études en Sciences Sociales, Paris (1999). Prof. Derani has also been visiting Professor at Pablo de Olavide University, Seville (2001–07), Maison des Sciences de l'Homme (2004) and J.W. Goethe Universität (2005). She was also invited by the Brazilian government to participate at Conference of Parties (COP) VI and VII of the Biodiversity Convention. Previously to her current occupation, she was Professor of São Paulo University (1997–2004); at Santos Catholic University (2000–10); and at State of Amazonas University (2004–10). Prof. Derani is a Recognized Researcher for the Brazilian Research Council (Cnpq); and Director of research group Advanced Studies on Environment and Economics in International Law.

Anaïs Guerry is a Ph.D Candidate at Sciences Po Law School in Paris. She holds a Bachelors degree in Political Science from the Franco-German Campus of Sciences Po Paris (2009) and a Masters degree in Economic Law from the Sciences Po Law School (2012). In 2011, she took part in the six months' International Parliamentary Scholarship run by the German Parliament. There, she had the opportunity to follow the work of a federal representative, member of the Environmental and Nuclear Security Commission (Ausschuss für Umwelt, Naturschutz und Reaktorsicherheit) directly after the collapse of Fukushima. When she returned to France, she decided to write a Masters thesis on the legal challenges of the integration of renewable energies in the electricity sector in France (2012), which was rewarded by the Paris Bar and the University of Paris Dauphine in 2013. In October 2013, she began a Ph.D on the legal governance of energy transition with a comparison between France and Germany under the supervision of Guillaume Tusseau (Professor of Public Law at Sciences Po Law School) and Gilles J. Martin (Emeritus Professor of Private Law at the University of Nice Sophia-Antipolis). She gives lectures in constitutional law, European law and social corporate responsibility at Sciences Po. Her research is supported by the French Agency for Energy Management (ADEME), the Institut for Sustainable Development and International Relations (IDDRI), and by Energycities, a European association of local authorities supporting a locally-led energy transition.

Elodie Le Gal is a French-Australian academic lawyer and postdoctoral research fellow who is researching various legal and institutional aspects of natural resource management issues at the Australian Centre for Agriculture and Law (University of New England, New South Wales, Australia). She has been involved in various natural resource management (NRM) projects focusing on different theoretical and practical aspects of environmental sustainability. These include: conservation finance mechanisms; the use of e-technology professional development programmes for farming and rural communities; an international aid training programme for addressing the food crisis in Africa; and research projects for improving NRM governance. She obtained her Ph.D at the University of New England in 2013 and her Master of Laws (Diplôme d'Etudes Approfondies) in Private International Law/International Business Law from the Pantheon-Assas Faculty of Law, Paris, in 1998. One of her research interests is to understand the nature and the extent of the economic, political and social risks to which communities around the world are exposed to further propose new methods and approaches for addressing them.

Lye Lin-Heng, LLB (Sing.), LLM (King's College, London, United Kingdom), LLM (Harvard, United States), is Director of the Asia-Pacific Centre for Environmental Law (APCEL), at the Law Faculty, National University of Singapore (NUS). Her areas of teaching and research are in environmental law and property law. She chairs the Programme Management Committee for the University's multi-disciplinary and inter-disciplinary programme, the MSc. (Environmental Management), hosted by the School of Design and Environment. She is former Vice-Dean of the Law School at NUS, and former Vice-Chair of the IUCN Academy of Environmental Law. She was a member of the Academy's Board of Governors, representing Southeast Asia, for many years. She is a Visiting Associate Professor at the Yale School of Forestry and Environmental Studies and has taught at the Law School, University of Sydney. She was Honorary Legal Advisor to the Nature Society in Singapore for many years. She is a member of the Ministry of Environment and Water Resources Committee on Clean Drinking Water Standards for Singapore. She is also a member of the Strata Titles Board, and a former Board Member of the Housing and Development Board in Singapore.

Melissa Low is currently a Research Associate at the Energy Studies Institute at the National University of Singapore, which she joined in September 2010. She holds an MSc. in Environmental Management (MEM), a BSoc.Sci. in Geography (with Honours), and a minor in Urban Studies, from the National University of Singapore. For her Masters thesis in the MEM programme, entitled *Past and Contemporary Proposals on Equity and Differentiation in Shaping the 2015 Climate Agreement*, Melissa was awarded the Shell Best Dissertation Award in 2013. She is currently working towards an LLM in Climate Change Law and Policy at the University of Strathclyde (distance learning). Melissa Low has participated in the United Nations Framework Convention on Climate

Change (UNFCCC) Conference of Parties (COP) talks since December 2009. Her current research areas are the 2015 climate change agreement and the analysis of greenhouse gas emissions and mitigation potential of different countries.

James R. May is a Distinguished Professor of Law and Director of the Global Environmental and Natural Resources Law Institute at Delaware Law School of Widener University, where he also serves as Chief Sustainability Officer and as an Adjunct Professor of Graduate Engineering, and founded and co-chairs a programme on marine policy. May's fields include constitutional, First Amendment, administrative, civil procedure, environmental, international environmental and global environmental constitutionalism law, and engineering. May is a former federal civil litigator, and mechanical engineer. Prof. May is the author of five books and more than 80 articles and book chapters. His recent books include *Global Environmental Constitutionalism* (with Erin Daly, Cambridge, 2015) and *Principles of Constitutional Environmental Law* (American Bar Association, 2011). Forthcoming books include *Environmental Constitutionalism in Context* (with Erin Daly, Edward Elgar, 2016), and *Shale Gas and Sustainability* (with John Dernbach (eds), Edward Elgar, 2016). May is a Member of Faculty to the National Judicial College; a Fellow of the American College of Environmental Lawyers; and a committee member of the International Union for the Conservation of Nature's Awards and Assessment Committee. He is also licensed to practice law before the US Supreme Court and numerous federal circuit and district courts in the United States, and in the Commonwealth of Pennsylvania.

Eloamaka Carol Okonkwo is a Nigerian-born legal practitioner. She earned her first degree (LLB) from the University of Benin, in Nigeria, and barrister-at-law (BL) from the Nigerian Law School, Abuja. She worked for a few years as a solicitor and advocate of the Supreme Court of Nigeria in a wide range of professional capacities in both private and public sectors before she proceeded to the United Kingdom in 2009 to pursue Masters of Law (LLM) at the University of Strathclyde, Glasgow. She is currently a researcher at the Strathclyde Centre for Environmental Law and Governance, University of Strathclyde, Glasgow. Her recent publications include contributions to the *Journal of Sustainable Law and Development*, of the Institute for Oil, Gas, Environment, Energy and Sustainable Development at Afe Babalola University, Nigeria, and to the *Journal of Sustainable Development in Africa*, of the Clarion University of Pennsylvania.

Richard L. Ottinger is Professor and Dean Emeritus of Pace Law School, where he has been on the faculty since 1984 and was Dean 1994–99. He established at Pace the first Energy and Climate Change Center, a leading national and international clean energy research centre. He has published and authored or co-authored a dozen books and more than 100 articles on sustainable energy and climate change. A 16-year Member of Congress, he chaired the Energy Conservation and Power Subcommittee of the House Energy and Commerce Committee, where he pioneered in establishing the country's energy efficiency and renewable energy laws. He was a founder, former Board Chair, and now Chair Emeritus of the Energy and Environmental Study Institute (EESI) in Washington, a leading advocate for sustainable energy before Congress. He now devotes himself to addressing international climate change issues, assisting developing countries adopt sustainable energy programmes. Much of this work is carried out in his capacity as Chair of the Energy Law and Climate Change Specialty Group of the IUCN World Commission on Environmental Law. He is a graduate of Harvard Law School and Cornell University.

Chiara Pappalardo is a Visiting Scholar in International and Comparative Environmental Law at American University Washington College of Law and an attorney qualified in Italy. She holds a Master of Laws degree in Energy and Environmental Law from the George Washington University Law School, where she received recognition for her outstanding *pro bono* service on the Deepwater Horizon Oil Spill in 2011. Her essay on *A Vision for the Decade Sustainable Energy for All (2014–2024)* was selected among the top finalists of the Global Energy Essay Contest in 2013. She is a practitioner member of the Legal Aspects of Sustainable Energy for All Community of Practice (SE4All-CoP), a leading forum of researchers, practitioners and policy-makers created to support the United Nation's broader SE4All initiative and which is part of the Global Forum on Law, Justice and Development's Thematic Working Group on Environmental and Natural Resources Law. Her current research focuses on energy and environmental governance, sustainable energy and new regulatory models for distributed energy and water supplies.

Teresa Parejo-Navajas, Ph.D, LLM on EU Law, is Associate Professor of Administrative Law at Carlos III University (Madrid, Spain) and member of the Pascual Madoz Institute of Spatial Planning, Urbanism and Environment at that same University. She has published two books, one of which received an award in 2004, as well as numerous articles on the environmental and spatial planning fields in Spanish and international journals. Previous to her collaboration with the Sabin Center (Columbia

University), she has been Visiting Scholar in various European and US Universities, such as the Università di Bologna (Italy), Oxford University (United Kingdom) and Fordham University, New York (United States). She received a research award in 2012 for her curricular merits.

Manuel Peter Samonte Solis decided to pursue his Ph.D in 2012, after almost two decades as a lawyer in the Philippines and working as a legal and policy advisor to multilateral financing and development institutions such as the World Bank and United Nations Development Programme. His Ph.D thesis examines the intersection of international human rights, energy, climate and environmental law, particularly the legal significance of adopting a human rights-based approach to provide universal access to modern energy services. While undertaking his Ph.D, he was a Teaching Fellow at the Adelaide Law School from 2013 to 2014. He also assumed various teaching roles at Carnegie Mellon University and the University of South Australia. He received a number of awards for his research, including the Dean's Commendation for Doctoral Thesis Excellence in 2015, the South Australia Governor's International Student Postgraduate Academic Excellence Award in 2014, and the International Union for the Conservation of Nature (IUCN) Academy of Environmental Law Best Graduate Student Paper Award in 2014. Appointed as Lecturer at the Adelaide Law School in 2015, he teaches in property law, foundations of law and human rights law.

Melissa K. Scanlan is the Associate Dean of the Environmental Law Program and Director of the Environmental Law Center at Vermont Law School (VLS). Prior to joining VLS, she was the University of Wisconsin Law School's Water Law and Policy Scholar, where she led a pilot project on interdisciplinary water research and teaching. She was also a lead consultant involved in launching the Center for Water Policy at the University of Wisconsin-Milwaukee's School of Freshwater Sciences 2011. Over a decade earlier, she received a competitive Equal Justice Works Fellowship (formerly NAPIL) and an Echoing Green Fellowship to found and direct Midwest Environmental Advocates, Wisconsin's first non-profit environmental law centre. Selected as a Wisconsin Super Lawyers' Rising Star in 2006, 2007 and 2008, Prof. Scanlan has represented clients in high impact lawsuits and shaped public policy in areas ranging from the Great Lakes Compact and water supply issues to enforcement and implementation of the Clean Water Act. Melissa Scanlan earned a law degree and Master of Science in Environmental Science, Policy and Management from the University of California-Berkeley. Her scholarly articles have focused on the public trust doctrine, the Great

Lakes Compact, adaptive management and empirical research about water management.

Jessica Wentz is Associate Director and Postdoctoral Fellow at Sabin Center for Climate Change Law, Columbia Law School. She joined Columbia Law School's Sabin Center for Climate Change Law in September 2014 as an Associate Director and Postdoctoral Fellow. Her work at the Sabin Center spans a variety of topics related to climate change mitigation and adaptation, sustainable development and environmental justice. She currently conducts research on US regulation of greenhouse gas emissions under the Clean Air Act; legal requirements for disclosing climate-related considerations during environmental assessments; and international strategies for addressing climate-induced displacement and migration. Prior to joining the Center, Jessica Wentz was a Visiting Associate Professor and Environmental Program Fellow at the George Washington University Law School. She is a 2012 graduate of Columbia Law School, where she was awarded the Alfred A. Forsyth Prize for 'dedication to the advancement of environmental law'. She also has a BA in International Development from the University of California, Los Angeles.

Abbreviations

BTU	British Thermal Unit
EDP	environmentally displaced person
EEO	Energy Efficiency Obligation
EPC	Energy Performance Certificate
ESA	Energy Service Agreement
ESCO	energy service company
ETS	Emissions Trading Scheme
EV	electric vehicle
FAO	Food and Agriculture Organization
FIT	feed-in tariff
GHG	greenhouse gases
IEA	International Energy Agency
IEG	Independent Evaluation Group (World Bank)
IMF	International Monetary Fund
LF	load factor
MDG	Millennium Development Goal
MHS	micro-hydropower system
NGO	non-governmental organization
PPA	power purchase agreement
PV	photovoltaic
RE	renewable energy
SEFA	Sustainable Energy For All (UN)
SME	small- and medium-sized enterprise
SPD	small power distributor
SPP	small power producer
TIESR	Toronto Initiative for Economic and Social Rights
UNDP	United Nations Development Programme

UNEP	United Nations Environment Programme
UNFCCC	UN Framework Convention on Climate Change
WHO	World Health Organization
WTO	World Trade Organization

1. Energy governance: a key challenge in the era of globalization

Jordi Jaria i Manzano, Nathalie Chalifour and Louis J. Kotzé

Societies need to build material infrastructures and feed their reproduction through energy production and consumption. A fundamental element of this social metabolism, conceived as the complex interaction between society and nature where human beings obtain resources and produce waste, is the energy cycle. It is now informally recognized that we are possibly living in a new geological epoch called the Anthropocene where social metabolism is increasing with the expansion of our capitalist world-system. Within this trajectory of exponentially growing energy consumption, environmental impacts are simultaneously increasing and the Earth and its systems are being pushed towards critical tipping points which might eventually mean an end of life as we know it. This accelerated growth and its concomitant anthropogenic impacts is arguably the greatest challenge facing contemporary societies today.

To respect the biological thresholds of the planet, it is imperative that our social metabolism is adapted to a fragile and closed Earth system which consists of humans, non-human but living entities, and non-living entities. The aggressive and massive energy consumption by humans during the last two centuries (a distinct period since the Industrial Revolution) has obvious and alarming consequences for the functioning of the biosphere. Since cheap and easily accessible sources of energy, such as coal and oil, were available during this period, social metabolism has increased as a result with no chances of replenishing such non-renewable energy resources. The consequences are immense resource depletion, significant environmental pollution and associated socio-economic crises all over the world, suggesting that a new approach in energy governance is urgently required. While technological innovation will play a decidedly important role, law and governance as socio-institutional regulatory interventions will also have their part in creating more sustainable futures for societies. Therefore, this fundamental transition to sustainable and just forms of energy production has deep implications for law and lawyers.

Recognizing the centrality of and urgent need for innovative modes of energy governance in contemporary societies, the International Union for Conservation of Nature's Academy of Environmental Law (IUCNAEL) organized its twelfth annual colloquium under the title 'Energy for a Fair Society on a Safe Planet', which sought to cover a wide range of energy-related topics, ranging from social energy needs to environmental justice and safety issues. Held at the Universitat Rovira i Virgili, in the Catalan town of Tarragona, the colloquium benefited from several original contributions prepared by leading scholars and specialists from all over the world. Debates around the issue of energy were critical, at times deeply unsettling, but with little exception, future-oriented and constructive. This book is a direct scholarly product of this high level meeting of global experts. It presents a selection of representative, innovative, high-quality papers that contain cutting edge research on the future of energy governance and the role of law within the energy governance paradigm.

Confronted as we are by climate change and resource depletion, thinking about energy transitions and environmental justice has become an important concern that reaches into the deepest realms of the global ecological and existential crisis through which humankind is living. In this context, this book attempts to offer the reader some novel insights into contemporary debates on energy governance from a juridical perspective. The different authors in their respective chapters show a deep commitment to and acquaintance with the social relevance of knowledge, contributing with their scholarship to the ongoing discussions revolving around energy governance. The book is organized into three related and sequentially organized parts: Foundations, Experiences and Governance Gaps. The first Part offers conceptual and theoretical contributions which help lay the groundwork in understanding the challenges and elaborating new approaches. The second Part showcases concrete innovative experiences in energy governance from around the globe. The third Part focuses on critical approaches to current social metabolism relating to energy.

I FOUNDATIONS

The first Part begins with a thought-provoking contribution by Klaus Bosselmann (University of Auckland). Being faithful to his radical ecocentric approach aiming to envisage deep changes in social patterns,

Professor Bosselmann commences from the profound implications of the *Energiewende* (energy transition) to challenge lawyers' attitudes in the process of social change. This chapter defines a space for debate, while at the same time addressing an alternative approach to energy governance. From this point of departure, the author argues that the social role of experts demands from them a deep social involvement where they act as agents of social change. He reminds us that traditionally lawyers have been merely reactive, being entrenched as they were (and continue to be) in formalism and specialization. Bosselmann criticizes this reductionism, pleading for a deeper engagement in ethical and political issues. In this context, the author offers a consequential reflection focused on climate governance that is based on the consideration of the atmosphere as a concern of the global commons.

James R. May and Erin Daly (Widener University, Delaware Law School) deliver an insightful chapter addressing the constitutional foundations of energy governance, especially in the area of shale gas. They point out that hydraulic fracturing ('fracking') demands new legal responses, which cannot be limited to a restricted sectorial approach, but should be opened to a more comprehensive constitutional approach. May and Daly consider that environmental constitutionalism is particularly relevant in order to enhance the potential for sustainability in the domain of shale gas. The ten good practices defined in the text can be seen as means in this constitutional framing of fracking. Finally, attempting to practically illustrate their approach, the authors analyze a landmark American court decision (*Robinson Township et al.* v. *Commonwealth of Pennsylvania*), which shows the relevance of constitutional considerations in relation to fracking and the role that the constitutional perspective could play in such matters.

Constitutionalism is not limited today to nation-states, but is growing within a complex network of constitutional 'sources' ranging from international law to intra-state and transnational developments. Human rights are often seen as the core of the (international) constitutional paradigm. Manuel Peter Samonte Solis (Adelaide Law School), offers a comprehensive contribution addressing universal access to energy services framed in terms of a critical rights-based approach. Solis argues that the lack of universal access to modern energy services continues to drive a widening gap between the 'haves' and 'have-nots', resulting in the marginalization of a significant segment of society – chiefly the poor. With this marginalization, the human rights dimension of poverty due to the lack of access to modern energy services comes to the fore, as poverty results in disempowerment and gives rise to equity considerations. Intuitively, these are matters that typically fall within the purview of human rights conversations; a conversation that he critically pursues in his chapter. In his chapter, Solis examines in broad terms the merits and limits of the language of needs compared to the language of rights in the context of the challenge of enhancing universal access to modern energy services. While doing so, the chapter also investigates the plausibility of integrating needs-talk into rights-talk.

Environmental justice is an important conceptual, theoretical and practical notion, developed during the last three decades since the seminal grassroots activism in Warren County, North Carolina, in 1982. Elodie Le Gal (Australian Centre for Agriculture and Law, University of New England), focuses on environmental justice in the domain of energy and addresses the key question of risk analysis. The author underlines that energy technology innovations carry their own risks of social failures, threatening effective advancement in the construction of an equitable social metabolism. The parochial debate in this domain is often centred on securing energy supply and combating climate change, but Le Gal shifts the focus towards environmental justice, exploring how this approach could potentially provide a new framing for the discussion and new foundations for regulation in this domain.

A proper energy transition from non-renewable to renewable sources should in theory move society to a decentralized, more equitable and less aggressive model of energy governance, based on a rapprochement between sources and consumption focuses. This is the topic addressed by Jessica Wentz (Columbia Law School) and Chiara Pappalardo (American University Washington College of Law) in their chapter on microgrids. By initially showing the many shortcomings of energy supplies at the global level, the authors consider that community-based renewable energy microgrids are potentially a more feasible way to ensure more sustainable energy production, supply and access, especially in developing countries such as India and in Southern Africa. By focusing on several useful case studies, the authors illustrate the many benefits of renewable energy microgrids. They specifically focus on community-based projects, and provide recommendations on how policies and regulations could feasibly be (re)structured to most effectively harness those benefits. They address two critical issues for 'scaling up' the deployment of these systems: namely, removing restrictions on the collection of electricity tariffs, and designing a national programme that will attract external investment in these projects.

Finally, Richard L. Ottinger and John Bowie (Pace Law School) provide an analysis of financing for renewable energy projects, which is a key issue for energy transition. Their chapter is premised on the assumption that renewable energy is central to any future-oriented development agenda. The authors focus on the issue of securing financing for renewable energy projects, noting that the renewable energy market is growing mainly as a result of innovative financing techniques around the world. The authors specifically focus on recent innovative methods for financing the high initial capital costs of many renewable energy resources, with case studies of their application.

II EXPERIENCES

Part II of the book is devoted to analyzing different experiences in innovative energy governance, providing a birds-eye view of innovative and cutting edge approaches in this domain. The first chapter of this section is devoted to the relevance of the emergent idea of the smart city and its connection with energy law and governance. Lye Lin-Heng and Melissa Low (National University of Singapore) propose a comprehensive and innovative vision of smart cities and energy using the city of Singapore as a case study. They analyze a wide range of measures that are meant to pave the way to change the energy consumption patterns of the city-state. The authors propose legal solutions that are based on a clean energy model and they identify and discuss financial instruments that could be used in a smart city's energy transition.

Trevor Daya-Winterbottom (University of Waikato) provides a detailed account of the New Zealand courts' reaction to the many new, diverse and often complex legal developments and socio-juridical concerns in the domain of energy law and governance. The chapter is richly documented and analyzes a series of decisions of New Zealand courts regarding use of renewable energy, as well as the social implications of fossil fuel and climate change and their relationship. The author indicates that there is considerable existing investment in renewable energy in New Zealand and there are significant prospects for future renewable energy projects. Nevertheless, the slow evolution of government policy regarding climate change and renewable energy has left a vacuum that has resulted in significant judicial involvement in determining policy questions regarding renewable energy and climate change governance.

By using France and Germany as case studies, the chapter of Anaïs Guerry (Sciences Po Law School, Paris) focuses on the extent to which law and governance is instrumental in facilitating the much needed energy transition from non-renewable to renewable energy resources. The chapter commences by establishing the meaning of 'energy transition' (*Energiewende*), and by distinguishing between governmental strategies addressed to modify dynamics of energy production and consumption that should lead to a deeper cultural change in society in this domain. The author then shows how legal instruments are used in France and Germany to achieve an energy transition in two decisive fields: distribution networks and cooperative companies that produce energy. Guerry underlines the importance of social commitment to reach success in this complex transition process, while emphasizing the roles of cities and the legal framework in this respect.

A particularly important topic in energy law and governance is the energy efficiency of buildings which are said to be responsible for almost half of the total greenhouse gas emissions in urban areas. Teresa Parejo-Navajas (Carlos III University) addresses this issue in her chapter by comparing the measures taken in Europe and in the United States to achieve more energy-efficient buildings. The author underlines the importance of taking measures with respect to existing buildings, which are many more than the new built ones. Parejo-Navajas finds that the European Union has taken the lead in this particular field, being a potential global inspiration for new advancements in energy-efficiency measures for buildings. The chapter considers that there is sufficient legal room to address energy efficiency in existing buildings, while highlighting the different strategies that can be used to do so.

Although energy consumption is a source of waste, Melissa Scanlan's (Vermont Law School) chapter demonstrates that energy-related waste can also be harnessed as a source of energy. More specifically, the author underlines the carbon footprint of traditional urban wastewater treatment and investigates the potential of wastewater as a renewable source of energy. This innovative reconfiguration of energy consumption into potential energy production is illustrated through three case studies that showcase best practices in reducing carbon emissions in municipal wastewater treatment facilities and opportunities for wastewater treatment systems to become net energy exporters. Scanlan's chapter also identifies several policy drivers that could facilitate a transition away from fossil fuels towards renewable energy from sewage.

III GOVERNANCE GAPS

Energy governance, as a crucial aspect of social metabolism, is flawed because of the internal imbalances of social reproduction at the global level. There are significant differences between countries situated in the developing South and countries in the developed North. Such inequalities and socio-economically constructed hierarchies often lead to grave injustices. In order to address these injustices, sustainable energy law and governance strategies must also have a very strong social justice dimension to them. The two final chapters of the books seek to vividly illustrate some of the many challenges apparent in global energy governance and the disproportionate impact and resultant injustices that often fall on countries and people in the global South as opposed to those situated in the global North.

The first of the chapters is devoted to a particularly serious case of environmental injustice that is related to exploitation of energy resources in a developing county by multinational companies, namely, that of the Niger Delta that has been devastated by the consequences of oil and gas extraction for decades. Eloamaka Carol Okonkwo (Strathclyde Centre for Environmental Law and Governance) addresses one of the gravest consequences of corporate greed in the Niger Delta, that is, environmentally displaced persons. By focusing on the dire negative impacts that oil exploration and extraction is having on local communities in the Delta, the author discusses the notion of environmentally displaced persons and contextualizes this discussion in terms of the realities that prevail in that particular geographical area. The chapter concludes that environmentally displaced persons in the Niger Delta are not adequately protected, neither under international law, nor under Nigerian law. It recommends interim actions within the human rights framework, followed by the enactment of a legally enforceable regulation that should ideally be built on internationally agreed principles.

The final chapter in this volume focuses on energy consumption in the agricultural sector, which is particularly relevant in the global South, where agriculture is often the main source of income and serves as the origin for much of the world's food resources. In this chapter, Cristiane Derani (Federal University of Santa Catarina) points to the interlinked nature between global agriculture, transportation and energy consumption, showing that the current dynamics of food distribution are particularly intensive in terms of energy. The author argues that this global network of food production, distribution and consumption is inefficient with respect to energy use, and she argues for policies in the international arena oriented towards transforming these unsustainable patterns of social behaviour into sustainable ones.

PART I

Foundations

2. Germany's '*Energiewende*': what can environmental law scholarship learn from it?

Klaus Bosselmann

I INTRODUCTION

The term *Energiewende* (energy transition) has entered the international vocabulary. It signals what many perceive as a general transition from the fossil fuel age to an age of renewables and sustainability. It certainly offers an opportunity to pause, take a breather and explore some wider cultural, social and legal issues surrounding the energy transition.

This chapter explores some of the legal and constitutional origins of the *Energiewende* and the particular role of environmental lawyers in this context. The point of departure here is that environmental law scholars should never be mere bystanders or commentators, but original thinkers and activists with a powerful message. So the first part of this chapter will focus on ecological sustainability as the overarching objective of all environmental law. The second part looks specifically at the importance of the *Energiewende* for more effective climate governance.

To this end, I want to show how the general discourse is moving away from internationally negotiated targets and timetables to domestically driven reforms. To an extent, the *Energiewende* is the result of internal rather than external forces combining a desire for technological effectiveness and economic competitiveness with genuine climate responsibility. My thesis here is that the atmosphere is increasingly accepted as a global commons and not merely treated as a commodity to suit market realities and property rights. We may be seeing signs of a shift from property rights rationality to a commons rationality, with important implications for a much more effective global climate change regime.

II THE 'ENERGIEWENDE': ITS POLITICAL, LEGAL AND CONSTITUTIONAL ORIGINS

Ending a debate of several decades, the German Parliament passed legislation in 2011 to reduce greenhouse gases up to 95 per cent by 2050 and increase renewable energy to a 60 per cent share by 2050. The combination of phasing out nuclear power, saving energy and shifting to renewable energy became known as the energy transition or *Energiewende*.

The *Energiewende* has been described as the biggest infrastructure project since post-Second World War reconstruction. And while driven by a desire for technological and economic innovation, its roots are less of an economic, but rather of an ecological nature. In an ecological paradigm, energy appears as an issue either threatening or preserving the natural conditions of life. In Germany, energy has always been discussed in the context of ecologicalization and democratization rather than as a purely technological issue.

It was 40 years ago when, in 1974, the Federal Environment Agency was established and the first energy conservation initiatives started. In 1980, the study entitled *Energiewende* was published[1] and the Greens were founded. Then, in 1983, they entered the German Parliament to help mainstream the idea of 'ecological modernization' (*Ökologische Modernisierung*).[2] This idea embraced virtually all aspects of moving towards a sustainable society. In a more narrow sense, ecological modernization meant technological innovation based on greater environmental efficiency. In a broader meaning it encapsulated political and legal measures and ultimately the concept of a sustainable society based on ecological values and principles.

(1) The Greening of Environmental and Energy Law

In the 1980s a key aspect of ecological modernization was the 'ecologicalization of the law' (*Ökologisierung des Rechts*).[3] At its core was

---

[1] Florentin Krause, Hartmut Bossel and Karl-Friedrich Müller-Reißmann, *Energiewende – Wachstum und Wohlstand ohne Erdöl und Uran* (S. Fischer, 1980).

[2] Martin Jänicke, *Umweltpolitische Prävention als ökologische Modernisierung und Strukturpolitik*, Wissenschaftszentrum IIUG Discussion Paper 84-1 (1984).

[3] Klaus Bosselmann, 'Wendezeit im Umweltrecht: Von der Verrechtlichung der Ökologie zur Ökologisierung des Rechts' (1987) *Kritische Justiz* 345; Klaus

the attempt to conceptualize human rights and laws from an ecological perspective. And it was a rather successful attempt that started with a jurisprudential debate around rights of nature in 1986[4] and culminated in a constitutional review of the Federal Government (1986–89) on the question whether the German Grundgesetz (Basic Law, in other words, German Constitution) needed a major reform.

At the centre was the question whether ecological realities require a redefinition of human rights and a special obligation of the state to protect the environment 'for its own sake' as well as for future generations. We (in other words, Institute für Umweltrecht/Institute for Environmental Law and Verein für Umweltrecht/Association for Environmental Law) proposed that ecological boundaries should define human rights, such as the right of liberty or freedom of research and teaching and particularly the concept of property. In essence, the use of natural resources on the whole would no longer be protected, but only their *sustainable* use. Reflecting the precautionary principle, the onus would be on a person or company to demonstrate that their proposed activity would not negatively affect the integrity of relevant ecosystems. Remarkably, our proposals were supported by the Bundesrat, the Upper House where *Länder* (states) are represented, and triggered a full review by the Joint Constitutional Commission.[5] The Commission did not resolve these issues and instead called for a wider public dialogue precisely because they are so important:

> The question of either an anthropocentric or ecocentric approach to the constitution is of such fundamental importance, that the Commission did not see itself as mandated to answer it. Instead the Commission calls for a wide expert and public dialogue before considering such a change.

Then, in 1989, The Wall came down and German unification ended the debate, at least for while. In its 1993 Report, the Constitutional Commission reversed its call for public dialogue and declared the matter closed:

Bosselmann, 'Einführung: Vom Umweltrecht zum ökologischen Recht' in Christopher Stone, *Umwelt vor Gericht* [*Should Trees Have Standing?*] (Trickster, 1987), pp. 9–23; Carl Böhret and Hermann Hill, *Ökologisierung des Rechts- und Verwaltungssystems* (Nomos, 1994).

[4] Klaus Bosselmann, 'Eigene Rechte der Natur? Ansätze einer ökologischen Rechtsauffassung' (1986) *Kritische Justiz* 1.

[5] Klaus Bosselmann, *The Principle of Sustainability* (Ashgate, 2008), p. 138; and Klaus Bosselmann, *Ökologische Grundrechte* (Nomos, 1998), pp. 80–126.

> The environment cannot be subject of protection in its own right, especially cannot claim unilateral priority. Rather it needs to be seen in the context of multifaceted situations of conflict, for example, with economic growth, industrial development, creation of jobs, housing, energy supply or transport services ... There was no support for the introduction of ecological limitations to individual fundamental rights, for example, property.

This was in stark contrast to what the environmental movement demanded. In 1991, a broad alliance of professors, activists and parliamentarians had symbolically adopted a 'New Constitution for Germany'[6] in the historic Paulskirche in Frankfurt (where the first German Constitution was adopted in 1848). This would have been an extraordinary achievement: based on the fundamental principle of sustainability, it included all our proposals on ecological limitations of human rights and property rights and a state obligation to protect the environment for its own sake. While this constitution remained a draft, political pressure on the government continued and several amendments to the Grundgesetz reflect a notable move away from anthropocentrism. The 1994 amendment of Article 20a, for example, established a new state obligation: 'The state, also in its responsibility for future generations, protects the natural foundations of life'[7] – not just 'human' life – following engaged parliamentary debate on anthropocentrism vs ecocentrism.

There is no direct link between the constitutional movement of the 1980s and the energy law reforms of the late 1990s, any more than there is any link between the environmental movement and the Renewable Energy Act (EEG) 2000. However, both the origins and the contents of this revolutionary Act have their roots in the strong advocacy of the 1980s towards ecocentrism. The EEG was the archetype for many similar laws around the world and was revolutionary in the sense that it provided investment security for energy providers and, at the same time, had its purpose in ecological sustainability as an overarching objective.[8] This purpose has not changed throughout the various amendments of the EEG with its ever more ambitious energy targets.

The bottom line of all the efforts towards constitutional and legal reform has always been the concern for ecological sustainability (not

---

[6] Kuratorium für einen demokratisch verfaßten Bund deutscher Länder, *Vom Grundgesetz zur deutschen Verfassung. Denkschrift und Vergassungsentwurf* (Nomos, 1991). See also Bosselmann, *Ökologische Grundrechte*, above n. 5, at 98.

[7] Translations from German by the author.

[8] EEG 2000/2012, s. 1.

some vague idea of sustainable development). It is important to distinguish between the core idea of sustainability, which is addressed to maintaining social reproduction given the limitation of resources, and the idea of sustainable development, which tries to face up to this limitation without renouncing development, that is, growth.[9]

It is worth noting that, like the German Grundgesetz, virtually all European Constitutions have since the 1980s been amended in the light of sustainability challenges. Previously, some European Constitutions were originally drafted with this in mind, such as the Constitutions of Greece (1974), Portugal (1976) and Spain (1978). Worldwide, 147 countries have enacted constitutional provisions for environmental rights and responsibilities. Approximately 100 countries have incorporated a state obligation to protect the environment; of those, 60 national Constitutions also recognize a human right to a decent environment, while 60 Constitutions include collective and individual responsibilities for the environment.[10] The most ambitious of all is in the Pachamama approach of some Latin American Constitutions, especially Ecuador's (2008) and Bolivia's (2009). In the latter case, legislation has deepened this approach (Ley marco de la Madre Tierra/Law of Mother Earth, 2012).[11]

(2) Role of Environmental Lawyers

In the context of this chapter, even more notable is the specific role that environmental lawyers have played in all this. As mentioned, the German constitutional initiative behind the energy law reform was driven by environmental law scholarship rooted in ecological thinking. It is also clear that Germany's mainstream environmental law scholars, for the most part, stood at the sidelines, merely observing the ethical and constitutional debate rather than engaging in it.

The gap between legal scholarship and legal activism has puzzled me throughout my career. To me, environmental law is neither neutral nor peripheral to the legal system. To the contrary, I see environmental law as

---

[9] Karin Mickelsen and William Rees, 'The Environment: Ecological and Ethical Dimensions' in Elaine L. Hughes, Alastair R. Lucas and William A. Tilleman II (eds), *Environmental Law and Policy* (Emond Montgomery, 1993), pp. 1–29.

[10] Bosselmann, *The Principle of Sustainability*, above n. 5, at 125–7.

[11] Jordi Jaria i Manzano, 'The Rights of Nature in Ecuador: An Opportunity to Reflect on Society, Law and Environment' in Robert V. Percival, Jolene Lin and William Piermattei (eds), *Global Environmental Law at a Crossroads* (Edward Elgar, 2014), pp. 48–62.

the key driver for a much needed transformation of law and governance, but very little has been achieved so far.

One of the pioneers of environmental law, the late Staffan Westerlund, Professor at the University of Uppsala, went so far as to say that the entire academic discipline of environmental law over the last 30 years has failed. Rather than looking at sustainability from the perspective of law, we should have looked at the law from the perspective of sustainability. This paradigm shift has never entered mainstream environmental law scholarship. According to Westerlund, the central reference point of environmental law is not some undefined 'environment' or 'sustainable development', but sustainability with ecological integrity at its core.[12]

In the same vein, Douglas Fisher, one of Australasia's pioneers of environmental law, argues that politicians, administrators and judges reach decisions without a specific environmental 'point of commencement'. In his recent book entitled *Legal Reasoning in Environmental Law* (2013), Fisher explores what criteria decision-makers are employing and how much weight they actually give to environmental concerns. According to his findings, legal practitioners and judges readily employ the general criteria of human well-being, economic development, property protection, and so on with the environment being just one factor, among many others, for decision-making. What's more, the environment usually appears as an unknown entity, too abstract and not nearly as well defined as human rights or property rights. As a consequence, mainstream economic considerations tend to trump soft environmental concerns. Fisher's book concludes with a plea for 'processes of legal reasoning which reflect the fundamental *grundnorm*s of the system – the rule of law in general and sustainability in the context of environmental governance'.[13] These *grundnorms* are indeed largely missing in international and municipal legal systems.

So far, environmental laws tend to refer to the environment either as a general, largely undefined concern or they focus on individual environmental aspects (water, air, biodiversity, etc.) without defining them to a degree that enables decision-makers to draw the line between acceptable and unacceptable public action. Yet, a clear definition is readily available, that is, the integrity of ecological systems as the core of sustainability.

---

[12] S. Staffan Westerlund, 'Theory for Sustainable Development Towards or Against?' in Hans-Christian Bugge and Christina Voigt (eds), *Sustainable Development in International and National Law* (Europa Law, 2008), pp. 48–65.

[13] Douglas Fisher, *Legal Reasoning in Environmental Law: A Study of Structure, Form and Language* (Edward Elgar, 2013), p. 433.

(3) Ecological Sustainability as an Overarching Objective

The concept of ecological integrity has its origins in the 1972 US Clean Water Act and in the 1974 Great Lakes Water Quality Agreement between Canada and the United States. It has since been used in conservation legislation in North America and Europe, but not in other countries, as notably in New Zealand. We can say that the Resource Management Act's definition of its purpose in section 5(2) comes close to it if understood correctly (as was the case back then in the mid-1990s). We can also find express reference to the integrity concept in annual reports of the Department of Conservation (DoC). Until 2009, DoC consistently described the central 'outcome' of its work in this way:

> The aim is to, as far as possible, maintain or restore marine, terrestrial and freshwater sites on public conservation lands and waters to a healthy, natural functioning condition. This condition is described as 'ecological integrity'.

However, since then the annual reports have shifted to utilitarian language. References to 'ecological integrity' have been replaced with the notion 'environmental, social and economic benefits from functioning ecosystems'.[14]

The concept of ecological integrity is well known in international environmental law. In fact, no less than 23 international soft and hard law agreements contain specific references to this concept. The first of such agreements was the Convention on the Conservation of Antarctic Marine Living Resources adopted in 1980, which recognized in its Preamble the importance of 'protecting the integrity of the ecosystem of the seas surrounding Antarctica'. Another example is the Preamble to the 1992 Rio Declaration on Environment and Development which calls for 'working towards international agreements which respect the interests of all and protect the *integrity* of the global environmental and developmental system'. Then, Principle 7 of the Rio Declaration provides: 'States shall cooperate in a spirit of global partnership to conserve, protect and restore the health and *integrity* of the Earth's ecosystem'. This is repeated in key documents such as Agenda 21 or the 2002 Johannesburg Declaration. Even the 2012 Rio+20 outcome document *The Future We Want,* widely perceived as unambitious and weak, calls for holistic and integrated approaches to sustainable development to guide humanity for restoring the health and *integrity* of the Earth's ecosystem (II.40).

---

[14] Outcome statements in the Annual Reports for 2010–13.

Finally, the Brundtland Report itself described the 'integrity of the natural system' as the basic condition for 'the survival of life on Earth' and in this way described the core idea behind sustainability as a prerequisite for development.[15]

Applying the usual standards for the recognition of concepts as international law, we can say that the repeated and consistent references to ecological integrity amount to an emerging fundamental objective or *grundnorm* of international environmental law.[16] But even independently of any legal status under international law, the fundamental importance of ecological integrity should be without dispute. Surely, no one would doubt the need to keep the Earth's life-supporting systems intact.

Energy policy and law needs to be embedded in a wider understanding of preserving the integrity of the Earth's ecological systems. Such an understanding is the essence of sustainability. The example of Germany's legal development leading to the *Energiewende* shows this and how this is possible. Of course, there is a long way to go before we can meaningfully speak of sustainability as an overarching legal objective either in Germany or anywhere else. But on our way towards such an objective, it is important to think of some ethical implications that are relevant here.

If we are concerned about preserving and restoring the integrity of the Earth's systems, then fundamentally we are taking a stance of stewardship or guardianship or trusteeship. Such a stance is the essence of caring for the environment. With respect to climate change this means caring for the atmosphere as a global commons.

In the following we ask how energy policies and laws can be informed by a sense of trusteeship for the global commons. We will first reflect on some current reform proposals for global climate governance to then argue that there is a need for institutional change, in essence, a global climate authority based on a trusteeship mandate.

---

[15] World Commission on Environment and Development, *Our Common Future* (1987), Part I.1.A.I: 'Nature is bountiful, but it is also fragile and finely balanced. There are thresholds that cannot be crossed without endangering the basic integrity of the system. Today we are close to many of these thresholds; we must be ever mindful of the risk of endangering the survival of life on Earth'.

[16] Rakhyun Kim and Klaus Bosselmann, 'Towards a Purposive System of Multilateral Environmental Agreements' (2013) 2 *Transnational Environmental Law* 285, available at www.journals.cambridge.org/action/displayAbstract?fromPage=online&aid=8943677.

III THE ATMOSPHERE AS A GLOBAL COMMONS

Intuitively, the atmosphere is a global commons. Somehow we all know that the atmosphere belongs to no-one, cannot be owned in a legal sense and must be available to any person, any country, any time. In fact, before global climate change became an issue, in the 1980s, the environmental literature typically described areas outside national jurisdiction (oceans, atmosphere, outer space and polar regions) as 'shared natural resources' or 'global commons'.[17] There was a general assumption that these areas could not be nationalized, privatized, commercialized or otherwise appropriated in any way by some at the expense of others.

This assumption rested on the long-standing tradition of all cultures that you cannot own what essentially belongs to all or nobody. In Western legal history, the concept of 'the commons' dates back to Roman law distinguishing things that can be owned individually (*res privatum*) from things common to all (*res publicum*). By definition, the commons required a form of governance that ensured their sustained availability for all. Governance of this kind was inevitably grounded in a sense of stewardship or trusteeship.[18] It can't be any other way: if you are asked to manage what belongs to someone else, you are essentially acting as a trustee for the benefit of someone else.

The relationship between *res publicum* and governance based on trusteeship is an essential part of public law doctrines (especially in civil law traditions, less so in common law traditions). This understanding has never changed and is probably still being taught in any public law course.

What has changed is the law itself. In most jurisdictions, *res privatum* thinking now dominates what essentially belongs to *res publicum*. We

---

[17] See, for example, IUCN/UNEP/WWF/UNESCO, 'The Global Commons' in *World Conservation Strategy* (1980); Elinor Ostrom, *Governing the Commons: The Evolution of Institutions for Collective Action* (Cambridge University Press, 1990); Klaus Bosselmann, *When Two Worlds Collide: Society and Ecology,* (RSVP, 1995); Peter Sand, 'Trusts for the Earth: New Financial Mechanisms for International Environmental Protection' in Werner Lang (ed.), *Sustainable Development and International Law* (Martinus Nijhoff, 1995), pp. 167–84; K. Baslar, *The Concept of the Common Heritage of Mankind in International Law* (Martinus Nijhoff, 1998); Klaus Bosselmann, Ron Engel and Prue Taylor, *Governance for Sustainability: Issues, Challenges, Successes* (IUCN, 2008).

[18] Peter Linebaugh, *The Magna Carta Manifesto: Liberties and Commons for All* (University of California Press, 2008); Jeanette Neeson, *Commoners: Common Right, Enclosure and Social Change in England, 1700–1820* (Cambridge University Press, 1996).

have only to think of the massive wealth accumulation around privately owned assets over the last 25 or so years, to appreciate the significance of private property and how effectively it isolates itself from responsibility for the commons. The big divide between the increasing wealth of the few and the decreasing wealth of many (including states) is, of course, the result of economic liberalism and free market ideology. But less known is perhaps the specific role that the law played in this process.

Legal theorists widely accept that law reflects dominant values of society, but also entrenches them. Moral values and legal norms are not entirely separated as political liberalism would prefer, they are in a dialectic relationship. This means that hard law trumps soft morality, but also that morality can change and in doing so shapes new law. What has happened over the last few decades is an incremental change of public morality that favours acceptance of market demands and private goods (*res privatum)* over governance of common goods (*res publicum*). With respect to the global commons such as the atmosphere, this shift of morality has meant that the atmosphere has been treated as a *res nullius,* a legal no-man's land, a void that has been filled with open access to anyone wishing to deposit carbon and other greenhouse gases.

Arguably, a global climate regime would have been far more successful if climate change was in the public arena *before* economic neoliberalism began its course. As illustrated above, during the 1980s public morality was much more supportive of pro-active and innovative measures of environmental protection. I was a member of the German delegation at the 1992 Rio Earth Summit and recall how we referred to the atmosphere as a global commons that needs to be guarded by humanity as a whole. Such sentiments have completely vanished and replaced by an attitude that regards the atmosphere as *res nullius* and subject to state negotiations in the same vein as state negotiations over free trade. The atmosphere degenerated from a global commons to a mere commodity.

The point to be made here is not how badly things went and how states surrendered to free market ideology, but how we can perceive a return to ethically-based rational governance.

The disappearance of the global commons is not just a physical, but a legal phenomenon as we have seen, so chances are that the law – as a cultural and social construct – can make a difference to the way we govern ourselves. Considering that public morality can change and given that we can build on centuries old traditions of effective governance of the commons, it is at least conceivable that an international climate regime can be based on the notion of the global commons.

In the following I want to explore two different avenues of climate governance; both are in response, and partly in contrast, to the states-negotiated global agreements. One is the avenue of incremental reform usually advocated by climate economists and more in line with existing practices (carbon pricing, state negotiations, market conform instruments). The other avenue is a transformation from state-centred governance to Earth-centred governance. The two avenues are not mutually exclusive, but complementary and certainly reflective of an increased sense of global commons governance. This is particularly important regarding energy, which is a key issue in terms of design of global commons governance, as will be set out in the following paragraphs.

(1) Improving Climate Governance

Ideas and trends around improved governance of the atmosphere focus on three areas: carbon pricing and taxation; global cooperation; and national and sub-national action.[19]

(i) Climate rent and carbon tax

To an extent, we can judge emissions trading schemes (no matter how inefficient they have been so far) as an acknowledgement of the polluter pays principle. Underpinning the polluter pays principle is the concern for a commons to keep it protected from individual overuse. In reality, however, emissions trading has been guided by the opposite concern. Many of its flaws around offsetting, permits, perverse incentives and general inefficiency are rooted in concerns for protection of property rights rather than the commons.

Crucial here would be a global carbon budget that is tightly monitored and fairly allocated. If that happens, the character of governance changes from a state-negotiated minimal compromise ('business as usual') to governance of a global commons assuming some kind of common property of humanity. The 'owner' is all humanity and charges the user of its property in the same way as landlords charge their tenants. We can then meaningfully speak of a 'climate rent'.[20] The concept of climate rent reflects common ownership and common responsibility. If used intelligently, a climate rent, such as a global carbon tax scheme, would not

---

[19] Ottmar Edenhofer, Christian Flachsland, Michael Jakob and Kai Lessmann, *The Atmosphere as a Global Commons: Challenges for International Cooperation and Governance* (Harvard Project on Climate Agreements, Harvard Kennedy School of Government, 2013).

[20] Ibid. 10.

only generate huge revenue, but restrict the use of the atmosphere as a carbon sink. As a consequence, property titles of the owners of coal, oil and gas would be devalued. Eventually, fossil fuels would become uneconomical.

The counter-argument against such a global rent or tax scheme is the usual concern for property rights – which from a commons perspective shouldn't be an argument at all. By definition, private property interests are subordinate to the inherent interests of the common good. Only from a libertarian perspective does this smack of unlawful expropriation and communism. From any other perspective, including legal history and contemporary constitutionalism, it is clear that private property is never absolute, but embedded in social relationships. The idea that private property in natural resources is ethically justified only if it serves the common good is as old as the very institution of private property itself. It goes back to the concept of property in Justinian codification (sixth century), sits among Thomas Aquinas's (1225–74) 'first principles of action' and even conforms with John Locke's (1632–1704) so-called 'enough and as good' proviso, which aims for an equal share of each person in the Earth's material resources.[21]

So there is nothing revolutionary in the idea to restrict private property for the sake of the common good. For example, Article 14(2) of the German Basic Law states: 'Property entails obligations. Its use shall also serve the public good'. Article 14(3) allows for 'expropriation … for the public good' and Article 15 specifically provides that 'Land [and] natural resources … may for the purpose of socialization be transferred to public ownership'.

The ethical and legal argument for the priority of the common good over private property protection is indeed compelling.[22] What is lacking, of course, is the political support for it. And this isn't just a matter of good political argument. We are talking about nothing less than trying to tame capitalism and reconcile it with an overarching concern for the atmosphere, the global commons, social justice and ultimately human survival. Currently, the dynamics of global capitalism and prospects for sustainability are at odds with each other, to say the least, so everything

---

[21] Helga Varden, 'The Lockean "Enough-and-as-Good" Proviso: An Internal Critique' (2012) 9 *Journal of Moral Philosophy* 410.

[22] Klaus Bosselmann, 'Property Rights and Sustainability: Can They be Reconciled?' in David Grinlinton and Prue Taylor (eds), *Property Rights and Sustainability: The Evolution of Property Rights to Meet Ecological Challenges* (Martinus Nijhoff, 2010), pp. 23–42.

depends on a strategy that is both ambitious and feasible. In this pursuit, we can now look at the challenge of global cooperation.

(ii) Global cooperation

The slow and cumbersome process of international climate change negotiations is well known and subject to much criticism. At the core of the critique is what I have called the dilemma of international environmental law.[23] On the one hand, it might be expected that the natural world forms a non-negotiable absolute for any agreement. On the other hand, nation-states see the natural world merely as relative, competing with other concerns such as economic prosperity, political strategizing or down-right power interests. This creates the dilemma of wanting to be seen as ambitious without actually being committed. Inge Kaul describes this phenomenon as a 'sovereignty paradox' explaining it in the following way:

> (T)he paradox is that states, notably their governments, are losing policy-making sovereignty precisely because they hold on to conventional strategies of realizing sovereignty, which make them shy away from international cooperation. If nations want to win back their policy-making capacity, only one path remains: cooperation.[24]

Much has been written about the free rider problem,[25] about the prisoner's dilemma,[26] the chicken game,[27] and other obstacles[28] in

---

[23] Klaus Bosselmann, 'Losing the Forest for the Trees: Environmental Reductionism in Law', *Environmental Laws and Sustainability*, Special Issue, (2010) 2(8) *Sustainability* at 2428, available at www.mdpi.com/2071-1050/2/8/2424/; see further Kim and Bosselmann, above n. 16.

[24] At the launch of *The Governance Report* (Hertie School of Governance, 2014) on 23 February 2014, available at www.governancereport.org/media/news/the-sovereignty-paradox/.

[25] Martin Weitzman, 'On Modeling and Interpreting the Economics of Catastrophic Climate Change' *The Review of Economics and Statistics* XCI (2009), 1–19.

[26] Andreas Lange and Carsten Vogt, 'Cooperation in International Environmental Negotiations due to a Preference for Equity' (2003) 87 *Journal of Public Economics* 2049.

[27] Carlo Carraro and Dominico Siniscalco, 'Strategies for the International Protection of the Environment' (1993) 52 *Journal of Public Economics* 309.

[28] Karen Pittel and Dirk Rübbelke, 'Transitions in the Negotiations on Climate Change: From Prisoner's Dilemma to Chicken and Beyond' (2012) 12 *International Environmental Agreements, Politics, Law and Economics* 23.

international negotiations. The game theory literature is full of descriptions why consensus building among states is so difficult. Game theorists, however, also offer strategies for improvement. One popular idea is that the very existence of international environmental agreements may change the rules of the game. With new treaties and their associated bureaucracies cooperation becomes more likely than non-cooperation.[29] Moreover, recent studies have shown that catastrophic events (tornados, hurricanes, tsunamis, severe draughts and floods) can substantially increase the desire for cooperation.[30]

In time, Mother Nature may well be the most powerful driver for cooperation, but for now we are probably well advised not to expect too much from the new Paris Agreement. The hard work has yet to begin.

(iii) Regional, national and sub-national levels

A promising upside of the failure of global climate change policy is that a number of regions adopt their very own climate policies. Frustrations with international passivity, especially of the United States, are endemic, perhaps most so in Europe, and quite possibly, unilateral actions are becoming more important than the international negotiation process. The EU has adopted a far-reaching package of climate policies and aims to reduce greenhouse gas (GHG) emissions by 20 per cent in 2020 (relative to 1990) and an increase of renewable energies by 20 per cent in 2020.[31]

I mentioned Germany, in particular. The goal of the *Energiewende* is to simultaneously phase out nuclear energy and reduce GHG emissions by 40 per cent in 2020 and up to 95 per cent by 2050, relative to 1990.

Beyond the EU, we can point, for example, to China with its economic transformation towards more renewables and its highly developed industry of cheap production of solar panels, wind generators and energy storage systems. Five Chinese cities and two provinces have set up an emissions trading scheme[32] and overall you get the impression that China has been more committed to a low-carbon economy than its counterpart United States, although this may all change now.

---

[29] Michael Hoel, 'International Environmental Conventions: The Case of Uniform Reductions of Emissions' (1992) 2 *Environmental Resource Economics* 141.

[30] Scott Barrett, 'Rethinking Climate Change Governance and its Relationship to the World Trading System' (2011) 34 *The World Economy* 1863.

[31] See generally, Sebastian Oberthür and Marc Pallemaerts (eds), *The New Climate Policies of the European Union: Internal Legislation and Climate Diplomacy* (VUB Press, 2011).

[32] Edenhofer *et al.*, above n. 19, at 15.

The US National Climate Assessment from May 2014[33] and proposals of the US Environment Protection Agency announced in early June 2014 seem to signal a turnaround, although President Obama will have an uphill battle to convince Congress of effective climate policies and laws.

Overall, 118 countries in the world have adopted renewable energy targets through feed-in tariffs, renewable quotas or investment programmes. China leads investment into renewables (NZ$60 billion), followed by the United States (NZ$58 billion) and Germany (NZ$31 billion).[34]

Also important in this context is low-carbon technology. Countries like Germany, Finland, Sweden, the Netherlands and, to some extent, China, Japan and South Korea, are very much driven by technological innovation. They clearly see low-carbon technology as a win-win option: it reduces GHG emissions and increases international competitiveness.

On the sub-national level, in 2013 California put a cap-and-trade system in place and just a few months ago the Governor of Washington State imposed an executive order to implement a cap-and-trade programme, eliminate coal power and fund green energy projects.[35] There are similar developments in other federal countries such as Canada, Germany and Australia.

Last, but not least, there is the ever-increasing role that local communities and local governments play in combatting climate change. Typically, they do more than their national governments. There is a worldwide trend of big cities acting to improve urban transportation and reduce GHG emissions. To some extent, big cities lead the way towards a low-carbon future as they feel the pressures most directly in the form of traffic congestion and pollution.

Smaller communities have the advantage of more effective citizen engagement and can be highly innovative. Consider the example of mid-size German cities such as Freiburg, Giessen or Marburg. They have adopted local planning statutes that make it compulsory for every new-built house to produce their own energy and become independent from the public grid. People want to have direct control over what happens in their communities and want to know how cultural commons such as schools, libraries, health institutions or community centres, but also natural commons (public spaces, parks, air, water, etc.) are protected from the austerity and privatization ideology of central governments.

---

[33] See http://nca2014.globalchange.gov.

[34] Edenhofer *et al.*, above n. 19, at 15.

[35] See http://dailycaller.com/2014/04/29/washington-governor-imposes-cap-and-trade-through-executive-order.

Overall, there has been a dramatic surge of local climate initiatives over the past decade that shifted the focus of climate policies from the global to the local. Recently, Christiana Figueres, Executive Secretary of the United Nations Framework Convention on Climate Change (UNFCCC), went so far as to speak of new metrics of the global conversation where no longer just states, but civil society and in particular local communities, engage in the actual decision-making process.[36]

Considering that nearly half of the world population is, in some form, represented in the global organization Local Governments for Sustainability (ICLEI),[37] the voice of local communities is indeed strong and able to elevate the global conversation to a new level.[38]

Overlooking the three mentioned areas of more effective climate governance, we can summarize them as playing fields for the development of governance of the atmosphere as a global commons. Each playing field has its own dynamics and we cannot be sure to what extent they are informed by a sense of actual governance of the global commons as distinct from traditional state-centred global governance. But they are relevant and deserve a lot more attention than, for example, the issues which public media usually report on.

It is simply not enough to assess global climate protection purely through the lenses of state negotiations. Somewhat cynically one could say that states are no longer in charge, they are bystanders in a world increasingly shaped by corporate forces, on the one hand, and active citizens and communities, on the other.

(2) Transforming Climate Governance

This brings us to the aforementioned transformational approach. As remarked earlier, governance of the commons is inherently stewardship or trusteeship governance. I also argued that legal regimes around the commons have a long tradition in all cultures including European history. What remains to be shown now is that trusteeship is an equally

---

[36] Address to the C40 City Mayors Summit, Johannesburg, 5 February 2014, available at http://unfccc.int/files/press/statements/application/pdf/20140502_c40_check.pdf.

[37] See www.iclei.org/index.php?id=9.

[38] Elinor Ostrom, *A Polycentric Approach to Cope with Climate Change*, Policy Research Working Paper 5095 (World Bank, 2009); Elinor Ostrom, 'Polycentric Systems for Coping with Collective Action and Global Environmental Change' (2010) 20 *Global Environmental Change* 550.

well-known concept and arguably the most effective form of caring for the global commons. Essentially, I am suggesting a shift away from state-centred to Earth-centred governance.[39] The difference between the two may appear as paradigmatic, but could also be seen as gradual, as Earth governance involves nation-states, the United Nations and global civil society alike.

Earth governance is a partnership model as perceived, for example, by the UN-initiated Commission on Global Governance. Its 1995 report *Our Global Neighbourhood*[40] calls for a 'global civic ethic' around social justice, intergenerational justice and ecological integrity and recommends institutional reform based on a partnership between states and civil society. The Report specifically acknowledges the Earth Charter[41] as an overarching and all-inclusive framework and blames the rigidity of state sovereignty as the main reason for the failure of global governance. It concludes:

> We propose, therefore, that the Trusteeship Council be given the mandate for exercising trusteeship over the global commons. Its functions would include the administration of environmental treaties … It would refer any economic or security issues arising from these matters to the Economic Security Council or the Security Council.[42]

Trusteeship over the global commons provides the basis to levy user fees, taxes and royalties for permits to use the global commons. The global commons are defined to be 'the atmosphere, outer space, the oceans and the related environment and life-supporting systems that contribute to the support of human life'.[43] This broad definition would give the UN authority to interfere with states if they do not comply with their duties to protect the environment within their borders. By implication, states are assumed to perform trusteeship functions with respect to both their

---

39 Klaus Bosselmann, *Earth Governance: Trusteeship of the Global Commons* (Edward Elgar, 2015).

40 Commission on Global Governance, *Our Global Neighbourhood* (Oxford University Press, 1995).

41 The Earth Charter, adopted in 2000 in the Peace Palace in The Hague, is the most inclusively negotiated global document to date and represents a consensus across cultures, religions and peoples. It can be perceived as having the status of constitutional founding document for global civil society. See, for example, Klaus Bosselmann and Ron Engel (eds), *The Earth Charter: A Framework for Global Governance* (KIT, 2010).

42 Commission on Global Governance, *Our Global Neighbourhood*, above n. 40, at 252.

43 Ibid.

domestic territory that they control and the global environment that they are part of.

The idea of trusteeship governance for the atmosphere is not new and has been further developed in a number of recent books.[44] My own book on the subject[45] particularly looks at the United Nations' own history and experience with trusteeship models to argue the feasibility of trusteeship. Apart from a possible revival of the dormant Trusteeship Council,[46] which has been strongly advocated by several countries, in particular Malta, but at some point also by New Zealand, there are other UN-affiliated bodies that perform trusteeship functions. For me, prominent examples include the World Health Organization (WHO) which has its *raison d'être* (reason for existence) not in serving states, but in serving human health. In this function, the WHO has some far-reaching powers, including setting of norms and standards and monitoring compliance of states.

Even more powerful is the World Trade Organization (WTO) with its *raison d'être* of promoting free trade. It has the world's only judiciary body that can hold members states directly accountable and against their will to be tested in an international court of justice. WTO's foundational and organizational documents specifically refer to trusteeship as its key function. While the ethical motives for creating such a strong organization may be questionable, it does demonstrate that states are quite capable to confer trusteeship functions on international organizations. Obviously, the eradication and control of global diseases finds the undisputed agreement of states. Likewise, free trade is very high on the list, if not at the top, of states' concerns. It is therefore quite ironic, but also telling, that the protection of the global commons – a prerequisite for human survival – seems to be of much less concern.

---

[44] See, for example, Peter Barnes, *Capitalism 3.0: A Guide to Reclaiming the Commons* (Berrett-Koehler, 2006); Ken Coghill, Charles Sampford and Tim Smith (eds), *Fiduciary Duty and the Atmospheric Trust* (Ashgate, 2012); Michael Blumm and Mary Wood, *The Public Trust Doctrine in Environmental and Natural Resource Law* (Carolina Academic Press, 2013); Mary Wood, *Nature's Trust: Environmental Law for a New Ecological Age* (Cambridge University Press, 2014).

[45] Bosselmann, *Earth Governance: Trusteeship of the Global Commons*, above n. 39.

[46] See, for example, Catherine Redgewell, 'Reforming the UN Trusteeship Council' in Bradnee Chambers and Jessica Green (eds), *Reforming International Environmental Governance: From Institutional Limits to Innovative Reforms* (UN University Press, 2005), pp. 66–92.

The only plausible explanation for this is the sheer weakness of states in standing up against multinational corporate power. They simply can't cope with the conflicting interests of climate protection, on the one hand, and economic dependence on corporates, on the other. Precisely this weakness makes it unlikely for states to accept a new global body acting as a trustee for the atmosphere (or any other global commons). The United States, in particular, is known for blocking every single initiative towards trusteeship governance (except of course for those performed by the World Bank, International Monetary Fund (IMF) and WTO).

IV FINAL REMARKS

As a conclusion of the previous pages, one could say that we are confronted with a dilemma. We can either hope for gradual improvement of climate governance (through negotiations or local initiatives) even if it means that any real action may come too late. Or we can insist on a radical turnaround through institutional reform at all levels – despite ongoing opposition of states. In practical terms, both strategies could possibly go hand-in-hand, and I have suggested that all genuine reform proposals are ultimately rooted in the idea of stewardship or trusteeship for the global commons.

Fundamentally, the issue is one of ethics. Shifting to renewable energy is a reflection of changed ethics and so is our awareness and concern for the global atmosphere. The shift from 'business as usual' to genuine commitment can only ever be facilitated by states and corporate organizations; its origins are in social change initiated by activists and civil society – hopefully including environmental lawyers.

3. Ten good practices in environmental constitutionalism that can contribute to sustainable shale gas development

James R. May and Erin Daly

I INTRODUCTION

Natural gas is considered by many to be a bridge fuel to a more sustainable energy state that produces less carbon, primarily because it produces less carbon than other fossil fuels for a comparable delivery of energy.[1] Likewise, constitutionally-embedded guarantees to environmental quality, stewardship and participation – or what we refer to as 'environmental constitutionalism' – are thought to serve an important function in advancing sustainable environmental outcomes by embodying the recognition that the environment is a proper subject for protection in constitutional texts and for vindication by constitutional courts worldwide.[2] This chapter examines whether and the extent to which best practices in environmental constitutionalism can contribute to the sustainable development of shale gas reserves worldwide.

---

[1] See generally, J.C. Dernbach and J.R. May, *Shale Gas and the Future of Energy Law and Policy for Sustainability* (Edward Elgar, 2016); J.C. Dernbach and J.R. May, *Can Shale Gas Help the Transition to Sustainability*, available at: http://www.environmentmagazine.org/Archives/Back%20Issues/2015/January-February%202015/shale-gas-full.html.

[2] See generally J.R. May and E. Daly, *Global Environmental Constitutionalism* (CUP, 2015); J.R. May and E. Daly, 'Global Constitutional Environmental Rights' in Shawkat Alam, Jahid Hossain Bhuiyan, Tareq M.R. Chowdhury and Erika J. Techera (eds), *Routledge Handbook of International Environmental Law* (Routledge, 2012); J.R. May and E. Daly, 'Vindicating Fundamental Environmental Rights Worldwide' (2010) 11 *Oregon Review of International Law* 365; J.R. May and E. Daly, 'New Directors in Earth Rights, Environmental Rights and Human Rights: Six Facets of Constitutionally Embedded Environmental Rights Worldwide' (2011) *IUCN Academy of Environmental Law E-Journal* 1; J.R. May and E. Daly, 'Constitutional Environmental Rights Worldwide' in J.R. May (ed.),

Because it is thought to be more climate-benign, natural gas can serve as a preferred alternative to the combustion of other fossil fuels. Increased demand for natural gas has in turn increased pressure to deploy unconventional methods to improve yields; the most prominent of these methods is known as horizontal hydrofracturing, or fracking, otherwise known as unconventional shale gas development. Unconventional shale gas development is a process that involves injecting a medium under extreme pressure (as much as 14,000 psi) deep into the Earth's crust to shatter shale strata and thereby liberate and capture the gas embedded within it.

Unconventional shale gas development was first employed on a large scale in around 2000 in the Barnett shale formation in Texas, and then in other shale formations.[3] US production has grown at a prodigious pace 'from 0.3 trillion cubic feet in 2000 to 9.6 trillion cubic feet in 2012'.[4] Canada, China, Argentina and Algeria, are just a few of the dozens of countries that are thought to possess vast recoverable reserves of unconventional shale gas.

Shale gas development has myriad environmental and health impacts, many of which are yet to be ascertained. These include adverse air and water quality impacts, methane leakage, and community disruption. A recent study commissioned by the European Union concerning the environmental and public health impacts of shale gas development, found that '[r]obust regulatory regimes would be required to mitigate risks and to improve general public confidence'.[5] The European Commission's 'minimum principles' recommend that Member States 'prepare a strategic environmental assessment to prevent, manage, and reduce the

---

Principles of Constitutional Environmental Law (ABA Publishing, Environmental Law Institute, 2011); J.R. May, 'Constituting Fundamental Environmental Rights Worldwide' (2006) *Pace Environmental Law Review* 23.

[3] US Energy Information Administration, *Technically Recoverable Shale Oil and Shale Gas Resources: An Assessment of 137 Shale Formations in 41 Countries Outside the United States* (2013), p. 13, available at www.eia.gov/analysis/studies/worldshalegas/pdf/overview.pdf.

[4] Ibid.

[5] AEA Technology LLC, *Support to the Identification of Potential Risks for the Environment and Human Health Arising from Hydrocarbons Operations Involving Hydraulic Fracturing in Europe* (2012), xv, available at http://ec.europa.eu/environment/integration/energy/pdf/fracking%20study.pdf.

impacts on, and risks for, human health and the environment' before allowing exploration or development.[6]

Despite these opportunities and challenges, the United States Congress has not exhibited much, if any, appetite for regulating shale gas. In fact, Congress has created a host of exemptions to many federal environmental laws for the shale gas industry[7] – although many risks from shale gas fall within the ambit of long-standing and still applicable federal laws including the Clean Air Act, the Clean Water Act, the Safe Drinking Water Act, and the Resource Conservation and Recovery Act. Nonetheless, owing to historical norms and entrenched notions of federalism, most regulation of unconventional shale gas development in the United States occurs at the sub-national and local level.

Most applicable sub-national and local laws concern casing requirements (for example, cementing, well diameter, and thickness of boring pipes), setback requirements (buffer zones between operational well pads and neighboring residences, commercial districts, schools and hospitals, and water supplies), and operational requirements (hours of operation, noise limits, and traffic patterns). In addition, industry best practices on many aspects of unconventional drilling are evolving rapidly.[8]

Resources for the Future compared 25 separate aspects of shale gas regulation in 31 states with actual or potential shale gas production.[9] It found wide variation among State regulation of unconventional shale gas development.[10] State disclosure laws also vary considerably. Only half of the 29 states with unconventional shale gas development require any form of public disclosure of the composition of chemicals used in the

---

[6] Commission Recommendation on minimum principles for the exploration and production of hydrocarbons (such as shale gas) using high-volume hydraulic fracturing, 22 January 2014 [2014] OJ L39/72–8.

[7] J.R. Nolon and S.E. Gavin, 'Hydrofracking: State Preemption, Local Power, and Cooperative Governance' (2013) 63(4) *Case Western Reserve Law Review* 1.

[8] American Petroleum Institute, *Overview of Industry Guidance/Best Practices on Hydraulic Fracturing (HF)* (2012), available at www.api.org/~/media/files/policy/exploration/hydraulic_fracturing_infosheet.ashx.

[9] N. Richardson, M. Gottlieb, A. Krupnick and H. Wiseman, *The State of State Shale Gas Regulation* (Resources for the Future, 2013), available at www.rff.org/files/sharepoint/WorkImages/Download/RFF-Rpt-StateofStateRegs_Report.pdf.

[10] Ibid. 18.

extraction process, and none require comprehensive disclosure.[11] The absence of public information about such chemicals only exacerbates public concerns.[12]

Far from regulating it, some states have enacted legislation that promotes and protects unconventional shale gas development. For example, in 2012, Pennsylvania enacted a law ('Act 13') that endorsed shale gas development by, among other things, requiring local governments to permit shale gas facilities in all zoning districts, including residential districts.

Courts are playing an increasingly prominent role in resolving policy questions about unconventional shale gas development, most profoundly in constitutional contexts.[13] For example, in *Robinson Township v. Pennsylvania Department of Environmental Protection*, the Pennsylvania Supreme Court invalidated Act 13, finding that it contravened a constitutional requirement to manage natural resources in furtherance of public trust.

As *Robinson Township* demonstrates, constitutional protections are playing an increasingly important role in advancing environmental outcomes. Such environmental constitutionalism can offer a framework for resolving some of the issues that arise with unconventional shale gas development. Accordingly, this chapter proposes ten 'good practices' in environmental constitutionalism for advancing positive environmental outcomes relating to development of unconventional shale gas reserves. The next section examines these practices, by which environmental constitutionalism can lead to positive environmental outcomes. Section III then explains how the *Robinson Township* decision from Pennsylvania's Supreme Court illustrates how good practices can have a positive impact on environmental outcomes in practice.

---

[11] M. McFeeley, *State Hydraulic Fracturing Disclosure Rules and Enforcement: A Comparison* (Natural Resources Defense Council, 2012), available at www.nrdc.org/energy/files/Fracking-Disclosure-IB.pdf.

[12] B.D. Goldstein, 'Transparency, Sustainability and Public Health: Why Act 13 is not Sustainable', paper presented at Widener University Law School Conference, Harrisburg, PA, 27 September 2013.

[13] May and Daly, 'Vindicating Fundamental Environmental Rights Worldwide', above n. 2.

II TEN GOOD PRACTICES IN ENVIRONMENTAL CONSTITUTIONALISM

This section identifies ten 'good practices' in environmental constitutionalism; while they are not indispensable, they can contribute to environmental sustainability in the development of unconventional shale gas reserves. These are:

(1) Situate environmental constitutionalism in systems that are amenable to social, economic and cultural rights, and those with civil law traditions.
(2) Clearly articulate a positive individual or collective right, such as 'everyone has an enforceable right to a quality environment'.
(3) Make provisions self-executing by placing them in a 'Bill' or 'Declaration' of rights, making them on a par with traditional first order rights.
(4) Align substantive, policy-based, and procedural provisions.
(5) Recognize emerging areas of environmental constitutionalism including sustainability, public trust, climate change and biocentrism.
(6) Scaffold additional statutory and regulatory means to implement constitutional prerogatives.
(7) Liberalize access to judicial vindication by permitting open standing, special procedural rules and fee-shifting for public interest litigation.
(8) Install complementary national and sub-national layers of environmental constitutionalism.
(9) Bundle constitutional recognition of substantive rights with procedural rights to information, participation and access to justice.
(10) Develop quality jurisprudence in environmental constitutionalism.

We do not mean to suggest that adherence to any particular practice or combination of practices assures a particular outcome, including the effective deployment of environmental constitutionalism. To be sure, any attempt at identifying good practices involves a tincture of magical thinking, and is certain to invite, at least, good criticism. We simply suggest that bearing in mind these ten correlative but not causative considerations increases the likelihood of positive environmental outcomes in general, and in promoting sustainable development of unconventional shale gas reserves in particular.

(1) Situate Environmental Constitutionalism in Systems that are Amenable to Social, Economic and Cultural Rights, and Those with Civil Law Traditions

The first good practice in deploying environmental constitutionalism to advance sustainable shale gas development is finding a suitable fit, that is, a constitutional and governance structure that is amenable to environmental constitutionalism. Countries that demonstrate a constitutional commitment to social, economic and cultural rights (SECRs) seems to be those most amenable to environmental constitutionalism. SECRs are designed to protect human well-being and quality of life, aiming to foster minimum standards of or access to economic and social security. They include rights to work, to form or join a trade union, to strike, to social security, to child protection, to food and housing, to healthcare and to education. Because rights to a quality sustainable environment, and to clean air and water have social, economic and cultural implications, they are more likely to be found in constitutions that recognize other SECRs.[14]

A sweeping report from the Toronto Initiative for Economic and Social Rights (TIESR) dataset supports the observation that national acceptance of SECRs correlates with good practices in environmental constitutionalism. The TIESR study measured the presence, absence and justiciability of 17 SECRs,[15] including a right to a healthy environment, among Constitutions worldwide.[16] Importantly, the TIESR study showed a strong correlation between SECRs in general and environmental rights in particular. It showed that countries with multiple SECRs are more apt to enshrine a right to a quality environment. The TIESR study concluded that 73 countries (or about 53.7 percent of the survey field) of those countries with SECRs also constitutionally enshrine a right to a quality environment.[17]

Gellers concludes that external normative influences tend to have the most profound effect on a country's predisposition toward recognizing

---

[14] Courtney Jung and Evan Rosevear, 'Economic and Social Rights Across Time, Regions, and Legal Traditions: A Preliminary Analysis of the TIESR Dataset' (2012) 30 *Nordic Journal of Human Rights* 374.

[15] The TIESR report refers to these as 'Economic and Social Rights' or 'ESRs'.

[16] The TIESR dataset is available at www.tiesr.org.

[17] Jung and Rosevear, 'Economic and Social Rights Across Time, Regions, and Legal Traditions', above n. 18, at 381.

social and economic rights, including environmental rights.[18] Indeed, the external normative pressures may be culturally, historically or geographically contingent: the common values shared by many Latin American countries, many of which are committed to a deep form of environmental constitutionalism, may be distinct from those shared by Middle Eastern countries, or Asian countries, thus accounting for regional differences in approaches to constitutionalism and to environmentalism.

Moreover, environmental constitutionalism tends to enjoy more success in constitutional systems grounded in civil law traditions than those that operate under other legal traditions. This is significant considering that governance structures worldwide predominantly reflect civil law traditions.[19] Common law systems are less likely to embody environmental constitutionalism, although more likely than Muslim or customary law-based systems, which are least likely to reflect environmental constitutionalism.[20]

(2) Clearly Articulate a Positive Individual or Collective Right, Such as 'Everyone Has an Enforceable Right to a Quality Environment'

The next good practice for using constitutionalism to advance sustainable shale gas development is to guarantee individuated (or collective) environmental rights clearly and directly, such as by recognizing that 'everyone' has the right to an 'adequate', 'clean', 'healthy', 'productive', 'harmonious' or 'sustainable' environment.

Where the Constitution is not explicit on the question of environmental protection, courts in some countries (particularly in India and its neighbors[21]) have inferred it from other constitutional rights such as the right to life, to health or to dignity.[22] While these innovations are welcome from the standpoint of environmental protection, they may not be as

---

18 See generally J.C. Gellers 'Explaining the Emergence of Constitutional Environmental Rights: A Global Quantitative Analysis' (2015) 6(1) *Journal of Human Rights and the Environment* 75.

19 The TIESR study distinguished Constitutions as follows: Civil Law, n =112; Common Law, n =35; Customary Law, n =57; Muslim Law, n =34. Jung and Rosevear, 'Economic and Social Rights Across Time, Regions, and Legal Traditions', above n. 18, at 388.

20 Ibid. 394.

21 See generally, Vijayashri Sripati, 'Human Rights in India: Fifty Years after Independence' (1997) 26 *Denver Journal of International Law and Policy* 93, at 100.

22 Carl Bruch, Wole Coker and Chris VanArsdale. 'Constitutional Environmental Law: Giving Force to Fundamental Principles in Africa' (2001) 26

durable as judicial vindication of clear constitutional mandates: in environmental constitutionalism as elsewhere, the more grounded in constitutional text the judicial consecration, the less susceptible it is to criticism, repudiation, or reversal.

A related good practice is to provide constitutional drafting history, which can assist with interpretive questions. Environmental provisions are often enacted with little if any guidance on threshold questions. Save some exceptions, there is little evidence of the intent of the drafters of these provisions that would provide guidance to their interpreters.[23] A good practice, which is seen far more often in the breach, is to include some explanation or interpretive guidance about the environmental provisions in the constitutional drafting history. Where this is done, as it was in the adoption of the rights of nature provision in Ecuador, it can be of enormous utility and persuasive authority for a court seeking to interpret the constitutional text.[24]

(3) Make Provisions Self-executing by Placement in 'Bill' or 'Declaration' of Rights, Making Them on a Par with Traditional First Order Rights

Another way that constitutionalism can help to advance sustainable shale gas development is to ensure that environmental rights protections are self-executing. Self-executing provisions may be enforced without the need for interceding legislative action. Indeed, the whole point of entrenching a right is to ensure that the value remains protected even if (and especially when) a political majority does not support it.

Self-execution can be expressed either structurally or syntactically. Substantive environmental rights provisions that appear structurally in a constitution alongside first-generation constitutional rights are those most

---

Columbia Journal of Environmental Law 166 (discussing constitutional interpretation in Tanzania, India, Pakistan, Bangladesh, Nepal, Columbia, Ecuador, Costa Rica, and some countries in Africa).

[23] The lower court in the Ecuadorian rights of nature case constitutes one exception, as it quotes at length from the speech of Alberto Acosta, President of the Constituent Assembly, to understand more fully the purpose of constitutionalizing the rights of nature. See *Wheeler* v. *Director de la Procuraduria General del Estado de Loja Juicio*, No. 11121-2011-0010, available at http://blogs.law.widener.edu/envirolawblog/2011/07/12/ecuadorian-courtrecognizes-constitutional-right-to-nature/.

[24] *Wheeler*, above n. 23, quoting the Chair of the constitutional drafting commission Alberto Acosta on the importance of the rights of nature.

likely to be self-executing.[25] Some nations place substantive environmental rights among other first-generation civil and political rights by designating them as an express 'Right', or as a 'Major', 'Human', 'Fundamental', 'Basic' or 'Guaranteed' right.

The Constitutions of the majority of nations that have adopted substantive environmental rights seem to classify them as self-executing rights. Such structural placement makes it more likely that such provisions are self-executing and enforceable. For example, when the Pennsylvania Supreme Court finally came to take seriously that State's constitutional environmental right, it noted that the placement of the provision within the Declaration of Rights of the Pennsylvania Constitution gives the rights protected therein the same degree of protection as any other individual right:

> The right delineated in the first clause of Section 27 presumptively is on a par with, and enforceable to the same extent as, any other right reserved to the people in Article I. See PA. CONST. art. I, § 25 ('everything' in Article I is excepted from government's general powers and is to remain inviolate).[26]

Whatever constitution drafters can do to reinforce the importance, if not the primacy, of constitutional rights will promote their efficacy. Some Constitutions allow the government to elevate environmental values over others. Some allow the government to restrict private property rights in favor of environmental policies, including Mongolia's ('The State shall have the right to … confiscate the land if it is used in a manner adverse to the health of the population, the interests of environmental protection and national security'). Chile's Constitution even contains a 'trump' card over all other rights in favor of the environment: 'The law can establish specific restrictions on the exercise of certain rights or freedoms in order to protect the environment'.

(4) Align Substantive, Policy-based and Procedural Provisions

Aligning environmental rights, policies and procedures with constitutional structures can also better advance sustainable practices in shale gas development. Many Constitutions contain elaborate articulations of the

---

[25] See Tim Hayward, *Constitutional Environmental Rights* (Oxford University Press, 2005), pp. 93–128 (examining the challenges of judicial enforcement of fundamental environmental rights).

[26] *Robinson Township* v. *Commonwealth of Pennsylvania* 52 A.3d 463, 494 (Pa. Cmwlth, 2012).

rights, values, processes and justifications for environmental protections. South Africa's environmental provision (from 1996) embraces both an individual right and a set of directive principles aimed at preventing pollution, promoting conservation and securing sustainable development. Argentina's 1994 Constitution protects the interests of present and future generations, and requires the government to repair environmental damage, use natural resources 'rational[ly]', preserve Argentina's natural and cultural heritage and biological diversity, and requires environmental information and education.[27] Likewise, France's Constitution requires environmental education and training ('Education and training on the environment shall contribute to the exercise of the rights and obligations defined by this Charter'). Thus, another good practice about textual instantiation of environmental values is that the more detailed the provision, the better.

Some environmental provisions specifically address certain types of activities that may be especially harmful to the local environment. For example, several countries prohibit the disposal of nuclear or hazardous wastes or substances that are imported from another country, including Niger ('The transit, importation, storage, landfill, [and] dumping on the national territory of foreign pollutants or toxic wastes, as well as any agreement relating [to it] constitute a crime against the Nation, punished by the law').

The Constitutions of other countries expressly restrain or restrict energy-related activities that could adversely affect the environment, including Ecuador's ('The State shall promote, in the public and private sectors, the use of environmentally clean technologies and nonpolluting and low-impact alternative sources of energy. Energy sovereignty shall not be achieved to the detriment of food sovereignty nor shall it affect the right to water').

Addressing rights to water is another common good practice. Indeed, about 30 Constitutions provide for rights to water as a human or environmental right, including at least one dozen countries that instantiate a human right to a fair distribution of clean, safe or potable water.[28] For example, South Africa's Constitution makes a strong commitment to

---

[27] Argentina Constitution (1994), art. 42.

[28] These are: Bolivia (art. 16(I)); Colombia (art. 366); Democratic Republic of Congo (art. 48); Ecuador (art. 12); Ethiopia (art. 90(1)); Gambia (art. 216(4)); the Maldives (art. 23); Panama (arts 110 and 118); Swaziland (art. 215); Switzerland (art. 76); Uganda (arts XIV(b) and XXI); Uruguay (art. 47); Venezuela (arts 127 and 304); and Zambia (art. 112(d)).

acknowledging water as a fundamental human right by asserting an enforceable individual right to access to drinking water.[29]

Ecuador's protection for the rights of nature[30] is another example of the alliance between substantive environmental rights and other constitutional guarantees whose combined effect is to strengthen the hand of courts when they attempt to vindicate environmental rights. The Ecuadorian provision further confirms that this right is not merely hortatory in that it empowers each 'person, community, people, or nationality'[31] to exercise public authority to enforce the right, according to normal constitutional processes.[32]

(5) Recognize Emerging Areas of Environmental Constitutionalism, Including Sustainability, Public Trust, Climate Change and Biocentrism

Another good practice for advancing sustainable shale gas development is to constitutionalize emerging areas in environmental constitutional protection, including sustainability, rights of nature, public trust and climate change, discussed below.

(i) Sustainability

Environmental sustainability is an amorphous concept that stands for the proposition that present generations should use resources so as to preserve opportunities for future generations. Nearly 20 countries expressly recognize a constitutional goal of 'sustainability' or 'sustainable development' though most of these are in sections of the Constitutions or written in language that indicates that they are not amenable to judicial enforcement. For example, Switzerland's Constitution contains a specific section entitled 'Sustainable Development', which provides that 'The Confederation and the Cantons shall endeavor to achieve a balanced and sustainable relationship between nature and its capacity to renew itself and the demands placed on it by the population'.

Sustainability recognizes responsibilities owed to those who follow. The Constitutions of about a dozen countries give at least a passing nod to 'future generations'. For example, Papua New Guinea's Constitution

---

[29] South Africa Constitution, ch. 2, art. 27(1)(b): 'Everyone has the right to have access to: (b) sufficient food and water'.

[30] Ecuador Constitution, title II, ch. 7, art. 71 and arts 72–4.

[31] Ibid. art. 71.

[32] Ibid.

requires the state to hold environmental resources 'in trust for future generations' and 'for the benefit of future generations'.

The strongest embodiment of environmental sustainability would seem to stem from those Constitutions that promote sustainable development *for the purpose of* protecting the interests of future generations. The Constitutions from around 18 countries contain this sort of hybrid pronouncement. For example, Mozambique's Constitution requires that the state:

> [w]ith a view to guaranteeing the right to the environment within the framework of sustainable development ... shall adopt policies aimed at ... guaranteeing the rational utilization of natural resources and the safeguarding of their capacity to regenerate, ecological stability and the rights of future generations.

The Constitutions of some countries require that specific resources be developed with future generations in mind. For example, the Dominican Republic provides that 'nonrenewable natural resources, can only be explored and exploited by individuals, under sustainable environmental criteria' and provides for the protection of the environment 'for the benefit of the present and future generations'.

(ii) Public trust

Environmental constitutionalism can sometimes reflect public trust notions. The Constitutions of half a dozen countries reference holding or protecting resources for the 'public trust' or some variation of that terminology. These tend to impose a trust responsibility upon policy-makers, rulers or citizens to hold resources in trust for current or future generations. Some specify trust responsibilities as a general governing norm. For example, the Ugandan Constitution provides that:

> the Government or a local government as determined by Parliament by law, shall hold in trust for the people and protect, natural lakes, rivers, wetlands, forest reserves, game reserves, national parks and any land to be reserved for ecological and touristic purposes for the common good of all citizens.

Reflecting traditional views of sovereignty, some Constitutions invest public trust in a supreme leader. For example, Ghana's Constitution provides that 'All public lands in Ghana shall be vested in the President on behalf of, and in trust for, the people of Ghana', and:

> every mineral in its natural state in, under or upon any land in Ghana, rivers, streams, water courses throughout Ghana, the exclusive economic zone and

> any area covered by the territorial sea or continental shelf is the property of the Republic of Ghana and shall be vested in the President on behalf of, and in trust for the people of Ghana.

Some constitutional provisions hold citizens accountable to hold resources in trust for future generations. For example, Tanzania's Constitution provides that 'all citizens together possess all the natural resources of the country in trust for their descendants'.

(iii) Climate change

Shortcomings in international and domestic responses to climate change create opportunities for tactical deployment of environmental constitutionalism. Thus far, however, very few countries have seen fit to address climate change constitutionally. The Dominican Republic's Constitution is explicit on the point, with a provision under 'The Organization of the Territory' that provides for a 'plan of territorial ordering that assures the efficient and sustainable use of the natural resources of the Nation, in accordance with the need of adaptation to climate change'.

Environmental constitutionalism might play an important if limited role in local approaches to climate change. Constitutions can, for one, direct governments to enact and implement policies to address the effects of climate change in ways not accomplished through existing international and national laws. And once absorbed into constitutional texts, courts can impel action by enforcing these provisions even through progressive realization.

(iv) Biocentric rights

Environmental constitutionalism advancing the right of nature is emergent and insistent, but still uncommon. The constitutionalization of the rights of nature is part of a slowly growing global movement highlighting the importance of the natural environment for its own sake and as a whole, rather than as an aggregation of resources to be harnessed by humans for various purposes.[33]

Environmental constitutionalism addressing nature appears as either governmental duties or substantive rights of nature. First, the Constitutions of some countries require all branches of government to protect nature. Germany's Constitution, for instance, requires the government to

---

[33] E. Daly, 'The Ecuadorian Exemplar: The First Ever Vindications of Constitutional Rights of Nature' (2012) 21 *Review of European Community and International Environmental Law* 1. See also rightsofnature.org and www.celdf.org/rights-of-nature.

protect 'the natural bases of life and the animals within the framework of the constitutional order by legislation, and in accordance with law and justice, by executive and judicial power'.

Second, biocentric environmental constitutionalism – recognizing the *right of nature* – has been pushed most emphatically so far by a couple of countries in South America. In 2008, Ecuador amended its Constitution to recognize the right of nature, providing that:

> Nature, or Pachamama, where life is reproduced and created, has the right to integral respect for her existence, her maintenance, and for the regeneration of her vital cycles, structure, functions, and evolutionary processes.[34]

Bolivia also has a framework law recognizing the rights of nature,[35] and discussions of constitutional reforms to recognize them have taken place in Turkey.[36] Moreover, rights of nature have recently found traction at the super-sub-national level, including in various municipalities in the United States.[37]

Even without explicit protection for the rights of nature, courts might be encouraged to interpret constitutional environmental provisions as protecting natural resources, the natural environment or the biodiversity within it. For instance, in vindicating the Chilean Constitution's right to a healthy environment, the Chilean Constitutional Court held that the right extends to cases involving environmental degradation *per se*, regardless of its effect on humans. This would include cases requiring the clean-up of beaches of Chañaral, Chile, for instance, where copper tailing wastes had been deposited for 50 years, destroying marine life.[38] Where this is the standard, the case would center on whether the environment itself is healthy, not on whether the environmental degradation induced any harm

---

[34] Ecuador Constitution, title II, ch. 7, arts 71–4. For an additional review of the judicial progressiveness in securing environmental rights in Ecuador, see Radden Patrick Keefe, 'Reversal of fortune: A crusading lawyer helped Ecuadorans secure a huge environmental judgment against Chevron. But did he go too far?', *The New Yorker*, 9 January 2012.

[35] John Vidal, 'Bolivia enshrines natural world's rights with equal status for Mother Earth' (10 April 2011), available at www.guardian.co.uk/environment/2011/apr/10/bolivia-enshrines-natural-worlds-rights.

[36] Global Alliance for the Rights of Nature, 'Turkey calling for ecological constitution' (23 May 2011), available at http://therightsofnature.org/rights-of-nature-laws/turkey-ecological-constitution/.

[37] See www.celdf.org.

[38] *Pedro Flores and others* v. *Corporacion Del Cobre, Codelco, Division Salvador*, Rol. 12.753 FS. 641 (Supreme Court of Chile, 1988).

to human beings. This is especially important with respect to water-related rights, where ecological concerns may be inconsistent with the human right to adequate water for personal and commercial uses.

(6) Scaffold Additional Statutory and Regulatory Means to Implement Constitutional Prerogatives

The impact of constitutional provisions advancing sustainable shale gas practices, whether elaborate or sparse, can also be enhanced by implementing legislation and regulation, or what we term 'extra-constitutional scaffolding'. In the Philippines and Argentina, elaborate statutory schemes promote and facilitate vindication of environmental constitutional rights. In the Philippines, the Supreme Court has developed a set of Rules of Procedure for Environmental Cases that encourage the vindication of constitutional and other environmental rights in extraordinary ways.

Importantly for environmental rights, the Philippine Rules provide for consideration of cases brought on behalf of nature, known as the 'writ of Kalikasan'. Such a writ can be pursued on behalf 'of persons whose constitutional right to a balanced and healthful ecology is violated, or threatened' by a public official or private entity, 'involving environmental damage of such magnitude as to prejudice the life, health or property of inhabitants in two or more cities or provinces'.[39]

Provisions making environmental information available, as well as requirements relating to standing, proof of injury and the allocation of fees and costs, can also promote or deter invocation of constitutional environmental rights provisions. These issues can be defined constitutionally or statutorily and can be articulated explicitly and exclusively for enforcement of constitutional rights or without any explicit reference to environmental rights at all. Here too, the more work done by the text, the less need for judicial interpretation and interpolation. All of this assumes what is perhaps the most significant determinant of the efficacy of constitutional environmental provisions: that they exist within a legal and political framework in which an independent and adequately funded judiciary has the authority, legitimacy and expertise necessary to meaningfully implement not only environmental rights but other constitutional guarantees as well. Constitutions in countries where the rule of law can be assumed to be entrenched and respected are likely to be effectively

---

[39] Supreme Court of Philippines, Rules of Procedure for Environmental Cases, Rule 7, s. 1.

implemented steadily over time. And environmental rights in particular require persistent application in order for the benefits to be realized.

(7) Liberalize Access to Judicial Vindication by Permitting Open Standing, Special Procedural Rules and Fee-Shifting for Public Interest Litigation

The next way to use environmental constitutionalism to promote sustainable shale gas practices is by liberalizing access to justice. For example, before a court reaches the merits of a constitutional claim, it will often consider the preliminary question of standing: whether the party who brought the suit has the right to invoke the court's jurisdiction. Most constitutional traditions have a standing doctrine, although they vary widely from country to country. Some constitutional systems limit those who can challenge government action to certain members of the government, or to an ombudsman, while others encourage anyone to seek judicial protection. Although sometimes seen as a fringe question, standing rules can have a dramatic effect on a nation's legal culture: where standing rules are broad and inviting, more people are encouraged to bring more cases to enforce more laws not only for their own private benefit but for the public good. Conversely, where courts restrict access to judicial fora, compliance with existing laws, as well as the progressive realization of constitutional promises, may be seen more as a matter of political discretion than of constitutional obligation.

Environmental cases in particular challenge conventional standing practices. Even where constitutional review is open to members of the public, standing has traditionally been limited to those who can assert well-recognized claims, including claims for harms recognized at common law (such as violations of property rights) or interests specifically identified in statutory provisions. In either case, the claims are personal, and standing rules tend to reflect the principle that only individuals who are personally and particularly injured may assert their interests against defendants and lay claim to scarce judicial resources.

Environmental harms, however, tend to affect groups of people generally and similarly. They may affect a whole community or culture or, in the case of climate change, all of humanity. Even where an individual can claim a particular harm (such as, for example, where a toxic leak proves carcinogenic) it is most likely that the plaintiff is not the only person so affected but that a whole community is affected by a greater incidence of cancer; indeed, the plaintiff is more likely to be able to show causation where the defendant's wrongful actions caused a broad-based injury rather than just her own illness. In even more difficult cases, the claim is based on the health not of an individual but of the environment in the abstract and may raise questions about environmental aesthetics or the health of a particular animal population that do not directly affect most people at all.

Consequently, the good practice is to relax or defray standing requirements to vindicate constitutional environmental rights. Some Constitutions make the decision for the court, clearly delineating who may sue and who may not, either for all claims or specifically in environmental cases. In Spain, constitutional environmental rights are protected, but they are enforceable only when an ombudsman initiates litigation. This contrasts markedly with the rest of the Spanish-speaking world, which tends to be receptive to constitutional environmental claims. The Constitutions of Argentina and Ecuador, for instance, invite any citizen to vindicate such rights, the latter even allowing claims on behalf of nature itself.[40] The Constitution of South Africa, too, adopts an open attitude toward standing, which is buttressed by legislation that reinforces the right of any person to approach the court to assert his or her own interest, the interest of another, or the public interest. The statutory authority to sue extends to suits on behalf of the environment.[41]

In Latin America, constitutional and statutory provisions have encouraged courts to expand standing for environmental cases even to those who cannot show a direct and individual injury; in India and its neighbors, courts have had to infer broad standing from legal and cultural norms. But in both of these regions, as well as in some other countries around the world, the commitment to opening the courthouse doors to environmental claimants is well established.

Even where the positive law is not as clear, some courts have opened their doors to environmental activists, often seeing these non-traditional stakeholders not only as litigants but as partners in an ongoing campaign in which the courts are equally invested.

---

[40] Argentina Constitution, Pt I, ch. II, arts 41–3; Ecuador Constitution, title II, ch. 7, arts 71–4.

[41] Louis J. Kotze and Anél du Plessis, 'Some Brief Observations on Fifteen Years of Environmental Rights Jurisprudence in South Africa' (2010) 3 *Journal of Court Innovations* 157, at 163–4 (discussing South Africa Constitution, art. 20 and the National Environmental Management Act 107 of 1998 (NEMA), art. 32).

(8) Install Complementary National and Sub-national Layers of Environmental Constitutionalism

Complementary national and sub-national constitutional enactments are another good device for advancing sustainable shale gas practices. Led by states in the Americas in general, and Brazil in particular, sub-national governments around the globe have seen fit to constitutionalize substantive and procedural environmental rights, environmental duties and sustainable development for present and future generations, often with much more specificity and enforceability than provided in national Constitutions.

Sub-national environmental constitutionalism can complement national efforts in several ways. First, sub-national Constitutions can reflect local environmental concerns that can be ignored or underserved by the national Constitution, even when those concerns may address global challenges. Second, sub-national Constitutions can fill gaps often left open in national Constitutions. Remarkable examples of this are found in Brazil, whose State Constitutions delineate extensive governmental functions in the service of substantive environmental rights, including promoting biodiversity and sustainability; protecting species and water quality; advancing conservation and environmental education; and enforcing environmental requirements. Complementarity like this reinforces the tenet that environmental protection is a shared obligation between the central and peripheral governments and relevant to both national identity and local control. Germany provides another example of rich State constitutional environmental protection that supports federal environmental constitutionalism. On the other hand, whatever environmental constitutionalism exists in the United States is more developed at the State level than at the federal level.

(9) Bundle Constitutional Recognition of Substantive Rights with Rights to Information, Participation and Access to Justice

Constitutional provisions that protect procedural rights, including principally rights to information on environmental matters, rights of participation in environmental decision-making and access to environmental justice can also advance sustainable development of shale gas.

The Constitutions of around three-dozen countries specifically recognize procedural rights in environmental matters, primarily to advance a human right to a quality environment. Such rights to information, participation and access to justice in environmental matters are a modern constitutional innovation. These sorts of provisions appear to serve both human and environmental interests, and can advance democratic values.[42]

Most of these constitutional procedural environmental rights provisions seem to be designed to help implement substantive environmental rights. For example, Ukraine's Constitution from 2004 creates an individual right to an environment that is 'safe for life and health' and further provides for damages when the right has been violated. It further provides for the right of access to and dissemination of information about the environment, as well as the quality of food and consumer goods.[43] Where such provisions expressly denote environmental concerns they are more likely to be invoked by litigants and recognized by courts in environmental cases, in part because the language itself suggests that they are designed to complement substantive environmental rights. But they can still be indispensable to the vindication of constitutional environmental rights even where they are of general applicability.

(10) Develop Quality Jurisprudence in Environmental Constitutionalism

The culminating good practice how environmental constitutionalism can advance sustainable shale gas development is to develop quality jurisprudence. Courts asked to apply constitutional environmental rights provisions face numerous difficult choices and have significant discretion in

[42] William Onzivu, 'International Environmental Law, the Public's Health, and Domestic Environmental Governance in Developing Countries' (2006) 21 *American University International Law Review* 597, at 672 ('International human rights law and national constitutions provide for procedural rights that are instrumental in the protection of human health and the environment. These rights include freedom of association, freedom of information, public participation in decisionmaking processes, and access to justice and judicial review'); B.W. Cramer, 'The Human Right to Information, the Environment and Information about the Environment: From the Universal Declaration to the Aarhus Convention' (2009) 14 *Communication Law and Policy* 74 ('The push for a fundamental human right to environmental protection is in turn inspiring demands for access to government documents and meetings that deal with environmental matters'); Gyula Bandi, 'The Right to Environment in Theory and Practice: The Hungarian Experience' (1993) 8 *Connecticut Journal of International Law* 450 (discussing the Hungarian Constitution's public participation provisions); Hayward, *Constitutional Environmental Rights*, above n. 29, at 200–3 (discussing procedural environmental rights in Africa and elsewhere).

[43] Ukraine Constitution (2004), ch. II, art. 50.

terms of interpretation, vindication and remediation. There are no generally accepted standards for identifying or vindicating these interests *as rights*, in part because, in straddling every familiar category of rights, environmental constitutionalism defies easy classification.[44]

Environmental rights include human rights as well as non-human rights, protecting such values as biodiversity and nature itself. As a human right, the environment can be protected through civil and political rights of participation and access to information, but it can also be protected as a social, economic and even cultural right. Environmental rights can be collective or individual and they can apply to the majority or to a discrete, insular and politically powerless minority. They can be treated as immediately enforceable or realized progressively over time, according to a legislative plan, and limited by the availability of fiscal resources. They can be implicit or explicit, procedural or substantive, and they can be amenable to judicial review or immune to it. They can be positive or negative or both (sometimes in the same case). They can be remedied injunctively or through compensation or declaration, for violations occurring in the past, as well as for harms as yet unknown and to people as yet unborn. In some ways, remedying environmental harms is long overdue, and yet the primary beneficiaries of environmental rights are those in the next generations. Environmental rights define the relationship between people and the world we live in, though invariably in broad and amorphous terms without clear foci or boundaries.

So how do courts give content to the concept of environmental rights without allowing them to swallow up every other right? One approach, which borrows from the discourse at the international level, is to limit the reach of environmental rights to already accepted human rights.[45] Environmental constitutionalism has pushed the conventional limits of this

---

[44] Hayward, *Constitutional Environmental Rights*, above n. 29, at 25–58 (making a case for a human right to an 'adequate environment'); Barry E. Hill, Steve Wolfson and Nicholas Targ, 'Human Rights and the Environment: A Synopsis and Some Predications' (2004) 16 *Georgetown International Law Review* 361: '[W]hile there appears to be a growing trend favoring a human right to a clean and healthy environment – involving the balancing of social, economic, health, and environmental factors – international bodies, nations, and states have yet to articulate a sufficiently clear legal test or framework so as to ensure consistent, protective application and enforcement of such a right'.

[45] Randall S. Abate, 'Climate Change, the United States, and the Impacts of Arctic Melting: A Case Study in the Need for Enforceable International Environmental Human Rights' (2006) 43 *Stanford Journal of International Law* 10 ('Existing sources of domestic and international law embrace a human-centered approach to environmental protection and recognize the connection

approach in two directions. Even where Constitutions do not specifically enumerate particular rights, courts have expanded the scope of interests that constitute violations of familiar human rights by recognizing, for instance, that environmental degradation can constitute a violation of privacy and family life, or that aesthetic and recreational environmental interests are essential to enjoying a dignified existence.

A slightly less anthropocentric option is explicitly to recognize environmental rights *as* a human right, so that environmental harms do not have to fit neatly into the other human rights boxes.[46] This view reflects an international environmental law approach and has been incorporated into Constitutions throughout the world. This also ensures that environmental values are given at least as much weight as other constitutional values, and perhaps more than some[47] and more than non-constitutional values such as development or some property interests.

An even less anthropocentric approach involves a class of rights somewhere between human rights and rights of nature that permit humans to commence constitutional environmental claims to protect nature or wildlife. A final approach would entirely reject anthropocentrism and recognize instead the rights of nature.

Admittedly, there is no 'best' practice here; the beauty of constitutionalism is that it takes a global problem and allows each nation to define for itself the particular balance of competing values that will produce the greatest benefit for each particular society. One country may be most concerned with protecting biodiversity, while the principal focus in another may be to ensure adequate water resources for everyone, while a third may be most concerned with promoting participatory environmental decision-making. Environmental constitutionalism permits each country

---

between human rights and environmental protection. These mechanisms can serve as a viable foundation upon which to build a new system to recognize and protect international environmental human rights'); Onzivu, 'International Environmental Law', above n. 46, at 667 ('An emerging right to a healthy environment favors the protection of public health. This is because such a right is viewed as anthropocentric and ecocentric, supporting environmental protection for both public health and intrinsic or aesthetic reasons').

[46] Dinah Shelton, 'Human Rights and the Environment: What Specific Environmental Rights Have Been Recognized?' (2006) 35 *Denver Journal of International Law and Policy* 129, at 163 ('Moreover, recognizing a right to environment could encompass elements of nature protection and ecological balance, substantive areas not generally protected under human rights law because of its anthropocentric focus').

[47] See *Wheeler*, above n. 23, noting that environmental rights should prevail over other constitutional rights.

to address its own priorities. The 'good practice' here is that each country's constitutional environmental framework should reflect those priorities in a robust and enduring way.

However, good practices require that as many aspects of litigation as possible be made express and comprehensive in advance, particularly where environmental rights confound ordinary expectations and assumptions generally applicable outside of environmental constitutionalism. For instance, while the beneficiaries of other constitutional rights are the putative litigants (think, for instance, of those who would claim the right to free speech or protection of property), the putative beneficiaries of environmental constitutionalism are often not obvious. For example, under a directive principle of state policy, the Indian Constitution requires the state to 'endeavour to protect and improve the environment and to safeguard the forests and wild life of the country'.[48] This protection seems to be as much for the benefit of the citizens as for the wildlife and even the forests themselves. But who can sue if the wildlife is not safeguarded? This is not only a question of standing but of the nature of the right and purpose of judicial intervention in the policy-making authority of the state. Is the court empowered to protect the flora and fauna or only to protect the people of the nation? Is a government constitutionally obligated to legislate for the benefit of the rivers, or may it limit its portfolio to helping the citizens directly? Can a Constitution protect non-human interests?

These difficult questions of public policy may, in some instances, even require recalibrating the boundaries between the public and private spheres. While some governments are held responsible for the environmental degradation caused by their licensees, some corporations are required to take on public goods like environmental clean-up. Environmental litigation may often in fact invert the normal expectations relating to the roles of public and private parties. Whereas traditional constitutional rights litigation pits the private individual against the public authority, environmental litigation often pits members of the public against a private entity (thus invoking the principle of the horizontal application of constitutional rights and obligations). Moreover, in many of these cases, private individuals are asserting public rights, whereas the government is facilitating private gain.[49] This does not mean just that

---

[48] India Constitution, art. 48A, 42nd Amendment (1976).

[49] See, for example, *Juan Antonio Oposa and others v. The Honorable Fulgencio S. Factoran, Jr.* G.R. No. 10183, 224 S.C.R.A. 792 (Supreme Court of the Philippines, 30 July 1993), reprinted in 33 I.L.M. 173 (1994) (involving government-issued timber licenses); Svitlana Kravchenko and John E. Bonine,

courts should consider standing questions expansively; rather, environmental litigation is increasingly forcing courts to adjust long-held views about the proper allocation of public and private power. It is therefore a good practice to be explicit about the putative beneficiary of the right, either in the Constitution itself or in early decisions from the interpreting court.

Indeed, it seems evident that no Constitution will address every issue, or even every major issue, that is likely to arise. Courts that interpret such provisions, therefore, have a significant and ongoing responsibility to decide these important questions and to use their opinions to explicate them; this would typically include not only explaining the interpretive choices, but also setting out the constitutional values and principles that underlie the associated decision.

These ten good practices in environmental constitutionalism promote sustainable practices in the development of unconventional shale gas reserves. Thus the next section examines a recent court decision that embodies some of these good practices.

III *ROBINSON TOWNSHIP V. COMMONWEALTH OF PENNSYLVANIA*: GOOD PRACTICES IN PRACTICE

The *Robinson Township* opinion from the Pennsylvania Supreme Court reflects good practices in constitutional environmental opinion-writing so as to advance sustainable practices in shale gas governance and development.

In *Robinson Township*, the Pennsylvania Supreme Court gave life to a State's constitutional environmental rights provision that had been adopted more than 30 years previously. It struck out as unconstitutional major parts of Act 13 of 2012, a state oil and gas law designed to promote the development of unconventional shale gas reserves in the State of Pennsylvania. The Environmental Rights Amendment to the Pennsylvania Constitution afforded rights and imposed public trust duties that were commensurate with other constitutional prerogatives: 'It is not a historical accident that the Pennsylvania Constitution now places citizens' environmental rights on a par with their political rights'.[50] Act 13 was enacted based on 'the mischief to be remedied and the object to be attained', namely, to address environmental degradation in the State

Human Rights and the Environment: Cases, Law and Policy (Carolina Academic Press, 2007) (referring to Hungary helping to sell off forests to private interests).

[50] *Robinson Township* v. *Commonwealth of Pennsylvania*, above n. 30.

by promoting individual environmental rights and requiring governmental authorities to hold natural resources in public trust.[51]

A plurality of the court determined that Act 13 contravened Environmental Rights Amendment, Article I, section 27's remonstration that the state holds natural resources 'in the public trust': 'we agree with the citizens that, as an exercise of the police power, [Act 13 is] incompatible with the Commonwealth's duty as trustee of Pennsylvania's public natural resources'. The plurality observed: 'As the citizens illustrate, development of the natural gas industry in the Commonwealth unquestionably has and will have a lasting, and undeniably detrimental, impact on the quality … of Pennsylvania's environment, which are part of the public trust'.[52]

The plurality's opinion in *Robinson Township* demonstrates good practices in environmental constitutionalism in large part because it represents an authentic attempt to engage the text of the Environmental Rights Amendment. First, the plurality noted that section 27 (much like many provisions that provide such rights) vests two rights in the people of the state. The first is a right to clean air, pure water, and to the preservation of the natural, scenic, historic and aesthetic values of the environment. The second is 'a limitation on the state's power to act contrary to this right'. Importantly, the plurality held that these rights are equal in status and enforceability to any other rights included in the State Constitution, including property rights.

Second, it enforced the 'public trust' provisions, that is, the obligations of the State to hold resources in public trust for all people. Because the State is the trustee of these resources, it has a fiduciary duty to 'conserve and maintain' them: 'The plain meaning of the terms conserve and maintain implicates a duty to prevent and remedy the degradation, diminution, or depletion of our public natural resources'.

The plurality in *Robinson Township* also made a point to note that the Environmental Rights Amendment served both present and future generations. Echoing sentiments from the majority opinion in *Minors Oposa*, it observed:

> By any responsible account, the exploitation of the Marcellus Shale Formation will produce a detrimental effect on the environment, on the people, their children, and future generations, and potentially on the public purse, perhaps rivaling the environmental effects of coal extraction.

---

[51] Ibid.
[52] Ibid.

In so doing, the plurality opinion in particular advanced the purpose of constitutional-enshrinement of environmental rights and public trust duties in the first place: to promote environmental protection and advance individual rights to a quality environment.

In some ways, *Robinson Township* is a more modern embodiment of good practices in environmental jurisprudence reflected in the *Minors Oposa* case, in which the Philippine Supreme Court laid the foundation for recognizing the rights of future generations to bring environmental claims:

> Petitioners minors assert that they represent their generation as well as generations yet unborn. We find no difficulty in ruling that they can, for themselves, for others of their generation and for the succeeding generations, file a class suit. Their personality to sue in behalf of the succeeding generations can only be based on the concept of intergenerational responsibility insofar as the right to a balanced and healthful ecology is concerned.

But the court went further and elucidated the meaning of the constitutional mandate to protect the 'rhythm and harmony of nature', stating that:

> Nature means the created world in its entirety. Such rhythm and harmony indispensably include, inter alia, the judicious disposition, utilization, management, renewal and conservation of the country's forest, mineral, land, waters, fisheries, wildlife, off-shore areas and other natural resources to the end that their exploration, development and utilization be equitably accessible to the present as well as future generations.

With this expansive and fundamental conception of nature, the court was able to justify its holding that children and future generations had legitimate and cognizable legal claims:

> Needless to say, every generation has a responsibility to the next to preserve that rhythm and harmony for the full enjoyment of a balanced and healthful ecology. Put a little differently, the minors' assertion of their right to a sound environment constitutes, at the same time, the performance of their obligation to ensure the protection of that right for the generations to come.[53]

Robinson Township well reflects the good practices outlined in the prior section. The underlying provisions were adopted in a governance structure that already recognized social, economic and cultural rights. The underlying rights were explicit and self-enforcing, and placed within an

---

[53] *Oposa*, above n. 49, at 9–10.

appropriate constitutional constellation. The rights were also coupled with evolving notions of environmental constitutionalism concerning sustainability, future generations, public trust and energy use, and afforded participatory rights in a scaffolded legislative and regulatory setting with complimentary municipal and local considerations.

The experience that courts have had in trying to make sense of and take seriously constitutional environmental rights reveals a lesson which, when learned, may significantly enrich the praxis of constitutional law generally. At bottom, adoption of good practices in constitutional incorporation of environmental rights, protections and procedures is multifaceted and serves as a proxy for social compacts with present and future generations.

IV CONCLUSION

Unconventional shale gas development is occurring at a breakneck pace, principally in North America, with vast reserves elsewhere. This development has placed new and unorthodox stresses on traditional environmental governance paradigms. Environmental constitutionalism offers an additional tool for engaging in sustainable practices in the development of shale gas. We identify ten 'good practices' in environmental constitutionalism including: situating it in systems amenable to social, economic and cultural rights, and those with civil law traditions; clearly articulating a positive individual or collective right; making provisions self-executing; aligning substantive, policy-based and procedural provisions; recognizing sustainability, public trust, climate and biocentrism; scaffolding additional statutory and regulatory means to implement constitutional prerogatives; liberalizing access to judicial vindication; combining national and sub-national environmental constitutionalism; adopting constitutional rights to information, participation and access to justice in environmental matters; and developing quality jurisprudence in environmental constitutionalism. Spotlighting the recently-decided *Robinson Township* decision from the Pennsylvania Supreme Court in the United States as an exemplar, we conclude that environmental constitutionalism can play a key role in promoting sustainable development of unconventional shale gas reserves, if at all.

4. Human rights versus human needs: debating the language for universal access to modern energy services

Manuel Peter Samonte Solis

I INTRODUCTION

Energy is indispensable to providing basic needs, eradicating poverty and meeting sustainable development goals.[1] This is because access to modern energy services[2] affects a variety of critical outcomes involving 'productivity, health, education, safe water and communication services',[3] among others. Yet 1.3 billion people remain without access to electricity.[4] Also, 2.6 billion people are still using traditional biomass fuels (firewood, charcoal, crop residues and animal dung) for their cooking needs with deleterious health consequences.[5] Unfortunately, these twin deficits add another significant dimension to poverty called 'energy poverty', which refers to the 'inability to cook with modern cooking fuels and the lack of a bare minimum of electric lighting to read

---

[1] General Assembly Resolution 67/215, Promotion of New and Renewable Energy Sources, at 3, para. 13, available at www.se4all.org/sites/default/files/l/2015/08/A-RES-69-225-2014-Promotion-of-new-and-renewable-sources-of-energy.pdf.

[2] The International Energy Agency defines 'modern energy access' as 'a household having reliable and affordable access to clean cooking facilities, a first connection to electricity and then an increasing level of electricity consumption over time to reach the regional average'. International Energy Agency, 'Energy for All: Financing Access for the Poor' in *Special Early Excerpt of the World Energy Outlook 2011* (IEA, 2011).

[3] Amie Gaye, 'Access to Energy and Human Development' in *Human Development Report 2007/2008* (2007).

[4] International Energy Agency, *World Energy Outlook 2012* (IEA, 2012), p. 529.

[5] Ibid.

or for other household and productive activities at sunset'.[6] In its expanded version, however, energy poverty encompasses 'lack of access to resources, denial of opportunities and choices in energy that is adequate, safe, and reliable for economic and human development'.[7]

By providing access to modern energy services like electricity, the poor are given the opportunity to move up the energy ladder, as it were, from traditional biomass fuels to modern energy, and reap its positive environmental and health effects.[8] Also, a variety of income-generating activities and business opportunities becomes possible.[9] In turn, this substantially benefits women and children, who are considered the 'prime beneficiaries of rural electrification'.[10] There is emerging evidence showing that women in households with electricity spend less time on fuel collection and other household chores, and more time on productive work, family, education and leisure activities.[11] Electric lighting and electric-powered water pumping facilities, for instance, 'are likely to reduce women's drudgery in fetching water and create opportunities to set up other businesses'.[12]

Moreover, access to modern energy services addresses critical safety and health-related concerns due to inefficient production and utilization of energy sources such as indoor air pollution, poisoning and fire hazards from the use of traditional biomass stoves, low-quality kerosene lanterns, and paraffin candles for lighting.[13] Alarmingly, the number of premature

---

[6] Gaye, 'Access to Energy and Human Development', above n. 3, at 4, quoting the United Nations Development Programme (UNDP) definition.

[7] United Nations Development Programme, *Towards an 'Energy Plus' Approach for the Poor* (UNDP, 2011), p. 19.

[8] World Bank, *The Welfare Impact of Rural Electrification: A Reassessment of the Costs and Benefits* (2008), p. 31: 'The energy ladder refers to the phenomenon of households and firms – and so, in aggregate, countries – shifting from low-efficiency fuels to high-efficiency ones as income per capita increases'.

[9] Benjamin Sovacool and Ira Martina Drupady, *Energy Access, Poverty, and Development* (2012), p. 46.

[10] Douglas Barnes, 'The Challenge of Rural Electrification' in Douglas Barnes (ed.), *The Challenge of Rural Electrification: Strategies for Developing Countries* (Resources for the Future, 2007), p. 5.

[11] Ibid.

[12] Paul Cook, 'Rural Electrification and Rural Development' in Subhes Bhattacharyya (ed.), *Rural Electrification Through Decentralised Off-grid Systems in Developing Countries* (Springer, 2013), p. 25.

[13] See Sovacool and Drupady, *Energy Access, Poverty, and Development*, above n. 9, at 48–9; Douglas Barnes and Willem Floor, 'Rural Energy in Developing Countries: A Challenge for Economic Development' (1996) 21 *Annual Review of Energy and the Environment* 499.

deaths – over 4 million per annum[14] – due to indoor air pollution alone exceeds those caused by malaria or tuberculosis.[15] Furthermore, access to modern energy services enables the delivery of social, health and medical services that enhance the attainment of the United Nations (UN) Millennium Development Goals (MDGs) on maternal health, infant mortality, and water and sanitation.[16] Therefore, access to modern energy services is inextricably linked to achieving international developmental goals in a definable and concrete sense.[17]

Essentially, the challenge lies in how to enhance access to modern energy services, particularly to those who live in impoverished rural areas of the developing world,[18] while achieving universal coverage and sustainable development at the same time. In response, the UN called the world's attention to this challenge and launched the 'Sustainable Energy for All' (SEFA) initiative, that focuses on three interlinked objectives: (1) enhancing universal access to modern energy services;[19] (2) improving the rate of energy efficiency; and (3) increasing the use of renewable energy.[20]

Beyond catalyzing global awareness,[21] the critical stage of turning the 'vision [of SEFA] into reality with concrete commitments to action' beckons.[22] The scale and magnitude of the challenge is such that in order

---

[14] World Health Organization, *Household Air Pollution and Health*, Fact Sheet No. 292 (March 2014), available at /www.who.int/mediacentre/factsheets/fs292/en/.

[15] International Energy Agency, United Nations Development Programme and United Nations Industrial Development Organization, *Energy Poverty: How to Make Modern Energy Access Universal?* (2010), p. 13.

[16] Sovacool and Drupady, *Energy Access, Poverty, and Development*, above n. 9, at 48–9.

[17] Yinka Omorogbe, 'Policy, Law, and the Actualization of the Right to Access to Energy Services' in Kim Talus (ed.), *Research Handbook on International Energy Law* (Edward Elgar Publishing Ltd, 2014), p. 361.

[18] According to the International Energy Agency, 84 per cent of 1.3 billion people without access to electricity live in rural areas. International Energy Agency, 'Energy for All: Financing Access for the Poor', above n. 2, at 3.

[19] The Secretary-General's Advisory Group on Energy and Climate Change, *Energy for a Sustainable Future: Summary Report and Recommendations* (2010), p. 13.

[20] A Vision Statement by Ban Ki-moon Secretary General of the United Nations, *Sustainable Energy for All* (2011), p. 4, available at www.se4all.org/sites/default/files/l/2014/02/SG_Sustainable_Energy_for_All_vision.pdf.

[21] International Energy Agency, *World Energy Outlook 2012*, above n. 4, at 531.

[22] Ban Ki-moon, *Sustainable Energy for All*, above n. 20, at 3.

to provide universal access to modern energy services by 2030 almost US$1 trillion in cumulative investment is required.[23] Clearly, the world has to act with urgency beyond the rhetoric, while moving away from a 'business as usual' approach. This means that change should happen, where the law plays a critical role in making this change happen; as Mary Robinson highlights '[l]aw is, first and foremost, a tool for change'.[24] Sonali Pachauri *et al.* warn that without innovative policies and increased investments, 'the goal of total rural electrification and universal access to modern cooking fuels and stoves by 2030 is unachievable'.[25] This is an unacceptable future,[26] which does not bear any good news for the energy poor.

Notably, the imperative of developing a coherent and appropriate legal response is vital to advancing the international and national development agenda and goals.[27] Along this line, it is posited that there is a need to embody the notion of basic needs such as access to modern energy services in 'clear, preferably legally binding standards'.[28] South Africa, for instance, has constitutionally entrenched a number of socio-economic rights, which allowed judicial determination of the meaning of the constitutional provisions on the rights of access to housing and healthcare, among others.[29] However, the legal response to the lack of access to modern energy services is, as a general rule, not clearly articulated,

---

[23] International Energy Agency, *World Energy Outlook 2012*, above n. 4, at 529.

[24] Mary Robinson, 'Preface', in Scott Leckie and Anne Gallagher (eds), *Economic, Social, and Cultural Rights: A Legal Resource Guide* (University of Pennsylvania Press, 2006).

[25] Sonali Pachauri *et al.*, 'Pathways to Achieve Universal Household Access to Modern Energy by 2030' (2013) 8 *Environmental Research Letters* 3.

[26] Omorogbe, 'Policy, Law, and the Actualization of the Right to Access to Energy Services', above n. 17, at 361.

[27] Adrian Bradbrook, Judith Gardam and Monique Cormier, 'A Human Dimension to the Energy Debate: Access to Modern Energy Services' (2008) 26 *Journal of Energy and Natural Resources Law* 552.

[28] Johannesburg Plan of Implementation, p. 5, para. 9(a), available at www.unmillenniumproject.org/documents/131302_wssd_report_reissued.pdf.

[29] For example, ss. 26, 27 and 29 of the 1996 Constitution provide rights of access to housing, health care, sufficient food and water, social security and basic education. The Constitutional Court of South Africa had on several occasions intervened and adjudicated cases on access to housing (Grootboom) and health (Soobramoney and Treatment Action Campaign). See Albie Sachs, 'Enforcement of Social and Economic Rights' (2007) *American University International Law Review* 22.

neither in the South African Constitution, nor elsewhere.[30] In the meantime, the lack of universal access to modern energy services continues to drive a widening gap between the 'haves' and 'have-nots', resulting in the marginalization of a significant segment of society, chiefly the poor.[31] With this marginalization, the human rights dimension of poverty due to the lack of access to modern energy services comes to the fore, as poverty results in disempowerment and gives rise to equity considerations.[32] Intuitively, these are matters that typically fall within the purview of human rights conversations, prompting some scholars to suggest taking a human rights approach to achieving universal access to modern energy services.[33] Yet the human rights perspective does not figure prominently in the SEFA initiative, with human needs being the preferred language of discourse.

Against this backdrop, the present chapter examines in broad terms the merits and limits of the language of needs compared to the language of rights in the context of the challenge of enhancing universal access to modern energy services. In doing so the chapter also investigates the plausibility of integrating needs-talk into rights-talk. In the process, the implications of couching universal access to modern energy services in the language of rights are amplified, including the potential of such discourse to accommodate and articulate the significance of the universal access to modern energy services targets within its moral and systematic fabric.

II LANGUAGE OF NEEDS IN LIEU OF RIGHTS

Although the language of rights has an impressive lineage and a deep intellectual allure in legal, moral and philosophical discourse, it has its

---

[30] Bradbrook, Gardam and Cormier, 'A Human Dimension to the Energy Debate', above n. 27, at 528.

[31] World Bank, *One Goal, Two Paths: Achieving Universal Access to Modern Energy Services* (2011), pp. 17–19, available at https://openknowledge.worldbank.org/handle/10986/2354.

[32] Based on the World Bank's 'Voices of the Poor' interviews where the poor defined 'poverty' as disempowerment, in United Nations High Commission for Human Rights, *Claiming the Millennium Development Goals: A Human Rights Approach* (2008), p. 9.

[33] See Stephen Tully, 'The Contribution of Human Rights to Universal Energy Access' (2006) *Northwestern Journal of International Human Rights* 4. Also see Adrian Bradbrook and Judith Gardam, 'Placing Access to Energy Within a Human Rights Framework' (2006) *Human Rights Quarterly* 28.

fair share of critics and detractors among thinkers, philosophers and scholars. One such critique comes from Mark Tushnet, who argues for the replacement of the language of rights with that of needs. The language of needs as a social theory has a long history that is traceable to Ancient times.[34] Early on, Seneca pointed to the evils of artificial needs to all civilizations, while Plato stressed that the basis of the state rested on reciprocal needs and services.[35] The preoccupation over the pursuit of pleasures – of what was true or false – and the gratification of needs found Stoics, Epicureans and Sceptics locked in heated and interminable debates.[36] It is no wonder that the discourse on needs 'always thrived in an atmosphere of sceptism and inquiry'.[37] In early writings, Karl Marx appeared to be fascinated by the Stoics, Epicureans and Sceptics.[38] In particular, Marx is seen as subscribing to the notion that the ideal society is one that satisfies real and authentic needs.[39] This is mainly premised on the proposition that 'human needs are expressions of our deepest natures',[40] and that the satisfaction of these needs is a precondition to being human.[41] But which need must be satisfied first? Abraham Maslow proffers an answer with a seminal theory on the hierarchy of universal human needs. Maslow identifies as basic human needs that must be satisfied in descending order: physiological (or biological), safety, love, esteem and self-actualization needs.[42] Moreover, Maslow argues that satisfaction of human needs is necessary to be considered fully human, and thus, human needs are tantamount to natural rights.[43]

Influenced by such eminent predecessors, Christian Bay finds affinity with their conception of needs and began with the premise that the justification and legitimacy of any government rests on its task of serving human need.[44] This need is defined as referring 'to any requirement for a

---

[34] Patricia Springborg, 'Karl Marx on Human Needs' in Ross Fitzgerald (ed.), *Human Needs and Politics* (Pergamon Press, 1977), p. 157.

[35] Ibid. 173.

[36] Ibid. 157.

[37] Ibid. 159.

[38] Ross Fitzgerald (ed.), *Human Needs and Politics* (Pergamon Press, 1977), p. x.

[39] Ibid.

[40] Ibid.

[41] Ibid.

[42] Abraham Maslow, *Motivation and Personality* (3rd edn, Harper & Row, 1987), pp. 15–22.

[43] Ibid. xxi; Fitzgerald, *Human Needs and Politics*, above n. 38, at xi.

[44] Christian Bay, 'Needs, Wants and Political Legitimacy' (1968) 1 *Canadian Journal of Political Science* 246.

person's survival, health or basic liberties; basic meaning that, to the extent that they are adequately met, mental or physical health is impaired'.[45] In addition, Bay continued that need pertains to those 'necessities for not only biological survival but also for the health and development (physical and mental growth) of persons as human beings'.[46] Moreover, Bay suggests that Maslow's needs-hierarchy provides a useful model in arranging priorities towards satisfying different human needs in the absence of a more feasible alternative.[47]

For Tushnet, rights in the abstract are meaningless and matter only in terms of being recognized or not recognized in a given social setting.[48] Once a right is recognized in a specific social setting, it becomes vulnerable, however, to instability, due to the possibility of changes in the social setting.[49] This is illustrated in the right to reproductive choice, which Tushnet contends is a matter that is contingent on technological and social facts that could undermine the earlier arguments for the exercise of such a right.[50]

Also, rights-talk suffers from indeterminacy. If a right is specified, it becomes 'either an act of political rhetoric or a commitment to social transformation', with liberal rights rhetoric usually failing in regard to the latter.[51] Pertinently, Mary Ann Glendon observes that as more rights are recognized 'the catalog of individual liberties expands without much consideration of the ends to which they are oriented'.[52] Worse, rights-talk allegedly offers promises instead of actually delivering on these promises.[53]

Moreover, the concept of rights suffers from reification, that is, it reduces real experiences to empty abstractions.[54] Tushnet illustrates this by citing the undeniable importance of experiences such as those of independence and solidarity. By characterizing them as abstract rights

---

[45] Christian Bay, 'Self-Respect as a Human Right: Thoughts on the Dialectics of Wants and Needs in the Struggle for Human Community' (1982) 4 *Human Rights Quarterly* 67.

[46] Ibid.

[47] Bay, 'Needs, Wants and Political Legitimacy', above n. 44, at 246–7.

[48] Mark Tushnet, 'An Essay on Rights' (1984) 62 *Texas Law Review* 1364.

[49] Ibid. 1363.

[50] Ibid. 1365–6.

[51] Ibid. 1380.

[52] Mary Ann Glendon, *Rights Talk: The Impoverishment of Political Discourse* (The Free Press, 1991), p. xi.

[53] David Kennedy, 'The International Human Rights Movement: Part of the Problem?' (2002) 15 *Harvard Human Rights Journal* 116.

[54] Tushnet, 'An Essay on Rights', above n. 48, at 1364.

instead of being real human experiences in themselves, experiences of solidarity and independence become reified.[55] As Costas Douzinas asserts, 'rights in the abstract does not mean much'.[56] Accordingly, Tushnet submits that the 'language of rights should be abandoned to the very extent that it takes as a goal the realisation of the reified abstraction 'rights' rather than the experiences of solidarity and individuality'.[57] This is because, as Tushnet asserts, it will be better to treat such experiences 'as directly relevant to … political discussions, instead of passing them through the filter of the language of rights', and thus, 'address the political issues at the appropriate level'.[58]

Lastly, Tushnet characterizes the use of rights-talk in contemporary discourse as a hindrance to progressive social forces.[59] This is illustrated by the existing imbalance between the positive rights to have various things and the negative rights to be free from interference, that is, to create more positive rights without sacrificing negative rights; a confluence that is pragmatically difficult to implement[60] (for example, extending the right not to be deprived of life, liberty and property without due process of law to guarantee the provision of basic services). In a similar vein, socio-economic rights as positive rights allegedly fail the test of practicability because, as Maurice Cranston writes: 'If it is impossible for a thing to be done, it is absurd to claim it as a right'.[61] If ever society accords recognition to positive rights, this is arguably done only through statutory entitlement programmes with very limited constitutional protection, as seen in the United States.[62] Accordingly, Tushnet suggests that abandoning the rhetoric of rights in favour of the language of needs is the more pragmatic and better path to follow, asserting that basics such as food and shelter are needed now, instead of discourse on the topic of the right to such sustenance:

> People need food and shelter right now, and demanding those needs be satisfied – whether or not satisfying them today persuasively be characterized

---

55 Ibid. 1382.

56 Costas Douzinas, *The End of Human Rights* (Hart Publishing, 2000), p. 232.

57 Tushnet, 'An Essay on Rights', above n. 48, at 1382–3.

58 Ibid. 1384.

59 Ibid. 1364.

60 Ibid. 1392.

61 Maurice Cranston, 'Are There Any Human Rights?' (1983) 112(2) *Human Rights* 13.

62 Tushnet, 'An Essay on Rights', above n. 48, at 1393.

> as enforcing a right – strikes me as more likely to succeed than claiming that existing rights to food and shelter must be enforced.[63]

Thus, as the argument goes, universal access to modern energy services is likely to be achieved as a need that must be immediately satisfied rather than one that must be enforced later as a right.

III IN DEFENCE OF THE LANGUAGE OF RIGHTS

Contrary to Tushnet's proposition that the language of rights should be abandoned in favour of the language of needs, Jeremy Waldron holds the view that the language of rights, which is underpinned by a moral system, is the preferred form of articulation for entitlement or claim. For Waldron it appears that Tushnet has pushed the discourse to one of 'genuine choice between the language of rights and the language of needs'.[64] Given such a choice, however, Waldron rejects Tushnet's position and explains the various reasons for doing so.

First, Waldron argues that claims of needs are at least as, if not probably more, indeterminate and contestable than claims of rights.[65] For Waldron there is no point in searching for definitional determinacy when political concepts 'simply are indeterminate and contestable'.[66] In effect, the indeterminacy critique of rights merely highlights the implausibility of providing any definitional determinacy to political concepts.[67] Thus, indeterminacy is merely the product of the highly contestable nature of political concepts, whether expressed in the language of rights or that of needs (although indeterminacy is worse in the case of the latter).[68]

Second, it is unlikely that needs-talk will be politically more compelling than rights-talk.[69] Rights-talk involves not only an acknowledgement that one has a duty or responsibility to secure whatever needs to be secured, but also an implicit commitment to action.[70] This makes a

---

63 Ibid. 1394.

64 Jeremy Waldron, 'The Role of Rights in Practical Reasoning: "Rights" versus "Needs"' (2000) 4 *Journal of Ethics* 115.

65 Ibid. 119.

66 Ibid. 121.

67 Ibid.

68 Ibid.

69 Ibid.

70 Ibid.

rights-statement more difficult to accept than a needs-statement.[71] However, action is still needed despite the comparative ease of the political acceptance of a needs-statement, because 'it is not straightforwardly prescriptive in the way that rights-talk is'.[72] Moreover, Waldron observes the passiveness of needs-talk asserting that 'a person with needs addresses others as a potential recipient of their concern and assistance'.[73] Admittedly, the language of rights with its connotation of independence and self-sufficiency resonates with an active voice, as against the suppliant and passive language of needs.[74] For this reason the idea of rights affords the individual the capacity to make a continuing demand until a right in its fullness is satisfied.[75] Effectively, the language of rights supplies the indispensable framework that underpins the moral status of a claimant, which the language of needs cannot provide on its own, because 'a claim of need, by itself, is merely a diagnosis ... of the predicament of some organism, animal or human'.[76]

Third, Waldron suggests that instead of considering needs as being alternative to rights, the former can be taken as a basis for the existence of rights, thereby imbuing needs with a certain sense of integrity and dignity.[77] As Waldron points out, a theory of rights establishes a viable system of relational responsibilities premised on equal respect for persons that gives form and substance to needs.[78] Also, a theory of rights transforms a list of demands to one that is capable of being organized into a vision of society grounded on equality.[79] This sets the language of rights apart from that of needs, because notionally there is an undercurrent of presumed inequality among individual members of society. Consequently, it is useful and sensible to couch the articulation of needs in the language of rights, which mode of discourse is underpinned by a heritage of theorizing that spans at least three centuries.[80]

Finally, Waldron concludes that rights-talk provides the moral framework to develop new ideas and approaches around the existing concept of rights. This opens up the opportunity to integrate social and economic

---

[71] Ibid.
[72] Ibid.
[73] Ibid. 123.
[74] Ibid.
[75] Ibid. 131–2.
[76] Ibid.
[77] Ibid. 132.
[78] Ibid.
[79] Ibid.
[80] Ibid.

needs into rights theory in a manner that befits the challenge confronted. Accordingly, Waldron views the moral framework of the language of rights as sufficiently extensive to accommodate the vocabulary of needs:

> Nothing less is promised by the integration of social and economic needs into a theory of rights. By themselves, claims of needs are nothing more than particular suppliant pleas. But taking their place in a theory of rights, they challenge us to develop new structures of thought about personhood, citizenship, universality, community and equality. The language of rights offers a framework and a sense of responsibility for articulating that challenge.[81]

Therefore, the language of human rights arguably has the capacity to accommodate access to modern energy services as a basic need and a subsistence requirement within its vast moral framework.

IV COUCHING UNIVERSAL ACCESS TO MODERN ENERGY SERVICES IN THE LANGUAGE OF RIGHTS

There are many compelling arguments in favour of either the language of needs or the language of rights. At the same time, there are convincing and corresponding critiques of both rights-talk and needs-talk that must be carefully considered. Accordingly, this part of the chapter sets out the underlying reasons for favouring Waldron's proposition to integrate needs-talk into rights-talk in the context of the challenge of enhancing universal access to modern energy services.

(1) Recasting Need in the Language of Rights

There is no iron curtain that strictly separates needs from rights or stipulating that one cannot be expressed in terms of the other. On the contrary, Waldron raises the possibility of integrating needs-talk into the theory of rights, as against Tushnet's attempt to reduce the discourse to simply a matter of choice between needs-talk and rights-talk. This proposition has the potential to translate needs into becoming moral

---

[81] Ibid. 134.

imperatives – human rights – that are traditionally considered to be of the highest order.[82] While this suggestion is not new, it still has considerable currency.

Much earlier than Waldron, Maslow believed in the existence of a system of self-validating human values that are intrinsically good and desirable.[83] For this reason, Maslow asserts that 'it is legitimate and fruitful to regard instinctoid basic needs and the metaneeds as *rights* as well as needs'.[84] Similarly, Bay articulated the notion that 'needs establish rights'.[85] For Bay, the recognition of basic human needs lays the foundation for human rights, asserting that 'there can be no human right that does not meet, generally speaking, a human need'.[86] Thus, there is a closer relationship between needs and rights in the foundational sense than what Tushnet's proposition otherwise conveys.

However, there is an inherent danger in rooting rights in needs.[87] This becomes apparent in the absence of a list of needs comprehensive enough to give rise to a cogent set of human rights.[88] In such a context, needs become merely descriptive,[89] as opposed to being normative. In addition, Joel Feinberg argues that claims based on need alone without a consideration of duties speak in the 'manifesto sense' and offer mere 'permanent possibilities of rights', that is, they are not rights in the actual and real sense.[90] This is notably the point where this chapter slightly diverges from Waldron's suggestion of using needs as a basis or source for rights. Instead of grounding the substance of rights on needs, it is argued that the more cogent way to move forward is to take the normative and moral dimensions of needs and utilize the language of rights to express them. It would not be false to state that this proposition is not intended to force needs 'to fit the theoretical straightjacket of the rights-preferences

---

82 Jack Donnelly, *Universal Human Rights in Theory and Practice* (Cornell University Press, 2013), pp. 23–4.

83 Maslow, *Motivation and Personality*, above n. 42, at xx.

84 Ibid. xxi.

85 Bay, 'Self-Respect as a Human Right', above n. 45, at 67.

86 Ibid. 62.

87 Donnelly, *Universal Human Rights in Theory and Practice*, above n. 82, at 26–8.

88 Ibid.

89 Ibid. 28–9.

90 Joel Feinberg, 'The Nature and Value of Rights' in Morton Winston (ed.), *The Philosophy of Human Rights* (Wadsworth Publishing, 1989), p. 72.

couple'.[91] Instead, it explores the possibility of couching the idea of needs closer to the moral structure and authority of the language of rights.

As early as 1986, when the Brundtland Commission alerted the world to the importance of energy as a basic necessity,[92] and until the UN General Assembly's resolution adopted in 2013 declared the UN Decade of SEFA from 2014 to 2024, the appeal essentially remained grounded on the idea of human needs. Also, universal access to modern energy services is framed as meeting not only a basic need (for example, access to electricity) but also as enabling access to other basic services such as health and education.[93] Despite the apparent urgency of the matter, the number of people across the planet who lack access to modern energy services remains staggering.[94] Alarmingly, the lack of access to modern energy services poses a serious hindrance to eradicating absolute poverty that begets unwarranted inequities[95] and 'inhibits the full and effective enjoyment of human rights'.[96] This has prompted the UN Secretary General to demand the fast-tracking of the provision of universal access to modern energy services by 2030,[97] for the reason that the current situation is not only unacceptable, it is also abjectly wrong in the normative and moral sense. It is incongruent in modern times to still have a large segment of the global population without access to modern energy services.[98] Evidently, there is a clear moral imperative in this call to action.[99] However, the appeal to everyone to

---

91 Lawrence Hamilton, *The Political Philosophy of Needs* (Cambridge University Press, 2003), p. 22.

92 World Commission on Environment and Development, *Our Common Future: A Report of the World Commission on Environment and Development* (1986), available at www.un-documents.net/our-common-future.pdf.

93 World Health Organization and United Nations Development Programme, *The Energy Access Situation in Developing Countries* (2009), p. 3.

94 Ibid. 1.

95 International Energy Agency, United Nations Development Programme and United Nations Industrial Development Organization, *Energy Poverty: How to Make Modern Energy Access Universal?* (2010), p. 7.

96 Vienna Declaration and Programme of Action, Art 14, available at www.ohchr.org/EN/ProfessionalInterest/Pages/Vienna.aspx.

97 Ban Ki-moon, *Sustainable Energy for All*, above n. 20, at n. 1 quoting the *World Energy Outlook 2011*.

98 Donnelly, *Universal Human Rights in Theory and Practice*, above n. 82, at 241–3.

99 Chad Holliday and Yumkeh Kandella, Co-Chairs of the High-Level Group on Sustainable Energy for All, emphasize that: 'Supplying modern energy

address the matter as a basic human need amounts only to a universal plea for discretionary and benevolent action. As Michael Ignatieff points out, mere reliance on the claim that one is human and therefore deserves to live is 'the weakest claim that people can make to each other: it is the claim addressed to anyone, and therefore to no one'.[100] There is no one in particular or no named juridical entity such as the UN itself or any of its organizations, which is duty-bound to act on such a plea because, in the words of Feinberg, the claim is made merely in the 'manifesto sense'.[101] This is arguably the most expedient way to address the issue of lack of universal access to modern energy services, because, as Michael Freeman points out, 'human-rights declarations are cheap, whereas human-rights implementation is rather expensive'.[102] Accordingly, access to modern energy services as a need is something that is brought about adventitiously.

Alternatively, this chapter suggests the need for a deeper consideration of the moral dimension of universal access to modern energy services that allows it to find its place within the language of rights. To amplify: the notion that access to modern energy services must be universal can be linked closely to the concepts of the rights to dignity, subsistence and equality. In the language of rights, access to modern energy services is deemed consistent with the intrinsic worth of the human person to enjoy a subsistence right (for example, adequate housing), including its constitutive and enabling elements, for the enjoyment of other associated rights.[103] Also, it is presumably to be secured for all human beings equally, because a lack of access to modern energy services creates a disparity in economic and social conditions in society.[104] This brings the provision of access to modern energy services a step closer to the moral imperatives of rights. In effect, there is a greater possibility of a claim for access to modern energy services based on need evolving later into an actual right, in other words, from being an object of charity to a justified

---

services to the billions who now lack electricity and clean fuels is not just a moral imperative but a unique business opportunity'. See Secretary-General's High-level Group on Sustainable Energy for All, *Sustainable Energy for All: A Global Action Agenda* (April 2012), p. 16, available at www.se4all.org/sites/default/files/l/2014/01/SEFA-Action-Agenda-Final.pdf.

[100] Michael Ignatieff, *The Needs of Strangers* (1984), p. 51.

[101] Feinberg, 'The Nature and Value of Rights', above n. 90, at 72.

[102] Michael Freeman, *Human Rights: An Interdisciplinary Approach* (Viking Penguin, 2011), p. 205.

[103] Committee on Economic, Social and Cultural Rights, *General Comment 4* (1991), available at www.refworld.org/docid/47a7079a1.html.

[104] World Bank, *One Goal, Two Paths*, above n. 31, at 17–19.

demand.[105] Otherwise the claim will share in the same frailties attributed to any other need that makes a claim against the world, albeit to no one in particular, in the sense that 'natural needs are real claims if only upon hypothetical future beings not yet in existence'.[106]

(2) Claim Not Charity

On another front this chapter agrees with Waldron's observation about the suppliant and passive nature of the language of needs. This highlights one of the fundamental differences between needs-talk and rights-talk. In needs-talk a plea for the provision of access to modern energy services as a need is essentially an appeal to the charity of others. Although this is politically easier to declare and accept, it lacks a moral imperative to meet the articulated need. As Gro Harlem Brundtland points out, the expression of need involves an appeal to 'charity that flows from the benevolent … when convenient'.[107] This means that in the case of needs-talk, intended beneficiaries cannot make active claims, as no one is bound to meet the claimed need.[108] Thus, the divide between 'need' and 'act' looms large in the horizon of the language of needs.

In contrast, a right entails 'obligations that, by definition, must be met by responsible duty-bearers'.[109] This creates 'a field of rule-governed interactions centred on, and under the control of, the right-holder'.[110] When recognition is accorded to beneficiaries as claim-holders, they are enabled to secure the fulfilment of their claim as a duty from those against whom it is held.[111] As Alan Gewirth writes, 'such mandatoriness distinguishes … human rights from virtues and other goods whose moral

---

105 Feinberg, 'The Nature and Value of Rights', above n. 90, at 72; see Brigitte Hamm, 'A Human Rights Approach to Development' (2001) 23 *Human Rights Quarterly* 1026.

106 Ibid.

107 Gro Harlem Brundtland, *Nutrition, Health and Human Rights*, SCN News 18 1999, p. 20, available at www.unscn.org/layout/modules/resources/files/scnnews18.pdf.

108 Urban Jonsson, *Historical Summary of the SCN Working Group on Nutrition, Ethics and Human Rights*, SCN News 18 (1999), p. 48, available at www.unscn.org/layout/modules/resources/files/scnnews18.pdf.

109 Brundtland, *Nutrition, Health and Human Rights*, above n. 107, at 20.

110 Donnelly, *Universal Human Rights in Theory and Practice*, above n. 82, at 21–2.

111 Jonsson, *Historical Summary of the SCN Working Group*, above n. 108, at 48.

status may be supererogatory, such as generosity or charity'.[112] Concomitantly, rights-talk introduces the element of accountability[113] that gives rise to a parallel commitment to action;[114] a word that is sorely missing in the vocabulary of needs. Effectively, rights-talk converts need into a matter of claim and not of charity,[115] and one that does not 'justify merely requests, pleas, [or] petitions'.[116] This is the beauty of the linguistic implications of 'making claims' in the language of rights: it puts the holder in a position to make a vigorous claim and to stand up with pride as a human being.[117] As Feinberg forcefully explains:

> Legal claim-rights are indispensably valuable possessions. A world without claim-rights, no matter how full of benevolence and devotion to duty, would suffer an immense moral impoverishment. Persons would no longer hope for decent treatment from others on the ground of desert or rightful claim. Indeed, they would come to think of themselves as having no special claim to kindness or consideration from others, so that whenever even minimally decent treatment is forthcoming they would think themselves lucky rather than inherently deserving, and their benefactors extraordinarily virtuous and worthy of great gratitude. The harm to individual self-esteem and character development would be incalculable.[118]

Imagine 1.3 billion people in suppliant plea, all together, for access to electricity. For this access to be universal, the investment required between 2016 and 2030 is estimated at US$477 billion.[119] This is the cost of benevolence. But whose kindness and beneficence is courted? Who is willing to shoulder the cost? From a needs perspective, it is a petition to those who are willing to be 'extraordinarily virtuous' benefactors, as Feinberg describes them. The likely result: a waiting game between an unnamed lucky beneficiary and a first mover without advantage. And this can go on forever. If the claim for the provision of access to electricity is

---

112 Alan Gewirth, 'The Epistemology of Human Rights' (1984) 1(2) *Social Philosophy and Policy* 2.

113 Jonsson, *Historical Summary of the SCN Working Group*, above n. 108, at 48.

114 Joseph Raz, 'On the Nature of Rights' in: Morton Winston, *The Philosophy of Human Rights* (Wadsworth Publishing Company, 1989), p. 55.

115 Hamm, 'A Human Rights Approach to Development', above n. 105, at 1026.

116 Henry Shue, *Basic Rights: Subsistence, Affluence, and U.S. Foreign Policy* (Princeton University Press, 1980), p. 14.

117 Feinberg, 'The Nature and Value of Rights', above n. 90, at 68–9.

118 Joel Feinberg, *Social Philosophy* (Prentice-Hall, 1973), pp. 58–9.

119 International Energy Agency *et al.*, *Energy Poverty*, above n. 95, at 22.

expressed in the language of rights instead of the language of need, the call becomes authoritative, confident and unabashed. It is 'no longer just a service, a gift, an aid; it is a duty and a contribution to the creation of claims'.[120] Suddenly, the passive appeal becomes an active, insistent and justified demand, as Henry Shue emphasizes.[121] Also, the Kantian argument that values individual autonomy and individuals' intrinsic worth becomes relevant. One can even hear John Rawls chanting the higher expectation from those in a better situation to improve the lot of the disadvantaged.[122] Clearly, there is much traction to be gained by couching the claim for the provision of access to modern energy services in the language of rights with its active tenor and 'distinctive force and remedial logic',[123] as value-added units to the rights conversation.

(3) Empowering Language of Rights

While the language of rights arguably has its own shortcomings as adverted to earlier in the chapter, an important point that Waldron raises that closely relates to accountability is that the language of rights is empowering, in comparison with that of needs. Aside from the empowering nature of the discourse, rights also benefit those who hold them.[124] This is so because the empowerment of citizens to make a claim and vindicate a right authorizes them to insist on the realization of certain standards,[125] or what Shue refers to as 'the line beneath which no one is allowed to sink'.[126] Moreover, rights are taken as allowing the needs of an individual to trump the collective goals of the greater number that are sometimes presented as sufficient justification for the imposition of loss or injury on the individual.[127] This serves not only as a form of counterweight to programmes or actions in the name of utility or social policy, but also to check the overreach of political justification.[128]

---

[120] Peter Uvin, *Human Rights and Development* (Kumarian Press, 2004), p. 179.

[121] Shue, *Basic Rights*, above n. 116, at 15.

[122] John Rawls, *A Theory of Rights* (Harvard University Press, 1971), p. 75.

[123] Donnelly, *Universal Human Rights in Theory and Practice*, above n. 82, at 21–2.

[124] Ibid.

[125] Ibid. 25–6.

[126] Shue, *Basic Rights*, above n. 116, at 18.

[127] Ronald Dworkin, *Taking Rights Seriously* (Duckworth, 1977), p. xi.

[128] Donnelly, *Universal Human Rights in Theory and Practice*, above n. 82, at 19–21.

Furthermore, the use of rights language endows a specific goal with an overwhelming priority in the use of resources and public policy.[129]

On the other hand, it is asserted that rights are only *prima facie* trumps, that is, not absolute, because they may be overridden or limited under justifiable circumstances.[130] Still, this does not substantially diminish the empowering language of rights in elevating the individual to being an effective claimant against the state and those who are duty-bound to meet the claim.[131] In effect, the language of rights has the potential to transform power relations in a way that the language of needs is unable to provide, because of the passive and suppliant nature of the latter.[132] This is particularly relevant to lack of access to modern energy services, as one of the undesirable facets of poverty that is deemed synonymous to 'vulnerability, voicelessness, and powerlessness'.[133] Lack of access to modern energy services represents a kind of social struggle that the language of rights has historically dealt with itself,[134] in other words, providing a voice to those who have struggled against colonialism and oppression. The language of rights is definitely preferred to the emotional appeal of the language of needs for its potential to bring about a social arrangement that benefits the poor and the weak. After all, as Shue emphatically argues, the language of rights 'provides the rational basis for a justified demand' and not merely a passive plea for benevolence.[135]

---

[129] Arjun Sengupta, 'The Human Right to Development' in Bard Andreassen and Stephen Marks (eds), *Development as a Human Right: Legal, Political and Economic Dimensions* (2nd edn, Intersentia, 2010), p. 33.

[130] Alan Gewirth, 'The Basis and Content of Rights' in Morton Winston (ed.), *The Philosophy of Human Rights* (Wadsworth Publishing Company, 1989), p. 194.

[131] Donnelly, *Universal Human Rights in Theory and Practice*, above n. 82, at 21–4. See, for example, Constitution of the Republic of South Africa, 1996, s. 36.

[132] Waldron, 'The Role of Rights in Practical Reasoning', above n. 64, at 123.

[133] Uvin, *Human Rights and Development*, above n. 120, at 123.

[134] According to Peter Uvin, human rights are 'but a subset of broader social struggles, many of which can properly be said to be about rights as well'. Ibid. 179.

[135] Shue, *Basic Rights*, above n. 116, at 13.

(4) Catalyst of Change

Finally, the unique attraction of the language of rights lies in its continuing insistence on questioning the status quo.[136] This is particularly significant in a society where many still remain trapped in the quagmire of poverty. The language of rights arms the citizenry to fight for the creation of a new order where they can enjoy the objects of their rights.[137] Also, instead of seeing poverty as a mere technical problem, it offers a view of the ills besetting society from the standpoint of dignity, which pushes 'the border of moral imagination and re-conceptualize[s] the nature of [the] change' being sought.[138] In turn, current institutions, practices and norms are challenged until the enabling environment for the recognition, fulfilment and enjoyment of the object of the right is put in place.[139]

Jack Donnelly aptly argues that the language of rights expresses claims not merely as 'aspirations, suggestions, requests or laudable ideas, but rights-based demands for change'.[140] Specifically, the language of rights speaks of demands as entitlements where the clamour for social change is stronger than whatever the language of needs will be able to conjure up.[141] Also, Henry Steiner and Philip Alston point out that rights 'are not static'; '[t]hey evolve'.[142] The language of rights is a language gifted with the ability to shape political society to realize the moral vision and possibilities of human nature.[143] Evidently, there is a sense of urgency that behoves society to bridge the gap between the 'haves' and 'have-nots'; between the now and the future; and between the vision and the reality. As Peter Uvin points out, the language of rights 'demands that we … render explicit the concerns of the oppressed and the poor when thinking through policies, and not make resource constraints as natural givens but treat them as the results of past choices'.[144]

---

[136] Uvin, *Human Rights and Development*, above n. 120, at 191.

[137] Donnelly, *Universal Human Rights in Theory and Practice*, above n. 82, at 25–6.

[138] Uvin, *Human Rights and Development*, above n. 120, at 179.

[139] Donnelly, *Universal Human Rights in Theory and Practice*, above n. 82, at 24–5.

[140] Ibid.

[141] Ibid. 29–30.

[142] Henry Steiner and Philip Alston, *International Human Rights in Context* (2nd edn, Oxford University Press, 2000), p. 181.

[143] Ibid.

[144] Uvin, *Human Rights and Development*, above n. 120, at 191.

Again, let us take up the case of those still without access to modern energy services, particularly electricity, in many dispersed rural areas of the world. There is a wide consensus that renewable energy plays a key role in filling that gap. The International Renewable Energy Agency notes, for instance, that decentralized solutions using renewable energy technologies offer 'the most economic option for off-grid electrification in most areas and, in locations with good resources, they are the best option for centralized grid supply and extension'.[145] Also, renewables are seen as a critical enabler to improve access to electricity.[146] However, the prevailing weak political support for the development of renewable energy gives the impression that the world wishes to preserve the status quo as long as possible, in other words, to keep renewable energy 'marginalised by distortions in the world's electricity markets created by decades of massive financial, political and structural support to conventional power technologies'.[147] This is the kind of barrier that makes the language of rights a strong medium in which to express the change that is needed to challenge the status quo. As such, the language of rights is imbued with a dynamic capacity to 'generate new duties with changing circumstances',[148] which makes it an attractive way to articulate the change being sought in a society disconnected by systemic distortions in the electricity infrastructure and a skewed technology preference for the status quo.

V CONCLUSION

The debate between rights-talk and needs-talk offers interesting perspectives on the proposal that the claim for the provision of universal access to electricity should be couched in the language of rights. Essentially, this finds justification in the extensive intellectual breadth and moral structure of the theory of rights developed over the centuries. However, the language of needs provides a counter-narrative that asserts the centrality of basic human needs in establishing human rights. It also advances the view that the satisfaction of basic needs is a prerequisite to being human, and thus arguably lends legitimacy and justification to the function of any

---

[145] International Renewable Energy Agency, *Renewable Power Generation Costs in 2012: An Overview* (2013), p. 12.

[146] World Energy Council, *2013 World Energy Issues Monitor* (2013), p. 7.

[147] European Renewable Energy Council and Greenpeace, *Energy Revolution: A Sustainable World Energy Outlook* (2010), p. 16.

[148] Raz, 'On the Nature of Rights', above n. 114, at 59.

government.[149] Tushnet accordingly suggests that the abandonment of the language of rights in favour of needs is the better path to follow due to the instability, indeterminacy, reification and pragmatic disutility of rights.[150]

On the other hand, Waldron asserts that the language of rights with its moral structure and reasoning is the preferred form of articulation for any claim or entitlement. The passiveness of the language of needs, including its weak correlation with duties, does not result in the moral upliftment of an individual's status in society.[151] Also, the suppliant nature of the language of needs is inconsistent with the inherent worth and dignity of individuals as self-respecting human beings. Instead, Waldron argues for the integration of needs-talk into the theory of rights to enrich and lend robustness to a language that apparently lacks the moral depth to sustain its place in political, legal and moral discourse.

From the foregoing discussions, this chapter argues that the language of rights has the greater potential to accommodate and articulate the significance of access to modern energy services within its moral and systematic fabric. First, in the last three decades the claim for the provision of universal access to modern energy services as a need has not resulted in the bold, immediate actions that are necessary to fight entrenched poverty, despite such provisions being deemed fundamental to human development, particularly in meeting other basic needs.[152] Second, couching access to modern energy services in the language of needs merely encourages charity that is not accordant with the dignity and intrinsic worth of the individual as a human being. Third, the language of rights demands action and accountability that is continuous and persistent until the provision being sought is fully and actually enjoyed. This is the kind of insistence and demand that must be made until access to modern energy services becomes a universal reality, especially in the developing world. Fourth, the empowering language of rights extends the rational basis to demand the realization of a minimum standard beneath which no one is allowed to fall; that is, access to modern energy services as a justified demand and the minimum standard for everyone, particularly

149 Bay, 'Self-Respect as a Human Right', above n. 45, at 246–7.

150 Tushnet, 'An Essay on Rights', above n. 48, at 1363–4.

151 Brundtland, *Nutrition, Health and Human Rights*, above n. 107, at 20; Jonsson, *Historical Summary of the SCN Working Group*, above n. 108, at 48.

152 Gaye, 'Access to Energy and Human Development', above n. 3, at 1.

those living in rural areas. Finally, the language of rights arms the plea for access to modern energy services with the zest and urgency of a continuing demand for change, targeting institutions, practices and norms until it is finally recognized and fulfilled.

5. Using social science perspectives on risk to implement an environmental justice analysis

Is this the right way forward to mitigate the social risks of low-carbon energy technologies and help policy-makers achieve renewable energy targets worldwide?

Elodie Le Gal

I INTRODUCTION

The aim of the Twelfth IUCNAEL colloquium was to explore energy themes relating to achieving a 'fair society in a safe planet'. In the context of global climate change and rising world energy demand putting increasing pressures on finite natural resources, new efficient and sustainable energy technologies are being developed to sustain human activities, combat climate change and protect global environmental assets.

While non-renewable fossil fuels such as oil, natural gas and coal are likely to remain the main sources of energy supply around the world in the near future,[1] different low-carbon technologies are being developed to maximize renewable energies to reduce greenhouse gas emissions. These technologies include wind power (on-shore and off-shore); solar (photovoltaic and solar thermal electricity); geothermal power; biomass; hydropower (small-scale and large-scale); biogas (including landfill and

[1] See graphic on Total Primary Energy Supply (TPES) outlook by fuel in International Energy Agency and Organization for Economic Cooperation and Development, *2014 Key World Energy Statistics* (OECD/IEA, 2014), p. 46.

sewage gas).[2] According to the International Energy Agency (IEA), renewable energy is one of the key pillars of a low-carbon economy, along with other elements such as energy efficiency, nuclear power and carbon capture and storage.[3]

However, in its Foresight Report, the United Nations Environment Programme (UNEP) identified emerging global environmental issues: specifically the need to overcome the barriers to implementing renewable energies and the importance of adopting new approaches for minimizing the risks of novel technologies.[4] These two key themes have thus been brought to the attention of policy-makers. The Chernobyl and Fukushima Daiichi nuclear accidents, on such catastrophic scales, highlight how the history of energy innovation can have environmental, social and economic consequences, and often at the expense of more vulnerable populations. New low-carbon energy technologies[5] are not risk-free to humans and natural systems and the regulations of these new forms of energy production can also impact vulnerable communities.

Throughout the world, international and domestic legal frameworks, informed by the concepts and tools associated with sustainable development, are attempting to achieve energy efficiency, climate change adaptation and a clean energy future. Innovative institutional arrangements, such as market-based instruments, are expected to trigger more sustainable energy consumption and production behaviours at various levels of society (for example, individuals, corporate, government). In the policy

---

[2] Clarisse Fräss-Ehrfeld, *Renewable Energy Sources: A Chance to Combat Climate Change* (Kluwer Law International, 2009), pp. 109–40.

[3] International Energy Agency, *Technology Roadmaps* (OECD/IEA, 2014), available at www.iea.org/roadmaps/.

[4] This chapter has used the definition adopted by the United Nations Environment Programme (UNEP) of emerging environmental issues. These are defined as 'issues with either a positive or negative global environmental impact that are recognized by the scientific community as very important to human well-being, but not yet receiving adequate attention from the policy community'. UNEP, *21 Issues for the 21st Century: Results of the UNEP Foresight Process on Emerging Environmental Issues* (UNEP, 2012), p. iv.

[5] Renewable energy is defined by the International Energy Agency as the '[e]nergy that is derived from natural processes (for example, sunlight and wind) that are replenished at a higher rate than they are consumed. Solar, wind, geothermal, hydro, and biomass are common sources of renewable energy'. See International Energy Agency, *Renewable Energy* (International Energy Agency, 2014), available at www.iea.org/aboutus/glossary/r/. Renewables which are not necessarily carbon neutral can also be referred to as low-carbon energy technologies. Overall, they have lower carbon impacts than traditional non-renewable fossil fuels.

arena, there are little or no signs of substantial contributions to social and environmental justice issues.[6] Renewable energy policy instruments, including market-based approaches and low-carbon energy technology projects, carry their own risks of social failures, thus jeopardizing the building of a fair and equitable society. So far, the focus of the energy debate remains mostly around energy security and climate change and the use of market-based approaches. The social and environmental injustice risks[7] arising from the emergence of new low-carbon energy technologies play a very minor part in the energy debate. This chapter redirects the discussion and intends to explore how the concept of environmental justice, combined with social science perspectives on risk, can create new theoretical frameworks and methods that can help integrate social justice considerations into energy legal and policy frameworks. Framing the energy debate differently, that is, through the lens of environmental justice and social sciences perspectives on risk, is likely to shape different types of regulatory responses that will be needed to address emerging social issues in the context of low-carbon energy technologies.

So far, the complex relationship that exists between environmental justice analysis, risk and social science research in the energy context has received very little attention from environmental and energy law scholars. This chapter intends to address this research gap. It argues that the law needs the support of other disciplines in social sciences to be able to create new methodological approaches that can contribute to achieving a clean energy future in a fair society.[8] Current risk-based approaches for

---

[6] As discussed in the following section of this chapter, the definition of environmental justice means different things depending on the sociological, political and cultural context. For the purpose of this chapter, social and environmental justice issues refer to any legal, policy or social norm that is likely to increase the vulnerability of certain socio-economic groups in the specific energy context. Examples of the nature and the extent of these issues are discussed later in this chapter.

[7] The concept of risk is defined in many different ways in the risk literature. For the purpose of this chapter, risk is defined as 'the potential to lose what we value due to uncertain (generally external) events. These events are called hazards'. This is the definition adopted in Paul Martin and Jacqueline Williams, *Policy Risk Assessment* (Cooperative Research Centre for Irrigation Futures, 2010), available at www.irrigationfutures.org.au/imagesDB/news/0310_web.pdf.

[8] In 1987, the American scholar, Richard Posner, already discussed the decline of law as an autonomous discipline. See Richard A. Posner, 'The Decline of Law as an Autonomous Discipline: 1962–1987' (1987) *Harvards Law Review* 100.

environmental protection are mostly technocentric and do not sufficiently incorporate community perceptions and community priorities into current legal frameworks.

The chapter draws upon a review of the national and international literature that focuses on different facets of environmental justice, risk, social sciences research[9] and low-carbon energy technologies. It is structured around two main sections. The first part explores the concept of environmental justice and discusses its significance for framing issues of social risk in the context of low-carbon energy technologies. The second part explores how social science perspectives on risk can produce useful knowledge for policy-makers to better incorporate social justice considerations into energy frameworks and understand why communities sometimes oppose low-carbon energy technology projects worldwide. Identifying the type and extent of the social risks that arise from low-carbon energy technologies and their underlying causes is important to better understand why national renewable energy targets may not be reached. The concluding section restates the key findings of the chapter, discusses research implications and provides further research directions.

II SIGNIFICANCE OF ENVIRONMENTAL JUSTICE ANALYSIS IN THE ENERGY CONTEXT

(1) 'Environmental Justice', a Multi-dimensional Concept

Justice and social justice are major themes in Western philosophical traditions. From the Greek philosophers, Plato and Aristotle, to more contemporary thinkers such as Hobbes and Rawls, all the greatest Western philosophers have explored the concepts of justice and social justice through different lenses. Philosophers have provided different

---

[9] As opposed to natural sciences methodologies which are embedded in the quantitative research paradigm and are predominantly guided by probabilistic and deductive reasoning, social science methodologies are embedded in the qualitative research paradigm and are to a wide extent informed by subjective methods and guided by qualitative inductive reasoning. See Norman K. Denzin and Yvonna S. Lincoln, 'Introduction: The Discipline and Practice of Qualitative Research' in Norman K. Denzin and Yvonna S. Lincoln (eds), *The Sage Handbook of Qualitative Research* (3rd edn, Sage Publications, 2005), pp. 10–12.

theories of justice,[10] including those involving the key concepts of corrective, retributive, procedural and distributive justice.[11] Over the centuries, these theories have informed Western democratic legal systems, symbolically represented by the lady of justice and sometimes the scales of justice. Inextricably linked with other concepts such as fairness, equity, social justice and human rights, the concept of justice is multifaceted.

With the environmental justice movement that began in the late 1970s and early 1980s in the United States, the concept of 'justice' was linked for the first time with the idea of 'environment'. Closely associated with the civil rights movement and the political fight against racial discrimination, this activist movement contributed to establishing the empirical evidence that belonging to certain racialized and/or socio-economic groups, such as African-American communities, was likely to increase someone's chance of living in certain geographical areas located near waste facilities. As a result, this would increase his/her chance of exposure to health risks from toxic waste.[12]

Whilst in the American context, the concept of environmental justice is historically linked to the idea of environmental racism in the specific context of waste sites,[13] it has since then travelled around the globe and expanded to include a much broader set of considerations of environmental inequalities in different contexts[14] (for example, air pollution,

---

[10] These are discussed in detail in Tom Campbell, *Justice* (3rd edn, Palgrave Macmillan, 2010).

[11] Richard A. Posner, *The Problems of Jurisprudence* (Harvard University Press, 1990), pp. 313–52.

[12] Commission of Racial Justice, *Toxic Wastes and Race in the United States: A National Report on Racial and Socio-Economic Characteristics of Communities with Hazardous Waste Site*s (United Church of Christ, 1987).

[13] For an overview of environmental justice milestones, see Robert D. Bullard *et al.*, *Environmental Milestones and Accomplishments 1964–2014, A Report Prepared in Commemoration of the Twentieth Anniversary of the Environmental Justice Executive Order 12898* (Texas Southern University, 2014), available at www.racialequitytools.org/resourcefiles/Enviromental_justice.pdf.

[14] For a discussion on how environmental justice is distinct from other concepts such as environmentalism and environmental equity, see Howard S. Schiffman and Paul Robbins, 'Environmental Justice (Ethics and Philosophy)' in Howard S. Schiffman and Paul Robbins (eds), *Green Issues and Debates: An A-to-Z Guide* (Sage Publications, 2011), pp. 3–4. In Australia, the Victorian Environment Defenders Office, which is a community environmental law centre, provides a brief overview of the literature relevant to environmental justice issues in different contexts. See Environment Defenders Office (Victoria) Ltd, *Environmental Justice in Australia*, Discussion Paper (EDO Victoria, 2011), available at

climate change). Some argue that environmental justice analysis should also be applied to the key issue of access to natural resources.[15]

As pointed out by Getches and Pellow, the term 'environmental justice' may mean different things in different contexts.[16] In the American context, the US Environmental Protection Agency (EPA) defines 'Environmental Justice' as:

> [T]he fair treatment and meaningful involvement of all people regardless of race, color, national origin, or income with respect to the development, implementation, and enforcement of environmental laws, regulations, and policies. EPA has this goal for all communities and persons across this Nation. It will be achieved when everyone enjoys the same degree of protection from environmental and health hazards and equal access to the decision-making process to have a healthy environment in which to live, learn, and work.[17]

Transposing the concept into the European context, Eloi discusses the similarities and differences in the American and European approach to environmental justice. He notes that:

> [W]hile distributional and procedural aspects are distinguished in both cases, Europeans highlight the social conditions producing injustices while Americans insist on the racial dimension of discriminations and exclusion from decision-making process that ethnic groups suffer.[18]

He explains that this difference is rooted in different philosophies of public policy:

> [T]he US approach traditionally recognizes the universality of natural rights granted to individuals and aims at curbing discriminations faced by them in

---

https://envirojustice.org.au/sites/default/files/files/Submissions and reports/environmental_justice_discussion_paper.pdf.

[15] See Gary Bryner, 'Assessing Claims of Environmental Justice: Conceptual Frameworks' in Kathryn M. Mutz, Gary C. Bryner and Douglas S Kenney (eds), *Justice and Natural Resources: Concepts, Strategies, and Applications* (Island Press, 2002), p. 32.

[16] David Getches and David Pellow, 'Beyond Traditional Environmental Justice' in Kathryn M. Mutz, Gary C. Bryner and Douglas S Kenney (eds), *Justice and Natural Resources: Concepts, Strategies, and Applications* (Island Press, 2002), pp. 17–23.

[17] US Environmental Protection Agency, *Environmental Justice*, available at www.epa.gov/environmentaljustice/.

[18] Laurent Eloi, 'Issues in Environmental Justice within the European Union' (2011) 70 *Ecological Economics* 1848.

> exercising those rights, while continental Europe countries usually focus on correcting the social processes that produce situations of inequalities.[19]

Drawing on the work by the OECD, the UK Environment Agency and Pye, Eloi then suggests that there are four key dimensions to environmental justice issues. These encompass concerns around exposure and access inequalities; policy effect inequalities; impact inequalities; and policy-making inequalities.[20]

In the Australian context, the definition of environmental justice is still in its infancy. The Environment Defenders Office in Victoria, an Australian not-for-profit community legal centre launched in the State of Victoria in 2011, is an environmental justice project that intends to explore through three case studies the applicability of the concept in the State of Victoria and in Australia.[21] It points out that:

> The concept of environmental justice started out as something quite narrow, but its application is much broader today, with a rapidly expanding application across a variety of disciplines and environmental themes. What it will mean in Australia is as yet unknown. Research on environmental justice specifically in Australian academia has been relatively sparse.[22]

Overall, the literature suggests that what falls within the ambit of environmental justice approaches still remains uncertain. It also suggests that its meaning is significantly contingent upon the sociological, political and cultural context in which it is meant to be applied. Different framing approaches to the concept also span a wide range of disciplines and sciences. These offer different perspectives, which in turn are likely to impact differently on the definition and the scope of the concept. Whilst distributive and procedural justice issues seem to be the most recurrent themes associated with the concept of 'environmental justice', there are other areas to be considered. For example, the human

---

[19] Ibid. 1849.

[20] Ibid.

[21] Environment Defenders Office (Victoria) Ltd, *Environmental Justice Project, Final Report* (2012), available at https://envirojustice.org.au/downloads/files/law_reform/edo_vic_environmental_justice_report.pdf.

[22] Environment Defenders Office (Victoria) Ltd, *Environmental Justice in Australia*, above n. 14, at 3.

geography discipline includes the corrective and retributive dimension of the concept of justice.[23]

In the energy context, justice issues seem to revolve around the following concerns:

- Distributive justice is concerned with ensuring that the environmental benefits and risks from the production of energy from low-carbon technologies are fairly and equitably distributed across society.
- Influenced by ideals of participatory and deliberative democracy, the concept of procedural justice focuses on the key idea that communities and citizens should be treated fairly in any dispute resolution mechanisms and litigation processes they may be involved with. Citizens have to be included in any decision-making processes that influence their life and well-being, including in the area of low-carbon energy technologies.
- Corrective justice provides the theoretical justification for using legal liability mechanisms to ensure that those who have been harmed by another person are being compensated.[24] In the energy context, this could mean that someone potentially impacted by low-carbon energy technologies could use liability mechanisms to return him/her to the position he/she would have been in had the hazard not occurred.
- As for the theory of retributive justice, it provides the conceptual foundation for using punishment, including criminal law and penalties against those who have breached the law, including energy laws.

In environmental politics, Schlosberg focuses on the notions of distribution, recognition, capabilities and participation.[25]

Reflecting the multi-dimensional nature of the term 'environmental justice', Bryner identifies five different theoretical frameworks applicable to assessing environmental justice issues.[26] These revolve around the

[23] As pointed out in A. Lehtinen, 'Environmental Justice' in *International Encyclopedia of Human Geography* (2009), available at www.sciencedirect.com.ezproxy.une.edu.au/science/article/pii/B9780080449104007732.

[24] This is discussed for example in Ernst Weinrib, 'Corrective Justice in a Nutshell' (2002) *University of Toronto Law Journal* 52.

[25] David Schlosberg, *Defining Environmental Justice: Theories, Movements and Nature* (Oxford University Press, 2007).

[26] Bryner, 'Assessing Claims of Environmental Justice', above n. 15.

following areas of concern: civil rights; distributive justice and ethics; public participation; social justice; and ecological sustainability frameworks. Underpinned by different assumptions, these theoretical frameworks emphasize various aspects of environmental justice issues. They provide different rationales for framing and addressing environmental justice issues in many different ways.[27] It is expected that using one framework rather than another is likely to shape very different regulatory responses to similar environmental justice issues.

Overall, the concept of environmental justice expresses a certain set of views on human relationships. It is a concept that implies there is a need to protect vulnerable communities against the risks they may be exposed to due to harmful human-induced environmental impacts, and that their well-being needs to be protected. The right to a clean and healthy environment, which is a key theme in the environmental justice literature,[28] also illustrates how environmental justice approaches closely relate to human rights concerns and concepts.[29] The goal of environmental justice analysis is to ultimately empower communities with tools to strengthen their resilience against the potential adverse social spillovers generated by environmental risks that have materialized.[30]

(2) Environmental Justice Issues in the Context of Low-Carbon Energy Technologies

This section describes the state of the literature on environmental justice issues with regards to low-carbon energy technology projects in different countries. Table 5.1 provides an overview of key studies in this area. Whilst some publications specifically used an environmental justice discourse predominantly framed around distributive and procedural justice, others discussed social risks more generally. Most of these studies

---

[27] Different problem-framing approaches will also shape the types of methodological tools used to answer key research questions in relation to environmental justice issues For an overview of research methods in the context of environmental justice issues, see Lui Feng, *Environmental Justice Analysis: Theories, Methods and Practices* (CRC Press, 2000), ch. 3 para. 3.2.

[28] See Commission for Racial Justice, *Toxic Wastes and Race in the United States*, above n. 12.

[29] See Robert D. Bullard, *The Quest for Environmental Justice: Human Rights and the Politics of Pollution* (Sierra Club Books, 2005).

[30] For a bibliography on issues revolving around environmental justice, energy use, see George Touché, 'Ecological Sustainability, Environmental Justice, and Energy Use: An Annotated Bibliography' (2004) *Journal of Planning Literature* 19.

contributed to identify the direct (first-order) social/environmental justice risks associated with low-carbon energy technology developments. They did not specifically investigate the types and extent of indirect (or second-order) social and environmental justice risks (also referred to as 'policy risks') that can also derive from laws and policies aimed at avoiding, controlling and managing first-order risks.

Overall, our literature review finds that low-carbon energy technologies are likely to involve a wide range of adverse environmental, political, regulatory, social and business uncertainties to human and natural environments, which are hard to measure in quantitative terms.[31] These uncertainties can only be amenable to subjective evaluation, which involves beliefs, values and preferences. They can also translate into social spillovers that can affect vulnerable communities.[32] The acceptable levels of risk that a society is willing to undertake to achieve a clean energy future are likely to depend on people's perception of the seriousness or severity of the threats that these uncertainties may raise.

Our literature review shows that most of the reasons for which communities oppose these projects are that these affect their lives and well-being in many different ways. The main environmental justice issues identified in these studies are: falling land values; noise pollution; impacts on non-use values such as aesthetic, cultural and spiritual values (for example, landscapes, endangered species and habitats); lack of community participatory decision-making processes; and unfair distribution of the risks and benefits of low-carbon energy technologies.

Whilst this literature review does not intend to be exhaustive, it tends to support the view that assessing claims of environmental justice is a challenge. This is already noted by Bryner, an American environmental justice scholar who stresses that there is a broader 'lively debate [that] exists about the nature of environmental justice, the extent and seriousness of the risks, and the causes and underlying factors'.[33] The difficulty in assessing claims of environmental justice is mostly due to the

---

[31] In 1921, the American economist Frank Knight established a distinction between the concept of risk, which relates to a 'measurable certainty' and the concept of uncertainty, which stands for an 'unmeasurable uncertainty'. See Frank H. Knight, *Risk, Uncertainty and Profit* (University of Chicago Press, 1971), pp. 19–20.

[32] See also, Economist Intelligence Unit, *Managing the Risk in Renewable Energy* (Report sponsored by Swiss Re, 2011), available at http://digitalresearch.eiu.com/risksandrenewables/report.

[33] See Bryner, 'Assessing Claims of Environmental Justice', above n. 15, at 31.

existence of informational gaps (or very scarce information) on the types and extent of the social/environmental justice risks involved with specific low-carbon energy technologies, such as hydropower.

Table 5.1 List of key studies providing an overview of key social/ environmental justice issues in the context of low-carbon energy technologies

Low-carbon energy technologies	*Authors*	*Geographical location*
Wind power	Walter and Gutscher[a] Gross[b] Ottinger *et al*[c] Ottinger[d] Pasqualetti[e] Wolsink[f] Hall *et al.*[g]	Germany, Austria and Switzerland Australia United States Not specified (general discussion) United States, Scotland, Mexico The Netherlands Australia
Solar (photovoltaic and solar thermal)	Mulvaney[h] Pasqualetti[e]	General discussion United States
Geothermal energy	Schneiderman et al[i] Pasqualetti[e] Kousis[j] Karuna[k]	Hawaii United States, Mexico Greece Hawaii
Bioenergy	Walter and Gutscher[a]	Germany, Austria, Switzerland
Hydropower (small-scale and large-scale)	Enrensu[l]	Turkey
Biogas (including landfill and sewage gas)	Magnani[m] Soland et al.[n] McGeehan[o]	Italian alpine valley Switzerland United States

[a] Götz Walter and Heinz Gutscher, *Public Acceptance of Wind Energy and Bioenergy Projects in the Framework of Distributive and Procedural Justice Theories: Insights from Germany, Austria and Switzerland* (Universität Zurich and The Advisory House AG, 2010), available at www.advisoryhouse.co.uk/UserData/Publication_00685_00.pdf

[b] Katherine Gross, 'Community Perspectives of Wind Energy in Australia: The Application of a Justice and Community Fairness Framework to Increase Social Acceptance' (2007) *Energy Policy* 35

[c] Gwen Ottinger, Timothy Hargrave and Eric Hopson, 'Procedural Justice in Wind Facility Siting: Recommendations for State-led Siting Processes' (2014) *Energy Policy* 65

[d] Gwen Ottinger, 'The Winds of Change: Environmental Justice in Energy Transitions' (2013) *Science as Culture* 22

[e] Martin J. Pasqualetti, 'Social Barriers to Renewable Energy Landscapes' (2011) *Geographical Review* 101
[f] Maarten Wolsink, 'The Social Impact of a Large Wind Turbine' (1988) *Environmental Impact Assessment* 32
[g] Nina Hall, P. Ashworth and P. Devine-Wright, 'Societal Acceptance of Wind Farms: Analysis of Four Common Themes across Australian Case Studies' (2013) *Energy Policy* 58
[h] Dustin Mulvaney, 'Opening the Black Box of Solar Energy Technologies: Exploring Tensions Between Innovation and Environmental Justice' (2013) 22 *SCI CULT* 230
[i] J.S. Schneiderman *et al.*, 'Geothermal Energy, Hawaii, and Environmental Justice' (1999) 31 *Geological Society of America* 137
[j] Maria Kousis, 'Collective Resistance and Sustainable Development in Rural Greece: The Case of Geothermal Energy on the Island of Milos' (1993) *Socio Ruralis* 33
[k] Amara Karuna, 'Geothermal Greenwashing and Injustice in Hawaii' (2013) *Communities* 43
[l] Sinan Erensu, 'When Green Energy Meets Environmental Justice: Contesting Small Hydropower Plants (SHP) in Turkey', paper presented to the Annual Meeting of the American Sociological Association, Las Vegas, 19 August 2011
[m] Natalia Magnani, 'Exploring the Local Sustainability of a Green Economy in Alpine Communities' (2012) *Mountain Research and Development* 32
[n] Martin Soland, Nora Steimer and Götz Walter, 'Local Acceptance of Existing Biogas Plants' (2013) *Energy Policy* 61
[o] Luke McGeehan, *Throwing Out the Trash: Waste to Energy in New York City, An Analysis of Environmental Justice and NIMBY Concerns* (Masters of Science, Columbia University, 2013), available at http://academiccommons.columbia.edu/catalog/ac%3A162105

(3) Policy Implications of Environmental Justice Analysis: An Overview

The case studies reviewed above underline:

- the importance of taking into consideration the characteristics and needs of the local socio-ecological systems in which renewable energy projects are conducted; and[34]
- that alternative low-carbon energy pathways can be found through community involvement and genuine dialogue about structural change with the communities concerned by new renewable energy projects.[35]

---

[34] See, for example, Natalia Magnani, 'Exploring the Local Sustainability of a Green Economy in Alpine Communities' (2012) *Mountain Research and Development* 32; Götz Walter and Heinz Gutscher, *Public Acceptance of Wind Energy and Bioenergy Projects in the Framework of Distributive and Procedural Justice Theories: Insights from Germany, Austria and Switzerland* (Universität Zurich and The Advisory House AG, 2010), available at www.advisoryhouse.co.uk/UserData/Publication_00685_00.pdf.

[35] See, for example, Magnani, 'Exploring the Local Sustainability of a Green Economy', above n. 34.

Overall, the studies suggest that environmental justice analysis can be a useful tool for:

- explaining community resistance to renewable energy projects and therefore better understanding public acceptance of new renewable energy projects that can contribute to achieving renewable energy targets;
- better understanding some of the tensions between energy technology innovation and environmental justice issues;[36]
- identifying principles and measures to promote distributional and procedural justice.

In all of the case studies, although it is not obviously stated, the subjective dimension of the concept of risk is central to understanding how communities perceive social risks and their motivation for opposing or accepting low-carbon energy projects. For instance, drawing upon analytical tools from the disciplines of psychology and sociology, the study conducted by Walter and Gutsher uses distributive and procedural justice theories to identify the main factors that influence community opposition or acceptance behaviours to wind energy and bioenergy projects.[37] Their study also contributes to explaining empirically the difference between risk perception among communities and renewable energy developers,[38] as well as between lay people and risk experts. These differences in risk perception are a main source of conflict in the low-carbon energy debate. They can also explain why and how people's behaviours, which are driven by how they make their own judgements and decisions, can jeopardize the transition towards a clean energy future. Public perception of risk in low-carbon energy projects is likely a key factor that explains the lack of progress towards a clean energy future and why renewable energy targets set by national energy policies worldwide may not be met.

As discussed in the following section, this chapter supports the view that environmental justice analysis combined with social science perspectives on risk can provide unique insights for:

---

[36] See, for example, Dustin Mulvaney, 'Opening the Black Box of Solar Energy Technologies: Exploring Tensions Between Innovation and Environmental Justice' (2013) 22 *SCI CULT* 230.

[37] Walter, and Gutscher, *Public Acceptance of Wind Energy and Bioenergy* Projects,above n. 34, at 6.

[38] Ibid. 7.

- identifying the types and extent of environmental injustice risks that can arise from low-carbon energy technologies and their underlying causes;
- explaining how people respond positively or negatively to new low-carbon energy technology projects, energy laws and policies;
- developing and implementing a new risk management strategy that is scientifically and empirically grounded and that effectively incorporates environmental justice considerations into legal and policy debates around energy issues.

In his book, *Thinking, Fast and Slow*, Daniel Kahneman, the father of behavioural economics, offers groundbreaking research on risk perception and demonstrates with empirical evidence how tools and methods from social sciences can provide evidence-based explanations on how people make the decisions and choices that drive their behaviours. This suggests that risk perception research in the area of low-carbon technologies can help policy-makers better understand how to trigger individual and corporate sustainable behavioural change and adopt a low-carbon development path.

III USING SOCIAL SCIENCE PERSPECTIVES ON RISK TO ACHIEVE A CLEAN AND FAIR ENERGY FUTURE

The laws and policies applicable to renewable energy in different national legal systems rely on a complex mix of instruments, including market-based approaches.[39] International and domestic legal frameworks through global and national mandatory renewable energy targets attempt to harness renewable energy markets[40] to support legal transitions towards a clean energy future. However, as illustrated in the case studies reviewed above, their effectiveness is likely to be jeopardized by key implementation challenges, among which is the lack of behavioural compliance due to public political opposition caused by the existence of social and environmental injustice risk issues.

---

[39] In the European context, see Fräss-Ehrfeld, *Renewable Energy Sources*, above n. 2. See also R. Saidur *et al.*, 'A Review on Global Wind Energy Policy' (2010) *Renewable Sustainable Energies Review* 14; K. H. Solangi *et al.*, 'A Review on Global Solar Energy Policy' (2011) *Renewable Sustainable Energies Review* 15.

[40] See www.iea.org/policiesandmeasures/renewableenergy/.

In this section, we argue that social science perspectives on risk, through the subjective assessment of social and environmental injustice risks, can contribute to activating the concept of environmental justice in the context of low-carbon energy technologies and mitigating the implementation risks from renewable energy policy failures due to community political resistance.

(1) Risk Concepts

(i) Risk and probabilistic thinking

In our technocentric Western societies, risk is strongly associated with probabilistic thinking.[41] As noted by Bernstein in his book, *Against the Gods: The Remarkable Story of Risk*, the concept of risk is strongly associated with the idea that human beings can control their destiny.[42] It is expected that by using mathematical probabilistic-based methods, human beings can, at a certain point in time, predict the future, including adverse events (such as environmental threats), by looking into the past. In this context, risk is to be understood as a statistical concept defined as 'the statistical frequency (or relative frequency) with which an event is expected to occur … [and] describes a chance process [which] exists, independent of our knowledge of it'.[43]

The probabilistic dimension of the concept of risk suggests that any risk can arguably be objectively assessed. Embedded in the quantitative research paradigm, the objective dimension of the concept of risk suggests that human beings can control and manage the risks they may have created or those they may be exposed to in the near future. It is through the use of statistics and probabilistic tools that risks can be identified and measured and risk management strategies designed and implemented. This underpins traditional risk management programmes, which as noted by Bekefi, Jenkins and Kytle, 'focus on operational and

---

41 For a philosophical approach to the concept of probability and risk, see Ian Hacking, *The Emergence of Probability: A Philosophical Study of Early Ideas about Probability, Induction, and Statistical Inference* (Cambridge University Press, 1975).

42 Peter L. Bernstein, *Against the Gods: The Remarkable Story of Risk* (John Wiley & Sons, 1996).

43 Mark Burgman, *Risks and Decisions for Conservation and Environmental Management* (Cambridge University Press, 2005), pp. 6–7.

compliance risks and are generally composed of point solutions: mitigation actions specific to particular sources or impacts of risk'.[44]

(ii) Subjective dimension of the concept of risk and social risks

It is our view that the objective assessment of social risks through probabilistic-based methods is of limited relevance in the context of low-carbon energy technologies. First of all, there are many different underlying factors that contribute to create social risks. As pointed out by Bekefi, Jenkins and Kytle:

> Point solutions can work for 'point' risks, where the main objective of risk management is to avoid or prepare for a particular event and, in so doing, reduce the associated cost. However, point solutions cannot work for strategic risks, such as social risk, where complex origins and impacts demand integrated management approaches.[45]

The second main argument that hinders the application of probabilistic methods to identifying and measuring social risks in the context of low-carbon energy technologies is that there is little to no statistical/historical data on the environmental injustice risks in the context of low-carbon energy technologies. This is because, similarly to climate change issues, environmental justice analysis involves new research fields.

Finally, the argument that vulnerable human beings and communities can control their destiny is highly arguable. Such a philosophical position provides the political rationale for a neo-liberal approach to public policy issues, which is characterized by the non-intervention of public authorities and the predominance of private market-based mechanisms to manage public interests. Our view is that legal and policy frameworks have to help vulnerable communities control their own destiny by strengthening their resilience and reducing their vulnerability.

Beyond its purely objective dimension, the concept of risk is concerned to a wide extent with judgements about uncertain future events, including social spillovers that have indeterminate impacts upon things that are socially valued. As explained by Berstein, the subjective dimension of the concept of risk relates to the 'gut view of probability',[46] that is the 'degree of belief or approvability of an opinion'.[47] It is closely

---

[44] Tamara Bekefi, Beth Jenkins and Beth Kytle, *Social Risk as Strategic Risk*, Harvard Kennedy School Working Paper No. 30 (2006), p. 1, available at www.hks.harvard.edu/m-rcbg/CSRI/publications/workingpaper_30_bekefietal.pdf.

[45] Ibid 2.

[46] Bernstein, *Against the* Gods, above n. 42, at 49.

[47] Ibid.

associated with the idea of approbation and the key question of 'how much can we accept of what we know?'[48] In other words, the subjective dimension of the concept of risk is concerned with people's acceptability criteria for managing certain types of risks, including social and environmental injustice risks from low-carbon energy technologies.

On this particular point, it is important to note that in all the case studies reported in Table 5.1, the acceptability, or rather the non-acceptability, of the social and environmental injustice risks associated with low-carbon energy technology projects is the main point of focus. The main reasons why communities worldwide oppose these projects is that they consider, for instance, that it is unacceptable that certain low-carbon energy technologies pollute too much and endanger the native fauna that they value. These projects may also be considered unacceptable because they expose certain groups of people to certain social risks that other communities are not exposed to. Overall these projects are being judged as unacceptable and contested because the costs of a clean energy future are being borne by those who may not have the full resources to deal with the types and extent of the social risks those projects may create and the communities affected were not given the opportunity to express their views and beliefs. In brief, community opposition often arises in the low-carbon energy technology context because people are not given the opportunity to express their views on what an acceptable level of risk should be in the clean and renewable energy context and they are not integrated in a fully democratic decision-making process.

(2) Social Science Perspectives on the Concept of Risk and Environmental Justice

The subjectivity that is inherent in the concept of risk provides the rationale for using social science research methods to better understand how people perceive and respond to risks, including environmental injustice risks. These methods rely extensively on qualitative research methods such as focus groups, in-depth interviews and open-ended questionnaires. As opposed to quantitative research methods, these methods often explicitly acknowledge the key role that value judgements play in the decision-making process.[49]

---

[48] Ibid.

[49] Renn proposes a systemic classification of different perspectives on the concept of risk, which encompasses both social and non-social sciences. See Ortwin Renn, 'Essay 1: A Guide to Interdisciplinary Risk Research' in *Risk*

The relationship between environmental justice analysis, the concept of risk and research methods (including social science research methods) remains under-explored in the literature. However, we have found two publications, which discuss the methodological dimension of this research field. Lockie and Measham point out that there are risk situations where risk cannot be assessed technically with probabilistic-based methods. They argue that social science research is needed 'to better reflect the diversity of risk calculation and management activities in which environmental managers, both public and private are engaged'.[50] They argue that environmental justice movements are historical examples of 'situations characterized by a lack of confidence in the capacity or trustworthiness of expert and/or risk regulating institutions'.[51] These authors also argue that social science perspectives on risk mostly focus on catastrophic events to the detriment of less 'spectacular' and 'mundane' risky situations.[52] As for Schiffman and Robbins, they highlight how opponents of environmental justice argue that risk assessment methods should be used in environmental decision-making, as an alternative to the environmental justice discourse.[53] These authors argue that environmental justice analysis amplifies the risks to which communities are exposed, which distort risk prioritization in the environmental decision-making process.

In this chapter we argue that social science risk research, which is a component of social and behavioural sciences, should inform the legal discipline to improve energy legal frameworks and to better understand the environmental injustice issues that arise from low-carbon energy technology projects. This is mostly because the literature reported in Table 5.1 suggests that environmental justice risks, rather than technological risks, are the main barriers to the adoption of new forms of clean and renewable energy. It is our view that risk research in the social

---

Governance: Coping with Uncertainty in a Complex World (Earthscan, 2008), p. 15. As for Lockie and Measham, they provide an overview of non-social disciplinary perspectives on risk. See Stewart Lockie and Tom Measham, 'Social Perspectives on Risk and Uncertainty: Reconciling the Spectacular and the Mundane' in Tom Measham and Stewart Lockie (eds), *Risk and Social Theory in Environmental Management* (CSIRO Publishing, 2012), p. 3.

[50] Ibid. 1.

[51] Ibid. 4.

[52] Ibid. 1.

[53] Shiffman and Robbins, 'Environmental Justice (Ethics and Philosophy)', above n. 14, at 9.

sciences can offer unique tools and methods for better understanding and analyzing the human and institutional dimension of energy issues.

Two American researchers, Prewitt and Hauser, have highlighted how behavioural and social sciences could contribute to evidence-based policies for improving people's livelihoods in the context of health care and national security. They note that:

> It is within the reach of political science, decision theory, cognitive psychology, behavioural economics, and systems theory to focus analytically on the use of 'science as evidence in public policy'.[54]

It should be noted that risk research falls precisely within the scope of these disciplines. This is for example illustrated by Jasanoff, who explores the political science of risk perception.[55] The work developed by Daniel Kahneman in the area of decision theory, behavioural economics, cognitive psychology and risk perception,[56] as well as the exploration by Japp and Kusche of the intersection between systems theory and risk,[57] are other examples of risk research in social sciences.

Yet as noted by Prewitt and Hauser, the contributions of social and behavioural sciences (and therefore social sciences risk research) 'are not always apparent to the broader science community and the public or in policy settings'.[58] They add that '[t]his lack of visibility risks underutilizing the nation's [United States'] capabilities as new challenges emerge'.[59] This suggests that further investigation is needed to explore how new and existing methodological tools informed by social and behavioural sciences can be used to better understand and manage the various environmental justice issues that may arise from low-carbon energy technology projects.

---

[54] Kenneth Prewitt and Robert Hauser, 'Applying the Social and Behavioural Sciences to Policy and Practice' (2013) *Issues in Science and Technology* 54, available at http://issues.org/29-3/prewitt/.

[55] Sheila Jasanoff, 'Political Science of Risk Perception' (1998) 59 *Reliability Engineering and Safety Systems* 91.

[56] See, for example, Daniel Kahneman, *Thinking, Fast and Slow* (Macmillan, 2011).

[57] Klaus J. Japp and Isable Kusche, 'Systems Theory and Risk' in J.O. Zinn (ed.), *Social Theories of Risk and Uncertainty: An Introduction* (Wiley-Blackwell, 2009), p. 76.

[58] Prewitt and Hauser, 'Applying the Social and Behavioural Sciences to Policy and Practice', above n. 54, at 53.

[59] Ibid.

IV CONCLUSION

This chapter has attempted to provide insights into the complex relationship that exists between environmental justice, risk and social sciences disciplines. The rationale was to explore whether new methodological tools and instruments for designing and implementing innovative risk management strategies could effectively incorporate social and environmental justice considerations into energy policy and legal frameworks. This chapter was also motivated by the desire to better understand and manage the social risks that are likely to arise from induced technological changes from low-carbon energy technology projects. One of the key findings of this chapter is that whilst the concept of environmental justice seems to be useful for addressing environmental justice issues that emerge in the transition towards a clean energy future, our review of the literature on environmental justice has also demonstrated that further research is needed to document the nature and the extent of environmental injustice issues in different low-carbon energy contexts.

The second finding of this chapter is that risk research in the social sciences, supported by environmental justice analysis, has the potential to offer unique tools and methods for better understanding and analyzing the human and institutional dimension of energy issues and better designing evidence-based policies that are behaviourally effective in the energy context. This is mainly because risk perception issues explain why communities may oppose low-carbon energy technology projects, as evidenced by the literature. From a philosophical point of view, acknowledging the subjective rather than the objective dimension of the concept of risk implies that vulnerable communities are not necessarily in control of their destiny. Instead, to achieve a fair society, those who conceive, draft and implement new laws and policies should protect vulnerable communities by incorporating new research methods from social and behavioural sciences that incorporate environmental justice considerations.

We acknowledge that there are still conceptual and methodological grey areas that need to be clarified for the purpose of designing and implementing new tools that incorporate social considerations into legal energy frameworks. However, framing the clean energy debate through the lens of environmental justice and the subjective dimension of the concept of risk provides an interesting alternative to conceptual frames that focus exclusively on energy security and climate change. Methodological tools often reflect political beliefs and values. Therefore, in the background of this chapter remain two key political questions. The first one is: what kind of society do we want to live in? The second question asks what new research tools of the future we want to create that are aligned with our beliefs and values in the energy context.

In a complex technological world governed by uncertainty, there are many risks and uncertainties surrounding legal transitions towards low-carbon economies. As pointed out by Renn and Klinke, risk knowledge is characterized by complexity, scientific uncertainty and socio-political ambiguity.[60] We acknowledge that, as with environmental justice research, risk and uncertainty research is still in its infancy, particularly in energy and environmental law scholarship. But these under-explored research areas provide unique research opportunities for reimagining how human systems interact with natural systems. There are interesting research initiatives being undertaken for improving people's livelihood and national legal and policy frameworks. For example, in 2012, the American National Research Council launched the Social and the Behavioural Sciences in Action project. This project intends to investigate how social and behavioural sciences can support intelligence analysis and improve evidence-based public policies. Such an initiative could, for example, be adopted to explore how risk research in the social sciences could contribute to design and implement effective new risk management strategies to avoid and manage the environmental injustice risks from low-carbon energy technologies.

---

[60] Ortwin Renn and Andreas Klinke, 'Complexity, Uncertainty and Ambiguity in Inclusive Risk Governance' in Thomas Measham and Stewart Lockie (eds), *Risk and Social Theory in Environmental Management* (CSIRO Publishing, 2012).

6. Scaling up local solutions: creating an enabling legal environment for the deployment of community-based renewable microgrids

Jessica Wentz and Chiara Pappalardo

I INTRODUCTION

In 2013 the International Energy Agency (IEA) estimated that there were over 1.3 billion people without access to electricity and 2.6 billion people without clean cooking facilities.[1] More than 95 percent of these people live in Sub-Saharan Africa or Southeast Asia and 84 percent live in rural areas. The link between energy access and socio-economic development is well documented, and addressing energy poverty is now a major focus of the sustainable development agenda.[2] Energy poverty has adverse impacts on income generation, economic growth, public health, education, the environment and many other social indicators.[3]

To address this problem United Nations (UN) Secretary General Ban Ki-moon launched the 'Sustainable Energy for All' ('SE4All') initiative, which aims to achieve three goals by 2030: (1) ensure universal access to

[1] International Energy Agency, *World Energy Outlook 2013* (OECD/IEA, 2013).

[2] Joy Clancy, Nthabi Mohlakoana and Margaret Matinga, 'Energy Poverty: Have We Got the Measure of It?', paper delivered at the UK DSA Annual Meeting, University of Birmingham, November 2013; International Energy Agency, 'Modern Energy for All: Why it Matters' available at www.worldenergyoutlook.org/resources/energydevelopment/modernenergyforallwhyitmatters/.

[3] Benjamin K. Sovacool, 'Design Principles for Renewable Energy Programs in Developing Countries' (2012) 5 *Energy and Environmental Science* 9157; Eva Rehfuess, *Fuel for Life: Household, Energy and Health* (WHO, 2006); John P. Holdren and Kirk R. Smith, 'Energy, the Environment, and Health' in UNDP *et al.* (eds), *World Energy Assessment: Energy and the Challenge of Sustainability* (2000), ch. 3.

modern energy services; (2) double the global rate of improvement in energy efficiency; and (3) double the share of renewable energy (RE) in the global energy mix.[4] The IEA estimates that over 40 per cent of capacity installed to meet the access target can be most economically delivered through mini- and microgrids.[5] Based on this projection, practitioners have determined that these systems represent a 'high-impact opportunity' for achieving SE4All.[6]

This chapter highlights the benefits of RE microgrids, with a focus on community-based projects, and provides recommendations on how policies and regulations can be structured to most effectively harness those benefits. We address two critical issues for 'scaling up' the deployment of these systems: (1) removing restrictions on the collection of electricity tariffs; and (2) designing a national programme that will attract external investment in these projects. We find that projects like the Multiuser Solar Microgrid installed in the small village of Monte Trigo in Cape Verde constitute successful models that could be replicated in an enabling regulatory environment. In addition, we find that ambitious national programmes such as Nepal's Rural Energy Development Programme can catalyze multi-stakeholder finance in these projects and thus expedite progress towards universal electrification and sustainable development.

II COMMUNITY MICROGRIDS: A NEW PARADIGM FOR ELECTRIFICATION AND SUSTAINABLE DEVELOPMENT

Electrification efforts in low-income countries have generally followed the Western paradigm of centralized generation and transmission. Although this is often viewed as the most efficient approach, it has some disadvantages that have impeded electrification efforts in low-income countries. These include the following.

Transmission costs: Many of the people without access to electricity live in remote locations, sometimes separated from population hubs by geographic features such as mountains and water bodies. Connecting

---

[4] Ban Ki-moon, Secretary General of the United Nations, *Sustainable Energy for All* (UN, 2011), p. 4.

[5] International Energy Agency, *World Energy Outlook 2011* (OECD/IEA, 2011).

[6] UN Sustainable Energy for All, *SE4All High Impact Opportunity Clean Energy Microgrids* (2015), available at www.se4all.org/sites/default/files/l/2014/08/HIO_CEMG_Publication_2015.pdf.

these communities to a central grid is viewed as cost-prohibitive due to the expense of constructing and maintaining expansive transmission infrastructure and the existence of a weak customer base.[7] Utilities have no incentive to make large transmission investments to reach a customer base with very little purchasing power.[8] Expanding transmission infrastructure also has other environmental and social costs associated with its impacts on landscape.

Poor utility performance: Many studies have documented the poor performance of both public and private utilities in low-income countries.[9] These performance issues are often attributed to a lack of adequate economic incentives for improvement (for example, market competition).[10] To make electricity affordable, many developing countries have introduced electricity consumption subsidies. Unfortunately, these subsidies tend to undermine managerial incentives to improve the efficiency of operations, expand services to new customers, or improve the quality of service for existing customers.[11] Consumption subsidies are also poorly targeted, because they only reach citizens that already have

---

[7] Charles Kirubi *et al.*, 'Community-Based Electric Micro-Grids Can Contribute to Rural Development: Evidence from Kenya' (2009) 37 *World Development* 1208.

[8] Lorenzo Pellegrini and Luca Tasciotti, 'Rural Electrification Now and Then: Comparing Contemporary Challenges in Developing Countries to the USA's Experience in Retrospect' (2013) 1 *Forum for Development Studies* 161; Uwe Deichmann *et al.*, 'The Economics of Renewable Energy Expansion in Rural Sub-Saharan Africa' (2011) 39 *Energy Policy* 215; Michel Sinn, *Cost Recovery of Isolated Microgrids in Sub-Saharan Africa: Causalities and Prerequisites* (Master's Thesis, Chalmers University of Technology, 2014).

[9] John E. Besant-Jones, *Reforming Power Markets in Developing Countries: What Have We Learned?*, Energy and Mining Sector Board, Discussion Paper No. 19 (World Bank Group, 2006); Heloisa Marone, *The Pillars of Utilities Provision: What is the Role of the Public in Public Utility Provision?* (UNDP, 2007); Katharina Gassner, Alexander Popov and Nataliya Pushak, *Does Private Sector Participation Improve Performance in Electricity and Water Distribution?*, Trends and Policy Options No. 6 (PPIAF, World Bank, 2009).

[10] Besant-Jones, *Reforming Power Markets in Developing Countries*, above n. 9, at 10; Gassner, Popov and Pushak, *Does Private Sector Participation Improve Performance*, above n. 9, at 15.

[11] United Nations Environmental Program, *Reforming Energy Subsidies: Opportunities to Contribute to the Climate Change Agenda* (2008); Cecilia Briceño-Garmendia and Maria Shkaratan, *Power Tariffs Caught Between Cost Recovery and Affordability*, Policy Research Working Paper 5904 (World Bank, 2011).

access to electricity.[12] Other factors that impede utility performance include capacity and resource constraints, internal corruption and regulatory capture.[13] These problems are not unique to large utilities, but the consolidation of managerial authority tends to amplify the problems associated with poor performance and corruption. One way to mitigate this problem is to have a larger pool of actors involved in the generation and distribution of electricity.

Limited socio-economic development impact: One justification for the subsidization of electricity tariffs is the assumption that electrification will induce economic growth, thus helping to build a solvent consumer base with higher electricity demand (which is necessary for the long-term financial viability of the electricity sector). However, the centralized approach to electrification has failed to produce the anticipated levels of economic growth and very few utilities have become economically self-sustaining through this process.

As a result of these and other problems, support is mounting for a decentralized electrification approach which directs public investment toward small-scale projects like microgrids and minigrids.

(1) Microgrids

Although the terms 'minigrid' and 'microgrid' are often used interchangeably, a microgrid is a particular type of minigrid that incorporates 'smart grid' technologies. Broadly defined, a microgrid is a localized network of electricity sources and loads that can be controlled to ensure reliable operation when the system is isolated or connected to another grid.[14] Microgrids contain technologies and design features that allow for

---

[12] Kristin Komives *et al.*, *Water, Electricity, and the Poor: Who Benefits from Utility Subsidies?* (World Bank, 2005); Diego Ángel Urdinola and Quentin Wodon, 'Do Utility Subsidies Reach the Poor? Framework and Evidence for Cape Verde, Sao Tome, and Rwanda' (2006) 9 *Economics Bulletin* 1; Trevor Alleyne, *Energy Subsidy Reform in Sub-Saharan Africa Experiences and Lessons* (IMF, 2013).

[13] 'Regulatory capture' occurs when regulated entities co-opt a regulatory programme to advance their own interests, rather than the interests of the general public. See Emmanuelle Auriol and Aymeric Blanc, 'Capture and Corruption in Public Utilities: The Cases of Water and Electricity in Sub-Saharan Africa' (2009) 17 *Utilities Policy* 203; Ernesto dal Bo and Martin A. Rossi, 'Corruption and Inefficiency: Theory and Evidence from Electric Utilities' (2007) 91 *Journal of Public Economics* 939.

[14] John Romankiewicz *et al.*, 'International Microgrid Assessment: Governance, Incentives, and Experience (IMAGINE)' (2014) 67 *Energy Policy* 198.

optimized load management, thus reducing system capacity requirements and contributing to a higher load factor.[15] This second feature is particularly important for low-income communities, since the efficiency of the system (as reflected by the load factor) influences the cost of the system. Whereas utility-scale systems are constructed to meet peak demand, microgrids can be scaled efficiently to reflect average electricity consumption.[16]

Microgrids achieve this level of control through a variety of design elements which differ depending on local context (see Figure 6.1).[17] These features include:

- complementary generation resources, including dispatchable and intermittent resources;
- energy storage systems and back-up generators;
- software that monitors and manages generation and consumption and makes adjustments as needed to maintain system reliability and achieve other goals (for example, optimizing the load factor or maximizing RE).[18]

Microgrids are also frequently deployed in combination with demand-side management (DSM) strategies and technologies to promote end-user efficiency.[19] Some examples include:

---

[15] Ramon Zamora and Anurag Srivastava, 'Controls for Microgrids with Storage: Review, Challenges, and Research Needs' (2010) 14 *Renewable and Sustainable Energy Reviews* 2009; Nikos Hatziargyriou *et al.*, 'Microgrids' (2007) 5 *Power and Energy Magazine* 83; Djiby-Racine Thiam, 'Renewable Decentralized in Developing Countries: Appraisal from Microgrids Project in Senegal' (2010) 35 *Renewable Energy* 1620.

[16] Mohammed Yekini Suberu *et al.*, 'Renewable Energy Distributed Electricity Generation and Microgrid Implementation in Rural Villages: A Review' (2013) 8 *ARPN Journal of Engineering and Applied Science* 149.

[17] Romankiewicz *et al.*, 'International Microgrid Assessment', above n. 14, at 7; Mahesh Illindala *et al.*, 'Localized Aggregation of Diverse Energy Sources for Rural Electrification Using Microgrids' (2007) 133 *Journal of Energy Engineering* 121.

[18] For example, many systems contain software that distinguishes between critical loads and non-critical or 'controllable' loads, and automatically terminates power to controllable loads when demand exceeds generation to prevent service interruptions to important end-users like hospitals.

[19] J.D. Kueck *et al.*, *Microgrids and Demand Response: How Software Controls Can Bridge the Gap Between Wholesale Market Prices and Consumer Behavior* (2003), available at www.consultkirby.com/files/Tech_Corridor.pdf; R.

- smart meters that allow for the two-way exchange of pricing, usage data and electricity;
- smart appliances and lighting that are programmed to come online when the system is generating excess electricity;
- usage limits, for example, customers pay a fixed monthly rate for a pre-determined amount of electricity.

These features facilitate the efficient design and operation of microgrids.

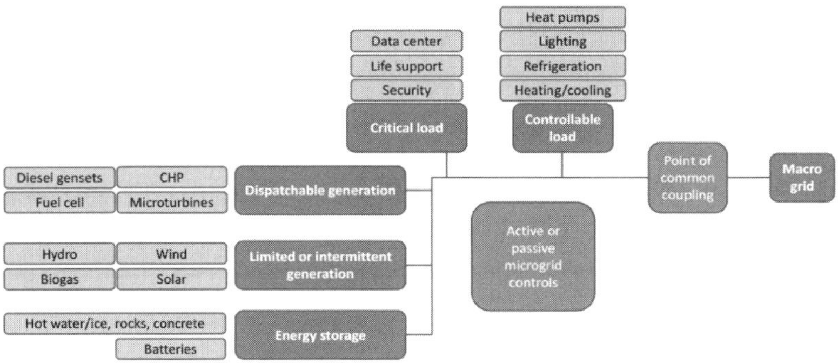

Source: John Romankiewicz *et al.*, 'International Microgrid Assessment: Governance, Incentives, and Experience (IMAGINE)' (2014) 67 *Energy Policy* 198.

Figure 6.1 Overview of the main components in a common microgrid

In light of these factors, microgrids are a prudent option for electrification in low-income areas, where there is insufficient capital to invest in excess generation capacity. The small scale of these projects means that they require a smaller upfront investment and can be deployed more rapidly than utility-scale projects. In addition, load management features and stakeholder planning can reduce uncertainty about future patterns of production, consumption and revenue, which in turn reduces investment risk.

Due to their generation and load controls, microgrids are also particularly well-suited for the integration of intermittent renewables.[20]

Palma-Behnke *et al.*, *Energy Management System for a Renewable-based Microgrid with a Demand Side Management Mechanism* (Computational Intelligence Applications in Smart Grid, IEEE Symposium, 2011).

[20] Suberu, 'Renewable Energy Distributed Electricity Generation and Microgrid Implementation in Rural Villages', above n. 16.

Microgrids are highly versatile since they can operate in isolation and when connected to a grid. They are an ideal solution for islands and remote areas, but they are also suitable in urban and suburban areas where the central grid is not providing adequate or reliable service. When connected to the central grid, microgrids can provide additional generation, energy storage, and other ancillary services to help maintain the safe, reliable and secure transmission of electricity within the networked system.[21]

Finally, microgrids have the transformative potential to 'democratize' the management of energy resources.[22] Under the centralized paradigm, control over energy resources is highly concentrated in the hands of a few policy-makers and utility decision-makers.[23] Individual end-users and communities have very little input on how energy resources are managed and how costs and benefits associated with electricity production are distributed. With the deployment of microgrids, there is an opportunity for greater levels of local participation in these decision-making processes as well as local ownership of energy resources.

Looking to the future, planners and regulators must contemplate how centralized and decentralized solutions can be integrated in order to develop electric systems that are efficient, reliable and resilient. With public oversight and coordination, it could be possible to have a fully operational network of locally managed renewable microgrids supplying a substantial proportion of energy needs in low-income countries and elsewhere. This network could be coordinated with utility-scale projects to develop a truly robust and diversified electricity system.[24]

While the technical advantages of a microgrid are clear, there are also costs associated with the advanced design of these systems. Fortunately, the technologies for automated management, storage and small-scale renewable energy production have declined sharply in recent years,[25] and this trend will probably continue with the increased deployment of

---

21 M. Gomes and J. Saraiva, 'Allocation of Reactive Power Support, Active Loss Balancing and Demand Interruption Ancillary Services in Microgrids' (2010) 80 *Electric Power Systems Research* 1267.

22 John Farrell, *Democratizing the Electricity System: A Vision for the 21st Century Grid* (Institute for Local Self-Reliance, 23 June 2011), available at https://ilsr.org/democratizing-electricity-system-vision-21st-century-grid/.

23 Kari Alanne and Arto Saari, 'Distributed Energy Generation and Sustainable Development' (2006) 10 *Renewable and Sustainable Energy Reviews* 539.

24 Emma Marris, 'Energy: Upgrading the Grid' (2008) 454 *Nature* 570.

25 Energy Sector Management Assistance Program, *Energy: CY2007-FY2008 Annual Report* (International Bank for Reconstruction and Development/World Bank Group, ESMAP, 2009); S. Szabó *et al.*, 'Energy Solutions in Rural Africa:

microgrids across the world.[26] Entrepreneurs have also begun to offer 'microgrid kits' and related installation services to reduce the costs of these systems.[27]

(2) Harnessing the Benefits of Microgrids through Integrated Development Programmes and Local Stakeholder Empowerment

Access to energy is a critical driver of poverty alleviation, economic productivity and social welfare, and RE projects can yield development co-benefits that 'far exceed their costs' relating to income generation, economic growth, technology use and social welfare.[28] However, energy access 'does not itself guarantee social progress or economic development'.[29] The Independent Evaluation Group (IEG) of the World Bank examined this issue in 2008 and found limited evidence to support long-standing assumptions about the welfare impacts of electrification projects.[30] The IEG concluded that '[t]he full benefits of providing electricity to the poor are not being realized' because electricity was not being used for productive purposes, projects were not targeting the poorest households, and the projects rarely contained elements to ensure that the intended development outcomes actually occurred.[31]

One way to address this situation is to approach electrification as part of a broader development approach. This can be accomplished by combining electrification projects with complementary infrastructure,

---

Mapping Electrification Costs of Distributed Solar and Diesel Generation Versus Grid Extension' (2011) 6 *Environmental Research Letters* (No. 3).

[26] N.W.A. Lindula and A.D. Rajapakse, 'Microgrids Research: A Review of Experimental Microgrids and Test Systems' (2011) 15 *Renewable and Sustainable Energy Reviews* 186.

[27] *Rural Microgrid* (Gham Power, 2014), available at http://ghampower.com/products/rural-solar-microgrid/.

[28] Sovacool, 'Design Principles for Renewable Energy Programs in Developing Countries', above n. 3, at 9161.

[29] Kirubi *et al.*, 'Community-Based Electric Micro-Grids Can Contribute to Rural Development', above n. 7, at 1209–10. See also Sylvain Quoilin and Matthew Orosz, 'Rural Electrification Through Decentralized Concentrating Solar Power: Technological and Socio-Economic Aspects' (2011) 1 *Journal of Sustainable Development of Energy, Water and Environment Systems* 199.

[30] World Bank Independent Evaluation Group, *The Welfare Impact of Rural Electrification: A Reassessment of the Costs and Benefits, An IEG Impact Evaluation* (International Bank for Reconstruction and Development/World Bank, 2008).

[31] Ibid. xvi.

social services and business services.[32] Individual projects can also be designed to support small enterprises, public facilities or other productive uses of electricity.[33] Productive uses are not limited to income generating activities: they also include activities such as farming, domestic work, education, public health and communication services.[34]

By understanding electrification as part of a development process characterized by many causal links and feedback loops, policy-makers and practitioners can strategically harness opportunities for positive synergies (and avoid negative synergies).[35] Many countries are now operating within this integrated framework, developing plans and programmes to deliver electricity 'as part of a wider package of complementary infrastructure, including but not limited to roads, telecommunication, health, and educational facilities' and also 'prioritiz[ing] productive uses such as agricultural, commercial, and institutional activities'.[36]

One key component of this integrated approach is ensuring that local stakeholders play a significant role in designing, implementing and managing projects. Sovacool suggests that this will require a transition away from old models such as the donor gift and the market creation paradigm, in favour of a 'sustainable programme' paradigm in which public and private stakeholders work cooperatively to achieve the broader goals of energy development relating to environmental and social sustainability.[37] One iteration of this new paradigm is the emergence of

---

[32] Kirubi *et al.*, 'Community-Based Electric Micro-Grids Can Contribute to Rural Development', above n. 7, at 1218–19.

[33] Stephen Karekezi and Lugard Majoro, 'Africa: Improving Modern Energy Services for the Poor' (2002) 30 *Energy Policy* 1015; Hisham Zerriffi, *Rural Electrification: Strategies for Distributed Generation* (Springer, 2010); Diego Masera and Vittoria Paramithiotti, 'Enabling Environment for Promoting Energy as an Income Opportunity' in Emanuela Colombo, Stefano Bologna and Diego Masera (eds), *Renewable Energy for Unleashing Sustainable Development* (Springer, 2013), ch. 11.

[34] R. Anil Cabraal, Douglas F. Barnes and Sachin G. Agarwal, 'Productive Uses of Energy for Rural Development' (2005) 30 *Annual Review of Environment and Natural Resources* 117; Karekezi and Majoro, 'Africa: Improving Modern Energy Services for the Poor', above n. 33.

[35] Cabraal *et al.*, 'Productive Uses of Energy for Rural Development', above n. 34 highlight empirical evidence from rural India and Peru demonstrating that the joint provision of education and electricity is likely to yield higher household income than providing education without electricity.

[36] Kirubi *et al.*, 'Community-Based Electric Micro-Grids Can Contribute to Rural Development', above n. 7, at 1210.

[37] Sovacool, 'Design Principles for Renewable Energy Programs in Developing Countries', above n. 3, at 9161.

community-based microgrids (which include but are not limited to cooperatively owned projects) in Southeast Asia, Sub-Saharan Africa, and other parts of the developing world.[38] For the purposes of this chapter, we define community-based projects as projects that are characterized by meaningful levels of community input and participation (see Table 6.1).

Table 6.1 Examples of community participation in local electrification projects

Customer model	*Community input*	*Community contribution*	*Community ownership*
• Per kwH tariffs • Fixed fees • Pay for service	• Project design • Project operations • Payment scheme	• Monetary contributions • In-kind contributions • Labour, maintenance	• Grants, subsidies • Microfinance • Rent to own
Increasing degree of community involvement →			

Source: Constructed by authors (2014).

The advantages of community participation include benefits relating to the viability of a particular project, as well as enhanced realization of development co-benefits. With respect to project viability, studies have shown that the likelihood of project success (for small power projects and other infrastructural projects) can be significantly increased by involving end-users in decisions about project design, operations and payment

[38] Akanksha Chaurey, Malini Ranganathan and Parimita Mohanty, 'Electricity Access for Geographically Disadvantaged Rural Communities: Technology and Policy Insights' (2004) 32 *Energy Policy* 1693; A. Gerger and M. Gullberg, *Rural Power Supply with Local Management: Examples from Bolivia, India and Nepal* (Stockholm Environment Institute, 1997); C.E. Greacen, *The Marginalization of 'Small is Beautiful': Micro-hydroelectricity, Common Property, and Politics of Rural Electricity Provision in Thailand* (Doctoral Dissertation, University of California, Berkeley, CA, 2003); Thomas Bourgeois *et al.*, *Community Microgrids: Smarter, Cleaner, Greener* (Pace Energy and Climate Center, 2013); Seth Meyers, 'The Economic Challenge of Rural Electrification: Community Solutions Initiative in Africa', paper delivered at IEEE Global Humanitarian Technology Conference, 2013.

schemes.[39] End-users can provide valuable information about local conditions, energy demand, their ability to pay, productive uses and anchor tenants,[40] all of which can help establish an appropriately sized project and a financial plan.[41] End-users can also provide valuable inputs in the form of labour, in-kind or monetary contributions. To the extent that they feel as though they have some level of ownership over the project, end-users are more likely to behave in a cooperative manner so as to ensure the ongoing viability of the project, for example, paying bills on time, conserving electricity when needed, helping with project maintenance, refraining from or reporting electricity theft, etc.[42] In theory, these benefits can be maximized when local stakeholders own and manage the system collectively as a common property resource.[43]

The community-based approach also offers a number of co-benefits relating to local capacity-building and empowerment. For example, when local end-users participate in project development and management, they can acquire valuable experience in areas such as community organizing and financial planning, as well as technical knowledge about designing and operating a small power project.[44]

---

[39] Kirubi *et al.*, 'Community-Based Electric Micro-Grids Can Contribute to Rural Development', above n. 7; Bernard Tenenbaum *et al.*, *From the Bottom Up: How Small Power Producers and Mini-grids Can Deliver Electrification and Renewable Energy in Africa* (World Bank, 2014).

[40] Anchor tenants are larger customers with more consistent demand for electricity, such as community clinics, police stations, telecommunications towers and manufacturing facilities. Planning a microgrid with an anchor tenant can increase the likelihood that the project will generate sufficient revenue so as to maintain a 'virtuous cycle' since the anchor tenant is perceived as a more reliable and stable customer. Involving an anchor tenant can also yield important co-benefits, for example, a community clinic can improve public health, a manufacturing facility can create additional jobs, and a cell phone tower can improve communication in a region.

[41] Quoilin and Orosz, 'Rural Electrification Through Decentralized Concentrating Solar Power', above n. 29, at 200.

[42] Tenenbaum *et al.*, *From the Bottom Up*, above n. 39, at 290.

[43] Kirubi *et al.*, 'Community-Based Electric Micro-Grids Can Contribute to Rural Development', above n. 7 1211.

[44] Tenenbaum *et al.*, *From the Bottom Up*, above n. 39.

(3) Case Study: Mpeketoni Electricity Project

The Mpeketoni Electricity Project (MEP)[45] was a community-based diesel-powered microgrid in rural Kenya, which operated as a collectively owned system from 1994–2007, and has since been operated by the national government. The MEP illustrates how community-owned projects can contribute to local development and achieve a high degree of cost recovery, particularly when they are situated within a broader integrated approach to rural development.

The MEP was constructed as part of an integrated development programme sponsored by the national government of Kenya and the German Technical Cooperation (GTZ/GASP). The local community, including entrepreneurs, farmers and institutions, contributed approximately 30 per cent of the initial capital cost in cash and labour for the project. In addition to the MEP, the development programme included a package of complementary infrastructure consisting of roads, schools, markets and business services, which contributed to the development of a robust and diversified local economy. For example, GTZ/GASP helped educate farmers about crop diversity, provided business support services (for example, for financial planning), and was also instrumental in facilitating the opening of a local branch of the Kenya Commercial Bank. GTZ/GASP also employed local businesses and workers to implement its various development activities (for example, by having them construct furniture for classrooms, health centres and community halls). According to one study, 'GTZ/GASP's policy of purchasing locally produced goods had a significant effect in growing the local market and boosting revenues for the SMEs [small and medium-sized enterprises]'.[46]

The MEP was designed to serve a diverse customer base. SMEs consumed slightly more than half of the total energy supply each month, and were a vital revenue base for MEP, given that they paid higher fixed monthly service charges (US$6.70) than households (US$3.30). The single largest end-user was the Mpeketoni Secondary School, which each month used nearly half as much energy again as all households together (and thus served as a valuable anchor tenant).

Over the course of operations, the MEP made a significant impact on local economic and social development. Access to electricity enabled the use of electronic equipment by SMEs, thereby boosting productivity per worker by 100–200 per cent (depending on the product). At the same

---

45 Case study adapted from Kirubi *et al.*, 'Community-Based Electric Micro-Grids Can Contribute to Rural Development', above n. 7.

46 Ibid. 1217.

time it enabled and improved the delivery of social and business services from schools and financial institutions. The project also facilitated rural trade and commerce by providing electricity for banking and communication services, with Internet access playing a particularly important role in supporting local businesses, social services and the MEP itself.

Finally, the MEP demonstrated that 'community-led rural micro-grids have the potential to cover a substantial proportion of the operating costs from internal revenue derived from sales of electricity and other charges'.[47] By 2007, 'MEP had attained 94% cost recovery, nearly five times that realized by the diesel-powered micro-grids operated by the KPLC, the national utility'.[48] Kirubi and others attribute this to the collection of cost-reflective tariffs, the promotion of productive uses, and the integrated approach to local development.[49]

(4) Addressing Barriers to Microgrid Deployment

The technical and economic barriers to microgrid projects are closely related to the local context in which these projects are implemented. In many low-income countries, microgrids are not yet commercially viable and thus will require public support in the immediate and near-term.[50] In this context, the ongoing viability of a project (its ability to recover un-subsidized costs) depends on the design and management of the system as well as its contribution to local economic growth.

According to a survey by the UN Foundation, successful projects typically follow a 'virtuous' cycle where there is sufficient revenue to support the grid, as well as service and schedule reliability to retain loyal customers.[51] This is true with respect to for-profit projects, partially subsidized, and fully subsidized projects (where the required 'revenue' includes whatever subsidy is provided). In contrast, unsuccessful projects follow a 'vicious' cycle, 'characterized by a chain of poor maintenance, disappointed customers, insufficient revenue and dysfunctional community support'.[52] Under these conditions, the project ceases to generate sufficient revenue for effective operation and maintenance (O&M),

---

[47] Ibid. 1212.

[48] Ibid.

[49] Ibid.

[50] Sinn, *Cost Recovery of Isolated Microgrids in Sub-Saharan Africa*, above n. 8, at 4.

[51] Daniel Schnitzer *et al.*, *Microgrids for Rural Electrification* (UN Foundation, 2014).

[52] Ibid.

service is compromised, and customers become less willing to pay for the electricity provided by the project (see Figure 6.2).

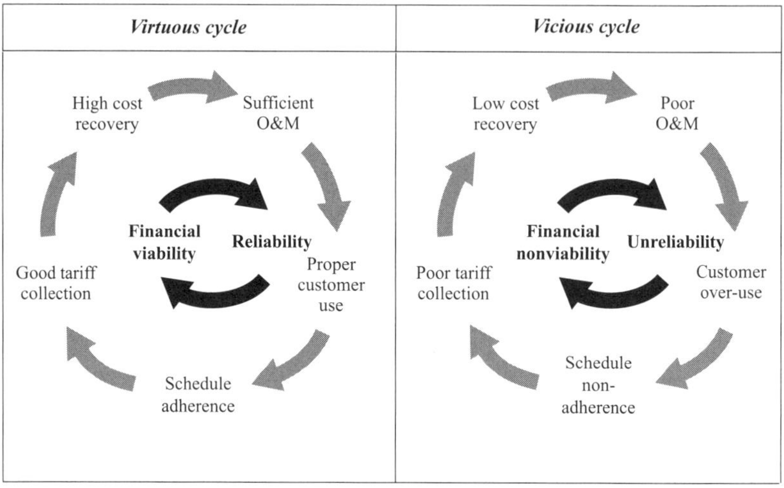

Source: Adapted from Daniel Schnitzer *et al.*, *Microgrids for Rural Electrification* (UN Foundation, 2014), p. 1.

Figure 6.2 Comparison of virtuous and vicious cycles

Tariff design is critical to project success. Ideally, tariffs are fully cost-reflective, but this is unfeasible in many developing and low-income areas.[53] Rather, a more common model, sometimes referred to as a break-even tariff, is to charge end-users a rate that will cover ongoing O&M, and cover upfront installation costs with public subsidies or donations.[54] For donor-supported projects, Pérez-Arriaga finds that the collection of a break-even tariff is the most important factor for sustainable operation.[55]

Another critical component of project viability is the quality of the initial design. In one Philippine programme, pressures to keep costs as low as possible resulted in the circumvention of technical standards and installation guidelines – and as a result, only 1 per cent of the projects

[53] S. Bhattacharyya, *Rural Electrification Through Decentralised Off-Grid Systems in Developing Countries* (Springer, 2012).

[54] Simon Rolland and Guido Glania, *Hybrid Mini-Grids for Rural Electrification: Lessons Learned* (ARE, 2011), p. 7.

[55] I.J. Pérez-Arriaga, *Regulation of the Power Sector* (Springer, 2013).

were still in operation after a few years.[56] In addition to high-quality components, the system should also be designed efficiently: demand needs to be calculated with enough precision to match generation capacity and justify infrastructure costs, in particular, distribution lines.[57] To accomplish this, end-users need to agree on a quantity of electricity that fits their needs and their ability to pay.

Ideally, the system would be designed to incorporate a variety of complementary load sources, such as households, small enterprises, public facilities and other productive uses. This helps distribute peak demand across different times, reducing the overall system capacity requirement. The system can then be designed and operated more efficiency, as indicated by the system load factor (LF).[58] For example, the MEP project was able to obtain an LF of 43 per cent (compared to 20 per cent for similar projects) because the end-user groups had different demand schedules, with enterprises peaking in the daytime and residences peaking at night.[59]

In addition, high-quality, consistent O&M are critical to the long-term sustainability of a project. This can be complicated in remote or isolated areas, where it is difficult to obtain technical experts, spare parts and other resources. Technical training programmes and other capacity building efforts are particularly useful for addressing gaps in local resources, and high-quality maintenance can help mitigate the need for spare parts.[60] Reliable performance is particularly important for maintaining satisfaction among end-users. This promotes on-time payments and reduces occurrences of individual abuse and consumption above the allocated household limit (that is, 'free rider' behaviour) that can disrupt the functioning of the microgrid.

Whether a project enters a virtuous or vicious cycle also depends on the legal context. Policy and regulations can either impede or enable the successful operation of a project (for example, by restricting the amount

---

[56] E, Martinot *et al.*, 'Renewable Energy Markets in Developing Countries' (2002) 28 *Annual Review of Energy and the Environment* 313.

[57] World Bank Group, *The Potential for Alternative Power Supply (APS) of Power in Developing Countries* (Final Report, June 2014), pp. 53–4.

[58] LF is a useful proxy for system efficiency and the financial viability of rural micro-grids. David J. Fulford, Paul Mosley and Alastair Gill, 'Recommendations on the Use of Micro-Hydro Power in Rural Development' (2000) 12 *Journal of International Development* 975.

[59] Kirubi *et al.*, 'Community-Based Electric Micro-Grids Can Contribute to Rural Development', above n. 7, at 1212.

[60] Quoilin and Orosz, 'Rural Electrification Through Decentralized Concentrating Solar Power', above n. 29.

that can be charged for electricity). Fortunately, many countries are reforming laws to better accommodate small power projects. One first step is the removal of barriers to market access for small power producers, including tariff restrictions and rules establishing exclusive service districts for utilities.[61] There have also been many efforts to clarify the legal status of and applicable regulations for small power producers, and to develop appropriate technical standards and interconnection procedures to ensure that these projects do not compromise grid reliability. Finally, some jurisdictions are attempting to develop standard power purchase agreements (PPAs) and other utility service contracts that can be used to streamline the sale of power from smaller projects.[62] A comprehensive discussion of all these regulatory issues is beyond the scope of this chapter. Rather, section 3 addresses the most critical legal barrier to microgrid development in low-income countries: national uniform tariffs.

III REMOVING REGULATORY BARRIERS: NATIONAL UNIFORM TARIFFS

Many developing countries have introduced national uniform tariff schemes that require utilities to charge the same tariffs for similarly situated customers. These tariffs sometimes differ based on the status of the end user, for example, whether they are a residential or industrial customer, and how much electricity they use, but they do not reflect differences in the cost of generating or transmitting electricity. Thus, they are intended to promote fairness rather than cost recovery. If a microgrid

---

[61] Tenenbaum *et al.*, *From the Bottom Up*, above n. 39.

[62] Examples of such jurisdictions include Tanzania, Kenya and Namibia. See Standardized Power Purchase Agreement for Purchase of Capacity and Associated Electric Energy to the Isolated Mini-Grid developed by the Energy and Water Utilities Regulatory Authority (EWURA) of Tanzania, available at https://energypedia.info/wiki/Standardized_Power_Purchase_Agreement_for_Purchase_of_Capacity_and_Associated_Electric_Energy_to_the_Isolated_Mini-Grid_%E2%80%93_Based_on_Tanzania/Kenya_Examples; Kenyan Regulatory Commission Standardized Power Purchase Agreement for Renewable Energy Generators of Less Than and Including 10 MW, available at www.renewableenergy.go.ke/asset_uplds/files/Standardized_PPA_for_Large_Scale_Generators_More%20than_10MW.pdf; Namibian Electricity Control Board Model PPA for Small Scale IPPs, available at www.ecb.org.na/images/docs/Regulatory_Support_Services/FINAL%20ANNEX%2011_%20Model%20PPA%20for%20Small%20Scale%20IPPs.pdf.

is involved in the sale of retail electricity, then it may be required to charge the uniform tariff, which is typically much lower than a break-even tariff.

There have been recent efforts to address this problem. Some of the most recent national electricity laws in Sub-Saharan Africa allow regulators to set cost-reflective tariffs rather than a uniform national tariff. But in most countries, the 'current reality is that most retail tariffs are both uniform and too low, particularly for isolated mini-grids'.[63] In India, for example, the national government recognizes a distinction between small power projects and utility-scale projects, but has stated that the retail tariffs for distributed generation projects must be comparable to the tariffs of nearby grid connected villages.[64] Some jurisdictions allow variances or waivers of the uniform tariff price for small power producers (SPPs), but the process of obtaining these can be unduly burdensome.

Finally, even if a microgrid project is not required to strictly adhere to the national uniform tariff scheme, these schemes can create major problems for microgrid operators because the national tariff establishes a *de facto* fair price in the eyes of customers, which will be too low to recover the microgrid operator's higher costs.[65] As a result, customers may be unwilling to pay higher costs for electricity from a renewable microgrid, or regulators may be hesitant to approve a waiver or variance from the national uniform tariff for fear of political reprisal.

(1) Case Study: Multisolar Microgrid in Monte Trigo

The Multiuser Solar Micro Grid (MSG) installed in Monte Trigo is another promising example of a community-based RE microgrid.[66] Monte Trigo is a small rural village in the island of Santo Antão in Cape Verde where people rely on fishing and trade with nearby islands for their survival. Until very recently, ice was not available in Santo Antão and villagers had to make five-hour boat trips to the nearest main island to purchase it. The only source of power was a three-phase 20kVA diesel generator providing electricity for four hours per day. Thanks to funds

---

[63] Tenenbaum *et al.*, *From the Bottom Up*, above n. 39, at 242.

[64] Ibid.

[65] Ibid.

[66] Matteo Briganti *et al.*, 'Implementation of a PV Rural Microgrid in the Island of Santo Antão (Cape Verde) with an Individual Energy Allowance Scheme for Demand Control' in *EU PVSEC Proceedings* (2012).

made available by the ACP-EU Energy Facility Programme,[67] a consortium of local entities was able to finance and develop an off-grid solar energy project with the assistance of an international consulting firm.[68] The facility installed is a photovoltaic generator with two storage batteries, monitoring, control and power conversion equipment, and low-voltage distribution lines that provides an aggregated value of 90kVA for 24 hours of electricity per day and relies on the old diesel generator only for back-up power. Permanent affordable electricity has changed the lives of Monte Trigans who can now trade fish more profitably, read at night, connect with the rest of the world, improve their standard of living and better sustain their economy.[69]

The project was built upon lessons learned in over 20 years of small-scale rural electrification experience and is generating a virtuous cycle for several reasons. First, project managers engaged with users at the outset in the design phase to tailor the system around their needs, preferences and financial capabilities. Second, they agreed with the community on a payment scheme based on a fixed amount of electricity paid by users at the beginning of each month, that provides both for predictability and certainty with regard to how much will be used and remunerated.[70] Third, several practical demonstrations and training sessions took place during the installation period to familiarize users, local technicians and operators with a new technology and teach them how to correctly use, maintain and operate the system in the long term. Fourth, developers adopted the concept of Energy Daily Allowance (EDA), which is a very efficient demand supply management tool that predicts and adequately controls electricity demand by limiting the power (kW) available to each user to an agreed maximum per day (kW/day), but that at the same time is flexible enough to respond to users' variable needs and variable generation capacity on sunny or cloudy days. Its implementation is based on an individual smart meter (electricity dispenser)

---

[67] The ACP-EU facility is a co-financing instrument launched by the European Commission in 2005.

[68] Trama TecnoAmbiental (TTA) is an international consulting and engineering company based in Barcelona (Spain) specializing in distributed generation through renewable energy sources with over 25 years of experience in rural electrification, available at www.tta.com.es/en/index.php.

[69] Workers were able to obtain the first welding machine to fix structures and many electricity users bought their first A+ energy rating refrigerators.

[70] This was critical since MSG cannot draw electricity from any other source if demand exceeds generation (except for using the old expensive diesel generator) and cannot recover costs if generation exceeds demand.

installed in each household that tells the user how much energy he has available and encourages or discourages consumption based on price options and on the plant's condition.[71]

Statistics show that Monte Trigans were very satisfied with the electricity service provided by the MSG.[72] They were able to adapt very quickly to efficient consumption habits and their on-time payment rate during the first six months of operations was 100 per cent. Also, they agreed with the developer and the local operator upon a tariff that reflects both constructing and operating costs, plus it provides a small return on the investment.[73] However, tariff regulation in Cape Verde presents some aspects of inflexibility that can compromise the expediting deployment of microgrid projects, despite these projects having received local consensus and being economically viable.[74]

Under current law, the provision of electricity is considered a public service and tariffs are established every five years by the national regulatory agency, Agência de Regulação Económica (ARE),[75] to provide

---

[71] Each user has a fixed EDA, that is, a fixed amount of electricity units determined by an agreed tariff. The maximum EDA available is 6 units (6kW/per day). Imagine the meter or energy dispenser as a 'tank' with a total capacity storage of 6 units. The tank is constantly filled with electricity. When the user consumes electricity, the level of the tank goes down. But since the tank refills automatically, if consumption is balanced the level of the tank remains constant. Users are rewarded if they keep their daily consumption under control: if their EDAs are between 0 and 3 units they pay electricity at the agreed rate; if their EDAs are between 3 and 6 units they pay 0.5 the tariff's value. If their consumption remains high and the dispenser shows a low level (< 10% EDA) after a warning signal the user is disconnected but the interruption only lasts a few minutes before the tank recharges. Users are encouraged to use the surplus of energy on very sunny days at no extra costs for them, meaning that when there is a generation surplus in the system, such energy is free.

[72] Briganti *et al.*, 'Implementation of a PV Rural Microgrid in the Island of Santo Antão', above n. 66, at 6, Figure 12.

[73] The tariff proposed by TTA is $.30/kWh.

[74] Cecilia M. Briceño-Garmendia and Daniel Alberto Benitez, *Cape Verde's Infrastructure: A Continental Perspective*, Policy Research Working Paper 5787 (World Bank, June 2011). The electricity sector in Cape Verde was liberalized in the early 1990s with the privatization of the national electricity company ELECTRA and a succession of laws opening the market to independent private producers to stimulate competition.

[75] ARE is an Independent Administrative Authority that regulates the water, energy and transport sectors. Its mission is to provide economic efficiency and the financial balance of the regulated sectors to ensure that services of public interest with benefits for society are offered, see www.are.cv/index.php.

fair and reasonable prices to everyone and guarantee the efficiency and reliability of the service.[76] Except for systems that are below 7.5 kVA, all power producers, whether public or private, need a concession or a licence to operate. Different tariffs are established for different categories of custumers and types of services (residential, commercial or industrial; high, medium or low voltage; public lighting; water production) and electricity is paid on a $/kWh (that is, a conventional tariff).

Law Decree No. 1/2011 recently introduced a simplified licensing regime for renewable energy microgrids in isolated areas, but power producers need the formal approval of the regulator before they can adopt a different tariff structure.[77] The law does not specify which criteria ARE has to take into account to evaluate applications, which creates great uncertainty for developers. In fact, the optimum tariff for Monte Trigo is a flat monthly fee as opposed to a conventional tariff based on users' consumption. The proposed tariff is also higher than the national tariff for residential and commercial custumers since it comprises capital and operational costs plus a small share of return on the investment. This contrasts with the regulator's view that in general a uniform tariff is better suited to provide a reasonable and fair price for electricity for everyone. At the time of the writing of this chapter, negotiations were still going on between the local operator and ARE.[78]

Monte Trigo is not an isolated case. Several other countries in Sub-Saharan Africa have similar laws in place that can discourage the implementation of renewable energy microgrid projects, thus setting back developers and investors.[79] For example, in Botswana a supplier of electricity (the licensee) is not allowed to adopt an agreed-upon tariff with any consumer different from the one established in its licence without prior approval by the Minister of Minerals, Energy and Water (MMEWR), making it difficult for suppliers to quickly adapt to changes in the markets they serve and scale up their businesses. Efforts should be made by policy-makers and regulators to remove these legal and regulatory barriers, as more flexibility would ease competition and market penetration by independent power producers.

That said, promising reforms are underway in many countries. Tanzania, for example, is in the process of modifying regulations to facilitate

---

[76] Decreto-Lei No. 14/2006.

[77] Decreto-Lei No. 1/2011, s. VIII.

[78] Interview with Matteo Briganti, Project Manager, TTA (22 March 2014).

[79] Botswana Electricity Supply (Licensing) Regulations of 1993, Pt II (6)(2). Two examples of countries with similar provisions are Malawi and Mozambique.

cost recovery in small electrification projects.[80] Under these regulations, small power producers (SPPs) and small power distributors (SPDs) would be authorized to charge tariffs that reflect 'the sum of operating costs, depreciation on capital, whether supplied by the operator or others, debt payments, reserves to deal with emergency repairs and replacements, taxes, plus a reasonable return on capital provided by the operator that reflects the risks faced by the operator'.[81] Such tariffs would presumably be higher than national uniform prices. Moreover, if an agreement is reached with an eligible group of costumers, the tariff does not need to be approved by the regulatory agency. Finally, the SPP or SPD 'may, in order to facilitate commercial sustainability, and subject to the Authority's approval, propose tariffs for specific customer categories or for customers within a single category, that take account of the ability to pay of the respective customers'.[82] Finally, SPPs and SPDs could propose to bill their customers using tariff structures that are different from the conventional kWh such as, for example, flat tariffs, power tariffs or even a combination of the two.[83]

IV BEYOND REGULATORY BARRIERS: SCALING UP THE DEPLOYMENT OF SUCCESSFUL MICROGRID PROJECTS

In addition to the removal of regulatory barriers such as tariff restrictions, policy-makers can support microgrid development with an enabling policy framework and a support programme that leverages public investment to attract additional resources to these projects. Some critical elements of this framework include:

- an overarching national policy for microgrid development accompanied by the preparation of periodic plans for implementing that policy;
- a programme that provides carefully targeted subsidies for qualifying projects and leverages this support to attract external resources; and
- an institutional architecture to support implementation.

---

[80] Tanzania, Proposed Amendments to the Electricity (Development of Small Power Projects) Rules (2014).
[81] Ibid. para. 48(1).
[82] Ibid. para. 48(2).
[83] Ibid. para. 50.

The articulation of clear policy goals with respect to microgrids and the development of plans to achieve those goals are essential, since they provide a coherent pathway for regulating and supporting microgrids, predictability for investors and other stakeholders, and legitimacy for public resources that are directed to these projects. In addition, national governments can more easily obtain development aid from other countries and institutions when goals and commitments are clearly articulated and formalized through legal decrees. Some examples of meaningful policies and plans include Nepal's National Rural Energy Policy (2006) and Rwanda's Sector-Wide Approach (SWAP) to Extending Access to Energy.

To overcome financial constraints for microgrids, national governments can also provide targeted support for promising projects. A programme to administer this support could be designed to attract funding and other resources from a variety of different stakeholders. Some authors view this multi-stakeholder approach to project finance as critical to the success of small energy projects in low-income communities.[84] One way to approach this would be a competitive solicitation which allows communities, business cooperatives, and other project proponents to submit proposals for local microgrid projects which describe the technical, financial and social elements of the project. A government agency such as a Rural Electrification Agency (REA) would review proposals (perhaps in conjunction with an independent institution) for compliance with the minimum requirements. The projects that pass initial review would then be compared, based on indicators such as need, stakeholder involvement, the potential for cost-recovery, and the potential for co-benefits.

This system could be used to determine *which* projects to support and *how* to support them, the goal being to match the most promising projects with appropriate resources, and then to monitor their implementation to assess performance to better understand the factors that contribute to project success. The programme could also be used as a mechanism for aggregating projects into portfolios to attract large-scale public and private finance.

One threshold question is whether or not resources are actually available at the national level to support such a programme. Given the amount of public funds that are expended on electricity subsidies each

---

[84] Tenenbaum *et al.*, *From the Bottom Up*, above n. 39.

year, we assert that national resources are indeed available for microgrid projects (see Figure 6.3).[85]

	% GDP	% Total Gov't Revenue	Value (USD)
Sub-Saharan Africa	**1.12**	**3.85**	**$13.5 billion**
South Africa	0.55	2.01	$2.21 billion
Uganda	1.32	8.95	$204.5 million
Malawi	1.60	5.43	$89.9 million
Tanzania	2.10	9.5	$501.3 million
Cape Verde	2.17	8.66	$40.4 million
Senegal	2.26	10.08	$326.3 million
Ghana	2.86	14.7	$1.13 billion
Zambia	4.85	21.59	$931.2 million
Mozambique	4.93	16.4	$619.7 million
Zimbabwe	14.52	47.02	$1.29 billion
World Total	**0.22**	**0.64**	**$150 billion**

Source: Constructed by authors (2014).

Figure 6.3 Pre-tax electricity subsidies in Sub-Saharan Africa, 2011

The critical question is how these subsidies can be more effectively targeted to achieve widespread electrification and sustainable development. As argued above, we believe that a portion of this spending could be used to expedite the deployment of 'best models' for microgrid development, and could also be leveraged to attract additional resources

[85] International Monetary Fund, *Energy Subsidy Reform in Sub-Saharan Africa: Experiences and Lessons* (2013), available at www.imf.org/external/pubs/ft/dp/2013/afr1302.pdf.

from public investors, private investors and local stakeholders. The history of micro-hydro development in Nepal provides an excellent model for how policy, planning and programmatic support can be combined to achieve both of these objectives.

(1) Case Study: Nepal's Rural Energy Development Programme

Experience from Nepal[86] provides valuable lessons regarding how national governments can 'scale up' small power projects through a multi-stakeholder approach. In 1996 the Nepalese national government launched a small pilot initiative, the Rural Energy Development Programme (REDP), in five remote districts, with assistance from the United Nations Development Programme (UNDP). The project aimed to provide energy services to remote and poor communities through off-grid decentralized approaches, specifically micro-hydropower systems (MHSs) and improved cooking stoves.

After an initial pilot programme proved successful, the initiative was scaled up to a total of ten districts by 1998, and 15 districts by 2000. The Nepalese government also enacted the Hydropower Development Policy of 2001, which had the following goals: (1) the generation of electricity at low cost by utilizing the water resources available in the country; (2) extending reliable, quality electric services throughout Nepal at a reasonable price; (3) integrating electrification with economic activities; (4) rendering support to the development of the rural economy by extending the rural electrification; and (5) developing hydropower as an exportable commodity. Importantly, this new policy explicitly recognized the connection between energy development, the productive use of energy and economic development.

By 2003 the REDP-I (Phase One) had supported the installation of 120 MHSs in cooperation with 100 Village Development Committees (VDCs), supplying electricity to over 10,000 new households. Phase Two was launched in 2003, with the World Bank joining as a partner organization to provide financial assistance for expanding REDP activities to an additional ten districts, bringing the total number of districts covered to 25. By 2006 approximately 130,000 individuals were receiving electricity from the MHSs. In 2006 Nepal also enacted a National

---

[86] Chanmi Kim, *Scaling Up Decentralized Energy Services in Nepal* (2011), available at www.undp.org/content/dam/undp/library/Poverty%20Reduction/Participatory%20Local%20Development/Nepal_REDP_web.pdf.

Rural Energy Policy which incorporated lessons learned from past experience.

In 2007 the REDP entered into Phase Three as a joint programme of the Nepalese government, UNDP and the World Bank, with the goal of implementing the Rural Energy Policy of 2006 in all 75 districts. By 2011 the programme had connected 59,172 households to 317 new micro-hydro plants with 5,747.2 kW of installed capacity. Due in part to the positive impacts of the REDP, the government of Nepal has set more ambitious renewable energy targets for the country as a whole, and has planned substantial investment in the rural energy sector by 2020.

Nepal's success in scaling up investment in these projects is due to a number of enabling factors. The provision of upfront public financing and clear policy support from the government of Nepal catalyzed investment from major partners including the UNDP, the Danish International Development Agency (DANIDA) and the World Bank. The support provided by these stakeholders also encouraged banks to provide loans for these projects. This facilitated larger contributions from households and individuals, with community contributions increasing over time to reach almost 40 per cent of investments in 2006. Another noteworthy feature of the REDP was its emphasis on capacity building at all levels. Capacity development costs represented a significant portion (56 per cent) of overall programme costs from 1996–2006. These investments were front-loaded to optimize the benefits associated with capacity development.

The outcomes of the REDP are impressive. Between 1996 and 2006, per-unit programme costs declined by 73 per cent, the decline being driven mainly by the decline in capacity development costs. As of 2010, some of the documented impacts of the programme included:

- reduced average annual household spending rates on energy to US$19, compared to US$41 spent by non-electrified households;
- average increase of US$121 (8 per cent) in annual household incomes with electricity access;
- 40 new businesses created per district following the installation of a micro-hydropower system, compared with only four established prior to electricity access;
- average of 11 health workers per 100,000 people in electrified areas, compared to two health workers per 1,000 people in non-electrified areas; and
- access to clean water and other health benefits.[87]

[87] Ibid. 6.

Broadly speaking, the MHSs served as an 'entry point for holistic development and poverty reduction' and helped Nepal make considerable progress towards implementation of the Millennium Development Goals.[88] In light of these benefits, the REDP provides an opportunity for 'south-south' learning on the design of national programmes to scale up the deployment of microgrids through multi-stakeholder financing and targeted support.

V CONCLUSION

Community-based renewable microgrids hold great promise as a mechanism for electrification and sustainable development, but they also face a variety of economic, technical and legal barriers. To fully harness the potential of these projects, we recommend that national policy-makers remove any legal barriers to cost-recovery and also provide a framework for directing financial and other resources to these projects. By supporting projects in this fashion, national governments can promote a new paradigm of energy management and service that empowers local stakeholders and delivers enhanced development co-benefits, as compared with traditional approaches.

---

[88] Ibid. 4.

7. Innovative financing for renewable energy

Richard L. Ottinger and John Bowie*

I INTRODUCTION

This chapter discusses currently implemented innovative methods for financing the high initial equipment costs of many renewable energy resources, with case studies of their application. Financial instruments for renewable energy installations are frequently dependent on physical and economic infrastructure. In response to this fundamental interconnectedness between infrastructure, the economy and financial instruments, this chapter follows a rough structure of financing methods used in: areas unserved by an electricity grid; areas of modest means served by limited transmission interconnections; and areas with developed regional or national grid connectedness.

Renewables have many benefits, but they also face challenges as they enter the existing market of entrenched and highly subsidized fossil fuels. Challenges take many forms but generally include: technical issues with balancing demand and electric system load; unpredictable or politically driven swings in tax structures; and resistance from existing corporate interests.

Traditional private sector financing also is often unavailable for many reasons, such as because projects are too small for funders to handle; funder ignorance of renewables; high front-end requirements of installation; lack of long-term performance information; risks of loan repayments, particularly in poor rural communities; mobility of residential customers in many areas; and landlord-tenant split-benefit issues. This chapter examines how innovative public and private financing can mitigate these issues and carry the industry forward.

* An unabridged and updated version of the chapter, which includes numerous examples, case studies and discussions of emerging issues relating to renewable finance appears in (2015) 32(3) *Pace Environmental Law Review*.

In addition to high capital costs and repayment, financing of renewable energy investments is the difficulty regarding the possibility of meeting the needs of landlords and tenants. Landlords have little incentive to incur a cost associated with an energy installation because they do not receive the direct benefit of the resulting electricity cost savings (they do not pay the electricity bill), and tenants have little incentive to incur the long-term cost because they are often transient.[1]

Furthermore, home-owners in some markets tend to be quite mobile.[2] A home-owner is likely to be reluctant to invest in renewable energy equipment having a high first cost if he or she intends to move or feels there is a high risk of his or her moving before the equipment's energy savings are realized.[3] The owner is unlikely to recover the full costs of the renewable energy investment in the selling price of the property.[4]

Several emerging innovative financing tools have proven able to address these problems and thus to increase the market penetration of renewable energy. The following sections explore selected approaches to financing renewable energy infrastructure.

II SELECTED INNOVATIVE APPROACHES TO RENEWABLE FINANCING

The following section describes innovative mechanisms currently in use in financing renewable energy. Some of these projects are still small, near-incubation phase financial tools, while others are entrenched in some areas, but may not yet be common practice in financing renewable

---

[1] United Nations Department of Economic and Social Affairs, Expert Group On Renewable Energy, *Increasing Global Renewable Energy Market Share: Recent Trends and Perspectives* (2005).

[2] World Bank, *Country Benchmarks: Internal Mobility: The United States* (World Bank, 2012), available at http://siteresources.worldbank.org/ECAEXT/Resources/258598-1284061150155/7383639-1323888814015/8319788-1324485944855/10_us.pdf.

[3] US Department of Energy, Energy Efficiency and Renewable Energy, *Clean Energy Finance Guide for Residential and Commercial Building Improvements* (2010), available at http://www1.eere.energy.gov/wip/solutioncenter/pdfs/revfinal_v3aafrontmatterdec9.pdf.

[4] Ben Hoen *et al.*, *An Analysis of the Effects of Residential Photovoltaic Energy Systems on Home Sales Prices in California* (Ernest Orlando Lawrence Berkeley National Lab, 2011), available at http://emp.lbl.gov/sites/all/files/lbnl-4476e.pdf.

energy. The purpose in documenting the following projects and programs is to chronicle and share methods that may be of benefit in new areas and markets. The general organization follows levels of infrastructure development, but this should not be construed as exclusive: financing mechanisms from less developed areas may be applicable to more developed regions, although the converse does not seem to be true.

Areas with no electricity access have a unique opportunity for renewable energy deployment. Renewable resources such as solar, wind, biogas, biomass, or micro-hydroelectric resources are often plentiful in developing regions, while more carbon-intensive traditional fuels may be unavailable or prohibitively expensive, especially if the extension of an electrical grid is required for their utilization. Even the often relatively expensive first costs of solar energy equipment and installation will frequently be cheaper than the use of conventional fuels in underdeveloped rural areas.[5]

Several energy companies and innovative financial institutions have recognized this mismatch of need with the shortcomings of traditional finance, with new technological opportunities. The following financing tools have helped to expand renewable energy production, and economic opportunity in underdeveloped off-grid markets. We illustrate each by means of an example.

(1) Microfinance

Microfinance systems provide alternative loans to individuals and small businesses lacking access to traditional banking and financial services.[6] The original intention of microfinance was to provide loans to very poor families, but this practice has gradually grown to include a broader range of small level financing.[7] Different microfinance providers have emerged,

---

5 Uwe Deichmann *et al.*, 'The Economics of Renewable Energy Expansion in Rural Sub-Saharan Africa' (2011) *Energy Policy* 215.

6 Consultative Group to Assist the Poor, 'What is Microfinance?', available at www.cgap.org/about/faq/what-microfinance.

7 Visions of Sustainability, *Microfinance and Renewable Energy: Investing in a Sustainable Future* (2006), available at www.gdrc.org/icm/environ/mf-renewablenergy.pdf. Specific examples from this report include: Revolving Fund for the Implementation of Small Hydro Schemes, Rural Housing Energy legislation, Rural Energy Enterprise Development Initiative, rural biogas plants. See also Anojl Viswanathan, *Energy Services for the Base of the Pyramid: The Role of Microfinance Institutions* (2009), available at www.slideshare.net/anoj.viswanathan/microfinance-and-renewable-energy.

including non-governmental organizations (NGOs), cooperatives, government agencies and community-based development groups.[8] A wide variety of microfinance products and services has rapidly expanded to renewable energy installations and infrastructure, helping to bring new energy online in previously underserved communities, as seen below.

Grameen Bank, a Bangladeshi bank focused on lending to the poor, presents one of the most established and successful examples of microfinance.[9] Grameen Bank created a family of micro-investment programmes to finance economic activities for poor communities in a variety of sectors, including Grameen Shakti, a programme devoted to financing rural renewable energy.[10]

Established in 1983, by visionary economist Muhammad Yunus, Grameen Bank now provides over 2.5 billion dollars of microloans to rural Bangladeshi families.[11] The Grameen Bank's *modus operandi* is to lend seed money to groups of people, mostly women, to start small economic enterprises under expert guidance and under strict conditions for quality control and repayment.[12] The bank receives an average of about 97 percent repayment of these community loans, largely as a result of peer pressure from other community borrowers.[13] The Grameen Bank has won several awards, including the 2006 Nobel Prize.[14] As of October 2011, the Grameen Bank had 8,349 million borrowers, 97 per cent of whom are women.[15] The bank's services cover 97 per cent of the total villages in Bangladesh.[16]

---

[8] Gerard Caprio and Doublas W. Arner (eds), *Handbook of Key Global Financial Markets, Institutions and Infrastructure* (2012). Other entities such as credit unions, commercial and state banks, insurance and credit card companies, telecommunications and wire services, post offices, and other points of sale, have emerged as viable candidates to provide microfinance services.

[9] Grameen Bank, 'A Short History of Grameen Bank', available at http://grameen-info.org/index.php?option=com_content&task=view&id=19&Itemid=114.

[10] Ibid.

[11] Ibid.

[12] Grameen Bank, 'About Us', available at www.grameen-info.org/index.php?option=com_content&task=view&id=16&Itemid=112.

[13] Grameen Bank reported a 97.28 per cent recovery rate in its May 2014 monthly update. Grameen Bank, *2014-04 Issue 412 BDT* (6 May 2014), available at www.grameen-info.org/index.php?option=com_content&task=view&id=1285&Itemid=422.

[14] Nobelprize.Org, 'The Nobel Peace Prize 2006', available at www.nobelprize.org/nobel_prizes/peace/laureates/2006/.

[15] Grameen Bank, 'Introduction', above n. 12.

[16] Ibid.

Building on success in other areas, Grameen Bank launched Grameen Shakti,[17] a Bangladeshi market-based company created to focus on microfinance for renewable energy. Grameen Shakti is a rural-based renewable energy company, founded as a biogas programme in 2005 that rapidly grew to include an Improved Cooking Stoves Programme in 2006, and later a Solar Home Systems (SHS) programme.[18] By December 2012, Grameen Shakti had installed more than 1 million SHSs in rural areas of Bangladesh.[19]

The company uses several options for microfinancing solar energy projects. Under each option, home-owners must make a down payment (15–25 per cent), and then pay off the balance in modest monthly installments over a period of two to three years.[20] Micro-utility customers must pay 10 per cent of the total price as down payment[21] with the remaining price to be repaid in 42 payments without any service charge.[22]

Through microfinance, Grameen Bank was able to effectively fund several types of development, including a robust biogas and home solar system. While Grameen is the paragon micro lender, several other providers now offer microfinance to different settings with similar success. Grameen Shakti demonstrates the potential for micro lending to transform and expand a rural renewable energy market.

(2) Margin Money Finance

The traditional loan structure typically includes a down payment requirement, also known as margin money.[23] Frequently a borrower seeking a loan for a renewable energy system would have the means to cover the term payments, but often would lack the ability to cover the margin money payment. Margin money finance support generally comes from government sources, because private financial institutions generally will

---

[17] See Grameen Shakti, available at www.gshakti.org/.

[18] Grameen Shakti, 'Grameen Shakti Evolving as a Social Business to Meet the Energy Needs of the Rural People', available at www.gshakti.org/index.php?option=com_content&view=article&id=57&Itemid=77.

[19] Ibid.

[20] Ibid.

[21] Ibid.

[22] Ibid.

[23] Chris Groobey *et al.*, *Project Finance Primer for Renewable Energy and Clean Tech Projects* (Wilson Sonsini Goodrich & Rosati, 2010), available at www.wsgr.com/PDFSearch/ctp_guide.pdf.

not take the concomitant risks of default. Subsidized relief for margin money financing has proven successful in several cases.[24]

The Indian government launched a successful margin money finance programme. This public programme demonstrates the viability of margin money financing as a method of encouraging investment in renewable energy. In this particular instance, the small government investment of margin money financing allowed rural and urban business owners without access to electricity to install reliable renewable energy generation.

(3) Financing Intermediate Community/Village-Scale Projects

Intermediate scale renewable energy development permits consideration of more financing options than rural non-grid installations. In terms of return on investment, the larger scale provides larger markets and greater resources to devote to renewable energy development. The previously discussed small-scale one-off projects provide some opportunity for a return on investment, but often fail to reach an economic scale that can attract larger investors. With larger-scale installations, community projects with microgrids become feasible and advantageous.

(4) Community Microgrid Projects

Community renewable energy projects at the village level with microgrid distribution tend to be anchored by larger community structures such as hospitals, military installations, schools and village halls or community centers that can afford to provide important financial assistance for solar projects.[25] The larger institution anchors electricity for residential use.[26]

Electricity distribution at the village or town scale permits larger capital projects that can attract more traditional investors to finance significant portions of a project. Changing demographics drawn to an expanding region may use more electricity (for example, air conditioning and refrigerators), in turn providing more return on investment. Institutional electricity customers may be able to raise funds from commercial sources more readily and can carry a higher debt-capital ratio than can an individual customer, making investment more attractive. As critical infrastructure receives power, additional opportunities for smaller community customers emerge to capitalize on the expanded capacity.

---

[24] Ibid.

[25] Daniel Schnitzer *et al.*, *Microgrids for Rural Electrification* (United Nations Foundation, 2014).

[26] Ibid.

In addition to encouraging potentially larger projects, a village-scale grid may also facilitate financing due to there being less risk of non-payment. The village scale may also make collecting payments on debt easier, including the fact that some stakeholders and investors may be the same people. Increased scale and a greater number of users require a more complex billing infrastructure that may not otherwise be affordable. There may even be less risk of non-payment than in large grid communities, due to peer pressures in intermediate village communities.[27]

Microgrids[28] have numerous benefits in terms of resilience, efficiency and reduced maintenance costs, so much so that there is currently a movement in developed nations to redevelop along the lines of a microgrid model.[29] The local nature of a microgrid encourages economic opportunities to spring up around the grid. Innovative companies have capitalized on this synergy to build renewable energy power grids that work in tandem with entrepreneurial programmes.[30]

Husk Power Systems (HPS),[31] an India-based company, specializes in the design, installation and operation of biomass-based power plants.[32] Each HPS biomass plant uses gasification technology to convert agricultural waste from local farms into electricity, which is then distributed to rural households and micro-enterprises through a micro-grid system.[33] Plants range from 25-kW to 100-kW and serve up to 4,000 inhabitants on a pay-for-use basis.[34]

---

[27] Kale Seagraves, 'How Grameen Bank uses peer pressure', *Poverty News Blog*, 6 August 2010, available at http://povertynewsblog.blogspot.com/2010/08/how-grameen-bank-uses-peer-pressure.html, citing Rana Foroohar, 'A Bank from Bangladesh brings Microlending to U.S.', *Newsweek*, 19 July 2010, available at www.newsweek.com/bank-bangladesh-brings-microlending-us-74333.

[28] 'A group of interconnected loads and distributed energy resources with clearly defined electrical boundaries that acts as a single controllable entity with respect to the grid [and can] connect and disconnect from the grid to enable it to operate in both connected or island mode'. See US Department of Energy, *2012 DOE Microgrid Workshop Report* (2012), available at http://energy.gov/sites/prod/files/2012%20Microgrid%20Workshop%20Report%2009102012.pdf.

[29] 'TechNavio's analysts forecast the Global Microgrid market to grow at a CAGR of 25.7 percent over the period 2012–2016': see Technavio, *Global Microgrid Market 2012–2016* (26 July 2013).

[30] Ibid.

[31] See www.huskpowersystems.com/.

[32] Ibid.

[33] Ibid.

[34] Ibid.

Frequently, this local source and distribution model provides a better quality, cheaper way to meet the community's energy needs.[35] HPS biomass systems embody the organic microgrid model by creating an 'ecosystem' that provides income opportunities for local farmers and entrepreneurs.[36] Since 2008, HPS has successfully installed more than 80 plants in Bihar, providing electricity to over 200,000 people across 300 villages and hamlets.[37]

(5) Distributed Finance: Internet Lending

The Internet is rapidly creating new avenues for fundraising and investment. Individual borrowers can now present their ideas directly to individual lenders, circumventing traditional financial institutions. Direct connections between lenders and borrowers promote transparency while reducing transaction costs.

In addition to the benefits of increased transparency and wider investor exposure, Internet funding options are also opening new markets. Cellular data infrastructure means that rural projects may have Internet access before reliable electricity. This paradox presents an opportunity for financing renewable energy projects. Direct lending between investors and borrowers through the Internet, frequently called peer-to-peer lending (and related crowdfunding),[38] has the potential to expand renewable energy in novel ways.

(6) Peer-to-Peer Funding

Peer-to-Peer (P2P) funding allows individuals and companies to invest without going through a traditional intermediary such as a bank.[39] This

---

[35] Ibid.

[36] Husk Power Systems, 'Community Impact', available at www.huskpowersystems.com/innerPage.php?pageT=Community%20Impact&page_id=81; see also 'How social entrepreneurs use rice husks to fuel micro power grids in India', *PBS Newshour*, 17 January 2013, available at www.pbs.org/newshour/bb/world-jan-june13-india_01-17/. 'Ecosystem' is the company's own description of their programme, implying a mimicry of the energetic relationships formed in nature – byproducts from one system become the fuel for another.

[37] Husk Power Systems, 'Community Impact', above n. 38.

[38] 'Crowdfunding' in *Merriam-Webster Online*, available at www.merriam-webster.com/dictionary/crowdfunding.

[39] Rupert Jones, 'Is peer-to-peer lending too good to be true', *Guardian*, 14 February 2014, available at www.theguardian.com/money/2014/feb/15/peer-to-peer-lending-nicola-horlick.

lending typically takes place online on a P2P lending website that connects lenders and borrowers. P2P lending is a direct relationship between one lender and one borrower. It allows potential investors to choose projects in which they are interested, promoting involvement, while providing both parties with the ability to minimize overhead transaction costs.[40]

Zidisha is a P2P lending website that connects lenders and borrowers directly across international borders.[41] Zidisha does not allow any third-party local organizations to post content for borrowers or act as managers for individual loans. Instead of third-party local organizations, Zidisha staff manages operations directly, including reviewing applications, loan disbursements and repayments.[42] Using this methodology, Zidisha achieves an average interest and fee rate between 5 and 9 per cent.[43] Zidisha's P2P model also implements an online social element, allowing lenders to post questions to entrepreneurs, while entrepreneurs can post progress and reports.[44]

(7) Crowd Funding

Crowd funding has also been successfully used to finance solar power projects. Crowd funding aggregates numerous individuals through an Internet lending source to support a project. Individual loans may be small, but the total aggregated amount may be a substantial loan. Under this model of crowd funding, as solar projects produce and sell electricity, investors are paid back with interest.

Mosaic is a US-based company[45] that uses Mosaic Notes as a written promise for money owed over a fixed term, and each payment account is Federal Deposit Insurance Corporation (FDIC) insured.[46] Mosaic is an Internet platform that connects multiple investors to solar projects through the Internet.[47] Mosaic has successfully funded several solar projects of varying scales including different generation capacities,

---

40 Ibid.

41 See www.zidisha.org/.

42 Zidisha, 'Frequently Asked Questions', available at https://www.zidisha.org/faq.

43 Ibid.

44 Ibid.

45 See https://joinmosaic.com/.

46 'How It Works', available at https://joinmosaic.com/how-it-works.

47 'About Mosaic', available at https://joinmosaic.com/about-mosaic.

returns on investments, yields and terms.[48] Mosaic projects range from just a few kilowatts to well over a megawatt.[49] Most present Mosaic investments, however, are currently limited to California. Guaranteed returns are created through the use of power purchase agreements.[50]

(8) Grid-served Communities

For larger community installations supported by a grid, the use of renewables will require smart grid technology to balance variable supply loads. In the absence of economic storage technology, the availability of solar and wind resources in particular fluctuates with the availability of adequate sunshine and wind, requiring back-up power when the resources are not adequate and sophisticated management to assure that electricity is smoothly available and not disrupted.[51]

(9) On-Bill Financing

On-bill financing is one of the most promising tools for use in renewable energy finance.[52] Under on-bill-financing the power utility or municipality provides, in effect as a loan, the initial capital to install renewable energy, which is usually hard to raise up front.[53] Repayment of this loan is then amortized and distributed as a charge on the customer's monthly utility bill or, in the case of municipal financing, a surcharge on the

---

[48] 'Browse Investments', available at https://joinmosaic.com/browse-investments.

[49] Ibid.

[50] Power Purchase Agreements are essentially long-term contracts for the purchase of electricity from a particular source. Investors prefer PPAs due to the security of long-term return on investment. For a more detailed discussion, see below, '(12) Existing Utility Programmes'.

[51] See Ruud Kempener *et al.*, *Smart Grids and Renewables: A Guide for Effective Deployment*, IRENA Working Paper (November 2013), available at www.irena.org/DocumentDownloads/Publications/smart_grids.pdf.

[52] Natural Resources Defense Council, *On-Bill Financing Programmes, Overview and Key Considerations for Programme Design* (July 2013), available at www.nrdc.org/energy/on-bill-financing-programmes/files/on-bill-financing-IB.pdf.

[53] Casey J. Bell, Steven Nadel and Sara Hayes, *On-Bill Financing for Energy Efficiency Improvements: A Review of Current Programme Challenges, Opportunities, and Best Practices*, Paper for American Council for an Energy-Efficient Economy (8 December 2011), available at www.aceee.org/research-report/e118.

property tax.[54] Often the energy savings from the financed energy efficiency or renewable measures can offset the repayment charges in whole or in part.

In addition to solving the problem of having to raise substantial amounts to pay for renewable energy equipment, on-bill financing eliminates the obstacles to renewable energy investment caused by landlord-tenant disincentives and those caused by the transient nature of home ownership, because the repayment obligation attaches to the utility bill or property tax, passing on the advantages of the energy savings and the obligations for repayment to successor lessees or property purchasers.

The costs of renewable energy and energy efficiency installations may be financed on-bill through monthly rates, property tax surcharges, and through amortized expected savings.[55] Each of these methods helps customers to finance energy investment while realizing the benefits of improved energy savings.

South Carolina electric cooperatives developed a Rural Energy Savings Programme to address the special challenges and opportunities facing rural communities to save energy, cut household utility bills and reduce greenhouse gas emissions.[56] The programme provides utility up-front finances for residential energy efficiency improvements, providing repayment through the co-op members' electric bills.[57] The Rural Energy Savings Programme also supports stable, high-skilled jobs and keeps more dollars in the local economy. The 'Help My House' pilot for this programme produced encouraging results, including participant energy bill reductions averaging 34 per cent, saving an average of US$288 per home per year after payments.[58] While this programme applied only to energy efficiency measures, its mechanism can also be applied to renewable energy investments.

---

[54] Ibid.

[55] James M. Van Nostrand, 'Legal Issues in Financing Energy Efficiency: Creative Solutions for Funding the Initial Capital Costs of Investment in Energy Efficiency Measures' (2011) 1(2) *Journal of Energy and Environmental Law*, available at http://groups.law.gwu.edu/jeel/ArticlePDF/2-1-Nostrand.pdf.

[56] Environmental and Energy Study Institute, 'Rural Energy Savings Program', available at http://www.eesi.org/projects/on-bill-financing.

[57] Ibid.

[58] Ibid.

(10) Pay As You Save (PAYS) Programmes

Pay As You Save or PAYS, is a variant of bill financing in which the customer agrees to pay a monthly surcharge which is lower than the independently verified, estimated savings. Money-saving energy efficiency products are purchased with no up-front cost or debt obligation to the consumer.[59] Instead, the customer pays a tariffed charge on the utility bill proportionate to efficiency savings.[60] Typically this applies to energy efficiency installations, but the principle could also be applied to renewable energy installations.

PAYS systems circumvent traditional barriers to finance by providing the up-front capital requirements. Participants do not take on any debt obligation for energy installations, making PAYS an attractive option for residential and business customers who may not be in a position to obtain a loan to pay for the up-front capital costs of the installed measures.[61] As an independent system, PAYS does not require credit checks or liens. Here, all obligations are attached to the meter, and dependent upon efficiencies.[62]

The system functions based on efficiency measures performing as advertised. Because of this, commissions or jurisdictions implementing PAYS systems must screen the products for eligibility. Utilities function as collectors in PAYS systems, imposing the charges as they would any other tariffed charge. PAYS systems have been applied to both energy efficiency investments and a growing number of renewable energy projects.

Aspiration Energy is a UK-based energy service company (ESCO) dedicated to providing solar solutions for industrial process heating and solar power.[63] Aspiration Energy finances its solar energy installations through a monthly performance-based energy charge model – a PAYS

---

[59] Clean Energy States Alliance, *Developing an Effective State Clean Energy Programme: Clean Energy Loanslenders Briefing Paper No. 4* (2009), available at http://perma.cc/L7SF-C6E2.

[60] Energy Efficiency Institute, Inc., *Pay-As-You-Save* (8 March 2005), available at www.eeivt.com/DTEpres.pdf.

[61] Charles Kubert and Mark Sinclair, *State Support for Clean Energy Deployment: Lessons Learned for Potential Future Policy* (National Renewable Energy Laboratory, 2011), available at www.nrel.gov/docs/fy11osti/49340.pdf.

[62] Ibid.

[63] See www.aspirationenergy.co.uk/.

system.[64] The Aspiration Energy system received the 2013 Parivartan Award for Innovation in the Business Model Category.[65] The company delivers solar hot water heating for industrial processes based on an 'energy as a service model', requiring no initial capital expenditure.[66]

One Aspiration Energy installation, Wheels India, used solar water heating to replace an oil boiler displacing nearly 7 million Indian rupees worth of fuel oil in the first 18 months of operation.[67] This translated to actual fossil fuel avoidance of 360 litres of fuel oil per day.[68] This economic and environmental success inspired the wheel producer to expand solar water heating to its factories across India.[69] In addition to solar thermal systems, Aspiration Energy has also operated as a PAYS ESCO for solar battery back-up systems and solar power for telecommunication networks.[70]

(11) Alternative Stock Trading Markets

Pioneering stock markets have taken a role in creating sources of capital for renewable energy projects. In addition to the basic listing requirements, several stock markets have added requirements for social responsibility, including environmental practices.[71] This allows the growing number of ethical investors to buy stock with confidence in the company's environmental and social virtues.[72]

---

[64] Aspiration Energy, 'Pay As You Save', available at www.aspirationenergy.com/index.php?option=com_content&view=article&id=79&Itemid=290.

[65] Parivartan Awards, *2013 Winners, Innovation in Business Model Category* (2013), available at www.parivartanawards.in/2013/application/process.

[66] Ibid.

[67] Global Solar Thermal Energy Council, 'Aspiration Energy', available at http://solarthermalworld.org/companies/aspiration-energy.

[68] Aspiration Energy, 'Success Story', available at www.aspirationenergy.com/index.php?option=com_content&view=article&id=83&Itemid=448.

[69] Ibid.

[70] Ibid.

[71] Social Stock Exchange, 'Our Admissions Panel', available at www.socialstockexchange.com/our-admissions-panel.

[72] See World Economic Forum, *From the Margins to the Mainstream: Assessment of the Impact Investment Sector and Opportunities to Engage Mainstream Investors* (September 2013), available at www3.weforum.org/docs/WEF_II_FromMarginsMainstream_Report_2013.pdf ('Investment industry thrives as a result of the pursuit of investment returns and businesses are not sustained without a profitable revenue model. However, the emerging generation of investors is also likely to seek achievement of social objectives in addition to financial returns'); see also Deloitte, *Deloitte's Global Millennial Survey 2013*

The Social Stock Exchange trades shares of companies that contribute to social or environmental projects.[73] This model takes the traditional benefits of raising capital through public trading and focuses on investments in companies promoting socially beneficial values such as renewable energy production.

Good Energy Group is a vertically integrated utility that seeks to lower UK carbon emissions by developing and distributing renewable energy within the United Kingdom.[74] The purpose of the Social Stock Exchange is to provide stakeholders with the information they need to identify and compare organizations based on their social and environmental values.[75] The exchange admissions process requires transparency and a disclosure of values and standards. Good Energy Group is one of the companies listed on the UK Social Stock Exchange.

Good Energy's mission is to 'keep the world a habitable place by offering consumers an active role in addressing climate change'.[76] Through the Social Stock Exchange reporting, Good Energy shares its impact report, outlining its key outcomes for the public.[77] In addition to these characteristics, Good Energy also shares financial information characteristics of a listed stock. This includes price, market cap, shares issued, and information on its securities.[78] Stock exchanges and funds, which help investors assess values through transparent listing principles, promise to promote this market growth even further. It has been

(2013), available at www2.deloitte.com/us/en/pages/about-deloitte/articles/millennial-survey-positive-impact.html (archived at http://perma.cc/MJM6-YQE2) ('Deloitte's Millennial Survey revealed that our world's future leaders are increasingly viewing business through the lens of social impact. More than half of Millennials surveyed (52 percent) believe business, more than any other area of society, will achieve the greatest impact in solving society's biggest challenges.').

73 Social Stock Exchange, 'Become a Member', available at http://socialstockexchange .com/become-a-member/.

74 Social Stock Exchange, 'Good Energy Group', available at www.socialstockexchange.com/members/good-energy-group.

75 Social Stock Exchange, 'What We Do', available at www.socialstockexchange.com/what-we-do.

76 Social Stock Exchange, 'Become a Member', above n. 74.

77 Social Stock Exchange, 'Impact Report', available at www.socialstockexchange.com/members/good-energy-group#ir.

78 Social Stock Exchange, 'Become a Member', above n. 74.

estimated that the market for global impact investing will be US$650 billion by 2020.[79]

Good Energy and the Social Stock Exchange are part of a greater overarching movement toward global sustainable economic growth. On 2 June 2014, the London Stock Exchange Group (LSEG) announced that it had joined the United Nations Sustainable Stock Exchanges (SSE) initiative as a Partner Exchange.[80] This partnership follows a trend toward stock exchanges promoting:

> good governance standards, encouraging best practice non-financing reporting, pioneering sustainable investing concepts ... providing access to capital for clean tech companies ... and dedicated programme[s] to support the growth and development of small and medium sized businesses.[81]

Within this partnership, the aforementioned Social Stock Exchange has brought over 160 listed clean tech companies to the global market.[82]

(12) Existing Utility Programmes

A major component of the financial packet for renewables is the stream of revenues from electric generation with which to develop a return to financial investors. There are various mechanisms in place to create these revenue streams, varying by jurisdiction, market, technology and other factors. Many US state utility programmes have been implemented that support the restructuring of the energy economy and increase the availability of financing for renewable energy infrastructure. The following sections briefly outlines these electric utility structures and how they promote renewable energy investment.

(i) Energy Service Agreement (ESA)

In the ESA model, an investment or public authority fund pays for and installs the project. An ESA is a contract that allows the capital investment in energy projects to be paid back over time by building owners or tenants.

---

[79] Social Stock Exchange, *Tomas Carruthers Appointed CEO of Social Stock Exchange* (8 December 2013), available at http://perma.cc/N2EJ-LPB6.

[80] London Stock Exchange, *London Stock Exchange Group Joining the UN Sustainable Stock Exchanges Initiative* (2 June 2014), available at www.lseg.com/resources/media-centre/press-releases/london-stock-exchange-group-joining-un-sustainable-stock-exchanges-initiative.

[81] Ibid.

[82] Ibid.

ESA contracts permit various costs, such as energy efficiency or customer-sited renewable energy generation equipment, to be packaged as a service that building owners pay for through savings.[83] Equipment upgrades installed through ESA contracts may require minimal to no up-front costs to the owners. ESAs can function as an alternative to using equity or a traditional loan to retrofit a building.

ESA providers generally assume the risk that energy savings performance will be sufficient to justify the up-front investment. Under ESAs, providers arrange for their own financing, which is a boon to property owners who may be concerned about using their own borrowing capacity to invest in their energy efficiency or renewable energy profile.[84]

Under the Con Edison NYCEEC Multifamily Energy Efficiency Loan Programme, New York City provides funding for qualified buildings to improve energy efficiency.[85] Qualified projects must include five to 75 units within the Con Edison utility service territory.[86] Once enrolled in the programme, building owners qualify for incentives for lighting upgrades; heating, ventilation and air conditioning (HVAC) systems; compact fluorescent lighting, and other projects.[87] The programme also aids multi-unit buildings to convert from oil to gas, thus reducing carbon emissions and air pollution.

(ii) Power Purchase Agreements (PPA)

Power Purchase Agreements (PPAs) are contractual arrangements in which a wholesale energy company may purchase exclusive rights to all or part of an energy provider's electricity.[88] PPAs allow the facility owner to secure a revenue stream from the project necessary to finance the project and determine the quality of credit.[89] The terms of PPAs address

---

83 New York City Energy Efficiency Corp., 'Energy Service Agreements', available at www.nyceec.com/.

84 Ibid.

85 Con Edison, 'Multifamily Energy Efficiency Program', available at http://www.coned.com/energyefficiency/residential_multifamily.asp.

86 Ibid.

87 Consolidated Edison, Inc., 'Multifamily Building (5–75 Units)', available at www.coned.com/energyefficiency/residential_multifamily.asp.

88 See for example, Bonneville Power Association, *Exhibit C. Example of a Purchase Power Agreement* (2002), available at http://perma.cc/P45W-XKUY (example of a Power Purchase Agreement, executed by the US Department of Energy acting by and through the Bonneville Power Administration).

89 Daniel A. Yarano, 'The Basics of a Power Purchase Agreement', *Biomass Magazine*, available at http://biomassmagazine.com/articles/2119/the-basics-of-a-power-purchase-agreement/.

issues such as the length of the agreement, the commissioning process, the purchase and sale of energy, price, curtailment, credit and insurance.[90]

PPAs are a standard financing mechanism for the grid-based power market, enabling wholesale purchasers, retailers and customers to buy and sell electricity through a distribution system. Innovations to these contracts are providing an excellent tool to augment and encourage renewable investment.[91] Like other programmes that finance renewable electricity, PPAs reduce the overall financing cost of renewable installations. In particular, a PPA allows renewable energy companies to diffuse the risk associated with selling their electricity directly to customers.[92]

The US Environmental Protection Agency (EPA) outlines specific recommendations for some Solar Power Purchase Agreements.[93] This subset of PPAs involves a financial arrangement in which a third-party developer owns, operates and maintains a photovoltaic (PV) system, and a host agrees to site the system on its property and purchase the system's electric output from the developer for a predefined period.[94] The developer under the solar PPA arrangement is also known as a 'solar services provider'.[95] Solar PPA arrangements enable host customers (those purchasing the power) to avoid many of the traditional barriers to adoption, including high capital costs, system performance risks, and design complexities.[96]

(13) Renewable Energy Certificates

Renewable Energy Certificates (RECs) represent the 'property rights to the environmental, social and other nonpower qualities of renewable electricity generation'.[97] By enabling producers to sell the rights separately from the underlying physical electricity associated with renewable generation, organizations can support renewable energy development and

---

[90] Ibid.

[91] Bonneville Power Association, *Exhibit* C, above n. 90.

[92] Ibid.

[93] US Environmental Protection Agency, 'Solar Power Purchase Agreements', available at www.epa.gov/greenpower/buygp/solarpower.htm.

[94] Ibid.

[95] Ibid.

[96] Ibid.

[97] US Environmenal Protection Agency, 'Renewable Energy Certificates', available at www.epa.gov/greenpower/gpmarket/rec.htm.

protect the environment when green power is not locally available.[98] RECs have become one of the most commonly used systems to finance the production and sale of renewable power in the United States.

(14) Feed-in Tariffs

Feed-in tariffs (FITs) are government-mandated renewable energy subsidies requiring utilities to purchase renewable energy at a subsidized rate.[99] Feed-in tariffs have played an important role in incentivizing the customer uptake of renewable energy.[100] These subsidized rates incentivize market participation from individual customers to add renewable electricity to the grid. FITs legally oblige utilities to purchase electricity from renewable energy producers at favorable, higher-than-market rates.[101] The favorable rates assured by FITs are typically guaranteed by the government for a certain period of time.[102]

Feed-in tariffs were pioneered in Germany and have been used very successfully there and in other jurisdictions to guarantee solar and wind energy installers a specified subsidized price.[103] The German FIT law, the Stromeinspeisungsgesetz (StrEG) (Original Electricity Feed Law), helped to finance renewable energy by securing a profitable business for renewable energy ventures.[104] This subsidized rate has led to high market penetration.[105] The solar sector alone has grown to include over 40

---

[98] Ibid.

[99] UNEP, *Feed-in Tariffs as a Policy Instrument for Promoting Renewable Energies and Green Economies in Developing Countries* (2012), available at www.unep.org/pdf/UNEP_FIT_Report_2012F.pdf.

[100] Germany has used feed-in tariffs to encourage a variety of renewable energy sources. See Matthias Lang and U. Mutschler, 'German Feed-in Tariffs 2012', *German Energy Blog*, available at www.germanenergyblog.de/?page_id=8617.

[101] E-Parliament, *Success Story: Feed-In Tariffs Support Renewable Energy in Germany* (2009), available at e-parl.net/eparliament/pdf/080603%20FIT%20toolkit.pdf.

[102] Ibid.

[103] See Miguel Mendonca, *Feed-in Tariffs: Accelerating the Deployment of Renewable Energy* (2009); see also Power-Technology.com, *Germany's Feed-in Tariffs Set the Example* (21 November 2008), available at http://perma.cc/Z3YA-ALYW / ('[Feed-in tariffs] were pioneered with success in Germany and have now been enacted by more than 30 other countries').

[104] 1990, BGBl I § 2633.

[105] A caution in implementing feed-in tariffs is the stress that excessive subsidies place on non-renewable customers.

companies and a revenue of €1.7 billion per year.[106] Favorable tariff structures, such as FITs, can thus possibly improve access to renewable energy financing by providing an enhanced revenue stream.

(15) Legal Structures Supporting Renewable Energy Investment

Certain corporate entities are expanding their objectives to capture emerging opportunities in renewable energy, while other novel corporate structures surface to realize the financial potential of the market. Flexibility in the corporate form, combined with the potential for raising capital through publicly traded securities, is allowing renewable energy to grow into a legitimate competitor to fossil fuel energy. The following legal structures demonstrate the potential for corporate forms and contract law to enhance channels for renewable energy finance.

(16) Energy Service Companies (ESCOs)

Energy Service Companies or ESCOs have also emerged as viable market participants supporting investment in renewable energy. ESCOs can serve a variety of functions. They can actively participate in the electricity generation market by developing, installing and arranging financing for energy projects. An ESCO essentially arranges the project, while the tenants or owners pay the project costs, usually over a seven- to 20-year term. The ESCO arrangement helps to catalyze renewable investment by shifting qualification for financing onto an ESCO specializing in renewable energy or energy investment installations.[107]

(17) Yield Companies (YieldCos)

Yield companies, or YieldCos, are publicly traded corporations that own and operate wind and solar power plants.[108] As a publicly traded corporation, a YieldCo enables sophisticated investors to own a share in renewable energy production. The ownership of renewable energy plants

---

[106] E-Parliament, *Success* Story, above n. 104.

[107] Epa and Energy Star Buildings, *Introduction to Energy Performance Contracting* (2007), available at www.energystar.gov/ia/partners/spp_res/Introduction_to_Performance_Contracting.pdf.

[108] See Alex Anich, 'The Emerging YieldCo Landscape', *Renewable Energy World.com* (24 October 2013), available at http://perma.cc/AE63-RQGT.

provides YieldCos with a steady stream of revenue at low cost.[109] The steady revenue stream helps the YieldCo to buy new plants from developer partners at favorable terms. The relationship between a YieldCo and a renewable energy developer allows developers to 'recycle' their capital.[110] Selling an existing plant to a YieldCo makes it cheaper to raise equity for subsequent plant investment.[111] Because the YieldCo owns a variety of renewable energy plants, investors are able to reduce risks by benefiting from diversification.

The YieldCo stimulates investment in renewable energy by avoiding risk through portfolio diversification, by providing wider access to capital through public investors, and ultimately by capturing the benefits of the zero-fuel cost of solar energy.[112] In many ways, the YieldCo represents the realization of a mature renewable energy market, providing the investor with the possibility of steady and solid yields.[113]

Renewable energy power production company, NRG Energy,[114] created NRG Yield, Inc.,[115] as a subsidiary company to own, operate and acquire renewable and conventional electricity generation.[116] Since its initial public offering in July 2013, NRG Yield has had a sales/revenue growth of 78.86 per cent, with a 2013 value of US$267 million.[117] Within its diversified portfolio, NRG Yield owns eight utility-scale solar and wind generation facilities and two distributed solar facility portfolios representing 1,324 megawatts (MW) of renewable generation capacity.[118] On

---

[109] See for example, Marketwatch.com, 'NRG Yield, Inc.: Company Overview', available at www.marketwatch.com/investing/stock/nyld. NRG Yield, Inc. operates as a dividend growth-oriented company, which owns and operates a portfolio of power generation assets and thermal infrastructure assets. It was formed to serve as the primary vehicle, through which NRG Energy, Inc. will own, operate and acquire contracted renewable and conventional generation and thermal infrastructure assets.

[110] Ehren Goossens, 'Expect More Renewable Energy Yieldcos Seeking Cheap Equity, Abengoa Says', *Renewableenergyworld.com* (7 April 2014), available at www.renewableenergyworld.com/rea/news/article/2014/04/expect-more-renewable-energy-yieldcos-seeking-cheap-equity-abengoa-says.

[111] Ibid.

[112] Anich, 'The Emerging YieldCo Landscape', above n. 111.

[113] Rocky Mountain Institute, *A Rock that Churns Out Cash: Solar YieldCos* (17 July 2013), available at http://blog.rmi.org/blog_2013_07_17_a_rock_that_churns_out_cash_solar_yieldcos.

[114] See www.nrgenergy.com/.

[115] See http://investor.nrgyield.com/phoenix.zhtml?c=251846&p=irol-irhome.

[116] Rocky Mountain Institute, *A Rock that Churns Out Cash*, above n. 116.

[117] See http://investor.nrgyield.com/phoenix.zhtml?c=251846&p=irol-irhome.

[118] Ibid.

4 June 2014, NRG Yield acquired the largest wind farm in North America, Alta Wind, thereby adding 947 MW worth of renewable energy to its portfolio.[119] Acquisition of the wind farm brought it 21 years of long-term power purchase agreements.[120]

NRG Yield closed a US$450 million secured revolving credit facility with RBC Capital Markets in April 2014.[121] The size of NRG Yield's revolving credit structure reflects the promise of large-scale renewable energy power purchase agreements, and the strength of a maturing, diversified renewable energy market.

III CONCLUSION

Renewable energy resources are an essential element of a global response to climate change and health-threatening coal power plant pollution. The sun and the wind are free and the lifecycle cost of the equipment needed to convert these resources to electricity is competitive with traditional electricity resources, particularly if the huge subsidies to traditional energy resources are eliminated and if the externality costs of the traditional resources and traditional energy subsidies are included.

The brief case studies discussed above include many active innovative financing mechanisms spurring investment in renewable power generation. Ranging from microfinance in off-grid rural applications, on-bill financing of community renewable energy programmes, to YieldCos acquiring increasingly larger-scale generation capacity, new models for financing are rapidly aiding growth in the renewable energy market. As the cost of infrastructure decreases and access to cheap finance becomes more readily available, renewable energy will become a more viable force to help bring global emissions from the power sector within safe and sustainable levels. The progress being made, as described in this chapter, is very encouraging.

---

[119] NRG Yield, Inc., *Press Release: NRG Yield, Inc. to Aquire Largest Wind Farm in North America* (4 June 2013), available at http://investor.nrgyield.com/phoenix.zhtml?c=251846&p=irol-newsArticle&ID=1937203&highlight=.

[120] Ibid.

[121] Ibid.

PART II

Experiences

8. Energy and smart cities: perspectives from a city-state, Singapore

Lye Lin-Heng and Melissa Low

I INTRODUCTION

The concept of the 'smart city' is a recent phenomenon. There is, as yet, no universally agreed definition, but the Smart Cities Council defines a smart city as one that 'has digital technology embedded across all city functions'.[1] It has identified the following as 'areas of responsibility' for a smart city: the built environment; economic development; energy; health and human services; payments; public safety and security; telecommunications; transportation; waste management; and water and waste water. Another team has identified eight key aspects that define a smart city: 'smart governance, smart energy, smart building, smart mobility, smart infrastructure, smart technology, smart healthcare and smart citizen'.[2]

On 24 November 2014, Singapore's Prime Minister Mr Lee Hsien Loong, launched its Smart City initiative, emphasizing that Singapore needs to be a 'smart city' to stay ahead.[3] This initiative 'was intended to bring the current piecemeal uses of technology into a cohesive, nation-wide whole, so as to "make our economy more productive, our lives

---

[1] Smart Cities Council, 'Definitions and Overviews', available at http://smartcitiescouncil.com/smart-cities-information-center/definitions-and-overviews. See also T. Giffinger, 'European Smart Cities', available at www.smart-cities.eu/team_1.html.

[2] S. Singh, 'Smart cities: a $1.5 trillion market opportunity', *Forbes*, 19 June 2014, available at www.forbes.com/sites/sarwantsingh/2014/06/19/smart-cities-a-1-5-trillion-market-opportunity/#2715e4857a0b321c2add7ef9.

[3] R. Au-Yong, 'Singapore needs to be "smart city" to stay ahead', *Straits Times*, 24 November 2014, available at www.straitstimes.com/news/singapore/more-singapore-stories/story/new-3d-map-collate-local-knowledge-part-smart-nation-pro.

better, and our society more responsive to people's needs and aspirations"'.[4] This chapter examines Singapore's efforts towards becoming a smart city in the context of energy. This entails an examination into 'smart energy': what does this mean, and to what extent has Singapore achieved smart energy? Again, as these are new concepts, there is difficulty in finding a universal definition. The authors prefer the definition crafted by a multi-disciplinary team of consultants from the Hoehner Research and Consulting Group, which defines smart energy as 'the intelligent integration of decentralized renewable energy sources and power consumption to form the future energy ecosystem'.[5] From this definition, smart energy comprises three independent building blocks comprising low carbon generation, efficient distribution and optimized consumption, that must be pieced together to form a complete smart energy solution.[6] This chapter thus focuses on what Singapore has done to achieve smart energy, critically examining its laws and policies towards greener energy sources and consumption, facilitated through the use of 'smart' technology and well-planned environmental management systems.[7]

II ENERGY AND THE ENVIRONMENT IN SINGAPORE

The tiny city-state of Singapore (715 sq km) is an enigma in many ways. Devoid of natural resources and left to fend on its own after leaving Malaysia in 1965, it has managed not only to survive but to thrive, becoming a highly efficient and technologically advanced city-state with the highest per capita GDP in Asia (in 2012),[8] and ranked third highest

---

[4] Ibid.

[5] Hoehner Research and Consulting Group, 'How Does 360|Consult Define "Smart Energy"', available at www.360consult.com/index.php?id=44. The first block comprises PV, hydro, solar heat pump, solar thermal, biomass and wind; the second includes IT, smart grid, infrastructure, direct marketing, energy trading and cross-border grids; and the third lists energy storage, intelligent services, e-mobility, smart metering and energy management.

[6] Ibid.

[7] For a detailed account of Singapore's environmental laws, see L.H. Lye, 'Singapore' in *International Encyclopaedia of Law* (Wolters Kluwer, 2013), pp. 1–156; and L.H. Lye, 'Environmental Law of Singapore' in N.A. Robinson, L.H. Lye and E. Burleson (eds), *Comparative Environmental Law and Regulation* (2013), vol. I, pp. 1–79.

[8] Knight Frank & Citi, *Wealth Report* (2012), available at www.private bank.citibank.com/pdf/wealthReport2012_lowRes.pdf. See also Global Property

per capita GDP worldwide (in 2014).[9] Although it does not produce oil, it is one of the world's major oil refining centres and houses many of the major global oil and gas corporations.[10] In recent years, its reliance on imports of energy and water and the challenges of climate change have compelled Singapore to examine its vulnerabilities and adopt practices towards ensuring resilience. Singapore has declared a goal of reducing emissions by 16 per cent below business-as-usual by 2020, contingent on a global agreement where countries adhere to their targets in good faith. It also aims to reduce energy intensity by 35 per cent from 2005 levels by 2030.[11] Achieving these targets would involve an in-depth examination and evaluation of its energy consumption patterns in various sectors and the adoption of appropriate mechanisms, such as laws and policies to help regulate energy management practices, as well as fiscal tools to steer the behaviour of consumers, particularly large corporations.

This chapter will explore the developments in Singapore's efforts towards becoming a low carbon, energy smart city, focusing on its new laws to promote clean energy and clean buildings, and its funding and incentive schemes for energy efficiency and research and development (R&D) in the energy sector. Section III examines the challenges of climate change in Singapore, particularly in the context of its obligations to reduce emissions as a party to the UN Framework Convention on Climate Change and its Kyoto Protocol, while being considerably disadvantaged in terms of alternative energy. Section IV examines Singapore's new laws and institutions that encourage and promote energy efficiency, cleaner energy and energy conservation. These new laws also facilitate and incentivize R&D in the energy sector. These efforts work towards making Singapore a 'smart' city in the context of energy. Section V critically evaluates these efforts as well as highlighting inadequacies in its legal framework. Section VI evaluates Singapore's efforts against the Hoehner Research and Consulting Group's three independent building

---

Guide, 'Asia: GDP per Capita', available at www.globalpropertyguide.com/Asia/gdp-per-capita.

[9] C. Harty, 'Singapore: GDP Per Capita: $64,584', *The Richest*, 14 May 2014, available at www.therichest.com/business/economy/the-10-nations-with-the-highest-gdp-per-capita/8/.

[10] For a history of Singapore's energy development and energy security, see L.H. Lye and Y.H. Chang, 'Singapore: Energy Security and Regional Cooperation' in B. Barton *et al.*, *Energy Security: Managing Risk in a Dynamic Legal and Regulatory Environment* (International Bar Association, Oxford University Press, 2004), ch. 26, pp. 391–412.

[11] Letter from Singapore to H.E. Yvo De Boer, Executive Secretary of the UN Framework Convention on Climate Change, 28 January 2010.

blocks for a smart energy solution, namely, low carbon generation, efficient distribution and optimized consumption. Section VII considers the role of non-state actors and section VIII details the inadequacies and limitations of the law, sectoral measures and non-state actors. Part IX concludes with recommendations for improvement.

III ADDRESSING CLIMATE CHANGE IN SINGAPORE

On 27 August 1997, Singapore ratified the United Nations Framework Convention on Climate Change (UNFCCC) three years after it entered into force on 21 March 1994. The UNFCCC's Kyoto Protocol, which legally binds 37 industrialized countries to emissions reduction targets, entered into force on 16 February 2005. Singapore ratified the Kyoto Protocol on 11 July 2006. Since the Bali Climate Conference in 2007, Singapore has participated actively in the international climate change negotiations to discuss and develop a universal agreement on greenhouse gas (GHG) mitigation to prevent further anthropogenic interference with the climate system. On 23 September 2014, during the Climate Summit in New York City, Singapore's Minister for Environment and Water Resources, Dr Vivian Balakrishnan, deposited an instrument of ratification of the Doha Amendment, which extends the Kyoto Protocol until 2020.

Despite being a non-Annex I country and not having any legally binding targets under the Kyoto Protocol, Singapore has voluntarily taken on an emissions reduction target since the Copenhagen Climate Conference in 2009. This is in spite of its lack of recourse to switching to alternative energy sources and its economic reliance on fossil fuel. It is important to note that the principle of 'common but differentiated responsibilities and respective capabilities' in Article 3(1) of the Convention emphasizes that developed countries should take the lead, since it would not be morally, legally or economically feasible to expect developing countries to pay the supplemental costs associated with leapfrogging the carbon-intensive stage of industrialization through which all developed countries have gone.[12] Articles 4.8(h) and 4.10 of the UNFCCC call for consideration in the implementation of the commitments of the Convention to be given to states parties that are highly dependent on fossil fuels and have serious difficulties in switching to

[12] United Nations Framework Convention on Climate Change (New York, 9 May 1992; in force 21 March 1994).

non-fossil alternatives.[13] Singapore has demonstrated clear commitment to address climate change by participating actively in multilateral negotiations.

Singapore has through the years sought to ensure sustainable development. It has adopted policies towards sustainable development and measures to mitigate and reduce the growth of GHG emissions. The country consumes fossil fuels for electricity generation and imports natural gas from its immediate neighbours Malaysia and Indonesia. Four offshore pipelines transport natural gas which constitutes 84 per cent of Singapore's current fuel mix.[14] Natural gas is the least carbon-intensive of all the fossil fuels, and from 2000 to 2006, the share of electricity generated from natural gas increased from 19 per cent to 78 per cent. This shift away from using oil as a source of energy was in part due to the investments of generation companies in natural gas and the subsequent use of highly efficient combined cycle generation turbines (CCGT). Today, the share of electricity generated from oil hovers around 12 per cent as compared to 81 per cent in 2000. Other sources of energy come from the incineration of municipal waste – this contributes to the remaining 4 per cent of fuel consumed.[15]

As a city-state, Singapore is able to govern effectively without the problems of federal-state conflicts. In 2007, an Inter-Ministerial Committee on Climate Change (IMCCC) was set up, chaired by the Deputy Prime Minister and comprising seven ministers from the Finance, Trade and Industry, National Development, Environment and Water Resources, Foreign Affairs, Law and Transport ministries. This Ministerial Committee is supported by an Executive Committee comprising the permanent secretaries of the seven Ministries.[16] A National Climate Change Secretariat (NCCS) was established in 2009, under the Prime Minister's Office, with the tagline 'Creating a climate resilient global city that is well positioned for green growth'.[17] The role of the NCCS is to translate

---

[13] Ibid. Art. 4.8(h) and 4.10. In this context, Singapore aligns itself with developing states, as its development is a recent achievement, attained only in some 40 years. See Lee Kuan Yew, *From Third World to First: The Singapore Story 1965–2000* (Harper Collins, 2000).

[14] Energy Market Authority, *Singapore Energy Statistics* (2013).

[15] Ibid.

[16] National Environment Agency Singapore, 'Behind the Negotiations with Ambassador Burhan Gafoor' (2013) 4 *Envision Issue* (May/June) 22.

[17] National Climate Change Secretariat, *Inter-Ministerial Committee on Climate Change*, available at www.nccs.gov.sg/about-nccs/inter-ministerial-committee-climate.

international climate change developments and Singapore's environmental commitments into domestic policies and promote action on mitigation and adaptation while facilitating opportunities for green growth. To do this, NCSS has to work with the research community to identify and explore technologies important to Singapore's emission reduction efforts. Singapore does not have a Ministry of Energy. An inter-agency Energy Policy Group (EPG) was set up in 2007 and chaired by the Permanent Secretary of the Ministry of Trade and Industry (MTI) to develop the national energy policy framework. Its role is to balance the policy objectives of economic competitiveness and energy security with environmental sustainability.[18]

Institutionally, it is clear that the Singapore government takes an inclusive approach by adopting a 'whole-of-government' approach when developing policies, and ensuring the passing of laws that ensure their implementation.

IV ROLE OF THE LAW

Law and policy play an important role in Singapore in influencing energy consumption and in creating a smart city. Although the right to a healthy environment is not specifically mentioned in the Constitution of Singapore, one significant constitutional amendment was made in 1990 to introduce non-constituency Members of Parliament (NMP) in order to bring more independent voices to Parliament. Since then, three NMPs in succession have raised various issues relating to the environment in Parliament, the most recent being Ms Faizah Jamal, a lawyer and keen member of the Nature Society, Singapore's oldest non-governmental organization (NGO).[19] It should be noted, however, that as NMPs serve a two and a half year term on the recommendation of a Special Select Committee of Parliament chaired by the Speaker, it is not ensured that a

---

[18] Ministry of Trade and Industry Singapore, *National Energy Policy Report: Energy for Growth* (2007), p. 5.

[19] *Singapore Parliamentary Debates,* Official Report 92 (5 August 2014), available at http://sprs.parl.gov.sg/search/report.jsp?currentPubID=00006482-WA. Ms Faizah Jamal, Nominated MP, raised questions on the enhancing of Singapore's commitments in dealing with climate change and on green procurement in the public sector.

NMP will have interests in the environment and will necessarily speak on such issues.[20]

Well-crafted and effective legislation is an important facet of good governance, as laws help give clearer structure to the environmental policies put forth by the government, outlining acceptable behaviour and imposing penalties for non-compliance.[21] Through the years, Singapore has put in place an effective legal and administrative system to effectively manage the environment. Singapore now has a sound environmental management system (EMS) comprising effective land-use planning, pollution and public health laws, and laws to protect its natural and man-made heritage.[22] To become an energy-smart city, Singapore has relied heavily on the law to govern and influence behaviour, enacting laws that contain both incentives and disincentives. In recent years, there has been a discernible push towards providing more incentives in the form of research grants to encourage adoption of smart technology for energy.

One example of the law making significant and wide-ranging changes to the industry and the energy market is the Energy Market Authority of Singapore Act.[23] This Act established the Energy Market Authority of Singapore (EMA), providing for its functions and powers. Introduced in April 2001, the Act set up the EMA to liberalize the electricity and gas markets, ensure security, reliability and adequacy of the power system. Together with the Electricity Act[24] and its subsidiary laws and codes of practice, these facilitated the creation of a competitive market framework for the electricity industry, making provision for the safety, technical and economic regulation of the generation, transmission and supply and use of electricity. This essentially was part of a move to restructure the

---

[20] In August 2014, nine people were selected as Nominated Members of Parliament. While NMPs are not affiliated to any political party and represent broad interest groups, it should be noted that of the nine, none of them explicitly said that they would represent views for the environment sector. See '9 new nominated Members of Parliament announced', ChannelNewsAsia, 11 August 2014, available at http://cached.newslookup.com/cached.php?ref_id=278&siteid=2219&id=7660583&t=1407753001.

[21] Center for Liveable Cities, *Environmental Trailblazing in Singapore* (CLC Lecture Series, URA Function Hall, 29 May 2012), available at www.clc.gov.sg/documents/environmental_trailblazing_in_singapore_lecture_report.pdf.

[22] For an in-depth look into environmental law and governance in Singapore, see L.H. Lye, 'A Fine City in a Garden: Environmental Law and Governance in Singapore' (2008) *Singapore Journal of Legal Studies* (31 July) 68.

[23] Act 9 of 2001, Chapter 92B, 2002 Rev. ed. All Singapore statutes and subsidiary laws are available at http://statutes.agc.gov.sg/aol/home.w3p.

[24] Act 10 of 2001, Chapter 89A, 2002 Rev. ed.

electricity industry in the mid-1990s, as parts of Europe were going through liberalization of their electricity markets.

It must be emphasized that Singapore firmly believes that in order not to distort prices and to ensure a level playing field, it should not subsidize energy. Instead, it seeks, through the use of incentives and grants, to encourage and support companies to pursue smart solutions to their energy problems, while ensuring the quality and reliability of the supply of electricity, gas and district cooling services.[25]

More recently, the Energy Conservation Act changed the energy landscape in Singapore even further.[26] The Act, which came into effect on 22 April 2013, requires large energy users to appoint an energy manager; monitor and report energy use and GHG emissions; and submit energy efficiency improvement plans by 30 June 2014 and each year thereafter. This is part of the government's plan to introduce minimum energy management standards for the industry sector and is a step towards setting a baseline for Singapore's energy consumption. Overall, this move to conserve energy in the industry sector has provided impetus for large industrial consumers of energy to increase energy efficiency through the implementation of more rigorous energy management practices nationwide.

V INCENTIVIZING SMART ENERGY BEHAVIOUR, RESEARCH AND DEVELOPMENT

In order to develop a truly energy-smart city without subsidizing energy (including renewables), Singapore has chosen to accelerate the growth of the green energy industry by initiating several funding and incentive schemes related to energy efficiency; clean energy; green buildings; water and environmental technologies; green transport and shipping; waste minimization; energy and GHG management; and environmental initiatives and training. A guide published online in 2012 counted at least 35 funding and initiative schemes.[27] The Singapore government has set

---

[25] Ministry of Trade and Industry Singapore, *National Energy Policy Report*, above n. 18, Part III, para. 6(d), (e), (f).

[26] Act 11 of 2012, Chapter 92C, 2014 Rev. ed.

[27] Green Future Solutions, *2012 Guide to Singapore Government Funding and Incentives for the Environment* (30 May 2012), available at www.greenfuture.sg/2012/05/30/2012-guide-to-singapore-government-funding-and-incentives-for-the-environment/.

aside more than SG$800 million[28] (US$640 million) to fund research and test-bed programmes in clean energy and water technologies.[29] By incentivizing companies to pursue green growth opportunities, the country is in fact raising the productivity levels of the workforce and enabling more efficient use of resources and decoupling economic growth from harmful GHG emissions.

Examples of energy related incentive and grant schemes include the Design for Efficiency (DfE) Scheme; Energy Efficiency Improvement Assistance Scheme (EASe); Grant for Energy Efficient Technologies (GREET); Singapore Certified Energy Manager (SCEM) Training Grant; and Energy Efficiency Financing Scheme.[30] Apart from helping companies to defray costs in integrating resource efficiency plans and honing energy management skills, investments in infrastructural or technical improvements are also eligible for grants through the One-Year Accelerated Depreciation Allowance for Energy Efficient Equipment and Technology (ADAS).[31] The inter-agency Energy Innovation Programme Office (EIPO) announced in 2011 the allocation of SG$195 million from the National Research Foundation (NRF) to promote R&D in the energy sector in the five-year period to 2015. Of the SG$195 million, SG$140 million was set aside for the Energy Innovation Research Programme (EIRP). In July 2013, the EMA awarded research grants totalling about SG$10 million to six research teams for projects on Smart Grid technologies under the auspices of the Energy Innovation Programme Office (EIPO). The six projects focus on ensuring the reliability and resilience of the electricity grid, and spans areas such as energy analytics, storage, condition monitoring and control systems.[32]

Mindful of impacts on smaller corporations, the Singapore government announced in July 2013 a National Small and Medium-Sized Enterprise Energy Efficiency (SME-EE) Initiative, pledging SG$17 million to help

---

[28] As at 12 October 2014 the exchange rate was SG$1 = US$0.80.

[29] Speech by Mr Choi Shing Kwok, Permanent Secretary, Ministry of the Environment and Water Resources, at the Green Growth and Business Forum, 4 June 2014, available at www.nccs.gov.sg/news/speech-mr-choi-shing-kwok-permanent-secretary-ministry-environment-and-water-resources-green.

[30] Energy Efficient Singapore, *Energy Efficiency Programme Office*, available at www.e2singapore.gov.sg/.

[31] See www.nea.gov.sg/grants-awards/energy-efficiency/one-year-accelerated-depreciation-allowance-for-energy-efficient-equipment-and-technology-(adas).

[32] Energy Market Authority, '$10 million awarded in research grants to support Smart grid innovation', *Media Releases*, 2 July 2013, available at www.ema.gov.sg/cmsmedia/News/Media%20Release/51d248adaa199020713_-_Press_Release_for_Smart_Grid_Grant_Call_Final_website.pdf.

some 300 SMEs achieve at least 10 per cent savings in energy costs over the next three years. Grant support will cover the initial energy audit, setting up of an Energy Monitoring System, implementation of efficiency projects and leadership training. This scheme was developed by SPRING Singapore[33] and is led by the Sustainable Energy Association of Singapore (SEAS),[34] with support from SPRING Singapore, the National Environment Agency (NEA)[35] and the Infocomm Development Authority of Singapore (iDA).[36] Thus, clearly even with the announcement of incentives and grants, these have to be coupled with an enabling environment for companies to fully utilize the incentives on offer.

VI SMART ENERGY

This section evaluates Singapore's efforts against the Hoehner Research and Consulting Group's three independent building blocks for a smart energy solution; namely, low carbon generation, efficient distribution and optimized consumption. Solar photovoltaics, smart grids and intelligent devices, and e-mobility have been chosen to be evaluated, and will be set in the broader context of Singapore's energy landscape.

(1) Low Carbon Generation: Solar Photovoltaics

Singapore is located just one degree north of the equator, and thus has a tropical climate. As most of the island is highly urbanized, this leaves very little space for the harnessing of renewable energy to replace its reliance on imported fossil fuels in the foreseeable future. Although sited in the tropics, with some 12 hours of sunlight each day, there is considerable cloud cover leading to diffused radiation which, in turn, reduces the efficiencies of solar photovoltaics (PV). The highly diffused solar radiation from cloud cover can potentially cause issues of intermittency in the power grid. Notwithstanding these challenges, the Singapore government, in an effort to encourage clean technology growth, announced plans to raise the adoption of solar power by government

---

[33] SPRING Singapore is an agency under the Ministry of Trade and Industry responsible for helping Singapore enterprises grow and building trust in Singapore products and services. See www.spring.gov.sg/About-Us/Pages/spring-singapore.aspx.

[34] Sustainable Energy Association of Singapore, see www.seas.org.sg.

[35] National Environment Agency of Singapore, see www.nea.gov.sg/.

[36] Infocomm Development Authority of Singapore, see www.ida.gov.sg/.

agencies to 350MWp in 2020. Installed solar PV capacity grew from 1.5MWac in 2009 to 13.9 MWac as at the end of March 2014.

In 2014, the Energy Market Authority (EMA) also announced plans in a paper in July to remove the 'hard cap' of 600 megawatt-peak (MWp) of solar energy that can be supplied to the grid. Instead, it would introduce a 'dynamic pathway' approach, where more solar power can be stored in reserve – and supplied to the grid – if more is generated. Consultations are ongoing to further enhance the regulatory framework to allow more intermittent sources of energy to be fed into the national grid.[37] This is a reassuring move, suggesting that the Singapore government is paying closer attention to the role of law in ensuring system reliability, quality and security of supply, as well as to eventually enable bi-directional flows from decentralized (renewable) production and demand response.

Singapore now serves as a 'living laboratory' for solar energy, with several pilot projects on solar leasing as well as floating solar systems on water catchment reservoirs announced over the last two years.[38] In July 2014, the EMA made several enhancements to the market and regulatory

---

[37] Energy Market Authority, *Proposed Modifications to the Market Support Services Code and the Metering Code* (9 March 2015), available at www.ema.gov.sg/cmsmedia/Consultation%20Paper_Proposed%20Modifications %20to%20MSS%20and%20Metering%20Code%20%23Final.pdf. See also Energy Market Authority, *Enhancements to the Regulatory Framework for Intermittent Generation Sources in the National Electricity Market of Singapore*, Consultation Paper (28 October 2013), available at www.ema.gov.sg/cmsmedia/Consultations/ Electricity/526a1e95d104b-Consultation_Paper_-_Enhancements_to_the_Regulatory_ Framework_for_Intermittent_Generation_28_October_2013_FINAL.pdf.

[38] In September 2013, the Housing and Development Board (HDB), the government's public housing authority, called for a tender for a solar leasing project to produce 5MW of electricity in optimum conditions, or 5 megawatts-peak (MWp) – enough to power more than 1,000 four-room HDB flats. HDB will offset up to 30 per cent of the start-up costs, and, in turn, buy the electricity for 20 years at a 5 per cent or greater discount off the prevailing market price. This electricity would power lights in corridors and common areas, lifts and water pumps. See www.pv-magazine.com/news/details/beitrag/singapore–housing-development-board-calls-largest-solar-leasing-tender_100012855/#axzz3 G0CObKcG. In May 2014, the Public Utilities Board (PUB) announced it had started two pilot projects to harness solar power at Choa Chu Kang Waterworks and installed floating systems on Tengeh Reservoir. In May 2011, HDB announced the launch of its first solar leasing scheme of 2 MW in 30 housing precincts. See www.pv-magazine.com/news/details/beitrag/singapore–hdb-launches-2-mw-solar-leasing-scheme_100003012/#axzz3G0CObKcG.

framework for intermittent generation sources, such as solar energy.[39] Overall, there has been increased interest and commercial viability of solar energy for power generation over the last five years. This was made possible by significant government initiatives such as the Building and Construction Authority (BCA) Green Mark Scheme, and the Economic Development Board (EDB) Solar Capability Scheme.[40] Coupled with innovative power purchase and solar leasing agreements, small- and medium-sized enterprises have also been able to participate.[41] The solar energy industry has also received a boost with the establishment of the world's largest solar panel manufacturing complex in Singapore by Norway's Renewable Energy Corporation (REC); investments in solar panel manufacturing by Solar Energy Power and Eco-Solar; and setting up of their Asia-Pacific headquarters in Singapore by leading solar and clean energy companies such as SolarWorld and Conergy.

The lack of space and high urban density further constrains development of other forms of renewables like wind or hydropower. Singapore's busy shipping lanes significantly reduce the likelihood of harnessing tidal energy, though the inter-tidal difference in the tropics is generally hardly enough to generate commercial interest. As for nuclear energy, the Singapore government did a pre-feasibility study on nuclear energy for Singapore in 2012, and concluded that it is not ready for deployment in Singapore due to national circumstances. However, the study said Singapore should continue to play an active role in global and regional cooperation on nuclear safety, monitor the development of nuclear energy technologies, and support research in nuclear science and engineering. Thus, a Nuclear Safety Research and Education Programme was recently launched in April 2014, with funding of some SG$63 million, at the National University of Singapore.[42]

---

[39] Energy Market Authority, *Enhancements to the Regulatory Framework for Intermittent Generation Sources in the National Electricity Market of Singapore: Final Determination Paper* (1 July 2014).

[40] Green Future Solutions, *2012 Guide to Singapore Government Funding and Incentives for the Environment* (30 May 2012), available at www.greenfuture.sg/2012/05/30/2012-guide-to-singapore-government-funding-and-incentives-for-the-environment/.

[41] V. Shah, 'Singapore's Sports Hub Marks New Dawn for Solar Industry', *Eco-Business.com* (24 June 2014), available at www.eco-business.com/news/singapore-sports-hub-marks-new-dawn-solar-industry/.

[42] National University of Singapore, 'Singapore Nuclear Research and Safety Initiative to be hosted at NUS', *NUS News*, 23 April 2014, available at http://news.nus.edu.sg/highlights/7618-singapore-nuclear-research-and-safety-initiative-to-be-hosted-at-nus.

(2) Efficient Distribution: Smart Grids

Cities like Singapore are hard-pressed to respond to the myriad pressures of population growth and economic development in the face of climate change and fiscal stress, by seeking new and more efficient ways of operating.[43] One of the main goals of creating and maintaining a smart city is to ensure sustainability and energy resilience. Despite substantial differences in energy market regulation and policy, there is a strong desire on a global scale to implement smart grids.[44] In Singapore, the Intelligent Energy System (IES) pilot is the first large-scale deployment to gather feedback on the energy distribution network, with SG$30 million investment funded by Singapore Power and the Singapore government. In collaboration with the Nanyang Technological University (NTU) and industry partners, the IES project will be testing various smart grid applications and solutions in real-life demonstrations for 4,500 customers.[45] The pilot phase, focusing on advanced metering infrastructure, took place from 2010 to 2012, and the second phase was conducted between 2012 and 2013, focusing on smart grid applications. So far, the agencies involved have not released information on whether the pilot has been successful and whether it will be implemented nationwide. There were two other test-beds completed in late 2011, including the Experimental Power Grid Centre (EPGC) and the Pulau Ubin Intelligent Microgrid project focusing on testing the integration of renewable energy sources in a grid-connected and off-grid environment, respectively.[46]

The EPGC, which is based at the A*Star's Institute of Chemical and Engineering Sciences on Jurong Island, has several collaborations, including with Hitachi, Vestas, Meidensha Corporation Japan and US-based National Instruments. The EPGC also works closely with several government agencies, including the Housing Development Board (HDB) and Building and Construction Authority (BCA). In 2014, after three years of joint research between BCA and Hitachi on converting

---

43 R. Puentes and A. Tomer, *Getting Smarter about Smart Cities*, Metropolitan Infrastructure Initiative Paper No. 79 of 91 (Brookings Institute, 23 April 2014).

44 eGov Innovation, *Singapore Among Top Ranking Smart Cities Globally* (24 February 2015), available at http://enterpriseinnovation.net/article/singapore-among-top-ranking-smart-cities-globally-52527604.

45 National Climate Change Secretariat and National Research Foundation, *Smart Grid Technology Primer: A Summary* (2011), available at www.nccs.gov.sg/sites/nccs/files/Smart%20Grid%20Primer.pdf.

46 Ibid.

waste heat from a combined heat and power (CHP) plant into viable electricity to power buildings' air-conditioning systems, plans were announced to commercialize this technology.[47] The SG$38 million facility on Jurong Island recreates grid-like conditions, allowing researchers to tinker around with experimental smart grid technologies. It is capable of generating up to 1 MW of power, enough to power 500 households. It remains to be seen whether this technology can be commercialized and is economically viable. If so, the law should compel or encourage its use in Singapore on a national scale so as to improve energy efficiency and contribute towards the nation's climate change mitigation targets.

The third smart grid pilot is the Pulau Ubin microgrid. As Pulau Ubin is an offshore island just off the Singapore mainland, the primary objective of the microgrid has been to promote the economic viability to lay power transmission cables due to the modest demand of the world's remote areas, which still lack proper access to electricity. With the intelligent microgrid, Singapore has test-bed close-to-market clean and renewable technologies, and intends to facilitate the deployment of market-ready ones. This test-bed aims to assess the reliability of electricity supply within a microgrid infrastructure using intermittent renewable energy sources, such as solar PV technology.[48] If successful, this microgrid model can be exported by Singapore to help remote communities in the Southeast Asian region gain access to distributed generation.[49]

(3) Optimized Consumption

(i) Intelligent devices and the smart consumer (the Internet of things)

Households account for about one-sixth of the electricity consumed in Singapore. In a typical home, air-conditioning and water heating account for the lion's share of electricity consumption. This is followed by refrigerators, computers and peripherals, and lighting.[50] Singapore

---

47 J. Lee, 'A*Star, Hitachi in joint energy research', *Business Times*, 27 August 2014.

48 Energy Market Authority, 'Pulau Ubin Microgrid Test Bed', available at www.ema.gov.sg/Pulau_Ubin_Micro-grid_Test_Bed.aspx#sthash.IObuAVMq.dpuf.

49 National Climate Change Secretariat and National Research Foundation, *Smart Grid Technology* Primer, above n. 45, at 11.

50 National Climate Change Secretariat, *Consultation Paper on Reducing Emissions in Households* (2011), available at www.nccs.gov.sg/news/government-seeks-views-singapore%E2%80%99s-climate-action-plans.

constantly explores new technologies and solutions to meet its energy needs, to build sustainable towns, and to empower residents to adopt a green lifestyle.

Policies and measures have been put in place over the years to promote energy efficiency in households. Under the Energy Conservation Act, all registrable goods must carry energy labels.[51] These include the Mandatory Energy Labelling Scheme (MELS), Minimum Energy Performance Standards (MEPS), and 10% Energy Challenge.[52] For its energy labels, Singapore has adopted a 'tick' rating system, with the lowest rating being one-tick that complies with the current MEPS level, and five-ticks for the highest which correspond to the highest equivalent bands in developed countries such as the European Union. Singapore's energy rating system extends to air-conditioners, refrigerators, clothes dryers and televisions.

The Energy Efficient Singapore (E^2Singapore) website[53] was set up to give comprehensive information on energy efficiency matters in Singapore. These schemes have been fairly successful in raising awareness, but a tender called by the National Climate Change Secretariat (NCCS) in 2013 on long-term economy-wide energy efficiency potential suggests that more work needs to be done to understand and quantify energy efficiency gains from policies and to be able to benchmark successes against best practices in other countries. There currently exists very limited data for electricity and town gas consumption by the different dwelling types in Singapore, particularly for common areas, as electricity consumption tends to be aggregated.[54] More recently, the HDB and EMA announced plans to establish a Smart Home Energy Pilot to explore a suite of different energy choices and solutions for HDB households in the future.[55] The study will assess the feasibility of integrating some of the following measures to increase energy efficiency in households:

---

[51] Energy Conservation (Energy Labelling and Minimum Performance Standards for Registrable Goods) Regulations 2013, S557/2013, Singapore Statutes.

[52] National Environment Agency, 'About Mandatory Energy Labeling', available at www.nea.gov.sg/energy-waste/energy-efficiency/household-sector/about-mandatory-energy-labelling.

[53] National Environment Agency, *Energy Efficient Singapore: An E^2PO Initiative*, available at www.e2singapore.gov.sg/.

[54] National Climate Change Secretariat, *Tender for Study on Long-Term Economy-Wide Energy Efficiency Potential*, Ref: NCCS-PPD-06/13 (2013).

[55] Energy Market Authority, 'HDB and EMA tie up with Panasonic to study the feasibility of establishing a Smart Home Energy Pilot for flats', *Media Release*, 3 June 2014, available at www.ema.gov.sg/media_release.aspx?news_sid=201406260pixO3k1aFUf.

(a) Time-of-Use Electricity Rate Packages;
(b) Home Energy Management Systems (HEMS); and
(c) Energy Aggregation Models.

The findings from the study will allow HDB, EMA and Panasonic to assess the feasibility of implementing the Smart Home Energy Pilot at 38 HDB blocks in Yuhua estate, HDB's Greenprint neighbourhood in Jurong East.

In February 2014, 260,000 consumers began participating in a new pilot by Singapore Power Services (SPS) and the EMA to use data and an electronic-billing account to monitor and reduce their electricity consumption. This smart feature allows consumers to compare their electricity consumption in the last six months against the national average consumption and the average consumption of their neighbours living in similar housing types.[56] The EMA hopes to raise customers' awareness of their consumption pattern and hence encourage better energy-saving habits.

Building on the progress made in its Intelligent Nation Masterplan (iN2015) set out in 2005, Singapore is now focusing on developing technical architecture for the home through the Internet of Things[57] @ Home (IoT@Home) standards. It is expected that smart embedded objects will become an important part of what is called the 'Internet of Things'. In 2014, the government appointed the Infocomm Development Authority of Singapore (IDA) to develop technical standards to identify ways to enable seamless inter-operability between connected smart devices, including wearables and home appliances, as they are applied in a home setting.[58] Because many of these home solutions typically work in silos and their functions are limited to within the device or those coming from the same brand, standards to create a common 'service

---

[56] Energy Market Authority, 'Using data to help consumers reduce their electricity consumption', *Media Release*, 18 February 2014, available at www.ema.gov.sg/media_release.aspx?news_sid=20140609S3zKFYtaqUG3.

[57] The 'Internet of Things' refers to the general idea of things such as everyday objects which are readable, recognizable, locatable, addressable, and/or controllable via the Internet, irrespective of the communication means. They can even include things we do not ordinarily consider electronic, such as people, location, time information and condition of various objects. See http://iotawards.postscapes.com/.

[58] Infocomm Development Authority of Singapore (IDA), 'Singapore unveils building blocks of Smart Nation Vision', *Media Release*, 17 June 2014, available at www.ida.gov.sg/About-Us/Newsroom/Media-Releases/2014/Singapore-Unveils-Building-Blocks-of-Smart-Nation-Vision.

layer' are expected to raise the potential of devices to provide stronger benefits and enhance user experience. This initiative focuses on key areas of application, including wellness, active ageing, home-based care and sustainable living. An Internet of Things Technical Committee (IoTTC) was therefore established to focus on the standardization of IoT technologies, including sensor networks, system interfaces, data management and security. Comprising two working groups on sensors and IoT reference architecture, the IoTTC also participates actively in the development of international standards such as the ISO/IEC JTC/SWG 5 Internet of Things (IoT).[59]

The legal criterion for standardization in Singapore is, however, lacking. The government appears to promote standards and conformance through publications such as newsletters and in high-level speeches. Within the European Union, in addition to the Third Energy Package provisions and Annex I.1 of the Electricity Directive explicitly asking Member States to assess the roll-out of intelligent metering systems as a key step towards the implementation of Smart Grid, many Member States have implemented provisions in their legislation, although some others are still lagging behind. In particular, Italy, Sweden, France, Malta, Finland and the United Kingdom are leading in investments in the deployment of smart meters. Thanks to legislation, investments in smart metering were developed fast and roll-out in a number of Member States was achieved on time.[60]

(ii) E-Mobility

Singapore also lends itself as a test-bed for transport efficiency. An inter-agency Electric Vehicle (EV) Taskforce was set up in 2011 to gauge different EV prototypes and charging technologies in the context of Singapore's urbanized environment and road conditions, before deciding on its implementation for mass adoption. Data for EVs have been collected and processed to examine issues relevant to policies regarding

---

[59] ISO/IEC JTC 1/SWG 5 Internet of Things (IoT) is a special working group (SWG) of the Joint Technical Committee JTC 1 of the International Organization for Standardization (ISO) and the International Electrotechnical Commission (IEC), which develops and facilitates the development of standards for Internet of Things (IoT).

[60] V. Giordano, F. Gangale, G. Fulli and M.S. Jiménez, *Smart Grid Projects in Europe, European Commission Joint Research Centre Institute for Energy Reference* (Report EUR 24856 EN, 2011), available at http://ses.jrc.ec.europa.eu/sites/ses/files/documents/smart_grid_projects_in_europe.pdf.

the implementation of EVs in the future.[61] As of 31 December 2013, there were 89 EVs registered under the test-bed, involving 53 organizations. To cater to the charging needs of the EVs, 68 normal charging stations (full charge within 7–8 hours) and three quick charging stations (full charge within 30–45 minutes) have been deployed.[62] But EVs are not the only solution Singapore has adopted in its bid to reduce emissions from the transport sector. Singapore has the world's highest prices for motor vehicles due to its many taxes and additional disincentives such as the need to bid for a limited number of Certificates of Entitlement (COE) to own and use a car.[63] Together, these apply the 'polluter pays' principle and have managed to curb growth in car ownership. A new Carbon Emission-based Vehicle Scheme (CEVS) was recently implemented, working essentially like a carbon tax on car emissions, penalizing cars in specific bands which exceed 231 CO_2g/km.[64]

VII ROLE OF NON-STATE ACTORS

Singapore has adopted a pragmatic approach towards energy governance by adopting a plethora of policies and measures which include legislation, incentives and grants, and capacity building. These measures complement policy shifts and ensure resiliency. As a small island city-state, it is important to stay relevant, given its inherent vulnerabilities to external shocks and changes in the world economy. Building a smarter, more livable city that efficiently utilizes the resources imported is a key to sustainable, low-carbon development. However, the creation of an energy-smart city is not built solely on infrastructure and hardware. While policies and measures are in place to change behaviours and regulate emissions from the various sectors, individuals and non-state actors also play a role in an overall mindset shift. Non-state actors can act as bridges to facilitate bringing workers and individuals up to speed

---

[61] The four EV models include the Daimler Smart electric drive, Mitsubishi i-MiEV, Nissan Leaf and Renault Fluence ZE.

[62] Energy Market Authority, *Electric Vehicle Test-Bed* (2012), available at www.ema.gov.sg/Electric_Vehicles_Test_Bed.aspx.

[63] See L.H. Lye, 'Environmental Taxation in the Management of Road Traffic in Singapore' in L.H. Lye, J.E. Milne, H. Ashiabor, L. Kreiser and K. Deketelaere (eds), *Critical Issues in Environmental Taxation: International and Comparative Perspectives* (Oxford University Press, 2009), vol. VII, 205–25.

[64] Land Transport Authority, *Tax Structure for Cars* (2014), available at www.lta.gov.sg/content/ltaweb/en/roads-and-motoring/owning-a-vehicle/costs-of-owning-a-vehicle/tax-structure-for-cars.html.

on the new regulations and mandatory energy management practices that can often be overwhelming. This section details the role of non-state actors in enabling an energy-smart city.

Non-state actors can be motivated to engage in networking, hold meetings among peers, find quick and effective solutions, debate new ideas and approaches, as well as present novel research findings.[65] In both national and international platforms, state and non-state actors help legitimize the process of policy-making, providing credibility and authority over time.[66]

(1) Sustainable Energy Association of Singapore (SEAS)

The Sustainable Energy Association of Singapore (SEAS) is a non-profit organization governed by a Council whose members comprise top management in sustainable energy firms in Singapore.[67] SEAS provides business-matching platforms, organize trade missions and networking sessions, forums, conferences and workshops. Representing the energy industry in Singapore, SEAS holds regular dialogues with government agencies and produces business intelligence reports. SEAS provides business advisory and technology facilitation services, enabling enterprises to access its growing network of sustainable energy players and technology access, product development and commercialization. SEAS also designs new courses and conducts workshops to help train manpower for the sustainable energy industry. In 2014, SEAS released a White Paper on accelerating renewable energy in Singapore.[68] The White Paper explains how renewable energy can generate 3,635 GWh of electricity each year, or approximately 7.3 per cent of Singapore's forecast 2025 demand, without government subsidies. SEAS has been instrumental in positing that great investment opportunities lie in renewable energy, and an even greater growth in the industry.

---

[65] For discussion on the politics of civil society in Singapore, see T. Lee, 'The Politics of Civil Society in Singapore' (2002) 26(1) *Asian Studies Review* 97.

[66] H. Schroeder and H. Lovell, 'The Role of Non-Nation-State Actors and Side Events in the International Climate Negotiations' (2012) 12(1) *Climate Policy* 23.

[67] Sustainable Energy Association of Singapore, see www.seas.org.sg/.

[68] Sustainable Energy Association of Singapore, *White Paper on Accelerating Renewable Energy in Singapore* (2014), available at www.seas.org.sg/resources/presentationpapers.

(2) Energy Studies Institute (ESI)

Another non-state actor in developing Singapore as a smart city is the Energy Studies Institute (ESI).[69] In 2007, the Singapore government set up the ESI at the National University of Singapore to promote and develop policy-oriented research on the economics, environment and international relations aspects of energy, as well as to contribute to energy dialogue and collaboration in the region. ESI has helped promote greater awareness by organizing and participating in high profile and impact conferences, seminars and platforms for information sharing. The Institute has worked closely with various government agencies in Singapore to produce policy reports and also host joint events. Their researchers have published papers in top ranking internationally peer-reviewed journals such as *Energy Policy* and *Energy Economics*. In 2014, ESI was ranked ninth out of 20 Top Energy and Resource Policy Think Tanks by the University of Pennsylvania's *Seventh Annual Global Go-To Think Tanks Report*.

(3) Solar Energy Research Institute of Singapore (SERIS)

The Solar Energy Research Institute of Singapore (SERIS) is Singapore's national institute for applied solar energy research.[70] The Institute is sponsored by the National University of Singapore (NUS) and Singapore's National Research Foundation (NRF) through the Singapore Economic Development Board (EDB). SERIS is structured as a National Laboratory at NUS and has the stature of an NUS University-level Research Institute. It is endowed with considerable autonomy and flexibility, including an industry-friendly intellectual property policy. In partnership with the Singapore government, SERIS conducted a study on the potential of solar PV adoption in Singapore.[71] In 2014, SERIS announced that it was conducting research with the Singapore Land Authority (SLA) to photograph and map (in 3D) the country's entire

---

[69] Energy Studies Institute, see www.esi.nus.edu.sg/.

[70] Solar Energy Research Institute of Singapore, see www.seris.sg/.

[71] Solar Energy Research Institute of Singapore, *Solar Photovoltaic (PV) Roadmap for Singapore: A Summary* (2014), available at www.nrf.gov.sg/docs/default-source/Publications/solar-photovoltaic.pdf?sfvrsn=0.

landscape and the potential to harness solar energy on rooftops in Singapore.[72]

(4) Other Tertiary Education Institutions

On 2 March 2012, the Ministry of Trade and Industry (MTI) identified that there was a need to build up manpower capacities and capabilities for Singapore's power sector. A Power Sector Manpower Taskforce (PSMT) was established and over the course of ten months consulted and gathered feedback through focus group sessions and personal interviews.[73] The PSMT report recommended that the government establish an 'Attraction, Retention and Development Framework'; embark on a sector-wide branding exercise; and adopt a coordinated approach to drive manpower efforts. In 2014, the EMA launched the Energy-Industry Scholarship (EIS) which was co-funded by the government and power sector companies. It aims to develop and nurture talent for the local power sector. Those pursuing relevant engineering courses at the local Institute of Technical Education (ITE), polytechnics and universities are encouraged to apply. The scholarships allow successful applicants to pursue internships and work attachments in the energy sector during their studies and upon completing their studies, scholars will join their sponsoring organizations.

VIII INADEQUACIES AND LIMITATIONS OF THE LAW, SECTORAL MEASURES AND NON-STATE ACTORS

It is clear that very positive steps have been taken towards ensuring that Singapore is a smart city. The administration functions well, thinks well ahead, and in the context of its energy future, has mobilized resources to encourage research and development, as well as reached out to the private sector towards effective partnerships in new energy initiatives. Indeed, from the standpoint of environment governance and management, Singapore stands out as a city with a well functioning environmental

---

[72] 'Solar power map to help Singaporeans see the light', *Straits Times*, 28 April 2014, available at www.straitstimes.com/singapore/solar-power-map-to-help-sporeans-see-the-light.

[73] Energy Market Authority, *Power Sector Manpower Taskforce Report* (18 December 2012), available at www.ema.gov.sg/cmsmedia/EPDD/PSMT Report.pdf.

management system (or EMS).[74] However, there are still inadequacies that should be addressed. In particular, these are the lack of laws mandating recycling, as well as the lack of laws mandating environmental impact assessments.

In 2008, incineration produced some 963 million kWh of electricity, representing 2 to 3 per cent of the total electricity generated in Singapore. However, more energy can be produced from incineration if wet wastes, such as food and other organic wastes, are first sorted out and separately treated. Legislation mandating this would greatly ease the efforts of the private sector to collect and appropriately treat such wastes. Food waste contributes to some 20 per cent of Singapore's total wastes. However, only 16 per cent of the 640,000 tonnes generated in 2013 was recycled. This is a long way off the target of 30 per cent by 2015, outlined nearly a decade ago, in the Singapore Green Plan 2012. Regrettably, Singapore's first and only food waste to energy plant, IUT Global, was compelled to close down in 2011 after three years of operation, due to the lack of laws mandating recycling.[75]

Singapore still does not have a law mandating environmental impact assessments. The nearest equivalents are sections 26 and 36 of the Environmental Protection and Management Act (EPMA).[76] Section 26 empowers the Director-General of Environmental Protection to require the owner or occupier of hazardous installations to carry out impact analysis studies. Section 36 authorizes the Director-General to require any person intending to carry out any activity that, in his opinion, is likely to cause substantial pollution of the environment or increase the level of such pollution, to carry out 'a study on environmental pollution control' and to submit for approval, within the specified time, a proposal for the implementation of such measures for pollution control as the Director-General may approve or specify. This is far short of requiring a comprehensive study on all possible environmental impacts, as advocated

---

[74] L.H. Lye, 'Environmental Law, Policy, Governance and Management for Cities: Getting it Right for a Sustainable Future – The Singapore Experience' in J. Huang and S. Gupta (eds), *Environmental Policies in Asia: Perspectives from Seven Asian Countries* (World Scientific, 2014), pp. 171–203.

[75] 'Food waste recycler folds', *Straits Times*, 18 November 2011, available at www.eco-business.com/news/food-waste-recycler-folds/.

[76] K.B. Foo, K.L. Koh and L.H. Lye, 'Environmental Protection: The Legal Framework' in G.L. Ooi (ed.), *Environment and the City: Sharing Singapore's Experience and Future Challenges* (Times Academic Press, 1995). See also the works by L.H. Lye cited above.

in Principle 17 of the Rio Declaration on Environment and Development[77] and as contained in Article 14 of the ASEAN Agreement on the Conservation of Nature and Natural Resources.[78]

Non-state or civil society actors in Singapore are sometimes limited in their sphere of influence on government policy-making. For example, in 2011, Tuas Power, the third largest power generator in Singapore announced that it would be building a new multi-utilities complex at Tembusu (the Tembusu Multi-Utilities Complex) to supply steam, chilled water and electricity, and treat industrial waste for up to ten petrochemical companies on Jurong Island. Powered by 80 per cent low-ash, low-sulphur coal and 20 per cent biomass comprising of waste woodchips and palm kernel shells, the plant is the first of its kind in Singapore. Citizens were concerned that coal burning was used and questions were raised by an opposition member of Parliament.[79]

The lack of access to information exacerbates the limited capacity of non-state and civil society actors. In Europe, the Convention on Access to Information, Public Participation in Decision Making and Access to Justice in Environmental Matters (better known as the Aarhus Convention) establishes a number of rights of the public in the context of environmental matters. In particular, these are, as the title suggests, the right of access to information; the right of public participation in decision-making; and the right of access to justice. The Convention recognizes that the ambit of these rights may be curtailed in the context of national security, but the recognition that such rights exist is in itself a huge step in the right direction.

---

[77] Principle 17 states: 'Environmental impact assessment, as a national instrument, shall be undertaken for proposed activities that are likely to have a significant adverse impact on the environment and are subject to a decision of a competent national authority'. See www.unep.org/Documents.Multilingual/Default.asp?DocumentID=78&ArticleID=1163.

[78] The Agreement, signed in 1985 by all six states parties to ASEAN, is still not in force as Brunei, Malaysia and Singapore are yet to ratify. See http://cil.nus.edu.sg/rp/pdf/1985%20Agreement%20on%20the%20Conservation%20of%20Nature%20and%20Natural%20Resources-pdf.pdf.

[79] *Singapore Parliamentary Debates,* Official Report 90 (13 March 2013). Mrs Lina Chiam, Nominated MP, asked the Minister for Trade and Industry: (a) why is the coal-burning Tembusu Multi-Utilities Complex on Jurong Island allowed to operate considering that coal is one of the most polluting sources of energy; and (b) whether Singapore has met its international obligations to reduce its carbon emissions. See www.mti.gov.sg/NewsRoom/Pages/Second-Minister-S-Iswaran's-reply-on-the-use-of-coal-at-Tembusu-Multi-Utilities-Complex-on-Jurong-Island.aspx.

IX CONCLUSION

In a short span of less than 50 years, Singapore has attained great economic success and enhanced its living environment. Its success was (and continues to be) motivated by economic growth. A robust and vibrant economy is dependent on a constant and reliable supply of energy. While Singapore has come a long way in developing an energy-smart city, it must continue to strive for excellence in all areas. This chapter has examined the role of the law, incentives, sectoral measures and non-state and civil society actors in enabling an energy-smart city. It has also highlighted several inadequacies and limitations. It is clear that Singapore's physical, economic and social environment will keep evolving and its administrators, civil servants and political leaders will need to strive to meet new challenges that arise, including dealing with climate change while ensuring economic growth, environmental sustainability and energy security. Even more can and needs to be done in the future, particularly in educating civil servants and the public on how to better manage energy resources and to shift mindsets when it comes to consuming and conserving energy. There is also a dire need for greater public participation in decision-making in the context of the environment, as a true measure of the partnership between the state and the people.

9. Judicial perspectives on renewable energy and climate change governance

Trevor Daya-Winterbottom

I NEW ZEALAND: AN OVERVIEW

The Waikato region of New Zealand stretches from the snowcapped mountains of the North Island's volcanic plateau surrounding Lake Taupo, through the broad Waikato River valley to the Tasman Sea. The region has the capacity to power up to 50 per cent of New Zealand, and exports over 75 per cent of the electricity generated to other regions.[1] The primary sources of electricity generation in the Waikato region are hydro, geothermal, and thermal (coal and gas); and recent growth in electricity development in the region has focused on geothermal and gas-fired generation. With peaking production from the Maui gas field offshore from the Taranaki coast of the North Island and the increased emphasis on a 90 per cent renewable electricity generation target by 2025 'the region is likely to play an important role in the development of future renewable electricity generation nationally'.[2]

For example, limited capacity for new hydro dams along the Waikato River and constraints on further assimilating discharges for cooling from thermal power stations due to increasing demand for freshwater underpin the continued interest in geothermal and wind power, and the interest in emerging technologies such as underground coal gasification and marine energy.[3] In particular, accessing north Waikato coal reserves (over 1 billion tonnes), which is currently an impractical and uneconomic proposition using conventional open-cast or deep mining methods, could

[1] Waikato Regional Council, *From the Mountains to the Sea* (Supplement to the proposed Waikato Regional Policy Statement, 2010), p. 53.

[2] Ibid. 53.

[3] Ibid. 54.

become 'a real possibility' using these new technologies.[4] Against this background, the Royal Society of New Zealand recommended that electricity generation should make the transition to renewable energy sources by 2020, including the use of less carbon-intense bridging fuels, and with a 'commitment to zero carbon emissions' from fossil-fuel generation through capture and storage techniques.[5]

II JUDICIAL PERSPECTIVES

Considering New Zealand's imminent move towards renewable energy, this chapter focuses on the role of the New Zealand judiciary in renewable energy and climate change governance. First, it examines attempts to mitigate the effects of greenhouse gas (GHG) emissions on climate change by including conditions on the grant of resource consents for gas-fired power stations requiring the planting of forest sinks, and the demise of this approach following the adoption of a policy preference for the introduction of an emissions trading scheme (ETS). Second, it examines uncertainty resulting from the 2004 amendments to the Resource Management Act 1991 (RMA) that attempted to prohibit local authority control of GHG emissions in light of the preferred policy package. Third, it examines attempts to regulate coal exports for burning overseas under the RMA. Finally, it examines the comparative ease with which renewable energy projects for wind, geothermal or tidal-energy can obtain resource consent under the RMA.

As noted in the introduction, there is considerable existing investment in renewable energy in New Zealand and there are significant prospects for future renewable energy projects. However, despite this position the slow evolution of government policy regarding climate change and renewable energy has left a vacuum that has resulted in significant judicial participation in determining policy questions regarding renewable energy and climate change governance.

---

4 Ibid. 54.

5 Royal Society of New Zealand, *2020: Energy Opportunities* (2006); Royal Society of New Zealand, *Climate Change Statement* (2008).

III CLIMATE CHANGE AND ELECTRICITY GENERATION

Electricity generation and GHG emissions have been controversial issues for New Zealand since the RMA came into force. For example, the proposed Taranaki power station was referred to a Board of Inquiry following the call-in of the resource consent applications by the Minister for the Environment. The Board found that the proposed 400MW combined-cycle thermal power station would increase total CO_2 emissions by 5 per cent.[6] While it found that further electricity generation would have a positive environment effect, it also found that there was 'no immediate need for the new power station' and that alternative generation technologies 'may become feasible in the future'.[7] As a result, the Board gave careful consideration to methods for mitigating the CO_2 emissions, including the removal of emissions from exhaust gases, controlling other power stations to guarantee that there would be no increase in overall emissions, and planting forest sinks. The Minister agreed with the Board's recommendation that a consent condition should be imposed, requiring mitigation, but provided for a more flexible approach that would (*inter alia*) take reductions at other power stations into account. The consent holder was therefore required only to take steps to mitigate 'the effects of the additional amount of CO_2 being discharged as a result of the exercise of this consent'.[8] Notwithstanding this change, the decision was criticized because the government was (at that time) developing a policy response to implement New Zealand's international obligations under the United Nations Framework Convention on Climate Change (UNFCCC) outside the RMA that provided for voluntary agreements and would have led to the introduction of a carbon tax in 1997 if emissions reduction targets were not being met.[9]

Subsequently, similar issues arose in relation to resource consent applications for new gas-fired thermal power stations at Otahuhu in

---

[6] *Proposed Taranaki Power Station, Air Discharge Effects: Report and Recommendations of the Board of Inquiry Pursuant to Section 148 of the Resource Management Act 1991* (Ministry for the Environment, 1995).

[7] Michael Sleigh, 'Stratford Power Station Decision', *Resource Management News* (February/March 1995), p. 25.

[8] Ibid.

[9] Paul F. Majurey, 'Proposed Stratford Power Station CO2 Decision: Aberration or Policy-U-Turn?', *Resource Management News* (May/June 1995), p. 8.

Auckland, and Stratford in Taranaki.[10] The decisions of the respective regional councils to grant consent without including any mitigation conditions were appealed to the Environment Court by the Environmental Defence Society, which sought that forest sink conditions should be imposed in both cases. The electricity generators argued that the proposed power stations would have a negligible effect on global emissions; that other less efficient generation from other power stations would be displaced; that sufficient forest sinks were already being planted by others; that no further mitigation was required; and that the government was formulating a revised policy position outside the RMA regarding climate change. However, the Society contended that climate change should be addressed under the RMA regardless of whether any adverse environmental effects would be local, national or global; that all CO_2 emissions should be mitigated notwithstanding any action by others; and that emerging government policy outside the RMA was irrelevant.

The Court considered that the assessment of environmental effects was not limited to merely local effects and observed that 'it would be artificial in the overall context to confine the environment to New Zealand'.[11] While the Court made no express finding about whether or not forest sinks planted by other persons should be taken into account, arguably this could be inferred from the judgment. The Court also held that New Zealand's international obligations under the UNFCCC were relevant, but found that these obligations should be applied in a way that was consistent with the preferred policy package then being developed by the government. As a result, although the Court accepted the scientific evidence regarding the adverse climate change effects of GHG emissions and the cumulative effect of the proposed power stations, it was reluctant to include conditions on the grant of resource consents that would be administered by the regional councils in the light of the need for a national approach advocated by the developing government policy. The appeals were subsequently dismissed. This led Van Bohemen to note that:

> Since these cases each concerned the discharge of over a million tonnes of CO_2 per annum, it is unlikely that the facts of other cases will dictate a different outcome. This suggests that it will rarely, if ever, be appropriate for a consent authority to require as a condition of a resource consent measures to

---

[10] *Environmental Defence Society Inc.* v. *Auckland Regional Council* [2002] NZRMA 492; *Environmental Defence Society Inc.* v. *Taranaki Regional Council* (A84/2002).

[11] Gerard van Bohemen 'Climate Change and Resource Consent Decisions' (2003) XI(1) *Resource Management Journal* (March) 16.

> mitigate climate change effects which manifest globally and which have no real local or even regional effect.[12]

Effectively, the decisions in the *Environmental Defence Society* cases confirmed the policy shift away from local authority involvement in climate change, and terminated any direct link between consenting new fossil fuel-fired power stations and planting forest sinks. As a result, the Taranaki Regional Council granted consent in 2003 for the cancellation of the condition requiring mitigation of CO_2 emissions relating to the Taranaki power station originally imposed by the Minister in 1995. The *Environmental Defence Society* decisions were remarkable in that they gave effect to intended government policy in advance of the relevant enabling legislation being enacted by Parliament. Notwithstanding the constitutional significance of the decisions,[13] no further appeals or applications for judicial review were filed with the High Court.

(1) RMA Amendments

Subsequently, the RMA was amended by the insertion of section 104E into the statute, which provides that local authorities 'must not have regard' to the effects of GHG discharges on climate change when deciding discharge permit applications, except to the extent that renewable energy use or development enables a reduction of GHG discharges 'in absolute terms' or 'relative to ... non-renewable energy' use or development.[14] The statutory amendment was intended to preclude local authorities from considering the 'effects on climate change' of GHG

[12] Ibid. 17. In addition, Van Bohemen also noted that three gas-fired power stations had been granted resource consent in the period 1995–2002 without any obligation to mitigate GHG emissions by planting forest sinks, and that the Minister for the Environment had subsequently agreed to cancel the general mitigation condition included on the grant of resource consent for the Taranaki combined-cycle power station in 1995.

[13] Compare: *Fitzgerald v Muldoon* [1976] 2 NZLR 615 where the executive action of the government based on its policy objectives absent any legislative basis was declared unlawful following judicial review.

[14] RMA, s. 104E; inserted by Resource Management (Energy and Climate Change) Amendment Act 2004, s. 3(b)(ii), available at www.legislation.govt.nz; Derek Nolan (ed.), *Environmental and Resource Management Law* (5th edn, LexisNexis, 2015), ch. 17; Peter Salmon and David Grinlinton (eds), *Environmental Law in New Zealand* (Thomson Reuters, 2015), ch. 15.

discharges.[15] The 2004 RMA amendments also preclude local authorities from preparing regional rules that have regard to the effects of GHG discharges on climate change, while requiring local authorities to have regard to the effects of climate change and the benefits derived from renewable energy development.[16] As a result, the 2004 RMA amendments attempted to confine local authority involvement in climate change to adaptation measures (for example, preparing coastal policies and rules to address the local effects of sea-level rise), while leaving considerable uncertainty about when the benefits derived from renewable energy would be relevant in the context of local authority decision-making. From a constitutional perspective the 2004 RMA amendments represent a seismic shift away from devolved environmental governance.

(2) Litigating the Benefits Derived from Renewable Energy

The interpretation of the 2004 RMA amendments came before the Court of Appeal in *Genesis Power Ltd* v. *Greenpeace New Zealand Inc.*,[17] where the decision to grant resource consent for the development of a coal-fired power station by Mighty River Power at Marsden Point, Northland, was appealed to the Environment Court by Greenpeace, who contended that the local authority should have considered the adverse effects of the proposal on climate change due to the extent that 'the proposal would diminish opportunities to use and develop renewable energy that would have reduced greenhouse gas emissions'.[18]

Mighty River Power successfully applied for strike-out of the appeal, and Greenpeace filed a further appeal in the High Court. The issue was whether section 104E of the RMA was relevant to deciding a resource consent application for energy development fuelled from non-renewable

---

15 Resource Management (Energy and Climate Change) Amendment Act 2004, s. 3(b)(ii), available at www.legislation.govt.nz; Nolan, *Environmental and Resource Management Law*, above n. 14, ch. 17; Salmon and Grinlinton, *Environmental Law in New Zealand*, above n. 14, ch. 15.

16 RMA, ss. 70A, 7(i), (j), inserted by Resource Management (Energy and Climate Change) Amendment Act 2004, ss. 6 and 5(2), respectively, available at www.legislation.govt.nz; Nolan, *Environmental and Resource Management Law*, above n. 14, ch. 17; Salmon and Grinlinton, *Environmental Law in New Zealand*, above n. 14, ch. 15.

17 *Genesis Power Ltd* v. *Greenpeace New Zealand Inc.* [2007] NZCA 569; [2008] 1 NZLR 803; [2008] NZRMA 125.

18 Janette Campbell and Brandon Watts, 'Considering the Effects of Greenhouse Gases on Climate Change' (2008) *Resource Management Journal* (April) 9.

sources. The High Court allowed the appeal, and found that this was a factor that the local authority could take into account, and rejected the proposition that section 104E of the RMA was not relevant when considering the proposed coal-fired power station or generating plant. Effectively, the High Court adopted a comparative approach:

> that permits consent authorities to balance the benefits, in terms of greenhouse gas reduction, of a hypothetical renewable energy project against the actual application concerning a non-renewable energy project.[19]

The decision was appealed to the Court of Appeal by Mighty River Power, but the appeal was abandoned when the company decided that it did not wish to proceed with the proposed Marsden Point power station. However, Genesis applied for a declaration regarding the issue, because it operated the 1,200 MW coal-fired Huntly power station in the Waikato region and wished to develop a gas-fired power station at Rodney, north of Auckland. The Court granted the declaration sought by Genesis regarding section 104E of the RMA, and considered that the response to climate change should 'be organised on a national rather than a regional basis'. In particular, the Court of Appeal found that:

> The effects of GHG emissions are not of a regional character. If regions adopt different standards, this would encourage selective behaviour, with projects being set up in regions which offered the least restrictions and with no net gain to the wider environment to which climate change is relevant. Further, given New Zealand's comparatively low contribution to worldwide GHG emissions and the infinitesimal contribution which any particular project would make, there would be no demonstrable linkage between GHG emissions associated with any particular project and climate change generally.[20]

The Court of Appeal decision in *Genesis* reflects the shift in government policy away from local authority involvement in climate change foreshadowed by the Environment Court in the *Environmental Defence Society* decisions. While the *Genesis* decision highlights the advantages of harmonizing laws to avoid new development being located in regions with less stringent environmental standards, it fails to recognize the economic reality of a small country such as New Zealand where activities are agglomerated in the metropolitan centres of Auckland in the North

---

[19] Ceri Warnock, 'Greenhouse Gases and Climate Change: Relevance to Discharge Permit Application' (2006) 6 *Butterworths Resource Management Bulletin* 191, 192.

[20] *Genesis*, above n. 17, [2008] NZRMA 125, paras [17]–[18].

Island, and Christchurch in the South Island, and their surrounding regions. More importantly, the Court of Appeal departed from the reasoning in the *Environmental Defence Society* decisions which found that arguments regarding the domestic scale of GHG emissions were not relevant in the context of a global environmental issue, and it presaged the current political fear about further Kyoto Protocol commitments prevalent in New Zealand and some other countries (for example, Canada).[21]

(3) *Genesis* in the Supreme Court

Greenpeace appealed the judgment to the Supreme Court, where the Court was divided regarding the intended effect of the 2004 amendments.[22] Chief Justice Elias considered that when read in the context of their legislative history, the amendments required a comparison between renewable and non-renewable energy development, otherwise section 7(j) of the RMA would be rendered neutral and irrelevant.[23] The majority of the bench, however, considered that the effect of GHG discharges on climate change would be relevant only in cases involving renewable energy use or development. Spiro noted that the decision was notable as a result of these 'starkly contrasting approaches', and because the decision highlighted the national response to climate change under the New Zealand ETS.[24] As a result, the majority decision from the Supreme Court further entrenched the policy shift away from dealing with GHG emissions under the RMA.

In the context of the *Genesis* cases, Bollard noted four distinct aspects of the New Zealand climate change debate, namely, the scientific basis, equitable considerations, policy design, and the role of the courts in

---

21 See below n 35 and related paragraph.

22 *Greenpeace New Zealand Inc.* v. *Genesis Power Ltd* [2008] NZSC 112; [2009] 1 NZLR 730; (2008) 15 ELRNZ 15.

23 RMA, s. 7(j) requires decision-makers to have particular regard to 'the benefits to be derived from the use and development of renewable energy', available at www.legislation.govt.nz; Nolan, *Environmental and Resource Management Law*, above n. 14, ch. 17; Salmon and Grinlinton, *Environmental Law in New Zealand*, above n. 14, ch. 15.

24 Matt Spiro, 'Greenpeace New Zealand Incorporated v Genesis Power Ltd' (2010) 8 *Butterworths Resource Management Bulletin* 11, 13; Climate Change Response (Emissions Trading) Amendment Act 2008.

resolving environmental conflict.[25] He drew on previous Environment Court decisions that identified various 'threads' which permeate the RMA, including intergenerational equity, and highlighted both the statutory purpose (sustainable management) in section 5 and the requirement in section 7(i) to have particular regard to the effects of climate change.[26] Bollard also noted the trend towards relying on strategies and regulations under other statutes to provide a national response to climate change rather than relying on policy statements and plans prepared by local authorities under the RMA.[27] He also foresaw a 'potential' increase in climate change litigation before the Environment Court concerning coastal risk management, competition for access to water resources, and the need to grant consent for new energy generation projects.[28]

Interestingly, Bollard indicated that the Court was not distracted by 'the merits of scientific dissent',[29] and in contrast with some Australian decisions the scientific basis for anthropogenic climate change has not been contested in any of the New Zealand cases.[30] However, Bollard's focus on the role of equitable considerations embedded in the RMA definition of sustainable management was no longer compelling and largely redundant at the time of writing as a result of the 2004 RMA amendments and the majority decision of the Supreme Court in *Genesis*. Policy design continued, but the work streams in the Ministry for the Environment during the period 2002–2008 were focused exclusively on development of the New Zealand ETS outside the RMA. Similarly, Bollard's projections about future climate change litigation failed to materialize in the way that he envisaged as the cases that have come before the courts regarding coastal risk management and competition for access to water resources have focused on jurisdictional and procedural issues, rather than any underlying substantive issues.[31] However, the

---

[25] Principal Environment Judge John Bollard 'Climate Change Issues from the Perspective of the Environment Court' (2008) 7 *Butterworths Resource Management Bulletin* 127.

[26] Ibid 127.

[27] Ibid 128.

[28] Ibid 131.

[29] Ibid 127.

[30] Trevor Daya-Winterbottom, 'Climate Change Litigation: The Xtrata Case' (2008) *Environmental Liability* 2; cf. *West Coast ENT Inc.* v. *Buller Coal Ltd* [2013] NZSC 87.

[31] See *Falkner* v. *Gisborne District Council* [1995] NZRMA 462 (HC) regarding whether common law rights to establish sea defences to prevent coastal erosion were overriden by statute law; *Central Plains Water Trust* v. *Ngai Tahu Properties Ltd* [2008] NZRMA (CA) and *Central Plains Water Trust* v. *Synlait*

Court's ongoing work in relation to consenting to new energy generation projects has been dominated by the consideration of contentious (primarily wind and tidal) renewable energy projects.

(4) Fear of Commitment Beyond Kyoto

Grinlinton highlighted the connection between GHG emission reduction targets and the uptake of renewable energy, but he observed that energy policies 'are generally aspirational', such as the 90 per cent target for renewable electricity generation under the New Zealand Energy Strategy.[32] While he considered that 'resource management regulation can be a powerful tool to restrict environmentally damaging forms of energy production', his argument (which relied on section 7(j) of the RMA) has been superseded by the Supreme Court decisions in *Genesis* and *Buller Coal,* which effectively removed GHG discharges from RMA regulation.[33] Grinlinton also noted the strong New Zealand commitment to reducing GHG emissions via the ETS, and the 'flexible target' of reducing emissions by 10–20 per cent below 1990 levels by 2020, which (paradoxically) is, *inter alia*, subject to 'major emitting countries taking action fully commensurate with their capabilities and contributions to global emissions'.[34]

Notwithstanding the concerns about significant increases in GHG emissions above 1990 levels by developing countries (for example, China, India and Brazil),[35] the export of New Zealand coal for burning overseas is not regulated by the New Zealand ETS.[36]

Ltd [2009] NZCA 609; [2010] 2 NZLR 363, regarding the procedural priority for deciding competing resource consent applications for the taking and use of water.

32 *New Zealand Energy Strategy 2012*, available at www.med.govt.nz.

33 Spiro, 'Greenpeace New Zealand Incorporated v Genesis Power Ltd', above n. 24.

34 David Grinlinton 'Achieving Emissions Reduction and Renewable Energy Targets: The Case for 'Feed-in Tariffs'' (2010) 8 *Butterworths Resource Management Bulletin* 68. Subsequently, New Zealand supplemented its 'flexible target' with a more modest 'unconditional target' for emissions reduction of 5 per cent below the 1990 levels by 2020, following the decision (9 November 2012) that New Zealand would not sign up to a second commitment period under the Kyoto Protocol. Both targets continue to apply in tandem.

35 Alison Arthur-Young and Rachel Boyte 'Fear of Commitment? NZ Dumps Kyoto' (2012) 9 *Butterworths Resource Management Bulletin* 188.

36 Warren Bangma 'Case Note: Coal, Climate Change and the Decision of the Supreme Court: West Coast ENT Incorporated v Buller Coal Limited' (2013) 10 *Butterworths Resource Management Bulletin* 94, 97.

IV BURNING COAL OVERSEAS

Subsequently, the consequential effects on climate change from land use activities (coal mining) came before the courts in *Buller Coal Ltd* v. *West Coast ENT Inc.*,[37] in declaratory proceedings regarding the approach to sections 7(i) and 104(1)(a) of the RMA. West Coast ENT contended that the local authority was required to have regard to effects on climate change when deciding the land-use consent application. However, the Environment Court rejected this argument in the light of the 2004 amendments and the previous decisions in the *Genesis* case.[38] In particular, the Environment Court found that the statutory purpose in section 5 of the RMA (sustainable management) was qualified by the 2004 amendments, and that there was no scope to interpret the relevant provisions in line with 'international obligations',[39] which the Court considered would only be relevant either where there was ambiguity in the legislation or some residual discretion left for the decision-maker. The Environment Court was therefore 'not persuaded that there is any discretion concerning interpretation, or any ambiguity or choice'.[40]

Steane noted that section 104E of the RMA was limited to discharge permits and that it did not expressly preclude local authorities from considering any effects on climate change in the context of land-use consent applications. In particular, he noted that:

> The present case may not have arisen had s 104E applied to all types of resource consent applications, particularly given the Supreme Court's decision in *Genesis* on the correct interpretation of s 104E.[41]

In addition, Steane observed that the Australian courts have found that effects on climate change could appropriately be considered in relation to land-use consent applications, and that consent conditions could validly be included in the grant of consent, for example, to offset GHG emissions from the coal-mining activity.[42] However, he noted that such

---

[37] *Buller Coal Ltd* v. *West Coast ENT Inc.* [2012] NZEnvC 40.

[38] *Greenpeace New Zealand Inc.* v. *Northland Regional Council* (A95/2006, unreported NZEnvC); *Greenpeace New Zealand Inc.* v. *Genesis Power Ltd*, above n. 22.

[39] *Buller Coal Ltd* [2012] NZEnvC 40, paras [49] and [37].

[40] Ibid. [38].

[41] Edward Steane 'Climate Change and Coal: Scope for Further Clarity' (2012) 9 *Butterworths Resource Management Bulletin* 145, 146–7.

[42] *Hunter Environmental Lobby Inc.* v. *Minister for Planning* [2011] NSWLEC 221; Judge Craig Thompson 'Case Note: Hunter Environmental

conditions had not ultimately been imposed in Australia due to the introduction of ETS legislation. In New Zealand, the Environment Court had expressed some disquiet about imposing similar conditions in the *Environmental Defence Society* cases, due to the government's policy preference for a national approach to GHG emissions, and while GHG discharges from the combustion of coal exported overseas would not be subject to the New Zealand ETS, drafting valid consent conditions to deal with such circumstances would be 'challenging' and might in practice be impossible.[43]

West Coast ENT appealed the Environment Court decision in *Buller Coal* to the High Court. Similar to its position before the Environment Court, West Coast ENT contended that section 104(1)(a) of the RMA does not contain any express or implied prohibition in a land-use consent context that would preclude the local authority from considering any effects on climate change from burning coal extracted from the mine; and that such matters were not addressed either by the 2004 amendments or by the Supreme Court decision in *Genesis*. These arguments were rejected by the High Court, which found that the 2004 amendments implied that any effects on climate change from GHG discharges should be addressed nationally, unless the position under the RMA had been altered by the promulgation of a national environmental standard (NES).[44] In particular, the High Court found that the RMA does not have extra-territorial effect beyond the 12 nm limits of the territorial sea, and that there was accordingly no jurisdiction under the statute to regulate the effects on climate change of burning New Zealand coal overseas. For example, Whata J observed that:

> One leviathan of environmental law [i.e., the RMA] is more than enough for lawyers, experts, environmental managers, planners, local authorities and the courts of this country. The prospect of a district council assessing whether an end use of coal … is subject to sustainable environmental policy … in Cambodia … China, in Japan or Brazil, Zimbabwe or Kenya … is palpably unattractive.[45]

Lobby Inc v Minister for Planning [2011] NSWLEC 221' (2012) 9 *Butterworths Resource Management Bulletin* 115; Daya-Winterbottom, 'Climate Change Litigation: The Xtrata Case', above n. 30.

43 Steane, 'Climate Change and Coal', above n. 41, at 147.

44 RMA, ss. 43–44A, available at www.legislation.govt.nz; Nolan, *Environmental and Resource Management Law*, above n. 14, ch. 17; Salmon and Grinlinton, *Environmental Law in New Zealand*, above n. 14, ch. 15.

45 *Royal Forest and Bird Protection Society of New Zealand Inc.* v. *Buller Coal Ltd* [2012] NZHC 2156, para. [53].

Leave was granted for appeal to the Court of Appeal, and leave was later granted for the appeal to be heard by the Supreme Court directly, thus leapfrogging the Court of Appeal.[46]

Chief Justice Elias delivered a minority judgment which concluded that GHG effects on climate change were not excluded from consideration under section 104(1)(a) of the RMA, and that interpreting in such a conclusion would be justified under the rules of statutory interpretation only where some ambiguity had been found regarding the meaning of the provision (which was not the case).[47] She also found that section 104E of the RMA pertaining to discharge permits was 'not directly relevant',[48] and that there was no relevant NES which permitted 'effects on climate change from the combustion of coal'.[49] As a result, Elias CJ held that both the adverse and positive effects of the proposed activity should be considered when the application was assessed under section 5 of the RMA.[50] However, the majority in the Supreme Court held that there was no 'overarching logic' to the literal interpretation of section 104(1)(a) of the RMA,[51] and that the approach taken by West Coast ENT would allow GHG effects on climate change to be taken into account in the context of land-use consent applications, whereas they could not be considered in the context of any related discharge consent application by virtue of section 104E of the RMA.[52] They also found that the consideration of any effects on climate change from burning New Zealand-mined coal overseas would give rise to difficult issues 'with assessing effects offshore'.[53] Overall, the majority found that precluding local authorities from considering GHG effects on climate change when deciding any resource consent applications:

> seems to us to be justified as a matter of necessary implication, essentially on the basis that, when the amended RMA is looked at as a whole, the limitation is so obvious that it goes without saying.[54]

---

[46] *West Coast ENT Inc.* v. *Buller Coal Ltd* [2013] NZSC 87, para. [112].
[47] Ibid. para. [24].
[48] Ibid. para. [70].
[49] Ibid. para. [73].
[50] Ibid. para. [77].
[51] Ibid. paras [151]–[153].
[52] Ibid. para. [157].
[53] Bangma, 'Case Note: Coal, Climate Change and the Decision of the Supreme Court', above n. 36, at 96.
[54] *Buller Coal*, above n. 46, [2013] NZSC 87, para. [173].

Rive noted that the Supreme Court decision in *Buller Coal* 'affirms the proposition' that the 2004 amendments prohibit local authority consideration of the effects of GHG discharges on climate change under the RMA, notwithstanding 'a considered and well-analysed dissenting opinion by the Chief Justice'.[55] He found that, effectively, GHG discharges are regulated nationally via the New Zealand ETS,[56] and the NES for Air Quality 2004 that regulates methane discharges from landfills.[57] This pragmatic result was not surprising, and was foreshadowed by the specialist decisions from the Environment Court in the *Environmental Defence Society* cases.[58]

The *Buller Coal* decisions reveal a deep-seated tension between the 2004 RMA amendments which (despite the political intent to remove GHG emissions completely from all local authority jurisdiction) focused exclusively in terms of their statutory drafting on removing the ability of regional councils to include rules in their regional plans governing GHG emissions or to include conditions on the grant of discharge permits controlling GHG emissions, and the resulting lacuna in the wording of the statutory amendments that do not include any express reference to territorial authorities or their ability to include rules in their district plans or include conditions on the grant of land-use consents. Both the Environment Court and the High Court (for different reasons) recoiled from identifying this lacuna and the potential need for further RMA amendments to complete the government's objective of removing GHG emissions from all local authority control. The reasoning of the Environment Court appears thin and unconvincing when considered against the common law canons of statutory interpretation,[59] whereas the High Court's jurisdictional focus on the limits of the territorial sea was not relevant when considering the jurisdiction of territorial authorities (whose jurisdiction does not extend beyond the mean high water springs of the

---

[55] Vernon Rive, 'A Climate Law Year in Review' (2013) 10 *Butterworths Resource Management Bulletin* 87.

[56] Climate Change Response Act 2002, available at www.legislation.govt.nz; Nolan, *Environmental and Resource Management Law*, above n. 14, ch. 17; Salmon and Grinlinton, *Environmental Law in New Zealand*, above n. 14, ch. 15.

[57] Resource Management (National Environmental Standards for Air Quality) Regulations 2004, available at www.legislation.govt.nz; Nolan, *Environmental and Resource Management Law*, above n. 14, ch. 17; Salmon and Grinlinton, *Environmental Law in New Zealand*, above n. 14, ch. 15.

[58] Trevor Daya-Winterbottom 'The Legitimacy of Climate Change Litigation: *Buller Coal* in the Supreme Court' (2014) 5 *IUCNAEL EJournal* 238.

[59] See Ross Carter, *Burrows and Carter Statute Law in New Zealand* (5th edn, LexisNexis, 2015), generally and pp. 512–18.

sea).[60] Overall, each of the decisions from the Environment Court, the High Court, and ultimately from the majority in the Supreme Court exhibit considerable political deference regarding the regulation of GHG emissions. Beyond that, the enforcement machinery in the RMA regarding compliance with consent conditions is devolved exclusively to local authorities, which as noted by Steane, will result in some practical difficulties with overseas enforcement in the absence of any national enforcement authority under the statute.

V GEOTHERMAL AND WIND ENERGY

Grinlinton drew attention to the public interest debate regarding landscape protection and wind energy development. He noted the rapid increase in the number of wind farms consented to in New Zealand since 2004, and the apparent bias in some Environment Court decisions where the benefits of renewable energy were given added weight.[61] For example, in *Genesis Power Ltd* v. *Franklin District Council*, regarding a 19-turbine wind farm located on the Awhitu Peninsula, south of Auckland, the Court found that:

> Notwithstanding the effects on the coastal environment we consider the proposal to be appropriate … We find that the benefits of the proposal, when seen in the national context, outweigh site-specific effects, and the effects on the local surrounding area.[62]

However, when allowing wind farm proposals in Hawke's Bay, the Court introduced a note of caution, and stated that renewable energy projects would not 'always be favoured in the balancing exercise', and that there may be locations where other factors (for example, iconic landscapes or the proximity to more densely populated areas) could result in a different

---

[60] RMA, s. 2(1), available at www.legislation.govt.nz; Nolan, *Environmental and Resource Management Law*, above n. 14, ch. 17; Salmon and Grinlinton, *Environmental Law in New Zealand*, above n. 14, ch. 15.

[61] David Grinlinton 'Property Rights, the "Public Interest" and Global Considerations: The Case of Wind Energy Development' (2008) 7 *Butterworths Resource Management Bulletin* 62, 64; *Meridian Energy Ltd* v. *Wellington City Council* (W31/07).

[62] *Genesis Power Ltd v Franklin District Council* [2005] NZRMA 541, para. [230].

outcome.[63] Subsequently, when considering an extension to an existing wind farm at Hastings on the east coast of the North Island, the Court found that adverse effects on amenity values (natural ridgelines) and Maori cultural and spiritual values outweighed the renewable energy benefits of the proposed activity, and stated that:

> Important as the issues of climate change and the use of renewable sources of energy unquestionably are, they cannot dominate all other values. The adverse effects of the proposal on what is undoubtedly an outstanding landscape, and its adverse effects on the relationship of Maori with both this land and the values it has for them, clearly brings us to the conclusion that the tipping point in favour of other values has been reached.[64]

Grinlinton considered that these decisions under-emphasized the cumulative effects of wind farms on outstanding landscapes, and suggested that a more principled approach to resolving environmental conflict between harnessing the benefits of renewable energy to reduce GHG effects on climate change and addressing the adverse effects of such development on outstanding landscapes could be achieved by preparing a national policy statement (NPS) to identify 'optimal wind generation areas' where such development would be acceptable.[65] However, this approach was not adopted. For example, the NPS for renewable electricity generation acknowledges that power stations will need to be developed in close proximity to renewable energy resources, encourages local authorities to have regard to 'offsetting measures and environmental compensation' where adverse effects cannot be avoided, and requires local authorities to include rules in plans regarding site identification and assessment, but does not require areas to be zoned for wind energy development.[66]

Subsequently the Environment Court adopted a more principled approach in *Maniototo Environmental Society Inc.* v. *Central Otago*

---

[63] *Unison Networks Ltd* v. *Hastings District Council* (W58/06); Kenneth Palmer 'Case Note: Unison Networks Ltd v Hastings District Council' (2008) 7 *Butterworths Resource Management Bulletin* 111.

[64] *Oustanding Landscape Protection Society Inc.* v. *Hastings District Council* (W24/07), para. [116].

[65] Grinlinton, 'Property Rights, the "Public Interest" and Global Considerations', above n. 61, at 65–6.

[66] National Policy Statement for Renewable Electricity Generation 2011, Policies E1–E4 and G, available at www.mfe.govt.nz; Nolan, *Environmental and Resource Management Law*, above n. 14, ch. 17; Salmon and Grinlinton, *Environmental Law in New Zealand*, above n. 14, ch. 15.

District Council,[67] where the Court refused resource consent for a 176-turbine wind farm at Lammermoor in the South Island. While the Court acknowledged the renewable energy benefits of the proposed activity, it was concerned about the potentially adverse effects of the activity on the surrounding outstanding landscape area. As a result, the Court found that a comprehensive cost-benefit analysis was required based on section 7(b) of the RMA, which obliges decision-makers to have regard to the efficient use and development of natural and physical resources. In particular, the decision required Meridian Energy to quantify the benefits and costs of the proposal, and to provide a comparative analysis of alternative methods and locations for securing the benefits that could be derived from the activity. This was partly influenced by the Court's finding that there were a number of wind energy projects under active consideration that could satisfy future energy needs over the next ten-plus years. However, Hassan and McIndoe criticized the decision on the basis that it was outside the Court's appeal jurisdiction regarding resource consent applications to require such a wide-ranging assessment, and because it would impose significant compliance costs on applicants. They also considered that the decision could establish an undesirable precedent for other infrastructure projects, and result in the process of gaining consent for notified infrastructure projects becoming more contentious through the intervention of other infrastructure providers joining the proceedings via the submission process (arguably) to advance trade competition arguments which the RMA generally seeks to prohibit. For example, Hassan and McIndoe considered that applicants:

> would be expected to demonstrate not only that the project represents the most efficient use that could be made of the resources, but that this benefit is greater than could be achieved by any other provider using a different set of resources.[68]

Meridian Energy appealed the decision to the High Court on questions of law – challenging, in particular, the Environment Court's requirement for a comprehensive cost-benefit analysis. After considering the statutory scheme of the RMA, the High Court found that this approach was not

---

[67] *Maniototo Environmental Society Inc.* v. *Central Otago District Council* (C103/09).

[68] John Hassan and Nicky McIndoe 'Project Hayes: Sand in the Gearbox for Consenting Infrastructure?' (2010) 8 *Butterworths Resource Management Bulletin* 108, 109.

justified in the context of resource consent applications and that, effectively, by implicitly asserting a role for the local authority or the Environment Court on appeal in deciding what may be the best use of resources, adopted a planning function beyond the scope of the RMA.[69] In addition, Rive noted that perversely the Environment Court decision 'would arguably have imposed a more stringent obligation on resource consent applicants concerning alternatives than currently exists for major public works under the designations regime of the RMA'.[70] Notwithstanding the High Court decision, Meridian Energy later announced on 20 January 2012 that it would not be proceeding with the project for commercial reasons.

Schofield examined geothermal and wind energy development and found that notwithstanding environment constraints geothermal energy development has maintained accelerated growth since 1998 with new geothermal power stations (with a combined capacity of 650 MW) being developed in the Waikato region at Nga Awa Purua, Ngatamariki, Te Huka and Tauhara.[71] In particular, Heffernan observed that commissioning the Ngatamariki power station in 2013 increased the geothermal electricity generation of Mighty River Power to 40 per cent of the company's output, and increased its overall generation from renewable sources to 90 per cent of its output. He also noted that geothermal energy provided 'steady base-load supply'.[72] Similarly, Schofield found that while wind energy proposals are frequently scaled back during the resource consent process, few developments are refused consent, and that in addition to 600 MW of installed wind energy development a further 3,000 MW has been consented or proposed but not yet constructed.[73]

The wind energy appeals are the antithesis of the climate change litigation envisaged by Bollard. In contrast, these cases were concerned with the actual or potential effects of wind energy projects on amenity values and outstanding natural landscapes. They have also resulted in divergent commentary. For example, Hassan and McIndoe focused on the resulting compliance costs for electricity generators arising from the

---

[69] *Meridian Energy Ltd* v. *Central Otago District Council* (HC Dunedin CIV 2009 412 980, 16 August 2010), para. [120].

[70] Vernon Rive 'Second Wind: Project Hayes in the High Court' (2010) 8 *Butterworths Resource Management Bulletin* 153, 157.

[71] Simon Schofield 'Geothermal and Wind Energy in New Zealand' (2013) 17 *New Zealand Journal of Environmental Law* 162.

[72] Doug Heffernan, *Mighty River Power* (Macquarie Conference, 2014).

[73] Schofield , 'Geothermal and Wind Energy in New Zealand', above n. 71, at 175 and 192.

appeal process, whereas Schofield offers a more neutral view and indicates that in practice few wind energy projects are refused resource consent and that significant electricity generation capacity has been expressly allowed under the RMA from this source. In addition, the direct commentary from Meridian Energy regarding Project Hayes indicates that compliance costs were not the underlying reason why the project did not ultimately proceed. Schofield's comparative analysis of wind and geothermal energy projects also highlights a significant difference in the public perception about different forms of renewable energy, and indicates that visual effects associated with wind energy projects may be of more concern to people and communities than the subterranean effects associated with geothermal energy development (for example, fluid re-injection and subsidence).

VI TIDAL ENERGY

While the Environment Court adopted a precautionary approach in *Crest Energy Kaipara Ltd* v. *Northland Regional Council*[74] regarding the proposal by Crest Energy to harness tidal energy from 200 marine turbines located in the Kaipara Harbour, it did not require comprehensive cost-benefit analysis of the proposed activity. Instead, the Court focused on the adaptive management regime proposed by Crest Energy for the staged development of the tidal energy project and the need to ensure that a robust environmental management plan would be in place under the consent conditions. In particular, the adaptive management regime required 'robust' baseline monitoring followed by regular periodic monitoring to ensure that the environmental effects of the tidal energy project would be within the parameters envisaged by the application before proceeding with subsequent stages of the project. For example, the Court was concerned about the effects on commercial fisheries, potential noise effects on marine fauna, effects on endangered marine mammals (Maui's dolphins), and effects on Maori cultural issues. As a result, the Court issued an interim decision to allow further evidence to be prepared on these matters, and for consultation with the parties to the appeals and expert witness conferencing. Overall, the Court was persuaded about the economic efficiency of the project and its renewable energy benefits under sections 7(b) and (j) of the RMA. For example, Bain observed that:

---

[74] *Crest Energy Kaipara Ltd* v. *Northland Regional Council* (A132/09).

> The Court … made positive findings under s 7(b) … and 7(j) of the RMA. With respect to economic efficiency, the Court concluded that the benefits to be obtained from the proposal were clear, and the production of electricity by harnessing the tidal flows of the Kaipara was a particularly efficient use of tidal energy … In addition, the proposal would assist in avoiding power shortages in Northland, minimising transmission losses by locating the plant close to energy demand, and reducing carbon emissions.[75]

Subsequently, the Court granted consent for the proposed tidal energy project. The final decision held that a three-year monitoring period would be sufficient for the first stage of the project, and that it was appropriate to require that Crest Energy should demonstrate that the environmental effects of the project were 'less than minor' before proceeding to implement stage two, while a less onerous standard was imposed for subsequent monitoring, whereby Crest Energy must demonstrate that environmental effects continue to be 'no more than minor' before proceeding with further stages. Initially, three turbines were approved for stage one. Subject to satisfactory monitoring, the proposed 200 turbines could, cumulatively, be installed by stage five. This approach to consenting by the Court led Wright to comment that:

> With growing interest in wave and tidal energy projects in New Zealand, the question of how such novel resource consent applications are likely to be dealt with by the Environment Court will become an issue of importance for this fledgling industry. In this regard, the Crest Energy case provides an optimistic indication of the willingness of the Court to facilitate the granting of consents for marine energy projects and some insights for marine energy companies into how best to approach the resource consent process.[76]

The complex issues related to the Crest Energy tidal energy project indicate the need for a more structured marine spatial planning approach to assist with identifying suitable locations for new tidal energy projects. But despite the long debate about oceans policy (2001–2007) and the subsequent enactment of the Exclusive Economic Zone and Continental Shelf (Assessment of Effects) Act 2012, marine spatial planning in New Zealand remains embryonic, with the first non-statutory marine spatial

---

[75] Jo Bain, 'Case Notes: Crest Energy Kaipara Ltd v Northland Regional Council' (2010) 8 *Butterworths Resource Management Bulletin* 123.

[76] Glen Wright, 'Crest Energy's Tidal Power Project Decision in Environment Court Leads Way for Marine Energy Projects' (2011) 9 *Butterworths Resource Management Bulletin* 66, 69.

plan currently being prepared for the Hauraki Gulf, offshore from the Auckland-Waikato coast.[77]

VII CONCLUSIONS

New Zealand has mature sources of hydro energy and geothermal energy, and emerging sources of wind and tidal energy that provide for the majority of the country's electricity generation needs.

Notwithstanding this focus on renewable energy, New Zealand has found it difficult to develop a coherent environmental policy regarding renewable energy or climate change. As a result, the courts have played a significant role in developing current policy via a series of decisions about the legality and enforceability of consent conditions requiring the planting of forest sinks and the interpretation of legislation seeking to remove climate change governance from local authority responsibility. The *Genesis* and *Buller Coal* decisions are remarkable due to their deference to government policy, pragmatic approach to statutory interpretation, and constitutional shift away from devolved environmental governance. Effectively, climate change litigation is unlikely to be tenable in New Zealand as a result of these decisions.

In contrast, the courts have successfully mediated apparently intractable conflicts between proposed wind energy projects and protecting outstanding natural landscapes, and have developed a robust approach to adaptive management that have allowed novel tidal energy projects to proceed. These substantive decisions are likely to assist in achieving the aspirational goal of generating 90 per cent of electricity supply from renewable sources.

---

[77] *Sea Change – Tai Timu Tai Pari, Hauraki Gulf Marine Spatial Plan*, available at www.seachange.org.nz.

10. A reflection on some legal aspects of decision control in the energy transition process: a comparison of France and Germany

Anaïs Guerry*

I 'ENERGY TRANSITION': THE TERM AND THE MEANINGS

In 2015, in France and Germany at least it is exceptional to go a single day without seeing or hearing those words: 'energy transition', '*Energiewende*', '*transition énergétique*'. They form part of what we might call the 'cultural *Zeitgeist*', reflecting the spirit of our time.[1] This expression is indeed ubiquitous, in newspapers, in universities, in political institutions… But, even though these words are often used, their meaning isn't unambiguous. To what exactly does this phrase refer? Sometimes the idea of 'energy transition' is associated with other expressions such as 'industrial revolution' or 'political reform'. At other times, it designates local initiatives, or it might even be used as the justification for the creation of new energy services and business models, etc. Moreover, 'energy transition' can also either reflect a moral imperative to save the planet for the sake of hypothetical future generations, or designate a rational and pragmatic response to both the current economic crisis and climate change. In short: this term is laden with many meanings.

* Anaïs Guerry is PhD Candidate at the Sciences Po Law School in Paris. Her research in law on the energy transition phenomenon is financed by the French Agency of Environment and Energy Management (ADEME), the Institute for Sustainable Development and International Relations (Iddri) and Energy Cities.

[1] The word 'transition' was chosen to be the word which most reflected '*l'air du temps*' (the feeling/spirit of the time) for the year 2014 in France, on the occasion of the Tenth Festival du mot (see www.motdelannee.fr/mot2014.pdf).

In order to clarify the different ideas collected under this umbrella term, this chapter recognizes two connotations. The first sense of 'energy transition' refers to a broad governmental strategy, which aims to transform one system of energy production and consumption into a more sustainable one. The *Energiewende* enacted by the German government in 2011 is one of the first examples of this. The second sense refers to a general cultural change, which aims to harmonize the link between man and nature, between individuals and their environment, and also the role, rights and responsibilities of citizens in a democratic legal system. Focusing on this second interpretation, this chapter will present two strategic fields, electricity distribution networks and renewable energy cooperatives, where members of civil society have used legal tools in order to influence local energy policy in Germany and in France.

II ENERGY TRANSITION AS A GOVERNMENTAL ENERGY POLICY: GERMAN ENERGIEWENDE AND FRENCH 'TRANSITION ÉNERGÉTIQUE'

(1) German 'Energiewende'

The roots of the German expression '*Energiewende*' are to be found in the United States, in one of the numerous books published by the famous American alternative energy activist, Amaury Lovins. In his book, *Soft Energy Paths: Toward a Durable Peace*,[2] published in 1977, he developed the concept of soft energy paths, which laid down for the first time the idea that renewable energies and energy efficiency could replace fossil fuels. Two years' later, attempting to transfer Lovins' idea to Germany, three members of the Öko-Institut wrote a book called *Energie-Wende – Wachstum und Wohlstand ohne Erdöl und Uran*.[3] According to one of the authors, Hartmut Bossel, the aim of this new word coining was to provoke the economists of the academic world, for whom the link between energy consumption and growth was a systematic connection.[4] Since the early 1980s, the expression '*Energiewende*' had

---

[2] Amaury Lovins, *Soft Energy Paths: Toward a Durable Peace* (Friends of the Earth International, 1977).

[3] Florentin Krause, Hartmut Bossel and Karl-Friedrich Müller-Reißmann, *Energiewende – Wachstum und Wohlstand ohne Erdöl und Uran* (Öko-Institut, 1980).

[4] 'The Energiewende', *ZeitOnline Wissen*, p. 3, available at www.zeit.de/2012/47/Energiewende-Deutsche-Begriffe-Englisch.

been much-used by anti-nuclear activists and pro-environmental associations.[5] But, it became known to a wider audience, in large part due to a conference held by the former Minister of Environment, Jürgen Trittin, in 2002.[6] On this occasion, the famous leader of the German political party the Greens, stated the need to formulate a responsible energy strategy which would be acceptable to citizens and would be based on renewable energies, energy savings and on the abandonment of nuclear power. On this occasion, '*Energiewende*' was endowed with an additional meaning, as the name of a certain type of national energy strategy.

The Fukushima catastrophe did not really open the debate in Germany but did cause the government to change the direction and subsequently the name of its energy strategy. In fact, the first legislative measure[7] in favour of renewable energies was introduced, not by the government, but by a parliamentarian[8] during the administration of Kohl's Liberal-Christian coalition in 1990. This measure was enacted and was later challenged before the European Court of Justice in a well-known case of the ECJ: *PreussenElektra*.[9] In March 2000, Schröder's government, which was composed of the Socialists and the Greens, with Jürgen Trittin as Minister in charge of the environment, introduced the famous Renewable Energy Act (Gesetz für den Vorrang Erneuerbarer Energien)[10] into the German legal system. This Act gave priority in electricity distribution networks to energy generated by renewable sources. In June 2000, the government made an agreement with German energy companies (*der Atomkonsens*) according to which they decided to phase out nuclear power by 2022. In September 2010, Angela Merkel developed a new energy strategy (*Gesamtstrategie*) to be achieved by 2050, known under the name of *Energiekonzept*. This strategy set several quantitative political objectives for Germany: the reduction of greenhouse gas emissions by 80 per cent (using 1990 as a base year), the reduction of energy

---

5 Ibid.

6 Lena Kayser, *Energiegenossenschaften ein Bürgerbeteiligungsmodell zur Bürgerbeteiligungsmodell zur Umsetzung der Energiewende? Möglichkeiten und Grenzen einer Möglichkeiten und Grenzen einer politischen Beteiligung*, KNI Working Paper 01/2014, p. 7.

7 Gesetz über die Einspeisung von Strom aus erneuerbaren Energien in das öffentliche Netz (Stromeinspeisungsgesetz), 7 December 1990, BGBl I No. 67, 14 December 1990, S. 2633–43.

8 Falk Illing, *Energiepolitik in Deutschland, Die Energiepolitischen Maßnahmen der Bundesregierung 1949–2013* (Nomos, 2012), p. 160.

9 C-379/98 *PreussenElektra AG*, ECJ, 13 March 2001.

10 Gesetz für den Vorrang Erneuerbarer Energien, BGBl I, 13 March 2000, S.305–9.

consumption by 50 per cent; and a 60 per cent increase in the share of renewable energies in gross final energy consumption.[11] In 2010, it was controversially decided to extend the deadline for the closing down of the country's nuclear power plants. In March 2011, the tragic events in Fukushima had a huge impact. Though as previously stated, the Fukushima catastrophe did not cause a huge debate in Germany about the existing energy transition strategy, it did cause the government to reconsider the risks of nuclear energy, later leading it to order the closing down of Germany's seven oldest reactors and set down in law a final phase-out of nuclear power by 2022. The name of the Germany energy strategy was also altered. It had been called *Energiekonzept* but was re-christened as *Energiewende*.

(2) French 'Transition Énergétique'

The French term '*transition énergétique*' may have been introduced into the French language as a translation of the German expression '*Energiewende*'. The first instance that the author has been able to find it is an article in the French press dating back to 2002, which reported on an international meeting organized by the collectivités territoriales (communes, départements, régions) in Strasbourg for the protection of the planet.[12] It is noticeable that the French speak about '*transition énergétique*' to designate their own national energy policy but they translate the German '*Energiewende*' as '*tournant énergétique allemand*' (the German energy turnaround). Indeed, the verb '*wenden*' means '*tourner*' (to turn). However, the German expression '*die Wende*' also has a special historical meaning,[13] as it refers to the fall of the Berlin Wall in 1989. As a result '*Wende*' tends to designate a process that might also be called a 'democratic transition' or an 'economic transition' towards a liberal economic system. To that extent, '*wenden*' is close to the Latin-rooted word '*transiter*' (*trans-ire*, to go beyond), the idea of going into another world, of changing from one model to another. But the idea of change signified by the French word '*transition*' seems to be weaker than that implied by '*Wende*', as '*transition*' also designates a progressive process, whereas '*Wende*' undertakes the meaning of a dramatic structural change.

---

11 Andreas Rüdinger and Noémie Poize, *Projets citoyens pour la production d'énergie renouvelable: une comparaison franco-allemande*, Working Paper 1/2014 (Iddri, 2014).

12 'Les collectivités locales et les entreprises se mobilisent dans la lutte contre le réchauffement de la planète!', *News Press*, 1 October 2002.

13 'The Energiewende', above n. 4.

So perhaps we could translate '*Energiewende*' as 'energy revolution', '*une révolution énergétique*'. With France's history, those words would undertake another dimension of change. But 'revolution' is also a term used in the economical field to designate certain paradigmatic changes, that is, 'industrial revolution'. In the field of energy economics, this expression is actually used, for example, by Jeremy Rifkin, for whom the energy transition represents the third industrial revolution. Nevertheless, in official French speeches several definitions have been given to the expression '*transition énergétique*': 'a profound change in our model of energy production and consumption, based on energy savings, energy efficiency, and the development of renewables energies'[14] or 'a complex expression, which means changing from a situation where we have no choice to an improved one, where we have the means, the opportunities and the political will to act collectively in a clear framework'.[15] However, there is confusion in France between '*transition écologique*' and '*transition énergétique*', so that the French Ministry of Ecology, Sustainable Development and Energy (MESDE) states: 'energy transition is one of the constituent parts of the ecological transition'. It means 'passing from a society based on a heavy consumption of fossil energies to a society which consumes less energy and emits less carbon [dioxide]'.[16]

Contrary to Germany, in France the Fukushima catastrophe sparked a new public debate on domestic energy policy, particularly one year later in 2012 on the occasion of the presidential campaign. As a presidential

---

[14] 'C'est un changement profond de nos modes de consommation et de production d'énergie. Elle sera fondée sur la sobriété, l'efficacité énergétique, ainsi que sur le développement des énergies renouvelables'. See City of Lyon official website for the National Debate on the Energy Transition, www.grandlyon.com/Transition-energetique.5655.0.html.

[15] '[M]ot un peu complexe – qui veut simplement dire que nous allons passer d'une situation telle que nous la subissons, à une meilleure situation parce que nous en avons les moyens, les opportunités et surtout la volonté collective d'agir ensemble avec un cadre clair'. Ségolène Royal, press conference, presentation of the Bill, 18 June 2014, available at www.developpement-durable.gouv.fr/Discours-Segolene-Royal-presente.html.

[16] 'La transition énergétique constitue l'une des composantes de la transition écologique. Elle traduit le passage d'une société fondée sur la consommation abondante d'énergies fossiles à une société plus sobre en énergie et faiblement carbonée. Un tel changement de modèle énergétique suppose de travailler à la fois sur les économies d'énergie et sur l'évolution du mix énergétique, avec une part accrue des énergies renouvelables'. See Ministry of Ecology, Sustainable Development and Energy, www.developpement-durable.gouv.fr/Qu-est-ce-que-la-transition.html.

candidate at that time, François Hollande undertook during his electoral campaign to reduce the proportion of electricity derived from nuclear power stations, as a share of the total amount of electricity produced, from 75 to 50 per cent by 2025. After his election, at the Environmental Conference of September 2012 Hollande announced the organization of a national debate on French energy policy. Between November 2012 and July 2013 there was a national debate on energy transition across the whole of France, which was organized in an innovative and participative manner. Indeed, a National Council of the Energy Transition Debate (Conseil National du débat de la transition énergétique) was created, specifically for this purpose, to be a forum where energy policy could be discussed. A monitoring committee (Comité de pilotage) was charged with making sure that the debate ran smoothly; it was composed of seven people responsible for facilitating dialogue between the participants. Eight commissions were requested to submit reports to the National Council of the Energy Transition Debate on different aspects of the energy transition, such as governance, energy efficiency, financing, competitiveness, job creation, etc.

In August 2013, a consultation commission called the National Council of the Ecological Transition (Conseil National de la Transition Ecologique) was created. Within the National Council of the Ecological Transition itself, a special taskforce was created to prepare the French energy transition Act. At the end of July 2014, Ségolène Royal submitted this Bill to the Assemblée Nationale. After several amendments, the Assemblée Nationale approved the Bill (14 October 2014) and submitted it to the Sénat (the Upper House of the French Parliament, which represents the collectivités territoriales) in accordance with the French legislative procedure. The Sénat passed its own version of the Bill on 3 March 2015.[17] It made several substantial amendments, particularly concerning the political objectives of the French energy policy contained in articles 1 and 2 of the Bill. Following the French procedural law, a joint committee (Commission paritaire mixte) comprising seven members from the Sénat and seven from the Assemblée Nationale, took place on 10 March 2015 in order to find a compromise between the legislative chambers. As no compromise arose from the meeting, the Bill was discussed a second time in the Assemblée Nationale and the Sénat, the Assemblée Nationale having the last word.

---

[17] 'Le Sénat adopte une loi de transition énergétique renucléarisée', *Le Monde*, 3 March 2015, available at www.lemonde.fr/planete/article/2015/03/03/le-senat-adopte-une-loi-de-transition-energetique-renuclearisee_4586720_3244.html.

Finally adopted by the Assemblée Nationale on 23 July 2015, the Bill was referred directly to the Conseil Constitutionnel (r) by 60 Senators and Deputies.[18] They particularly asked the Conseil Constitutionnel to review the compatibility between the objectives of the law and the fundamental rights of property and free enterprise. On 13 August 2015, the Conseil Constitutionnel rendered its decision,[19] which declared that the objective of reduction of electricity coming from nuclear sources in the energy mix is compatible with the fundamental rights of property and freedom of enterprise. Finally, the Act was promulgated on 17 August and officially published on 18 August 2015.[20]

The Act on the energy transition is defining a new French energy strategy by setting new additional political quantitative objectives.[21] In addition to the previous undertakings of the French government,[22] and the European Union's binding objectives with regard to renewables (energy from renewable sources must form 23 per cent of gross final energy consumption by 2020),[23] the current Bill[24] fixes five quantitative objectives for French energy policy:

- A 40 per cent reduction in greenhouse gas (GHG) emissions by the year 2030 (with 1990 as the base year) and a 75 per cent reduction by the year 2050.
- A 50 per cent reduction in gross energy consumption by the year 2050 (using 2012 as the base year) with an intermediate objective of 20 per cent by the year 2030.
- A 30 per cent reduction of primary energy consumption derived from fossil fuels by the year 2030 (using 2012 as the base year).
- The proportion of France's total electricity production deriving

---

[18] French Constitution, art. 61.

[19] Conseil Constitutionnel, Decision 2015-718, 13 August 2015.

[20] Loi no. 2015-992 du 17 août 2015 relative à la transition énergétique pour la croissance verte.

[21] I use the term 'political objectives' because, although they are stated in a Bill, which may become Law, the actual binding effect of these targets is uncertain.

[22] See the French Energy Policy Guidance Programme adopted in 2005 (*loi POPE*).

[23] Directive (EC) 2009/28 on the promotion of the use of energy from renewable sources [2009] OJ L140/16, Annex I.

[24] As approved by the Assemblée Nationale on 14 October 2014 and submitted to the Sénat by the Prime Minister for the first reading.

from nuclear energy to be reduced by 25 per cent by 2025 (this target has since been removed by the Sénat).[25]

- The proportion of total energy consumption deriving from renewable energies to increase to 23 per cent by 2020 and 32 per cent by 2030. In 2030, 40 per cent of the national electricity production must come from renewable energies, as well as 38 per cent of the final national heat consumption, 15 per cent of the fuels consumption and 10 per cent of the gas consumption.

The French expression '*transition énergétique*' with the sense of energy policy refers to this Act.

(3) 'Energy Transition' as a Cultural Change

The main hypothesis of this chapter is to distinguish a first meaning of the expression 'energy transition' as a governmental strategy from a second meaning, which refers to a broader cultural change. Indeed, 'energy transition' is often associated with other expressions such as 'paradigm shift' or 'global change'[26] in the scientific view of the world. This is expressed by the terms 'profound change' or 'passage from one situation to another' in the French definition of '*transition énergétique*' presented above. This idea corresponds to the recent general realization that human activities have a direct effect on the natural functioning of the planet in a way which can endanger it. This epistemological phenomenon is also presented as a new geological era, the Anthropocene era[27] and calls into question the modern idea of the world born from a complex of cultural and economic causes during the final stages of the Middle Ages. This meaning refers also to the emergence of a new type of social organization according to which individuals try to meet their needs through consuming resources available to them locally. This premise of social organization (new to the modern Western world) has already been sketched out by some intellectuals. For example, a new feeling of responsibility towards future generations according to Hans Jonas (1979); a new 'natural contract' according to Michel Serres (1992); or a 'new civilization based on the feeling of empathy' according to Jeremy Rifkin

---

[25] This disposition was discussed by the Senators, who wanted the deadline deleted for 2025 in the first reading of the Bill.

[26] Michel Serres, *Le contrat naturel* (Editions Champs Flammarion, 1992).

[27] Christopher Bonneuil and Jean-Baptiste Fressoz, *L'évènement anthropocène* (Editions du Seuil, Paris, 2013), p. 118.

(2011).[28] More concretely, this new social organization gives a deeper and broader sense to innovative local practices, described by Rob Hopkins in his *Transition Handbook* (2008),[29] whose scope goes beyond the sole issue of energy. Hopkins uses the concept of 'resilience' referring to the 'ability of human communities to not break down or collapse at the first sign of an oil or food shortage, but, on the contrary, to react to these crises by adapting'.[30] He looks at the potential of communities to organize themselves in order to live autonomously in their local area.[31] This explains the vision, which highlights the importance of the participation of citizens in designing an energy transition policy. While the principle of participation as a criterion of success for the energy transition is largely accepted in Germany,[32] it can also be found in the synthesis of the French National Debate on the Energy Transition, which highlighted the need to achieve a transition by all and for all, with the participation of citizens.[33] Finally, it is clearly stated in the explanatory memorandum of the current French Bill, which wishes to create an environment conducive to the emergence of an 'energy participative democracy' (*démocratie participative énergétique*).[34]

---

[28] Jeremy Rifkin, *Une nouvelle conscience pour un monde en crise, vers une civilisation de l'empathie* (Les liens qui libèrent, 2011).

[29] Rob Hopkins, *The Transition Handbook* (Green Books, 2008).

[30] 'La capacité des communautés humaines de ne pas s'effondrer au premier signe d'une pénurie de pétrole ou de nourriture, mais au contraire, de réagir à ces crises en s'adaptant'. Rob Hopkins, *Manuel de transition, de la dépendance au pétrole à la résilience locale* (Editions Ecosociétés, 2010), p. 60.

[31] Dobigny Laure, 'Produire et échanger localement son énergie. Dynamiques et solidarités à l'oeuvre dans les communes rurales' in Fabrice Papy, *Nouveaux rapports à la nature dans les campagnes* (Editions Quæ Indisciplines, 2012), pp. 139–52.

[32] 'Regierungserklärung zur Energiewende, eine 'Herkulaufgabe'', *Frankfurter Allgemeine Zeitung*, 9 June 2011, available at www.faz.net/aktuell/politik/energiepolitik/regierungserklaerung-zur-energiewende-eine-herkulesaufgabe-1657503.html.

[33] *National Debate on the Energy Transition's Final Synthesis* (July 2013), p. 16, available at www.developpement-durable.gouv.fr/IMG/pdf/dnte_synthese_web_bat_28-8.pdf.

[34] Ségolène Royal, *Explanatory Memorandum of the French Law Project on the Energy Transition* (30 July 2014), V, p. 12, available at www.developpement-durable.gouv.fr/IMG/pdf/0-_Expose_des_motifs.pdf.

Assuming that the energy transition is an 'alternative societal project'[35] according to its second meaning as described above, this chapter compares legal tools by means of which civil society (cities and citizens) attempt to gain more influence over local energy policy, in the sense of a bottom-up movement in Germany and France. For this purpose I have chosen two specific areas: the distribution networks, the control of which grants cities' influence over the sources of energy that feed and sustain them,[36] and the field of energy production (gas, heat or electricity).

III LEGAL ASPECTS OF CITIES' CONTROL OVER ELECTRICITY DISTRIBUTION NETWORKS

At the end of the nineteenth century, the industrial structures for the production and distribution of energy were organized by local production-distribution systems in a monopolistic manner. Local councils were the authorities charged with the organization of the public electricity service. This model was a compromise between the willingness of local politicians to encourage industrial development on their own territory (even where there were no private initiatives) and the wish of industrialists to secure exclusive rights over their activity even if it meant also giving back a part of their profit.[37] It was considered desirable for fierce competition because at this time technologies and investments were uncertain in Western Europe.[38]

Subsequently, two models of local gas and electricity organization have been developed: the direct responsibility model under the form of municipalities (Stadtwerke) in Germany; and the concessive model, which is still in force in France. This section aims to present the legal channels that enable civil society to influence the manner in which distribution networks are managed. In Germany, the movement called '*Rekommunalisierung*' shows that citizens and municipal councils have recourse to certain legal tools in order to control the networks, whereas in France local authorities have to overcome legal obstacles.

35 Aurélien Evrard, *Contre vents et marées, Politiques des énergies renouvelables en Europe* (Les Presses de Sciences Po, 2013).

36 Peter Becker, *Aufstieg und Krise der deutschen Stromkonzerne* (Ponte Press, 2010), p. 271.

37 Emmanuel Grand and Thomas Veyrenc, *L'Europe de l'électricité et du gaz, acteurs, marchés, régulations* (Economica, 2011), p. 77.

38 Ibid.

(1) German Trend of 'Rekommunalisierung' of Electricity Distribution Networks

Before explaining the movement of *Rekommunalisierung* of distribution networks in Germany, it might be useful to note that on a national level electricity transportation is performed by four companies (50Hertz, Amprion, Tennet, Transnet BW), each company responsible for one regional area. According to European legislation,[39] these four companies must be legally independent. However, the organization of electricity distribution is more complex. In Germany, according to the constitutional principle of independent administration (*Selbstverwaltungsprinzip*),[40] each local authority must itself provide or contract others to provide each *Daseinsvorsorge* (those economic, social and cultural goods and services which have been judged essential). As electricity has been judged in 1971 to be a common good by the German Constitutional Court, the distribution of electricity consequently falls into the scope of the *Daseinsvorsorge* and is thus one of the responsibilities of the German *Gemeinden*.[41]

The system for the local management of electricity distribution can take different legal forms in Germany. It can be placed under direct municipal management, known as Stadtwerke, which is the case for approximately 50 per cent of the total number. It can also be delegated to private companies under the form of a concession contract, or in a more cooperative model, the *Gemeinden* can buy shares in a private company whose activity is the distribution of electricity.

In total, there are 900 electricity distributors in Germany. But between them, 90 per cent of these distributors serve a total of only 100,000 customers. That is why the distribution sector in Germany has been seen as a market dominated by a small number of vendors. Moreover, big energy producer companies such as Eon, RWE, EnBW and Vattenfall actually have stakes in some of the smaller private distributing companies.[42] But, it is very interesting to note that in the period between

---

[39] Directive 2009/72 concerning common rules for the internal market in electricity, art. 9 [2009] OJ L211/55.

[40] German Constitution (Grundgesetz), art. 28-2.

[41] C. Nill-Theobald *et al.*, *Grundzüge des Energie-wirtschaftsrechts* (3rd edn, Verlag C.H. Beck, 2013), p. 3, available at www.beck-shop.de/Theobald-Theobald-Grundzuege-Energiewirtschaftsrechts/productview.aspx?product=12140469.

[42] French public budget's auditor, Cour des Comptes, *Les concessions de distribution d'électricité: une organisation à simplifier, des investissements à financer*, Annual Report (February 2013), p. 109.

2009 and 2015, 7,800 of the estimated 14,300 concession contracts were set to end. In fact, in the field of energy, in Germany, concession contracts have a maximum duration of 20 years.[43] At the end of the contract local authorities have the opportunity to decide to extend the contract of the concession company, or to directly manage the distribution of electricity for their citizens. During this decision-making process, local authorities have to respect the rules of standard competition law; for example, by publicizing the date that the contract is due to end two years in advance; and they must also justify why they want to end the concession. But the motivation of the local authority is broadly accepted through the force of the constitutional principle of self-administration.

This process of *Rekommunalisierung* first started after a wave of liberalization in the 1990s. Among several grounds to justify this trend, German literature highlights a new awareness on the part of local authorities of some of their powers and the revival of the idea of self-administration, the reduction of costs of public services, the maintenance of jobs and environmental protection.[44] There are several examples, which illustrate this trend of *Rekommunalisierung* well, but the cases of Schönau (1986) and Hamburg (2010) are particularly illuminating. After the Chernobyl accident, in Schönau, a small village in the south-west of the country, a local association tried to convince the city council and the local electricity distribution operator (KWR) to provide the city with energy from renewable sources. When its attempts were unsuccessful, the association forced a local referendum through the introduction of a popular initiative against the extension of the concession contract for the incumbent distribution operator (KWR). The association won the referendum and then assumed responsibility for the distribution of electricity in the town. In order to do so, the association founded a cooperative company called Elektrizitätwerke Schönau (EWS) in 1996. It is also worth noting that the new cooperative company had to buy the former distribution operator KWR's network in order to be able to use it. When the former operator set an inhibitive price, EWS began a national fundraising campaign and successfully gathered the necessary DM5.7 million. EWS became the first German electricity operator to use only renewable energies and become a symbol of responsible energy worldwide. Indeed, the director of the association and of the cooperative,

---

43 Energy Competition Law (EnergieWirtschaftsGesetz), 2005, s. 46.

44 Hartmut Bauer, 'Zukunftsthema, "Rekommunalisierung"' (2012) *DÖV* 329.

Ursula Sladek, received the Goldmann Environmental Prize from President Obama in 2011 and the German Environmental Prize in 2013.[45] Today, EWS is the third biggest vendor of green electricity (electricity generated by renewable energies) in Germany.[46]

Similarly, a local referendum in Hamburg approved public re-appropriation of the city's gas and electricity networks, as well as the district's heating network, on 22 September 2013 (the date of the federal election). The vote was 50.9 per cent in favour. The citizen initiative *Unser Hambourg – Unser Netz* ('Our Hamburg, our network'), composed of diverse groups of the general public, used legal tools to bring about a public consultation on the issue. Currently, purchase contracts are being negotiated with Eon and Vattenfall. On 3 November 2011, a similar referendum on the re-communizing of electricity distribution was held in Berlin. This procedure was introduced by a popular initiative led by the collective Energetisch. Although there were a majority of votes in favour of re-communizing electricity distribution in Berlin, since the required threshold of 25 per cent of voter participation was not met, the decision was considered invalid.

To conclude, German civil society has mobilized, using the tools of direct democracy such as popular initiatives and referendums, in order to obtain more influence over management of energy distribution in its cities. These democratic mobilizations were principally motivated by the environmental concerns raised by local energy policy. In so doing, 72 new energy municipalities (Stadtwerke), which directly manage their own electricity distribution, have been created since 2005.[47]

(2) Challenges Involved in the Organization of French Electricity Distribution

In 1884, the French Parliament gave municipalities (communes) the responsibility for organizing the distribution of gas and electricity.[48] Moreover, public property rights over distribution networks were given to

---

[45] Frédéric Lemaître, 'À Schönau, en Allemagne, l'électricité verte et citoyenne', *Le Monde*, 22 January 2014.

[46] Julia Wyssling, *Schönau face au monopole de l'énergie: le rachat du réseau électrique local par une coopérative énergétique citoyenne* (Energycities, 2013).

[47] Kurt Berlo and Oliver Wagner, *Stadtwerke-Neugründungen und Rekommunalisierungen. Energieversorgung in kommunaler Verantwortung* (Wuppertal Institut, September 2013).

[48] French Municipal Act (1884).

the communes by an Act of 1906.[49] Since then, the communes have theoretically been the authorities in charge of the organization of the distribution of electricity as a local industrial and commercial public service (*service public industriel et commercial*).[50] However, the communes can also form a grouping alongside other local communes in order to organize this public service in a public body for local cooperation (*établissement public de coopération communale*), such as a Syndicat intercommunal or a Syndicat départemental. Moreover, some départments traditionally perform this service.[51]

In 1946, the majority of the distribution companies were nationalized and gathered into one public entity called Electricité de France (EdF). However, some other public distributors stayed independent, which means that they haven't been nationalized; these are called '*entreprises locales de distribution*'. They are local public companies (*régies*) or even cooperative companies exploiting distribution electricity networks. When we count the communes and their intercommunal groupings, there are only 736 different *autorités organisatrices*, that have responsibility for the concessions of electricity distribution. Electricité Réseau Distribution France (ErdF), the subsidiary of EdF,[52] manages 95 per cent of the distribution network concessions in France. The remaining 5 per cent are formed by the *entreprises locales de distribution*.

Although in theory French law gives the property, and the consequent property rights, of the distribution networks to the relevant organizing authority in each area, in practice, the actual effective property rights of local governments over their networks can be considered limited for several reasons. The first reason is the legal monopoly of ErdF in the distribution sector. Indeed, French law and jurisprudence explicitly require local authorities to delegate this local public service to ErdF

---

[49] French Act on Energy Distribution (1906).

[50] French Energy Code, art. L.111-51; French General Local Authorities Code, art. L.2224-31.

[51] The FNCCR (Fédération Nationale des Collectivités Concédantes et Régies) is an association, which represents the interests of the communes and their groupings (établissement de coopération communal) in charge of local public services (such as water and electricity). Looking at the members of this association gives us an overview of the intercommunal cooperation which exist in France. Moreover, we can also learn that the départements of Sarthe and Loiret are in charge of their electricity distributional networks (www.fnccr.asso.fr/).

[52] Since the European Commission required the legal separation between distribution and transportation networks (Directive 2009/72/EC), ErdF and EdF are now legally separated, but ErdF remained a subsidiary of EdF.

except in the following circumstance: communes are able to delegate the responsibility of distributing electricity to an *entreprise locale de distribution*, but only if this *entreprise locale de distribution* was created before 1946.[53] Furthermore, the possibility of creating a new public company (a so-called '*régie*') is not envisaged in French law. For this reason, ErdF is called the 'obliged concessive company' of local authorities and the situation is fixed.[54]

The second reason for which the effective property of communes over distribution networks can be regarded as restricted is that local authorities cannot themselves decide the tariff on the use of their distribution networks. It is instead determined by the national energy regulator (Commission de régulation de l'énergie) and the Ministry in charge of the economy. Moreover, in 2013 the French government's auditory body (Cour des comptes) pointed out that the obligation to transmit information on the functioning of the distribution networks was not being respected[55] so that local authorities are not well-informed about the use of their own distribution networks.

This situation can be explained by electricity distribution's exemption from competition law in France and the European Union.[56] As a result of this exemption, the duration of concession contracts is not limited and varies between 25 and 40 years in France. Some commentators have stressed the fact that such a long duration has never been justified.[57] As a result, French local authorities do not have much leeway in order to renegotiate their contracts once they come to an end after several decades.

This mismatch between the letter of the law, which gives the property rights over the networks to communes (1906), and economic reality has

---

[53] French Energy Code, art. L.111-52.

[54] Rémi Barroux, 'Les villes veulent choisir leur avenir énergétique', *Le Monde*, 7 September 2012, available at www.lemonde.fr/planete/article/2012/09/07/les-villes-veulent-choisir-leur-avenir-energetique_1757100_3244.html.

[55] Cour des Comptes, *Les concessions de distribution d'électricité*, above n. 42, at 115.

[56] French General Local Authorities Code, art. L.1411-2; Sapin Act (1993), art. 41; Directive 2004/17 coordinating the procurement procedures of entities operating in the water, energy, transport and postal services sectors [2004] OJ L134/1 and Directive 2004/18 on the coordination of procedures for the award of public works contracts, public supply contracts and public service contracts [2004] OJ L134/114.

[57] Philippe Terneyre, 'Sur quelques problèmes juridiques contemporains à haute tension. A propos des concessions locales de distribution et de fourniture d'électricité' (2009) *AJDA* 1640.

caused legal challenges from civil society. For example since 2010, the Deputy-Mayor of Dijon, Jean-Patrick Masson, has refused to re-sign another concession contract with Gaz Réseau Distribution France (GrdF), which holds the monopoly in France for the distribution of gas, and has publicly said that he will also refuse to sign a new concession contract with ErdF.[58] Then, in the context of the current debate around a new law on the project of energy transition, cities and their lobbies are strongly advocating for more powers and responsibilities in the field of energy, particularly energy distribution.

However, the channel of legal challenges has been used. In a particularly interesting case the question of constitutional priority was raised by a French citizen (Raphael Claustre),[59] on the occasion of the extension of Paris's electricity distribution concession contract[60] by the town council on 15 December 2009. He asked the Administrative Court of Paris to declare this decision void, since such concession contracts are unconstitutional. His argument was that contracts of this kind violate three constitutional principles: that of the free administration of local government; that of the freedom of contracting; and finally the principle of equality between citizens (in this case discriminating between those whose commune had an ELD before 1946 and those whose commune did not). When he lost the case,[61] he appealed. However, the Court of Appeal returned a very curious decision, stating that the claim of Raphael Claustre was based on articles of the Energy Code,[62] which were codified in 2011, that is to say two years after the decision of the Council of Paris (2009). But those articles are exactly identical to articles 2 and 23 of the Law of Nationalization of 1946 and article 18 of the Law on the Modernization of the Electrical Public Service of 2000, as they were codified in the Energy Code. However, according to Parisian administrative judges, Raphael Claustre had explicitly based his claim solely on

---

58 Béatrice Mathieu, 'Quand les villes rêvent d'indépendance énergétique', *L'Expansion*, 2 September 2013, available at http://lexpansion.lexpress.fr/actualite-economique/quand-les-villes-revent-d-independance-energetique_1386459.html.

59 Raphael Claustre is the President of the Network for the Energy Transition (CLER), see www.cler.org/.

60 This concession contract was signed on 30 July 1955.

61 Administrative Court of Paris, Judgment no. 1011598/7-2, 30 November 2011.

62 French Energy Code, arts L.111-52 and L.111-54.

the relevant articles of the 2011 Energy Code, the question of constitutional priority was rejected and the questions raised remain unanswered.[63]

This notable case aside, French doctrine[64] does call into question the compatibility of French law with European jurisprudence in this field. The *Telaustria* case[65] (2000) is particularly telling, imposing as it does respect for the minimum competition principles based on an appropriate obligation of transparency when a concession is allocated.

However, things may be changing. The Council of State (Conseil d'État) recently confirmed[66] a judgment of the Administrative Court of Polynesia, which declared the extension of a concession contract for electricity distribution decided by a mixed intercommunal union (syndicat mixte d'intercommunalité) invalid on the grounds that it was not compatible with the general principles of public procurement. Indeed, the territory of Polynesia benefits from a particular autonomous status according to which it is not subject to French concessive law in the field of energy.[67]

Whereas German civil society is able to influence the management of distribution networks by mobilizing popular initiatives and referendums, this is not possible in France, where legal options to change situations are more limited. Such an example permits us to better conceptualize the link between an appropriate legal system and the realization of local citizen projects. The following paragraphs are dedicated to the sector of renewable energy production in which citizens tend to become more and more involved in establishing energy citizen projects. The efficiency of citizen participation depends on appropriate legal rules, as a Franco-German comparison shows.

---

[63] Administrative Court of Appeal of Paris, Judgment no. 12PA00593, 25 February 2013.

[64] Jérémy Bernard, 'L'attribution obligatoire des concessions de distribution publique d'énergie aux opérateurs historiques est-elle conforme à la jurisprudence Telaustria?', *Semaine juridique Entreprises et Affaires,* 8 October 2009, p. 41; Sophie Nicinsky, *Droit public des affaires* (LDGJ, Montchrétien, 2012), p. 678.

[65] C-324/98 *Telaustria Verlags GmbH* v. *Telekom Austria AG*, ECJ (2000).

[66] *Société Électricité de Tahiti*, Case no. 361607, French Council of State (Conseil d'État), 10 July 2013 (JurisData no. 2013-015608).

[67] Jean Sébastien Boda, 'Le Conseil d'État et la mise en concurrence des concessions de distribution d'électricité : le cas de la Polynésie française', *La Semaine Juridique Administrations et Collectivités Territoriales*, 3 February 2014, p. 5.

IV LEGAL ASPECTS OF CITIZENS' CONTROL OVER THE MEANS OF ENERGY PRODUCTION IN THE FIELD OF RENEWABLE ENERGY

In the 'energy transition process' understood as a cultural change, we can see that the finance models of energy production are also changing. Indeed, citizens and civil society seem to become more and more involved in controlling production infrastructures at a local level. In doing so, they reach a form of political autonomy in becoming independent from energy imports (which can be adversely affected by war and diminishing resources, among other factors) and in choosing their own development paths.[68]

In the public sector's point of view, including citizens in public-private financing models is also an instrument of governance, which has three advantages according to an analysis made by Andreas Rüdinger and Noémie Poize.[69] First, it permits the mobilization of citizens' savings in times of economic crisis. Secondly, it allows the development of local resources in order to keep them locally-owned. Lastly, it should guarantee against legal challenges by citizens and thus avoid the blockage of infrastructure projects by legal means.

Such participative energy production infrastructures are called 'citizen energy projects' ('*Bürgerenergieprojekt*' in Germany and '*projet d'énergie citoyenne*' in France). In Germany, researchers[70] have studied the concept of citizen energy projects, whereas in France the definition of citizen energy projects constitutes the core of the constitutional Charter of Energie Partagée[71] (an association, founded in 2010, which unites and represents citizen energy projects). According to the German understanding of the word, a *Bürgerenergieprojekt* is a group of actors aiming at financing undertakings in favour of renewable energies or energy savings. Such a project is composed of individuals, farmers or legal entities. However, the majority of the capital has to be held by individuals, who

---

[68] Dobigny Laure, 'Produire et échanger localement son énergie. Dynamiques et solidarités à l'oeuvre dans les communes rurales' in Fabrice Papy, *Nouveaux rapports à la nature dans les campagnes* (Editions Quæ Indisciplines, 2012), pp. 139–52.

[69] Rüdinger and Poize, *Projets citoyens pour la production d'énergie renouvelable*, above n. 11.

[70] Trend: research and University of Lüneburg Germany, *Definition und Marktanalyse von Bürgerenergie in Germany* (2013), p. 28. This is a study carried out on the initiative of the German Agency for Renewable Energies.

[71] Energie Partagée, see http://energie-partagee.org/.

also own the majority of the voting rights. It is particularly interesting that according to the *Regionalität* criterion, individuals taking part in a citizen energy project must come from the same administrative territory and they must also be united by a common feeling of identity.[72]

The French idea of *projet d'énergie citoyenne*, defined by the constitutional Charter[73] of the association Energie Partagée, which gathered those projects, is broader. It states that, a citizen energy project is voluntary engaged in the protection of the environment and in the reduction of energy consumption. It is locally based, which means that individuals (or groups thereof), or local authorities or Energie Partagée itself, control the project thanks to the ownership of the majority of the voting rights. In addition, its aim must not be to make a profit, and as a result such projects are characterized by a limited return on capital. Finally, the citizen energy project must adopt cooperative principles, in order to be fully democratic (using the principle of one vote per individual), as well as acting in a transparent and clear manner.

From a legal point of view, this raises the question of the most appropriate legal form to support such projects, characterized by such a variety of different actors. A large number of studies demonstrate that the cooperative model has been a real success in Germany whereas this is not the case in France so that cities and citizens are compelled to find other participative solutions.

(1) Success of the German Cooperative Legal Form 'Eingetragene Genossenschaft'

In Germany more than 50 per cent of renewable electricity production units built between 2000 and 2010 belong either to individuals (40 per cent) or farmers (11 per cent).[74] In contrast, the Big Four own just 7 per cent of the production capacity. The term 'individuals' used in this context encompasses not only individual households who have installed solar-power equipment on their roofs but also citizens' associations, which aim to produce electricity from wind or from biomass.

---

[72] Trend: research and University of Lüneburg Germany, *Definition und Marktanalyse von Bürgerenergie in Germany*, above n. 70, at 25.

[73] Energie Partagée, *La Charte Energie Partagée*, signed on 18 May 2010, available at http://energie-partagee.org/le-mouvement/la-charte-energie-partagee/.

[74] Trend: research and Klaus Novy Institut, *Marktakteure Erneuerbare-Energien-Anlagen in der Stromerzeugung* (2012); Rüdinger and Poize, *Projets citoyens pour la production d'énergie renouvelable*, above n. 11.

This impressive movement is to be linked with another phenomenon: the explosion of the number of new cooperative energy companies (Bürgerenergiegenossenschaften). There were 75 in 2006 and 754 in 2012. It is easy to count the number of Energiegenossenschaften, as a cooperative has to be registered. Naturally, there are also other legal forms, which are used for citizens' projects, such as associations or Limited Liability Companies, nevertheless, the increase in the number of cooperative companies in the field of energy is particularly striking.

However, this phenomenon hasn't occurred simply by chance. In Germany, the legal form of cooperative company (eingetragene Genossenschaft, eG) was created by law in 1869 but it was reformed in 2006 in order to make it more flexible. As a result, a German cooperative company has many attributes which make it well-suited to citizen energy projects. Just three people are needed in order to create a new cooperative company and no minimum capital is required. Also, only 5 per cent of the turnover must be kept in 'reserve', although a cooperative's members are free to set the reserve above this level if they wish. The amount of profit, which can be shared, isn't limited by law and the share of dividends can be counted as charges in order to reduce taxes. In addition, the German cooperative company is exempted from the requirements of the Prospectus Directive because it falls within the scope of its non-profit organization exemption.[75] This means that German cooperative companies are able to have recourse to public offerings in order to find new financial resources without paying for authorization from the German financial markets regulator (Bundesanstalt für Finanzdienstleistung Aufsicht). Security for investors is guaranteed by an audit carried out by the regional federation for cooperative companies, which checks the accounts and assets of the cooperative every two years.[76] Finally, a territorial authority can be financially involved in a citizens' project as long as its financial and management capacities are respected, the geographical area concerned corresponds to its own territory, and the local community has a sufficient role in the governance of the cooperative company.

The above reasons help to explain the successful use of the German cooperative company by citizens in order to be the legal base of their citizen energy projects. Even though such citizen projects are complex by

---

75 Directive 2003/71/EC on the prospectus to be published when securities are offered to the public or admitted to trading, 4 November 2003, art. 1-2 e).

76 Martin Wolters, 'Genossenschaftsanteile in öffentlichen Vertrieb', *Asscompact, Steuern und Recht* (2012), available at www.mzs-recht.de/fileadmin/user_upload/PDF-Dateien/AssCompact_03-12_Genossenschaftsanteile_im_oeffentlichen_Vertrieb.PDF.

their very nature and due to the diversity of the actors they unite, the way German law has developed seems to be encouraging such initiatives. On the contrary, the legal form of French cooperative companies is not so flexible and presents legal difficulties, which seem to obstruct the citizens' creative initiatives to produce renewable energy from renewable sources.

(2) French Alternatives to the Cooperative Company of Public Interest

Compared to Germany and other European countries (Denmark, Belgium and Holland), citizen energy projects are not so numerous or widespread in France and this phenomenon can be partly explained by legal barriers which exist in France.

Contrary to the German legislation on eingetragene Genossenschaften, French cooperative law is fragmented. The legal form of the cooperative company was created in 1947 by a general statute.[77] But there are different types of cooperative company according to the sector concerned (agriculture, production of goods, building sector) and each type of cooperative company benefits from specific legal rules and exemptions. Nevertheless, the form of cooperative company that citizen energy projects have to adopt is that of the cooperative company of collective interest (société coopérative d'intérêt collectif, SCIC), which was created in 2001.[78]

The SCIC has the advantage of permitting the inclusion of different types of actors within the same entity (private companies, users, employees, local authorities, individuals). However, this legal form also presents many difficulties, especially regarding the need to raise sufficient finance for the constitution of an energy citizen project (several million Euros). Secondly, investment in an SCIC is not very attractive since 57.7 per cent of the profits must be kept in 'reserve', and cannot be shared among the members of the cooperative. Moreover, the distribution of dividends is restricted to the average rate yielded by the bonds of private companies (2.28 per cent in September 2014 according to the Ministry of the Economy). An SCIC is not exempt from taxes but is in fact subject to all the same taxes as a normal commercial company.

---

[77] French Act no. 47-1775 Creating the Status of Cooperation (1947).

[78] French Act no. 2001-624 (2001), art. 36.

Before the new law on social economy came into force on 31 July 2014 (Loi relative à l'économie sociale et solidaire[79]), the total amount of shares that a single local authority could hold in any single such cooperative company was limited to 20 per cent. According to article 33 of the new statute, a local authority can hold 50 per cent of the shares of a SCIC, which might encourage the financing of such projects. However, an SCIC is not exempted from gaining the authorization of the national financial authority in order to make a public offering, unlike its German equivalent. For these reasons, even though the new law facilitates the participation of local entities in SCICs, this legal form has been criticized by French legal scholars because of its lack of flexibility.[80]

In order to avoid this type of legal difficulty, citizens have tried to find other incorporation forms, such as the simplified stock company (société par actions simplifiées, SAS). The SAS was legally brought into being in France in 1994 in order to remedy the complex rules attached to the traditional limited company (société anonyme, SA). Citizen energy projects can undertake the legal form of the SAS and still correspond to the cooperative governance criteria required by Energie Partagée. Indeed within an SAS, operating rules can be freely fixed by cooperators, so that they can choose to adopt cooperative rules.[81] By doing so, they avoid the regulatory difficulties of the SCIC.

However, an SAS cannot legally receive investment from a local authority according to the principle of freedom of commerce and industry.[82] But here once more, the situation is going to change, since the current Bill on energy transition allows local authorities to buy and hold shares in such companies since they are dedicated to 'the production of energy from renewable energies' (article 109). This new measure is particularly striking in French public economic law, especially because, as the Bill stands, there is no threshold limiting the percentage of investment from public bodies.

Another difficulty was due to the fact that, contrary to a stock company (SA) or a limited liability stock company (SARL), an SAS cannot make a public offer of securities,[83] except for a limited group smaller than 150

---

[79] French Act on Social Economy no. 2014-856 (2014), art. 33.

[80] Sophie Grandvuillemain, 'La société coopérative, un statut inutile?' (2012) *Semaine Juridique Entreprise et Affaires* 51.

[81] French Commercial Code, art. L.227-5.

[82] French General Local Authorities Code, art. L.2253-1.

[83] French Commercial Code, art. L.227-2.

people.[84] Nevertheless, this number remains too small for the financial needs of a citizen energy project.

Once again, in order to avoid French legal obstacles, French civil society found a solution in order to raise the funds required to launch renewable energy-producing projects. For example, they have resorted to solidarity financial funders known as CIGALEs (club d'investisseurs pour une gestion alternative et locale de l'epargne), clubs which favoured an alternative management of local savings. CIGALEs are small, socially responsible capital-risk companies created by (between five and 20) citizens who want to dedicate their savings to local projects. They are organized under a co-ownership agreement[85] (*convention d'indivision*) for five years. Usually, CIGALEs buy shares in local small enterprises in order to support local economic projects.

The best example of the use of this practice is the first citizen-led wind power project in France, in Bégannes, which groups together 53 clubs of private investors representing around 700 citizens, who supplied the amount of 1.4 million Euros for the creation of a project with a total budget of 12 million Euros.[86] Initiated by the association Éoliennes Pays de Vilain, which is comprised of 30 farmers, the project is supported by the SAS Bégawatts. The legal form of the SAS was actually chosen because of its flexibility. It is organized according to cooperative principles, which means that the group representing the citizens who launched the project has a blocking minority (one-third of the votes). The participatory wind power project in the Landes du Mené (in Brittany) is another illustrative example of this practice. Indeed, 140 households invested in this project through eight CIGALEs, which together provided 30 per cent of the required investment fund.

Then in 1991, an association called Phebus raised a subscription from 130 people in order to invest in photovoltaic roofs in Arièges. Between 1992 and 2008, five associations and social business banks have worked together within the framework of European projects dedicated to local energy investments (Welfi, Universol, DaSolaSol) in order to help with fundraising. Finally, with the help of the national agency for the environment and energy (Agence de l'environnement et de la maîtrise de l'énergie), a joint-stock company (société en commandite par action) was created in 2009 under the name of SCA Energie Partagée Investissement. After two decades of difficulties finding funding due to regulatory

---

[84] Ordonnance no. 2009-80 (2009).
[85] French Civil Code, art. 1873-1.
[86] Parc éolien de Bégannes, see www.eolien-citoyen.fr/gouvernance-65.html.

obstacles, the founders decided to adopt a Charter in order to guide future citizen energy projects in 2010. Finally, the company SCA Energie Partagée Investissement gained authorization from the French financial market authority on 19 September 2011 and was able to make a public offering, one for each local citizen energy project. In 2012, four solar energy projects, two wind power projects and one biogas heating project were supported by Energie Partagée Investissement. Currently, 10 projects are seeking investment through Energie Partagée's public platform. In total, 10 million Euros were subscribed by 4949 individuals in 2016 with an average of slightly less than 1,800 Euros per citizen.

Soon, the difficulty caused by legal barriers protecting a public offer of securities will be overcome. Article 111 of the Act on energy transition requires all citizen energy projects, which aim to produce renewable energy, to invite investment from local citizens to invest in it. The amount of capital reserved for citizen investment and the geographic scope of this offer will be determined by decree.

V CONCLUSION

The discussion in this chapter leads us to some conclusions. First of all, the mobilization of the traditional instruments of direct democracy for the *Rekommunalisierung* in Germany reveals obvious citizen concerns about their energy and whether it is produced sustainably. This trend, which comes from civil society, is a grassroots movement. As such, it can only be effective if associations, citizens and city mayors have the opportunity to participate in the public debate by taking part in important decisions, such as the manner in which local public services are managed. Germany's federal model seems to be better suited to this kind of citizen energy movement than a central democratic state, such as the French constitutional model, since it devolves more powers to local governments and citizens. Secondly, the principle of freedom of competition can be strongly linked with the principle of free administration, that is to say, freedom of choice for local governments as regards the way in which their local public services should be performed. To that extent, some of the most important principles of the welfare state (such as tariff equalization and the organization of certain public services as monopolies) should be viewed alongside other important concepts, such as freedom of choice (for cities and citizens). In this matter, the flexibility awarded to cooperative companies by German law, compared to the rigidity of the French legal system, shows that values such as investor and/or consumer protection should be weighed alongside new values such as individual risk and liability and environmental collective liability.

In summary, it seems that the establishment of a kind of environmentally-friendly participative democracy relies on politicians having more faith in the ability of citizens to be a good judge of what is beneficial to them and to their local area. Lastly, in terms of legal theory, the examples of the distribution networks and of the inadequacy of the cooperative legal forms highlight the fact that an easily navigable legal system, one which works *pro bono* the public, is a legal system which pays attention to the real world and its modern challenges.

11. Learning from Europe: some ideas for the energy improvement of the US existing building stock

Teresa Parejo-Navajas*

I INTRODUCTION

The stock of existing buildings represents a largely untapped opportunity for the reduction of greenhouse gas (GHG) emissions in the European Union and the United States. Existing buildings are responsible for 41 per cent of energy consumption and 36 per cent of carbon dioxide (CO_2) emissions in the EU,[1] and 39 per cent of total energy use and around 38 per cent of CO_2 emissions in the United States.[2] Understanding the energy consumption in buildings requires insight into the energy levels consumed over the years and the mix of fuels used in that energy consumption. Although there are several ways to reduce GHG emissions derived from energy use in buildings, scientists and governments agree that improving the energy efficiency of building systems and operations,

* This chapter was prepared as part of research conducted at the Sabin Center for Climate Change Law, Columbia Law School, Columbia University, under the supervision of Michael Gerrard and Michael Burger, to whom I am deeply indebted.

1 This is the largest end-use sector, followed by transport (32 per cent) and industry (25 per cent). European Commission, *Report from the Commission to the European Parliament and the Council, Financial Support for Energy Efficiency in Buildings*, Staff Working Document, COM(2013)225 final (2013), p. 6, available at http://eur-lex.europa.eu/procedure/EN/202562.

2 See www.epa.gov/greenbuilding/pubs/whybuild.htm. US buildings are responsible for more CO_2 emissions annually than those of any other country, except China. B. Kinzey, S. Kim and J. Ryan, *The Federal Buildings Research and Development Program: A Sharp Tool for Climate Policy* (ACEEE Buildings Summer Study, 2002), available at www.eceee.org/library/conference_proceedings/ACEEE_buildings/2002/Panel_9/p9_18/paper.

as well as investing in cleaner on-site power generation, is a highly effective approach.[3]

Accordingly, this chapter focuses on the improvement of the energy efficiency of the existing building stock, filling an important void in the literature on GHG emissions reductions strategies, as most laws and regulations adopted to improve energy efficiency have focused primarily on new buildings. For that purpose, this chapter shows the most interesting and innovative energy efficiency solutions in the EU and the United States, and outlines several recommendations for the energy improvement of the US existing building stock based on the European experience.

II EXAMPLES OF EUROPEAN BEST PRACTICES FOR THE ENERGY PERFORMANCE OF THE EXISTING BUILDING STOCK

The EU has traditionally led the fight against climate change. This makes its experience of remarkable value in finding best practices for energy efficiency improvement in other parts of the world, such as the United States. However, the EU is still behind schedule to achieving a 20 per cent increase in energy efficiency in 2020, set by the EU leaders in March 2007, although its leaders remain confident in the EU's capacity to achieve the target. Furthermore, during the last European Council of October 2014, the EU has assumed even more ambitious commitments. It is, therefore, clear that there is political determination in Europe to contribute to the objective of combating climate change and that energy efficiency measures will play an important role in that fight.

The 20-20-20 targets are 20 per cent reduction in EU GHG emissions from 1990 levels; share of EU energy consumption produced from renewable resources raised to 20 per cent; and 20 per cent improvement in the EU's energy efficiency. On top of that and since the year 2009, the EU is also offering to increase its emissions reduction goal to 30 per cent by 2020 if other major economies in the developed and developing world commit to undertake their fair share of a global emissions reduction effort. And furthermore, in July 2009, EU leaders and the G8 already announced a more ambitious GHG emissions reduction target, in the so-called Roadmap 2050, by at least 80 per cent below 1990 levels by

---

[3] Among others, Ch. Wilson, A. Grubler, K.S. Gallagher and G.F. Nemet, 'Marginalization of End-use Technologies in Energy Innovation for Climate Protection' (2012) 2 *Nature Climate Change* 780; European Commission, *Energy Efficiency Plan 2011*, COM(2011)109final (2011).

2050. Even more, in October 2009 the European Council had set the appropriate abatement objective for Europe and other developed economies at 80–95 per cent below 1990 levels by 2050. Finally, the European Council of October 2014 has committed Member States to an indicative target at the EU level of at least 27 per cent for improving energy efficiency in 2030 compared to projections of future energy consumption based on the current criteria, which will be reviewed by 2020, having in mind an EU level of 30 per cent.

The specific energy efficiency measures adopted in the EU in order to accomplish the targets are explained below.

(1) Regulatory Instruments and Voluntary Standards

From all the above, the EU has adopted an ambitious vision for the energy performance of buildings, which has led to regulation (mainly through Directives) aiming at complying with the Energy Efficiency 2020 goal.

As far as the existing building stock is concerned, it is important to keep in mind that its characteristics differ significantly between Member States in terms of age, type, ownership, renovation rates and energy performance. Therefore, while national policies and regulatory frameworks share common themes, measures to improve the building stock will have to take these differences into account. Indeed, building energy codes in Europe are typically developed at the national level, adopted at the state level, and implemented and enforced by local governments. In the EU, the regulation for energy efficiency in buildings is mainly based on Directives, which set minimum requirements for all Member States and have to be transposed into their legal systems (with equal or more stringent requirements) in order to be effective. The EU Directives include specific energy efficiency standards for both the new and the existing building stock.

In all, there are six main legislative instruments at the EU level to achieve the targets established to reduce the energy consumption of the existing building stock (or directly related to those objectives):

(i) Directive 2009/28/EC of the European Parliament and of the Council of 23 April 2009, on the promotion of the use of energy from renewable sources (and amending and subsequently repealing Directives 2001/77/EC and 2003/30/EC), establishing a common framework for the use of energy from renewable sources in order to limit GHG emissions (and to promote cleaner transport). This regulation is applicable to the building stock as it obliges Member States to set up sector-specific targets for renewable heating and cooling; requires them to adopt support policies for RES-H projects (for heating and cooling)[4] for new buildings and for existing ones that are subject to major renovations; defines technology-specific restrictions for heat pumps and bioliquids; and requires Member States to ensure that new public buildings that are subject to major renovation fulfil an important and exemplary role in the context of the use of RES-H projects.

(ii) Directive 2009/125/EC of the European Parliament and of the Council of 21 October 2009, establishing a framework for the setting of eco-design requirements for energy-related products (Ecodesign Directive), which sets minimum efficiency standards for technologies used in the building sector (for example, boilers, hot water generators, pumps, ventilation, etc.). The EU Ecodesign Directive was introduced in 2005 and updated in 2009. Within its framework, EU-wide minimum energy and environmental performance standards for products are set out to remove the most inefficient and poorest performing products from the market. It applies to energy-using products (EuPs) and energy-related products (ErPs), with specific measures implemented for over 20 product groups, with this number also increasing over time.[5]

(iii) Directive 2010/30/EU of the European Parliament and of the Council of 19 May 2010, on energy labels, which obliges Member States to establish efficiency labelling schemes for a number of technologies used in the building sector.

The mandatory EU Energy Label was first introduced in 1992 and was updated by the current recast Directive 2010/30/EU (and has been amended by Directive 2012/27/EU, as indicated below). It now applies to more than ten appliance product groups, with this number slowly increasing over time. The primary element of the label is a seven-class scale, A–G, which rates the energy efficiency of a product, which can be extended above class A with classes A+, A++ and A+++, where necessary, in which case the lowest class may be F, E or D, provided there are no longer products on the market belonging to the classes below them. The label also includes information on energy consumption and in most cases on other product-specific parameters, such as size/capacity, noise and water efficiency. Energy labels aim to enable consumers to make

---

4 The RES H/C SPREAD project aims at developing six regional pilot plans in the field of heating and cooling with renewable energies. The project involves six pilot regions pertaining to as many European countries representing the EU main climatic zones, with a prevalence of the Mediterranean nations. Available at file:///Users/tparejo/Downloads/intelligent_energy_europe_-_res_heating_and_cooling_-_strategic_actions_development_-_2014-08-21.pdf.

5 See www.eceee.org/ecodesign.

informed choices by providing accurate, relevant and comparable information on energy efficiency and other resource consumption of a product before consumers make their purchasing decision, thereby indirectly improving the overall efficiency of the products that are produced and purchased.[6]

(iv) Directive 2010/31/EU of the European Parliament and of the Council, of 19 May 2010, on the energy performance of buildings (also known as EPBD), which lays down a number of requirements that have to be implemented by the Member States, encouraging the introduction of intelligent energy consumption metering systems whenever a building is constructed or undergoes major renovation.

(v) Commission Regulation (EU) 244/2012, of 16 January 2012, supplementing EPBD, which establishes a comparative methodology framework for calculating cost-optimal levels of minimum energy performance requirements for buildings and building elements; and

(vi) Directive 2012/27/EU of the European Parliament and of the Council of 25 October 2012, on energy efficiency (also known as the Energy Efficiency Directive or EED, amending Directives 2009/125/EC and 2010/30/EU and repealing Directives 2004/8/EC and 2006/32/EC), which establishes a common framework of measures for the promotion of energy efficiency within the Union, in order to ensure the achievement of the Union's 2020 20 per cent headline target on energy efficiency and to pave the way for further energy efficiency improvements beyond that date. The obligation to renovate central government buildings stated in Directive 2012/27/EU[7] complements Directive 2010/31/EU, which promotes the improvement of the energy performance of buildings within the Union, taking into account outdoor climatic and local conditions, as well as indoor climate requirements and cost-effectiveness.

By the time the first energy efficiency Directive was introduced in 2003, most Member States had building codes but they varied in the level of performance required.[8] However, according to the Buildings Performance Institute Europe (BPIE) most current renovation activity is minor, resulting in much more modest levels of energy savings. This is due to the government's incentive programmes that encourage installation of single measures (efficient heating plants, renewable energy measures,

---

6 See www.eceee.org/ecodesign.

7 Directive 2012/27/EU, art. 5.

8 The Economist Intelligence Unit, *Investing in Energy Efficiency in Europe's Buildings: A View from the Constructor and Real Estate Sectors* (GBPN, BPIE, 2013), available at www.bpie.eu/uploads/lib/document/attachment/15/EIU_GBPN_EUROPE.pdf.

etc.), but are rarely geared towards achieving the maximum energy savings for the building as a whole.[9]

Despite the importance of this regulation, there are still problems to overcome. For one thing, construction works in existing buildings are treated differently by the general technical building regulations, and in more than half of EU countries there is not any specific regulation for existing buildings.[10] In addition, in all Member States the regulatory instruments are the dominating measures addressing heating consumption and electricity, either in the residential or the commercial sectors. Also, the obligation on Member States to achieve a certain amount of final energy savings to drive energy efficiency improvements frequently falls short in implementation. Moreover, while countries have to report their implementation progress to the EU, these reports often are not detailed enough and/or describe an overly optimistic picture. At the same time, statistical data about the energy performance of buildings and related indicators is irregular at best in most EU countries.[11]

Consequently, compliance and enforcement of building regulations remains a key issue in EU countries[12] as they are essential to deliver the full potential of energy efficiency savings. In 2010, the rates of compliance in the EU Member States varied from 45 to 55 per cent for existing buildings and 70 per cent for new buildings. Indeed, while the efficiency of new buildings has improved over time, most of Europe's existing

---

[9] Ibid.

[10] Exceptions are Austria, where there is no building regulatory law established on a central level, and Belgium, France and Portugal, which do not have a national law that directs the technical building regulations. In some cases, the Building Act is joined to the Planning Act, such as in Belgium, the Czech Republic, Finland, Germany and Sweden. P. Costa Branco de Oliveira, J.A. Meijer and F.M. Visscher, 'Technical Building Regulations in EU Countries: A Comparison of their Organization and Formulation', paper presented at CIB World Congress 2010, Building a Better World, 10–13 May 2010, pp. 2 and 11.

[11] According to a recent review of EU methodologies for energy benchmarking, at the European level, the unavailability of building energy use databases has restricted the development of benchmarking tools. T. Nikolaou, D. Kolokotsa and G. Stavrakakis, 'Review on Methodologies for Energy Benchmarking, Rating and Classification of Buildings' (2011) *Advances in Building Energy Research* 9.

[12] F. Klinckenberg and M. Suninkka, 'Better Buildings through Energy Efficiency: A Roadmap for Europe' in *Eurima Blueprint Project, Netherlands* (June 2006), p. 15.

building stock has yet to be affected by energy performance requirements.[13] For those who do not comply with the regulation, the European Commission can open an infringement procedure. In 2010, eight infringement proceedings for environmental and pollution control and boiler and air-conditioning system inspections were open. Enforcement is systematic in Denmark, Finland, the Netherlands and Belgium, but a failure in Spain.[14]

(2) Market-based Instruments

In Europe, energy performance contracts (EPCts) were first identified as a key instrument to finance and implement ambitious energy efficiency investments. In fact, Directive 2012/27/EU obliges Member States, among other things, to establish financing facilities for energy efficiency measures. However, there are still some barriers that need to be overcome, like the lack of understanding and information, distrust in suppliers, high transaction costs, inadequate accounting and procurement rules, different procedures in each country and problems accessing financing. This is why the use of EPCts though energy service companies (ESCOs) has been heterogeneous among Member States. The new *European Code of Conduct for Energy Performance Contracting* has been recently elaborated (July 2014) to define the basic values and principles that are considered fundamental for the successful preparation and implementation of EPCt projects in Europe.[15]

Also, Energy Efficiency Obligations (EEOs) have been used in the European energy efficiency market. Indeed, the EU Regulation[16] obliges Member States to introduce an EEO scheme as it states that the objective of the Union 2020 could be better achieved, at least at this stage, by means of national EEO schemes for energy utilities or other alternative policy measures that achieve the same amount of energy savings. The first scheme in the world with a white certificate-trading element was

---

[13] See http://europeanclimate.org/bpie/.

[14] Lawrence Berkeley National Laboratory, *BEE Best Practice Policies and Policy Packages: Executive Summary* (GBPN, 2012), pp. 56–8, available at www.gbpn.org/reports/building-energy-efficiency-best-practice-policies-and-policy-packages-0.

[15] See http://ec.europa.eu/energy/efficiency/financing/doc/2014_european_code_of_conduct_energy_performance_contracting.pdf.

[16] Directive 2012/27/EU, art. 7.

introduced in Australia,[17] and in the United Kingdom in Europe. Since then, governments around the world have endeavoured to improve end-use energy efficiency by designing and implementing EEOs schemes. Currently in the EU, the Danish EEOs are the strongest in relation to energy efficiency in the industry, in contrast to France, Italy and the United Kingdom, where households and the public sector dominate. However, EEOs are more frequently used in the United States than in the EU.[18]

More common than the two previous approaches are Energy Performance Certificates (EPCs). EU Member States use them as mandatory comparative performance labels. EPCs were introduced by Directive 2002/91/EC to be issued when a building is constructed, sold or let, and must include reference values, such as current legal standards, in order to make it possible for consumers to compare and assess energy performance. Also, they have to be accompanied by recommendations for cost-effective improvement options to raise the performance and rating of the building. Directive 2010/31/EU has strengthened the role of EPCs.[19]

Given the EU's subsidiarity principle,[20] there is significant room for Member States to detail the mechanisms and manner of implementation of EPCs. All EU Member States have adopted building energy labels based on rating systems, but implementation and effectiveness vary among them, depending on a range of factors, including the local

---

[17] P. Bertoldi and S. Rezessy, *Energy Saving Obligations and Tradable White Certificates, Report Prepared by the Joint Research Centre of the European Commission* (December 2009), p. 5.

[18] As of 2009, almost half of US States had some kind of energy efficiency or energy savings obligations, either as a stand-alone target (referred to as Energy Efficiency Resource Standards, EERSs) or as part of renewable energy obligations (referred to as Renewable Portfolio Standards, RPSs). Bertoldi and Rezessy, *Energy Saving Obligations and Tradable White Certificates*, above n. 18.

[19] European Commission (DG Energy), *Energy Performance Certificates in Buildings and Their Impact on Transaction Prices and Rents in Selected EU Countries, Final Report* (19 April 2013), p. 11.

[20] Article 5(3) of the Treaty on the European Union establishes that: 'Under the principle of subsidiarity, in areas which do not fall within its exclusive competence, the Union shall act only if and in so far as the objectives of the proposed action cannot be sufficiently achieved by the Member States, either at central level or at regional and local level, but can rather, by reason of the scale or effects of the proposed action, be better achieved at Union level'.

political and legal context, the related incentives and subsidies, and the characteristics of the local property market.[21]

The regional implementation of Directive 2010/30/EU on energy labels in Austria may be regarded as a best practice example. It is streamlined by a national guideline (OIB-Richtlinië) to help the regions with development of the major aspects of the Directive and, at the same time, give a level of flexibility to each region if necessary. In the Netherlands, many aspects concerning the implementation of the EPCs are regularly discussed in working groups composed of different relevant stakeholders in the field, and in Portugal, the energy agency ADENE has played a key role in the successful implementation of EPC schemes by actively getting relevant stakeholders involved in the process. Also, many Member States have implemented penalties for non-compliant building owners, as established in the Directive. Finally, in Denmark, years of consistent communication by the government that energy performance is important has raised awareness among its citizens.[22]

(3) Incentives

A number of incentive schemes have been developed across Europe to harness the huge potential to reduce energy use in the existing stock, both in residential and in non-residential buildings. These instruments essentially fall into eight categories: preferential loans; subsidies; grants; third-party financing; trading (white certificates/energy certificates); tax rebates; tax deductions; and value added tax (VAT) reductions.[23] However, most Member States have opted for more traditional financial instruments, such as loan and tax incentives, and less frequently for market-based ones, such as obligation schemes (sometimes structured in the form of white certificates or EEOs), audits, third-party financing (including financing offered through ESCOs), and feed-in tariffs (FITs).

---

[21] European Commission, *Energy Performance Certificates*, above n. 19, at 17–18.

[22] Buildings Performance Institute Europe (BPIE), *Energy Performance Certificates Across Europe: From Design to Implementation* (December 2010), pp. 20–22.

[23] Klinckenberg Consultants, *Making Money Work for Buildings: Financial and Fiscal Instruments for Energy Efficiency in Buildings* (EuroACE, 2010), pp. 4 and 16, available at www.euroace.org/MakingMoneyWorkForBuildings/September%202010%20-%20Making%20Money%20Work%20For%20Buildings%20-%20EuroACE.pdf.

Examples of grants and subsidies are found: (a) in Austria, with the KlimaAktiv project,[24] aimed at introducing and promoting climate-friendly technologies and services in existing and new buildings; (b) subsidies to households for improving energy efficiency in Belgium, through improvement in the insulation and the efficiency of electrical and heating equipment;[25] (c) the Green Saving Programme of the Czech Republic, for new and existing residential buildings,[26] focused on supporting heating installations utilizing renewable energy sources and investment in energy savings; and (d) in Germany the Bank aus Verantwortung (KfW) Energy-Efficient Rehabilitation Programme,[27] aimed at reducing energy consumption through insulation measures, improvement of heat pumps and ventilation of buildings, and the KfW Housing Modernization Programme for the rehabilitation or refurbishment of residential buildings through the renewal of central heating installations and other housing features. The success of the KfW programmes are mostly due to the fact that the KfW constitutes an immense fund.[28]

Some EU countries have set up energy and carbon taxes to internalize the negative externalities of energy consumption in the final prices of goods and services, such as Austria, Denmark, Finland, Germany, Italy, Sweden and the Netherlands, with very good results. The International Monetary Fund (IMF) has indicated that the carbon tax is the most effective instrument for encouraging businesses and individuals to reduce energy use and switch to cleaner fuels.[29] Denmark was one of the first countries in the world to introduce a carbon tax on both households and businesses, to reduce the use of coal and to promote the use of natural gas, as well as renewable sources of energy, and to decrease imports through lower private energy consumption. Sweden is another example of success. The Italian programme provides tax credits to households and companies for single retrofit measures such as thermal insulation, installation of solar panels, and replacement of heating and air-conditioning systems, or for comprehensive retrofit work, covering up to 55 per cent

---

24 More information available at www.klimaaktiv.at/english.html.

25 More information available at www.esv.or.at/.

26 More information available at www.zelenausporam.cz/sekce/582/about-the-green-savings-programme/.

27 KfW Development Bank is a bank and an institution specializing in developmental policy that helps reduce poverty and protect the climate and the environment. More information available at www.kfw-entwicklungsbank.de/International-financing/KfW-Entwicklungsbank/.

28 Ibid. 81.

29 See www.imf.org/external/np/exr/facts/enviro.htm.

of the energy-related cost, but not exceeding a maximum value indicated in the specific measure. From 6 June 2013 to 31 December 2013 (30 June 2014 for renovations in communal parts of apartment blocks), the tax credits were temporarily increased to 65 per cent of the purchase and installation costs.[30]

Loans offered by public entities, or managed by private commercial financial institutions in public-private partnership, are being used in countries such as Germany, Hungary, Latvia and Spain. In this last country, grants and preferential loans have financed the Spanish Energy Efficiency Action Plan (2008–2012), for the rehabilitation of the thermal envelope of existing buildings, improvements in existing thermal installations and internal lighting plants, and promotion of the rehabilitation of existing buildings with high-energy ratings.[31]

Also, the 'Green Deal' financial mechanism is an innovative variant of FITs introduced in the United Kingdom. It eliminates the need for the consumer to pay up front for energy efficiency measures and instead provides reassurances that the cost of the measures should be covered by savings on the electricity bill.

(4) Voluntary Actions

With respect to voluntary standards, although they are not as important as the mandatory regulations, one of them,[32] originally from Europe, has made important contributions to architectural techniques and, moreover, has created a 'whole-approach building philosophy'. The Passive House (*Passivhaus*, in German) is the oldest voluntary standard for super-efficient buildings in Europe[33] and refers to a rigorous, voluntary standard for energy efficiency in a building. It contains the most stringent standards with regard to heating requirements, which prescribes a heating load (assuming a uniform indoor temperature of 20ºC) of no more than 15 kWh/sqm/yr irrespective of the climate. It typically entails a high-performance thermal envelope combined with mechanical ventilation

[30] A. Albertini and A. Bigano, *How Effective are Energy-Efficiency Incentive Programs? Evidence from Italian Homeowners*, Economics Working Paper Series, ETH (October 2014), p. 5.

[31] The Plan is available in English at www.idae.es/index.php/id.67/relmenu.333/lang.uk/mod.pags/mem.detalle.

[32] There are other examples such as the Swiss MINERGIE Standards or the French Effinergie Criteria, but the most important one is the Passive House.

[33] For more information see C. Goodall, *Ten Technologies to Save the Planet: Energy Options for a Low-carbon Future* (Greystone Books, 2008), p. 132.

with heat recovery to ensure high indoor air quality. This standard represents a factor of 6–12 reduction in heating load in mild climates (such as Southern Europe) and up to a factor of 30 reduction in cold climate regions with minimal insulation requirements. Where buildings are not currently heated to comfortable temperatures, adoption of a high-performance envelope can aid in achieving comfortable conditions while still reducing heating energy use in absolute terms.[34]

Even though the Passive House standard has been used mostly for new buildings, it can also be applied to retrofitting projects. With respect to new construction, the first Passive Houses were built in Germany in 1991, and the vast majority of them are located in German-speaking countries and Scandinavia. Interestingly, this philosophy has inspired new holistic projects that have moved beyond energy efficiency, beginning to think about the other systems that are part of our buildings. This is the case, for example, of the 'Living Building Challenge' (International Living Future Institute),[35] a US building certification programme, advocacy tool and philosophy, which calls for the creation of building projects at all scales that define the most advanced measure of sustainability in the built environment possible today. With respect to the retrofitting of existing buildings with Passive House standards, there are examples in both Europe and the United States that show its success, such as the A-Zero project, which transformed an old cowshed into a family home in the United Kingdom,[36] the renovation of an American Ranch home in Michigan, and a house in Sonoma (California).[37] Although not very numerous, these examples show that this technique is also possible in major renovations.

(5) Informative Measures

An interesting example of informative measures is the Energy Efficiency Certificate (EEC) Register included in the most recent Spanish

---

34 'Buildings' in *IPCC Report* (2014), ch. 9, p. 20, available at www.ipcc.ch/report/ar5/wg3/.

35 For more information on the Living Building Challenge see http://living-future.org/lbc.

36 See www.a-zero.co.uk.

37 Passive House Alliance (United States), see www.phius.org/media/W1siZiIsIjIwMTIvMDEvMDQvMTFfMDZfMzJfNzc3X0Nhc2VfU3R1ZHlfMl9PX05laWxsX1Jlc19SZXRyb2ZpdEZJTkFMLnBkZiJdXQ?sha=0843d4cd.

regulation[38] (some other Member States also have created them, such as the United Kingdom), to comply with the requirements established by the European regulation.[39] The Register is a statistical inventory on the EECs registered in each Autonomous Community which assists the inspection and monitoring of activities, and which informs the public about the level of compliance with the energy efficiency objective.

III ENERGY EFFICIENCY MEASURES ADOPTED IN THE UNITED STATES

Policies and programmes have played an important role in reducing energy use and energy intensity in US States over the past 30 years. With less than 1.5 per cent of the US building stock built each year, improving existing buildings is critical to ameliorate building inefficiency. Knowing that, the Environmental Protection Agency (EPA) and the US Department of Energy (DOE) have jointly created the State Energy Efficiency (SEE) Action Network to help States achieve maximum cost-effective energy efficiency improvements in homes, offices, buildings and industry by 2020, through energy audits and retro-commissioning practices.

The federal government adopted a number of laws from 1975 to 1980 that established educational efforts and financial incentives, and authorized the setting of efficiency standards, and also made a significant investment in energy efficiency research and development and grants over the past 30 years. More recently, new regulations establishing minimum efficiency standards for a wide range of household appliances and major types of equipment for the commercial and industrial sectors were adopted. And, as will be explained, many states have implemented building energy codes, utility-based energy efficiency programmes, and other policies to complement these federal initiatives.[40]

---

[38] Royal Decree 235/2013, 5 April 2013, on the basic procedure for the energy efficiency certification of buildings, available in Spanish at www.boe.es/diario_boe/txt.php?id=BOE-A-2013-3904.

[39] Directive 2010/31/EU, art. 20.

[40] H. Geller, P. Harrington, R. Rosenfeld, S. Tanishima and F. Unander, 'Polices for Increasing Energy Efficiency: Thirty Years of Experience in OECD Countries' (2006) 34 *Energy Policy* 556.

(1) Mandatory and Regulatory Measures

In the United States, codes have been developed at State and local levels. These codes and standards provide a range of energy, environmental and economic benefits to the States and municipalities, and can be supported by utilities through helping their implementation, integrating them into resource planning, and advocating for the adoption of more ambitious regulation.

Also, energy codes in the United States regulate the residential and the commercial sectors separately. The States and municipalities (and tribes) across the United States select any of the existing codes in the world, adapting them to their specific needs. In this regard, the energy code that applies to most residential buildings is the International Energy Conservation Code (IECC),[41] which supersedes the Model Energy Code (MEC).[42] The federal Energy Policy and Conservation Act (EPCA) of 1992 requires States to review and adopt the MEC (and its successor, the IECC), or submit to the Secretary of Energy its reasons for not doing so. Most energy codes for commercial buildings are based on ASHRAE/ IESNA Standard 90.1, jointly developed by ASHRAE and the Illuminating Engineering Society (IES). In this case, EPCA requires States to adopt the most recent version of ASHRAE Standard 90.1 that the US Department of Energy (DOE) has determined will save energy. Alternatively, States can follow the commercial building provisions of the IECC.[43]

The main national policy instruments developed to promote green buildings are: (a) the National Action Plan for Energy Efficiency, Vision for 2025: A Framework for Change (November 2008); and (b) the Energy Efficiency and Conservation Block Grant (EECBG) Program, funded for the first time by the American Recovery and Reinvestment Act (Recovery Act) of 2009. At the same time, several States in the United States (mostly those on the east coast and in California) have developed energy efficiency innovations and plans, and have made a real commitment to

[41] The International Codes are also called I-Codes. The International Code Council is a member-focused association. It is dedicated to developing model codes and standards used in the design, build and compliance process to construct safe, sustainable, affordable and resilient structures. See www.iccsafe.org/AboutICC/Pages/default.aspx.

[42] For more information see www.epa.gov/cleanenergy/energy-programs/suca/resources.html.

[43] See www.epa.gov/cleanenergy/documents/suca/buildingcodesfactsheet.pdf, at 4.

energy efficiency targets as a unique opportunity not only to fight climate change but as an economic driver to improve quality of life. In fact, recent studies estimate that cost-effective energy efficiency improvements in the US building sector have the potential to reduce annual electricity and natural gas consumption by 20 to 30 per cent over the next 10 to 15 years, saving more than US$100 billion annually for consumers and businesses.[44]

Legislation passed in 1976 called for the adoption of national building energy efficiency standards, but the building industry opposed this policy, and it was eventually converted to voluntary guidelines and design tools.[45] Therefore, there is not a US building code at national level, but, as indicated before, codes have been developed at the State and local levels, giving rise to heterogeneous regulations.[46] However, model codes such as the IECC are widely followed by States and localities, bringing some uniformity to building energy codes,[47] but there are still some States that have not yet adopted a State-wide code.[48] Since then, the status of the adoption of the building codes has not changed much.[49] However, in many States, several municipalities are very active and have their own code. In fact, some States may also allow local jurisdictions to adopt more stringent code requirements, and some cities are using codes to encourage innovative building practices to pave the way for new building technology. Yet, among many States and cities with codes, compliance levels still lag behind expectations.[50]

But while most States in the United States have energy codes for new buildings, not all apply such regulation to retrofits of existing buildings.

---

[44] M. Eldridge, R.N. Elliott and S. Vaidyanathan, *North Carolina's Energy Future: Electricity, Water and Transportation Efficiency* (ACEEE, March 2010); H.C. Granade, J. Creyts, A. Derkach, P. Farese, S. Nyquist and K. Ostrowski, *Unlocking Energy Efficiency in the U.S. Economy* (McKinsey & Company, July 2009).

[45] Geller *et al.*, 'Polices for Increasing Energy Efficiency', above n. 40, at 563.

[46] The Economist Intelligence Unit, *Achieving Scale in the US: A View from the Construction and Real Estate Sectors* (GBPN, IMT, 2013), p. 6.

[47] Geller *et al.*, 'Polices for Increasing Energy Efficiency', above n. 40, at 563–4.

[48] According to 2007 data, South Dakota, Wisconsin, Tennessee, Mississippi, Alabama, Alaska, Colorado, Missouri and Arizona.

[49] To check the status of the adoption of the building codes and standards, see www.energycodes.gov/status-state-energy-code-adoption.

[50] Lawrence Berkeley National Laboratory, *BEE Best Practice Policies and Policy Packages*, above n. 14, at 11.

This shortage of coherent regulation, combined with the lack of harmonization across States, create reluctance among investors.[51] Aware of the regulation's dispersion in this matter, the federal government's Climate Action Plan (July 2013) contemplated the formalization of a memorandum entitled 'Implementation of Energy Savings Projects and Performance-Based Contracting for Energy Savings', inviting federal agencies, in support of the Better Buildings Challenge, to work together to synchronize building codes, leveraging those policies to improve the efficiency of federally owned and supported building stock.[52]

According to the 2014 International Energy Efficiency Scorecard of the American Council for an Energy Efficiency Economy (ACEEE), the federal government should update national model building codes and provide technical assistance to States implementing and adopting energy efficiency building codes.[53]

(2) Economic Instruments: Building Energy Labelling

US rating and disclosure policy is less expanded than in Europe; in fact, there is not yet a mandatory buildings energy label for buildings (or even a common approach for labelling) in the United States, but research based on the voluntary rating and disclosure of US buildings suggest that the US marketplace is already factoring energy efficiency into its real estate decision-making. Those labels and ratings are:

- The HERS is the most common home rating system in the United States, and it is required for a home to qualify for an energy efficiency mortgage, for ENERGY STAR labelling, and for many other energy efficiency programmes. As of today, more than 1 million US homes have received a HERS score, many in conjunction with ENERGY STAR and federal new home tax incentives.[54]
- The ENERGY STAR for homes[55] voluntary programme helps businesses and individuals save money and protect the climate

[51] The Economist Intelligence Unit, *Achieving Scale in the US*, above n. 46, at 10.

[52] The White House, *The President's Climate Action Plan* (Executive Office of the President, July 2013), p. 11, available at www.whitehouse.gov/sites/default/files/image/president27sclimateactionplan.pdf.

[53] See www.aceee.org/research-report/e1402, at 3.

[54] For more information on HERS, see www.resnet.us/hers-index.

[55] For more information on ENERGY STAR, see www.energystar.gov/about/.

through superior energy efficiency. Any home, new or existing, that can be field-verified to meet all EPA requirements for ENERGY STAR Certified Homes could earn the label.

- ENERGY STAR Portfolio Manager and ENERGY STAR Buildings and Plants are specific tools for commercial buildings. The first one is the most widely used benchmarking tool in the United States. It is the tool of choice among cities such as New York, Seattle and Boston that have passed mandatory benchmarking laws, and it is used by the Canadian government as the platform for their national energy-benchmarking programme for existing commercial and institutional buildings.
- The DOE Home Energy Score allows homeowners to compare the energy performance of their homes to other homes nationwide, while providing homeowners with suggestions on how to improve their homes' efficiency. As of June 2014, 11,372 home energy scores have been completed in the United States.[56]
- ASHRAE Building Energy Quotient (EQ)[57] is a voluntary certification programme for buildings that compares the building with an energy label to other buildings based on energy use intensity (per square foot). The *in operation* EQ rating provides information about the actual energy use of an existing building to provide valuable insight into how the building performs and opportunities for improvement.
- Green Building Rating is a type of rating which is also a label and is growing its presence in the United States (and also in the rest of the world) with different programmes at all levels. The most important one is Leadership in Energy and Environmental Design (LEED), administered by the US Green Building Council (USGBC). It has nine different categories,[58] and one of them is the LEED for Existing Buildings: Operations and Maintenance (LEED-EB). There are 168 LEED-EB platinum, 1,118 gold and 817 silver certified buildings in the United States.[59] By industry, the three

---

[56] More information available at http://energy.gov/eere/buildings/home-energy-score.

[57] More information available at <http://buildingenergyquotient.org/what-is-bEQ.html.

[58] New Construction (LEED-NC); Existing Buildings (LEED-EB); Commercial Interiors (LEED-CI); Core and Shell (LEED-CS); Schools (LEED for Schools); Retail (LEED-NC Retail); Healthcare (LEED-HC); Homes (new construction, LEED for homes); and Neighborhood Development (LEED-ND).

[59] See www.usgbc.org/projects?keys=existing+buildings.

sectors with highest penetration of Green Building rating are: (1) education; (2) health care; and (3) offices.[60]

- Federal Energy Management Program (FEMP), operated by the US government to improve energy efficiency in federal facilities. Some Executive Orders commencing in 1991 have instructed federal agencies to reduce their energy use per square foot of floor space. In order to accomplish this, the FEMP provides technical assistance, training and help with innovative approaches, such as ESCOs and EPCts, project financing and implementation.[61]

(3) Financial Instruments and Incentives

Direct payments and incentives (mostly tax credits and rebates) or low-cost financing play a key role in driving homeowners and businesses to invest in energy efficiency. The most common instruments used in the United States for that purpose are as follows.

(i) *Utility and ratepayer-funded programmes*: these account for the bulk of incentives for improved building energy performance in the United States.[62] Moreover, the investment in efficiency programmes has more than tripled since 1998, mainly targeting residential and commercial buildings, which received the largest share of programme funds.[63] Much of the increase in these programmes has to be attributed to the proliferation of State-level regulatory commitments to energy efficiency, especially through the Energy Efficiency Resource Standard or Energy Efficiency Obligation (EERS or EEO) that is in place in the majority of US States. It establishes specific, long-term targets for energy savings that utilities or non-utility programme administrators must meet through customer energy efficiency programmes. An EERS can apply to either

---

60 See www.usgbc.org/articles/green-building-facts.

61 Geller *et al.*, 'Polices for Increasing Energy Efficiency', above n. 40, at 566.

62 Lawrence Berkeley National Laboratory, *BEE Best Practice Policies and Policy Packages*, above n. 14, at 32.

63 The consortium for Energy Efficiency report indicated that electricity programme budgets were split among commercial and industrial efficiency programmes by 39 per cent, residential efficiency programmes by 23 per cent and low-income programmes by 8 per cent. In the case of gas programmes, 41 per cent of the budget was directed to the residential sector, followed by low-income with 27 per cent and then the commercial and industrial sectors, with a share of 24 per cent. Lawrence Berkeley National Laboratory, *BEE Best Practice Policies and Policy Packages*, above n. 14, at 28.

electricity or natural gas utilities, or both, depending on the State, and can be adopted either through legislation or regulation.[64]

Also, rebates are commonly used to reduce the initial cost of energy-efficiency investment, encouraging higher levels of investment in the market. At first, these programmes focused on high-efficiency appliances and equipment, but now they are targeting a comprehensive approach seeking better building performance.

In the residential sector, the US EPA has developed ENERGY STAR utility programmes with incentive structures for new and existing home retrofit markets, such as tiered incentives, equipment incentives, rating incentives and homeowner discounts. Specifically for existing homes, the ENERGY STAR Home Performance (HPWES) offers whole-house solutions to high-energy bills and homes with comfort problems. The assessment includes the heating and cooling systems, windows, insulation, flow of air into and out of the house, as well as a safety check of gas appliances.[65]

In the commercial sector, ENERGY STAR has recently launched a Building Performance Program (BPwES). It is designed to help utilities and energy efficiency programme sponsors engage their business customers and local trade allies in an ongoing relationship centered on strategic energy management and a path to help business meet efficiency programme goals through persistent savings in commercial buildings.[66]

(ii) *Tax incentives*: owners and designers of new and existing energy-efficient residential and commercial buildings may qualify for tax deductions under the Energy Policy Act (2005). These tax incentives are mostly designed to cover the very highest levels of efficiency sold in 2005 in order to minimize costs to the Federal Treasury and participants who would have purchased eligible products even if the tax credits were not available (free riders). Residential retrofitting accounted for most of the credits in windows, insulation and exterior doors. For commercial buildings, most credits were granted for deductions in energy use for lighting.

(iii) *Innovative financial mechanisms*: up-front costs continue to be high even with the incentives. Therefore, incentives alone are not sufficient to meet the needs for building retrofitting and must be complemented with other programmes. During the last decades, some

---

[64] See www.aceee.org/topics/eers.

[65] See www.energystar.gov/index.cfm?c=home_improvement.hpwes_sponsors_about.

[66] See www.energystar.gov/index.cfm?c=eeps_guidebook.eeps_building_performance.

innovative energy-efficiency financing programmes have emerged helping reduce the up-front costs of improvements. The most prevalent mechanisms in the United States are the following:[67]

(a) EPCt implemented by an ESCO: with the traditional ESCO using an EPCt (a partnership between a federal agency and an ESCO), the initial cost of the investment (for example, equipment) has to be self-funded by the host customer, especially if it is in the MUSH (municipal, university, school and hospital) market, as it has easier access to funding.[68] In its first stages in the United States, EPCts were popular in the MUSH market, and in recent years it has expanded to federal projects, though it remains less common in the private building sector.[69] The ESCO guarantees that the improvements will generate energy cost savings over the term of the contract (up to 25 years). After the contract ends, all additional cost savings will accrue to the agency.
(b) Energy Services Agreement (ESA) and Managed Energy Services Agreement (MESA) models: under these, the customer does not have to pay up front the cost of the project, but instead enters into an ESA or a MESA with an energy service provider which will finance 100 per cent of the improvement. The service provider owns the energy efficiency improvement, which is progressively paid through the energy service. The building owner, hence, can avoid the expensive initial payment of the project. These models are particularly suited for larger energy efficiency projects rather than small-scale ones.
(c) On-bill financing and repayment models (OBF/OBR): these are usually serviced by a utility company. In these programmes, the customer pays the utility's improvement through the monthly energy bill. Programmes can be tailored to the industrial, commercial or residential sector. Advantages of on-bill programmes

---

[67] C. Kim, R. O'Connor, K. Bodden, S. Hochman, W. Liang, P. Sheridan and S. Zimmermann, *Innovations and Opportunities in Energy Efficiency Finance* (Wilson Sonsini Goodrich & Rosati, May 2012), pp. 4–10.

[68] See http://energy.gov/eere/femp/energy-savings-performance-contracts.

[69] S. Bhattacharjee, M.S. Ghosh and D. Young-Corbett, 'Energy Service Performance Contracting in Construction: A Review of the Literature' in *Proceedings of the 46th Annual International Conference of Associated Schools of Construction* (2010), p. 1, available at www.mlsoc.vt.edu/people/young/images/energy-service-performance-contracting-in-construction.pdf.

include: the convenience of a single bill for the customer; the perception of a secure investment; the capacity to leverage a unique relationship between the utility and the customer, allowing easier ways to pay back the cost of the energy efficiency improvements; and creating potential for customers to gain access to financing through modified underwriting that takes bill payment history into account. But they still face some challenges, such as up-front costs to utilities; risk on payments of the finance charge; handling the transfer of property; finding capital; and addressing non-utility fuels.[70]

(d) Property-assessed Clean Energy Financing (PACE): this is a local government/community voluntary initiative that allows property owners to fund energy efficiency, water efficiency and renewable energy projects with little or no up-front costs through an assessment on their property tax bills for up to 20 years.[71] It eliminates up-front costs, providing low-cost long-term financing and making it easy for building owners to transfer repayment obligations to a new owner upon sale, hence, overcoming challenges that have hindered adoption on energy efficiency projects in buildings. This mechanism has been used nationwide for decades since its introduction in pilot programmes in 2008.

IV GENERAL RECOMMENDATIONS FOR THE ENERGY IMPROVEMENT OF THE US EXISTING BUILDING STOCK

Once the information about best practices is clear, improvement proposals may be suggested to arrive at specific conclusions for the improvement of the energy performance of the existing building stock in the United States, as follows.

(1) Strengthening national model building codes and assuring more homogeneity in the regulatory package and establishing a general framework setting out minimum requirements for energy efficiency measures in the existing building stock might assist market incumbents in their respective tasks.

---

[70] C.J. Bell, S. Nadel and S. Hayes, *On Bill Financing for Energy Efficiency Improvements: A Review of Current Program Challenges, Opportunities and Best Practices*, Report #E118 (ACEEE, December 2011), p. iii.

[71] See http://energycenter.org/policy/property-assessed-clean-energy-pace.

The most important issues that should be taken into account in making regulations more effective are:

- rigorous updating of standards to promote the development and use of new and efficient technology;
- announcing new codes and standards early so industry can prepare for more stringent codes;
- increasing training;
- demonstrating the feasibility of constructing progressively more efficient buildings that are cost effective;
- developing consistent mandatory regulation with increasing and effective penalties for those who do not comply with it, to help the energy efficiency market investment; and
- setting up accurate and accessible information, as well as rigorous compliance.

This way, the energy efficiency process would become:

(i) more mechanical, hence making it easier to establish a programme of action; and
(ii) simpler, resulting in lower costs and easier for compliance.

(2) Energy labels for home appliances have been very effective and appreciated by the general public as they are very easily recognizable. The next clear step in the United States is to move towards a labelling requirement. The labels should be:

- mandatory, the phase for voluntary labels now being over;
- clear, reflecting homogeneous information and easy to understand for the general public;
- flexible, which could be accomplished with gradual energy efficiency indicators; and
- strengthened, the label needing to be updated in accordance with technological improvements.

(3) There are a great variety of financial mechanisms and alternative measures to reduce end-use energy consumption. Opting for one or the other (or for a specific combination of them) is conditioned by the particularities of each region or nation. The key here is, therefore, to find the best combination of measures to suit each idiosyncrasy (for example, any type of tax will be the subject of controversy in most US States

whereas in Europe, they are more common and widely accepted). Here are some recommendations:

- a combination of different financial instruments (subsidies, EEOs, FITs, etc.) appropriate to each culture should be used to offset the high capital cost of projects;
- a carbon tax should be imposed on the use of carbon-based energy by households, according to income levels;
- other financial instruments, such as grants, subsidies, deferred payments (or any other innovative instrument that might eventually arise) should be considered in order to help overcome the added operational and maintainance costs of the building, especially for low-income households; and
- subsidies for investment in cleaner energy technologies should be put in place (FIT measures).

(4) Informative actions:

- informative measures need to complement the mandatory ones;
- educational campaigns are necessary to guide the behaviour of stakeholders, especially tenants, since they use the home appliances;
- a mandatory Energy Efficiency Certificate Register could help the general public and technical experts understand buildings' level of compliance; and
- the public sector should take the lead.

(5) Voluntary actions must be deployed to complement other measures, but clear informative campaigns are required to be effective.

(6) Public-private sector collaboration is necessary. The public sector, again, must set the standards.

(7) All measures should be complementary:

- enforcement of existing thermal regulations (switching to cleaner fuels), and implementation of subsidies and economic instruments like the Energy Performance Certificate for homes and for appliances that have been proven very effective;
- improvement in space cooling could be achieved with a mandatory energy label and helped by the use of vernacular buildings refurbishment like lowering heat loads by using shading devices or improving the insulation of roofs and ventilation systems (better if natural);

- enforcement of existing regulations for appliances and lighting is key to accomplishing energy efficiency goals; and
- buildings and their energy infrastructure need to be designed, built and used taking into account culture, norms and occupant behaviour. Technology can improve vernacular designs.

Table 11.1 Types of measure and recommendations

Type of measure	Recommendation
Regulation	Linked to technological improvements. Clear and accessible to general public. Enforced and controlled.
Economic instruments	Mandatory. Clear (homogeneous information and easy to understand). Flexible. Followed-up according to technological improvements.
Financial measures	Carbon tax on the use of carbon-based energy by households, according to income levels. Other measures to help overcome the added costs (subsidies, etc.). Subsidies for investment in clear energy technology.
Informative actions	Educational campaigns. A mandatory energy efficiency certificate Register.
Voluntary actions	Passive House standards for major renovations. Informative measures are key for voluntary actions.
For all measures	A combination of different measures is necessary. All measures should be complementary.
Public-private collaboration	The public sector should take the lead.

12. Sustainable sewage

Melissa K. Scanlan

I INTRODUCTION

Treating large amounts of human sewage is the often-criticized job of the municipal wastewater treatment facility. These facilities are sometimes spurned as bad neighbors, dischargers of raw or partially treated sewage during storms, and the cause of health advisories that keep people away from natural bodies of water. In the process of providing the necessary service of treating municipal sewage, these facilities can also have a large carbon footprint because cleaning municipal sewage is an energy-intensive process.[1]

Cleaning up urban sewage, however, does not necessitate a large carbon footprint nor fouled public waters. Some leading wastewater treatment facilities are charting a different course with renewable sewage-based energy and a prospect of becoming net energy neutral, and even energy producers. In light of climate disruption and the need to significantly reduce greenhouse gas emissions, redesigning municipal wastewater treatment to be more sustainable is an area where action is needed and which makes environmental and fiscal sense.

This chapter will show the renewable energy potential hidden in urban sewage, which if tapped can simultaneously reduce greenhouse gas emissions and energy costs. There are a variety of potential sources of renewable energy at sewage treatment facilities, but the single biggest source is biosolids, which can be anaerobically digested to make biogas.[2]

Municipal systems around the world, from Birmingham, England to Washington, DC, are redesigning their sewage treatment processes to

---

[1] Milwaukee Metropolitan Sewerage District, *Landfill Gas*, available at www.mmsd.com/sustainability/landfill-gas.

[2] Water Environment Research Foundation, *Energy Production and Efficiency Research: The Roadmap to Net Zero Energy* (August 2011), p. 4.

produce renewable sewage power.[3] This chapter provides three case studies of best practices that are already being implemented at municipal wastewater treatment facilities. The case studies come from Austria and the United States and cover facilities serving various sizes of populations (from 68,000 to 1.1 million). These facilities are simultaneously reducing dependence on fossil fuels and energy costs. The first case study is of the wastewater facility in Strass, Austria, which has been a net energy producer for a decade. The second case study is of a similarly-sized regional wastewater treatment facility in Sheboygan, Wisconsin, in the United States, which currently produces 90 percent of its annual electrical needs and 85 per cent of its heating needs.[4] The final case study is the Milwaukee Metropolitan Sewerage District in Wisconsin, in the United States, which is implementing and experimenting with a variety of renewable energy options with a goal of becoming net energy neutral by 2035. The case studies illustrate the energy demands of treating municipal waste, the energy potential contained in the waste, and specific steps facilities have taken to reduce their carbon footprint. The chapter identifies several drivers that have influenced changes at the facilities studied and further opportunities that could accelerate the transition from fossil fuels to renewable sewage power.

II MUNICIPAL WASTEWATER FACILITIES' TRANSITION TO SUSTAINABLE ENERGY

(1) Municipal Wastewater Energy Demands

Treating municipal wastewater is an energy-intensive process. A municipal wastewater treatment facility with an average flow of 10 million gallons per day uses as much energy as almost 3,000 average US homes.[5]

---

[3] Emily Atkin, 'People in England are Harnessing the "Power Locked in Poo" to Fuel Their Homes', *Climate Progress*, 3 October 2014, available at http://thinkprogress.org/climate/2014/10/03/3575503/the-power-of-poo/. A facility in Washington, DC, is converting sewage gas in order to fuel 11,000 homes in the DC, Maryland and Virginia area. Ibid.

[4] Sheboygan Regional Wastewater Treatment Facility, *Microturbines*, available at www.sheboyganwwtp.com/4a_microturbines.php.

[5] Author's calculations based on Water Environment Research Foundation Factsheet, *Energy Production and Efficiency Research: The Roadmap to Net Zero Energy*, Table 2, available at www.werf.org/c/RFP/2013/ENERc13/ENER1_Fact_Sheet.aspx.

For plants operating at 80 per cent influent capacity, primary source energy

In addition to a large carbon footprint, all this purchased energy costs a lot of money. In the United States alone, wastewater facilities spend around US$4 billion per year for energy.[6] In the United Kingdom, Severn Trent has switched to producing energy from sewage as a way to reduce expenses because 'energy is its second-highest operating cost … [and harnessing sewage power] enables the company to save as much as 1.7 million pounds a year on its gas bill'.[7]

It is typical for municipal wastewater facilities to meet their energy needs through fossil fuel combustion, and spend a large portion of their budgets on external purchases of energy.[8] However, as noted earlier, these facilities have the potential to be net energy neutral and even to be exporters of energy. 'The energy contained in wastewater and biosolids exceeds the energy needed for treatment by ten-fold.'[9] As will be illustrated in the case studies, wastewater treatment facilities can redesign

---

needs are 13.3 Gj/MG (13.3Gj/MG * 365 days * 10 MGD = 48545 Gj) (48545Gj = 13484722.2 kWh = primary source energy annually). Secondary source energy needs are 1,107 kWh/MG (1,107 kWh/MG * 365 days * 10 MGD = 4040550 kWh secondary source energy annually). 4040550 kWh + 13484722.2 kWh = 17525272.2 kWh (average home uses 6,000 kWh/yr so 17525272.2/6000 kWh = energy to power 2,921 homes annually).

[6] Milwaukee Metropolitan Sewerage District, *Sustainable Water Reclamation* (2012), available at www.mmsd.com/-/media/MMSD/Documents/Sustainability/Sustainability%20Plan.pdf. This chapter is focused on the energy footprint of treating municipal sewage. However, another angle on the water-energy nexus is the water footprint of energy. The production of electricity from fossil fuels and nuclear energy requires 190,000 million gallons of water per day, accounting for 39 per cent of all freshwater withdrawals in the United States. Ibid.

[7] Louise Downing, 'Severn Trent "Poo Power" Helps Fuel Homes, Save on Costs', *Bloomberg*, 1 October 2014, available at www.bloomberg.com/news/2014-10-01/severn-trent-poo-power-helps-fuel-homes-save-on-costs.html.

[8] 'As the largest source of U.S. greenhouse gas emissions, CO2 from fossil fuel combustion has accounted for approximately 78 percent of GWP-weighted emissions since 1990, and is approximately 78 percent of total GWP- weighted emissions in 2012.' See US Greenhouse Gas Emissions Inventory, *Executive Summary* (2014), para. ES-9. The greenhouse gas emission inventory presents emissions from fossil fuel combustion by 'end use sector', but these are so broad (for example, industrial, commercial, residential) that they do not show the level of municipal wastewater treatment. Ibid. para. ES-11. As noted above, in the United States, water reclamation facilities spend around US$4 billion for energy annually. Milwaukee Metropolitan Sewerage District, *Sustainable Water Reclamation*, above n. 6.

[9] Water Environment Research Foundation, *Energy Production and Efficiency Research*, above n. 5, at 1.

treatment processes to harness this renewable energy and reduce greenhouse gas emissions from fossil fuel combustion. A municipal sewage treatment facility that serves 2.5 million people in England projects that switching from fossil fuels to sewage power will result in a reduction in its 'carbon emissions by 300,000 metric tons, the emissions reduction equivalent of taking about 63,000 cars off the road'.[10]

The largest source of greenhouse gases (GHG)[11] in the United States comes from fossil fuel combustion by the electric power industry.[12] In addition to the GHG emissions from electricity municipal wastewater treatment facilities purchase from the power industry, the treatment of wastewater produces GHGs. According to the US greenhouse gas emissions inventory, wastewater treatment (not limited to municipal sewage) accounts for 2.2 per cent of US methane emissions, and 1.2 per cent of US nitrous oxide emissions.[13]

Because removing pollutants from municipal sewage is such an energy-intensive process, the first step in becoming net energy neutral is to make the facility more energy efficient. 'Approximately, 60% of the energy used at wastewater treatment facilities is for aeration.'[14] Changing biological treatment processes 'from aerobic to anaerobic or anoxic microbes' contains the greatest potential for energy reductions.[15] The second step is to capture the energy potential contained in the sewage and use it to power the municipal wastewater treatment facility. If more energy exists, it can be exported to other nearby users to replace their dependence on fossil fuel-based energy. The case studies below show how facilities have reduced energy demands to treat municipal sewage and describe several methods for capturing and using sewage energy.

---

[10] Atkin, 'People in England are Harnessing', above n. 3.

[11] 'Greenhouse gases trap heat and make the planet warmer. The most important greenhouse gases directly emitted by humans include CO2 [carbon dioxide], CH4 [methane], N2O [nitrous oxide], and several other fluorine-containing halogenated substances. Although the direct greenhouse gases CO2, CH4, and N2O occur naturally in the atmosphere, human activities have changed their atmospheric concentrations. From the pre-industrial era (that is, ending about 1750) to 2012, concentrations of these greenhouse gases have increased globally by 40, 151, and 20 percent, respectively'. See US Greenhouse Gas Emissions Inventory, *Executive Summary*, above n. 8, para. ES-2.

[12] Ibid. para. ES-22 and Figure ES-13.

[13] Ibid. para. ES-21.

[14] Water Environment Research Foundation, *Energy Production and Efficiency Research*, above n. 5, at 1. Aeration is providing oxygen for a biological system like activated sludge treatment. Ibid.

[15] Ibid. 4.

(2) Municipal Wastewater Energy Potential

After reducing energy demands, there are a variety of options to harness the energy contained within the wastewater process and use it to meet the facility's remaining energy needs. Municipal wastewater contains three different types of energy that can be harnessed: thermal, hydraulic and chemical. *Thermal energy* or the heat energy is the energy contained in the wastewater which is governed by the specific heat capacity of water. *Hydraulic energy* can be of two types. *Potential energy* is the energy due to the water elevation while *kinetic energy* is the energy from moving water (velocity). *Chemical (calorific) energy* is the energy content stored in the various organic chemicals in the wastewater. The organic strength is typically expressed as a chemical oxygen demand (COD) in mg/L.[16]

These potential sources of energy at wastewater treatment facilities can be harnessed and used in at least five ways: (1) fuel cells emit light energy that degrades organic compounds in wastewater, generating electrons that provide a renewable source of electrical power; (2) biosolids in wastewater can be anaerobically digested to make biogas; (3) algae can be grown in nutrient-rich wastewater and harvested to make biofuel; (4) wastewater's thermal energy can be harvested and used for heating and cooling; and (5) wastewater's gravity-driven movement can turn propellers and turbines to produce electricity.[17]

The most developed opportunity for energy recovery at treatment plants is from biosolids. Unprocessed biosolids typically contain 18,000 kJ/kg (8,000 BTU/lb) on a dry weight basis.[18] The most typical way to access this is through anaerobic digestion, where the volatile solids are converted to biogas, and then onsite power generation units convert the biogas to electricity.[19] The heat from the power generation units can be recovered and used to heat the digesters.[20] When combined with energy efficiency improvements to reduce overall demands, biogas production has the potential to move wastewater treatment facilities entirely off fossil fuels.[21]

---

[16] Ibid. 1.

[17] Ibid. 4–7.

[18] Ibid. 4.

[19] Ibid. 4. This biogas is composed of greenhouse gases (60–65 per cent methane and 35–40 per cent CO_2). Ibid.

[20] Ibid.

[21] Malin Jonasson, *Energy Benchmark for Wastewater Treatment Processes: A Comparison Between Sweden and Austria* (PhD Thesis, Lund University,

Some facilities are following the process used on some 200 farms in the United States, and creating biomethane, which is an upgraded biogas from anaerobic digestion:

> The normal biogas produced from anaerobic digestion is comprised of about 60 percent methane and 40 percent carbon dioxide. Biomethane is an upgraded version of biogas that can be injected and distributed through the natural gas grid, and can be used in vehicles the same way as natural gas.[22]

Further, this can be used in place of diesel. 'Western Washington University researchers estimate an engine powered with bio-methane emits about 95 percent less carbon than a traditionally fueled engine.'[23]

Some things that are seen as pollutants or waste to be disposed are actually bonus sources of energy for a properly-designed wastewater treatment facility. Adding high-strength organic waste, such as fats, oils and grease from food production, to co-digest with biosolids, can boost biogas production:[24]

> Other organic wastes that could be used in the co-digestion process include glycerin from biodiesel production, airplane de-icing fluid waste, manure, and other organic wastes (brewery, cheese production, etc.).[25]

After removing contaminants, biogas can be used as a vehicle fuel, injected into a natural gas pipeline, or the methane converted into liquid biofuel, methanol.[26]

Additionally, municipal wastewater facilities can build algae bioreactors. These use wastewater to grow algae to produce biofuels (including methane, biodiesel, ethanol, hydrocarbon chains and hydrogen).[27]

This chapter provides three case studies of urban sewage treatment facilities to illustrate how to implement strategies to become energy efficient and then meet remaining energy needs by using the energy potential contained in sewage.

2007), p. 56, available at www.iea.lth.se/publications/MS-Theses/Full document/5247_full_document.pdf.

22 Atkin, 'People in England are Harnessing', above n. 3.

23 Ibid.

24 Water Environment Research Foundation, *Energy Production and Efficiency Research*, above n. 5, at 5.

25 Ibid.

26 Ibid.

27 Ibid. 7. There are significant limitations to using algae to produce biofuels.

III THREE CASE STUDIES SHOWING A TRANSITION TO SUSTAINABLE SEWAGE ENERGY

(1) Strass im Zillertal, Austria

(i) Background

Located near Strass im Zillertal, the Strass wastewater treatment facility (Strass facility) serves 31 communities in the Achental and Zillertal valleys east of Innsbruck, in Austria. The plant provides wastewater treatment for a population that ranges from 60,000 in the summer to 250,000 in the winter tourist season. The peak winter flow and load is equivalent to a plant treatment capacity of 10 MGD. The Strass facility is one of the best performing wastewater treatment facilities in Europe and the most energy-efficient wastewater treatment plant in Austria. For a decade, the facility has been producing more energy than it requires for its operations.[28] It has been way ahead of other European facilities. For example, the first facility in the United Kingdom to be a net energy producer was just announced in 2014. It will 'make bio-methane power available to the public, injecting the biomethane into the electric grid'.[29]

As will be seen through a comparison to the case studies in the United States, although this facility produces less energy than the similar-sized one in Sheboygan, Wisconsin, it uses far less energy because of its focus on energy efficiency.

(ii) Energy demands and production

By 2005, the Strass facility was a net energy producer; the Strass facility consumed 7,860 kWh/day[30] and produced 8,490 kWh/day of electricity from the biogas-driven generators.[31] It became a net energy producer through a process of improvements that started with an intense focus on energy efficiency. It then effectively invested in technology that allowed it to capture the renewable energy contained in the municipal sewage. In 2001, the Strass facility installed a new, higher-efficiency, eight-cylinder, co-generation engine that provides 340 kW of power.[32] The new

---

[28] Water Environmental Research Foundation, *Sustainable Treatment: Best Practices from the Strass im Zillertal Wastewater Treatment Plant* (2010), available at www.werf.org/c/_FinalReportPDFs/OWSO/OWSO4R07b.aspx.

[29] Atkin, 'People in England are Harnessing', above n. 3.

[30] Water Environmental Research Foundation, *Sustainable Treatment*, above n. 28, at 3.

[31] Ibid.

[32] Ibid.

co-generation units convert biogas to electrical energy at an average efficiency of 38 per cent.[33] Between 1996 and 2005, the percentage of energy self-sufficiency improved steadily from 49 to 108 per cent,[34] and as of 2008, self-sufficiency reached 120 per cent.[35]

(iii) Overview of Strass' sustainable energy transition

Successive sustainability efforts since 1999 resulted in significant cost and energy savings. An overview of these efforts includes:

- reduction of chemical costs for sludge thickening by 50 per cent;
- reduction in sludge dewatering costs by 33 per cent;
- reduction in energy consumption on mass treated basis from approximately 6.5 euro/kg NH_4-n removed in 2003 to 2.9 euro/kg NH_4-n removed in 2007/2008;
- reduction in energy consumption for sidestream treatment from 350 kWh/d to 196 kWh/d by implementing a novel sidestream nitrogen removal system (DEMON®); and
- enhanced utilization of the digester gas by converting to a state-of-the-art cogeneration unit, boosting electrical efficiency from 33 to 40 per cent and overall usage efficiency from 2.05 to 2.30 kWh/m^3 of digester gas.[36]

(iv) Reducing Energy Demands Through Deammonification (DEMON process)

Nitrogen removal is the most costly and most energy-intensive part of wastewater treatment.[37] Energy is consumed in the powerful blowers during the aeration process, additional carbon (methanol) is needed as a fuel for the bacteria, and dewatering the sludge from sidestreams, which have a significantly higher nitrogen load than ordinary wastewater, is particularly costly.[38]

---

33 Ibid.

34 Ibid.

35 Dimitri Katehis, *Bay Area Clean Water Agencies, Enhancing Sustainability Practices of Wastewater Treatment: The Strass Case Study* (2011), available at http://bacwa.org/Portals/0/Strass%20Case%20Study.pdf.

36 Ibid.

37 Ibid. 4.

38 Ibid.

Using biological treatment processes are the most cost-effective ways to reduce energy consumption and chemical usage.[39] In recent years, the nitritation/denitritation and deammonification processes have been implemented successfully in Europe and are being adopted in the United States.[40]

The Strass facility engages in a two-stage primary and secondary biological treatment process. This two-stage approach removes organic compounds and converts organics to biogas.[41]

The Strass facility achieved energy savings from sidestream treatment using the patented DEMON® process for deammonification.[42] Bernhard Wett at the University of Innsbruck developed the DEMON® process.[43] The deammonification process utilizes the recently discovered Anammox bacteria, which requires no additional carbon and only 40 per cent of the oxygen required for conventional nitrogen removal.[44] The deammonification process can save up to 63 per cent of the oxygen demand compared to conventional nitrification/denitrification processes, with nearly 100 per cent reduction in carbon demand, 80 per cent reduction in biomass production, and no additional alkalinity requirement.[45] The deammonification process can achieve up to 95 per cent ammonia removal,[46] thus

---

[39] US Environmental Protection Agency (EPA), *Emerging Technologies for Wastewater Treatment and In-Plant Wet Weather Management* (2013), available at http://water.epa.gov/scitech/wastetech/upload/Emerging-Technologies-Report-2.pdf.

[40] Ibid.

[41] Water Environmental Research Foundation, *Sustainable Treatment*, above n. 28, at 2. In the first stage, they eliminate 55–65 per cent of the organic load and operate at a half-day sludge retention time (SRT). In the next stage, the low-loaded stage, eliminates nitrogen at an annual efficiency of about 80 per cent and is operated at a ten-day SRT. This two-stage approach 'results in high-rate entrapment of organics without excessive aerobic stabilization in the A-stage system. Due to the reduced SRT, organic compounds are removed mainly by adsorption from the A-stage onto solids and are immediately conveyed through thickening and digestion, where conversion of organics to biogas occurs'. Ibid.

[42] Ibid. 3.

[43] Thomas Wirthensohn, 'Turning Waste into Watts: Producing and Reducing Energy in U.S. Wastewater Treatment with Austrian Knowledge', *Bridges* (April 2009), p. 2.

[44] Water Environmental Research Foundation, *Sustainable Treatment*, above n. 28, at 2.

[45] US Environmental Protection Agency (EPA), *Emerging Technologies for Wastewater Treatment*, above n. 39, para. 3-16.

[46] Ibid. para. 3-17.

reducing costs and environmental impact.[47] The nitritation and denitritation process offers energy and carbon savings. Less carbon means as much as 40 per cent less sludge production.[48] The average nitrogen removal efficiency ranges from 85 to 95 per cent.[49]

The Strass facility successfully implemented the technology in 2002, which was a key to making the Strass facility Austria's most energy-efficient wastewater treatment plant.[50] By 2005, the Strass facility was the first to be operated successfully under a full load.[51] This process treats certain sidestreams with particularly high nitrogen loads, decreasing energy consumption by more than 50 per cent.[52]

(v) Benchmarking

Austria's success in energy-efficient wastewater treatment is due in part to the benchmarking process.[53] The first benchmarks were developed in 1999, and roughly 950 wastewater treatment facilities participated in the process, which annually compares individual costs to overall national performance.[54] Participating facilities compare their own data to the overall benchmarks, stimulating a competition between facilities and the drive to improve.[55] As a result, Austrian municipal wastewater treatment facilities have decreased their electricity costs by about 30 per cent since 1999.[56] Compared to Sweden, which initiated its energy saving programme in 2005, Austrian facilities use roughly 45 per cent less electrical energy.[57]

(vi) Conclusion

As noted by Wett *et al*:

---

47 Katehis, *Bay Area Clean Water Agencies,* above n. 35, at 45.

48 US EPA, *Emerging Technologies for Wastewater Treatment*, above n. 39, para. 3-20.

49 Ibid.

50 Wirthensohn, 'Turning Waste into Watts', above n. 43, at 5.

51 Ibid.

52 Ibid. 2.

53 B. Wett, K. Buchauer and C. Fimml, *Energy Self-Sufficiency as a Feasible Concept for Wastewater Treatment Systems* (Institute of Infrastructure and Environmental Engineering, University of Innsbruck, 2007).

54 Ibid.

55 Ibid.

56 Jonasson, *Energy Benchmark for Wastewater Treatment Processes*, above n. 21.

57 Ibid.

> in sum, those allegedly perfect European [wastewater treatment facilities] offer an astounding average energy saving potential of about 30–50% without the need to compromise on treatment efficiency. It is hence safe to assume that the worldwide existing energy saving potential … is enormous.[58]

The Strass facility case study shows that redesigning a 10 MGD wastewater treatment to be sustainable is an immediately viable option; the technology exists to substantially reduce energy usage related to sewage treatment and to meet the remaining energy demands with renewable sewage power.

(2) Sheboygan, Wisconsin, United States

(i) Background

Located near Lake Michigan, one of the United States' Great Lakes, the Sheboygan wastewater treatment plant (Sheboygan facility) serves seven communities with a total of 68,000 people in eastern Wisconsin in the United States.[59] The annual treatment capacity is the same as the Strass facility, at 10 MGD, which provides a solid comparison.[60] The Sheboygan facility is one of a few wastewater treatment plants in the United States that is producing most of the energy required to run the facility. This transition has provided financial benefits: the use of onsite renewable sewage power saves the facility about US$78,000 annually for electricity and US$60,000 for heat.[61]

(ii) Energy demands and production

In 2002, the facility did a study of its energy demands and renewable energy potential. Whenever an equipment upgrade is needed, they consider how the investment in new equipment can improve energy efficiency. The facility now uses 20 per cent less energy compared to a baseline figure in 2003.[62] The drive to make the facility more energy

---

58 Wett, Buchauer and Fimml, *Energy Self-Sufficiency as a Feasible Concept*, above n. 53, at 3.

59 Sheboygan Regional Wastewater Treatment Facility, see www.sheboygan-wwtp.com.

60 Ibid.

61 American Council for Energy Efficiency Economy, *Sheboygan Wastewater Treatment Plant Energy Efficiency Initiatives* (May 2012), available at http://aceee.org/sector/local-policy/case-studies/sheboygan-wastewater-treatment-plant-.

62 Ibid.

efficient was led by the facility Superintendent and facilitated by Wisconsin Focus on Energy, a State-wide ratepayer-funded energy efficiency programme. Focus on Energy provided technical assistance and grants to pay for the energy efficiency improvements.[63] Another nudge toward greater energy efficiency comes from the Wisconsin Department of Natural Resources, which encourages including energy considerations when conducting required project cost effectiveness calculations.[64] Facility staff are better able to assess and communicate the value of energy efficiency because they analyze the 'lifecycle cost of all projects, instead of implementing the least capital cost fix for replacing failing equipment'.[65]

Currently, the Sheboygan facility produces 90 per cent of its annual electrical energy and 85 per cent of its heat requirements. It uses the biogas it produces to fuel boilers that heat the anaerobic digesters and the plant buildings.[66] It also uses the biogas to produce electricity to power the facility's operations.[67] Processing 10 MGD of wastewater, the Sheboygan facility can produce biogas at a rate of 500,000 ft^3/day @ 65% methane.[68] The Sheboygan facility produces electrical and thermal energy at a rate of 16,500 kWh/day (at peak gas production) and 55 million BTU/day.[69] This is almost double the electricity production of the Strass facility, and yet the Strass facility is able to export the excess electricity it produces because it requires much less energy to run the Strass facility due to its even greater investments in energy efficiency.[70]

(iii) Overview of Sheboygan's sustainable energy transition

Although the Sheboygan facility has made strides to become more energy efficient, its greatest results have been in the second step in the sustainable energy transition: harnessing renewable energy from sewage. In order to transition to this more sustainable energy produced at the Sheboygan facility, they installed a variety of equipment in two stages.

---

63 Ibid. In 2006, Wisconsin's Focus on Energy produced *Water and Wastewater Energy Best Practice Guidebook.*

64 Ibid.

65 Ibid.

66 Sheboygan Regional Wastewater Treatment Facility, *Microturbines*, available at www.sheboyganwwtp.com/4a_microturbines.php.

67 Ibid.

68 Ibid.

69 Ibid.

70 The Strass facility produces 8,490 kWh/day of electricity from the biogas-driven generators. Water Environmental Research Foundation, *Sustainable Treatment*, above n. 28, at 3.

In 2006, the equipment improvements included: ten 30kW Capstone Micro-turbines, Unison Solutions Gas Conditioning Equipment, and two Cain Heat Recovery Units. In 2008, they started co-digestion of high strength wastes. This produced so much more energy that in 2010, they installed new equipment to utilize the additional biogas. They invested in two 200kW Capstone Micro-turbines to convert the biogas to electricity.[71]

(iv) Utilizing digester gas

The Sheboygan facility uses primary and secondary digesters with a total volume of 4,855,000 gallons. The sludge is retained in the digesters for 30 days:

> While the sludge is in the primary digesters, the sludge is heated and mixed to create the appropriate environment for the anaerobic bacteria to stabilize the sludge. The methane gas produced is used as a fuel to heat the digesters and to fuel 10 Capstone Micro-turbines that produce 30 kW each for a combined production of 2,300 megawatts of electricity annually. Excess methane gas can be used to fuel a caterpillar engine that powers one influent lift pump.[72]

In 2006, the Sheboygan facility initially installed these ten micro-turbines to produce electricity from the biogas, along with heat recovery units and gas conditioning system. The facility partnered with Alliant Energy – Wisconsin Power & Light, which provided the funding for the new equipment. The power company recovered its investment through the sale of electricity back to the Sheboygan facility. Eventually, in 2012, the Sheboygan facility exercised its option to purchase this equipment from the power company.[73] As the Sheboygan facility Superintendent explained, the transition to energy self-sufficiency made fiscal sense:

> With energy costs increasing each year, we were actively looking at different ways to reduce our total energy bill. Since we were wasting excess biogas produced at the wastewater treatment plant, it became evident that we could use the excess biogas as fuel for the Capstone Micro-Turbines and reduce our energy cost. Our partnership with Alliant Energy made this project a reality.[74]

---

[71] Sheboygan Regional Wastewater Treatment Facility, *Microturbines*, above n. 66.

[72] Sheboygan Regional Wastewater Treatment Facility, *Solids Handling*, available at www.sheboyganwwtp.com/4_solids.php.

[73] Sheboygan Regional Wastewater Treatment Facility, *Microturbines*, above n. 66.

[74] American Council for Energy Efficiency Economy, *Sheboygan Wastewater Treatment Plant Energy Efficiency Initiatives* above n. 61.

In 2008, the facility found it produced a lot more biogas when it started injecting high-strength organic wastes directly into the anaerobic digesters.[75] This is called co-digestion. The source of the high-strength wastes for the Sheboygan facility is food processing and ethanol production. Adding high-strength waste to their waste stream boosted biogas production by 150 per cent.[76]

In 2010, they installed two more Capstone micro-turbines to utilize the excess biogas produced as a result of co-digestion. These turbines each have the capacity to produce 200 kW. The Sheboygan facility's energy production capacity now stands at 700 kW of cogeneration and 2.4 million BTU of heat per hour.[77] The Sheboygan case study demonstrates the ability to produce significant amounts of energy from sewage, especially when boosting energy production with high-strength wastes from food and ethanol production.

It also provides an example of a facility that, despite its energy efficiency improvements of approximately 20 per cent, still uses much more energy to process 10 MGD of sewage than the Strass facility. Perhaps other countries could learn from Austria's successful policy of benchmarking to drive energy efficiency at wastewater treatment facilities. The Strass facility's reduction in energy usage was driven by Austria's benchmarking, in which approximately 950 wastewater treatment facilities compete in comparing their energy usage and costs to overall national performance of the sector.[78] Although the Sheboygan facility communicates its energy usage to its staff to encourage energy efficiency, there is not the same type of comparison and competition across the municipal wastewater sector in the United States.[79]

---

[75] Sheboygan Regional Wastewater Treatment Facility, *Microturbines*, above n. 66.

[76] Ibid.

[77] Ibid.

[78] Wett, Buchauer and Fimml, *Energy Self-Sufficiency as a Feasible Concept*, above n. 53.

[79] See http://aceee.org/sector/local-policy/case-studies/sheboygan-wastewater-treatment-plant-#performance.

(3) Milwaukee Metropolitan Sewerage District, Wisconsin, United States

(i) Background

The Milwaukee Metropolitan Sewerage District ('Milwaukee facility') is a regional government agency serving 1.1 million people in 28 communities in the Greater Milwaukee Area, in south-eastern Wisconsin, in the United States.[80] A large percentage of the Milwaukee facility's annual budget (18 per cent in 2012) is spent on purchasing energy.[81]

Just like the Sheboygan facility, the Milwaukee facility is in Wisconsin, a state where the utility rate structure 'favors the production of new energy by burning cheap coal'.[82] Yet, in 2005, the Milwaukee facility adopted a sustainability policy to:

> encourage and optimize the use of renewable, recyclable, eco-friendly materials; reduce energy consumption and emissions from fossil fuels; and have a positive impact on the region's economic, social and environmental resources while maintaining the desired level-of-services in a financially responsible manner.[83]

The Milwaukee facility's goal is to achieve complete energy independence by 2035.[84] Like the Sheboygan facility, this focus on sustainability appears to be driven in large part by the leadership of the facility and supported by the economic case.[85]

(ii) Energy demands and production

The Milwaukee facility has two sewage treatment locations: Jones Island and South Shore. As of 2012, the Milwaukee facility has been able to set up South Shore to create two-thirds of the energy it uses to run the treatment plant.[86]

---

80 Milwaukee Metropolitan Sewerage District, *About Us*, available at www.mmsd.com/about/about-us.

81 Milwaukee Metropolitan Sewerage District, *Sustainable Water Reclamation*, above n. 6.

82 Susan Nusser, 'A Giant of Renewable Energy', *Urban Milwaukee* (3 September 2013), available at http://urbanmilwaukee.com/2013/09/03/a-giant-of-renewable-energy/.

83 Milwaukee Metropolitan Sewerage District, *Sustainable Water Reclamation*, above n. 6, at 15.

84 Ibid. 42.

85 Ibid.

86 Ibid. 40.

(iii) Overview of Milwaukee's sustainable energy transition

The Milwaukee facility has continued to optimize its energy efficiency during the past several years by installing newer, more sustainable equipment and implementing new treatment technologies. At South Shore, these efforts start with reducing energy demands, which they have done through installing new high-efficiency blowers, new instrumentation and control systems and power monitors.

Two-thirds of the remaining energy needs are met by harnessing energy produced at South Shore. They installed new digester mixing systems to increase biogas production and produce more electricity to power the facility. They are adding high-strength wastes into digesters to generate more biogas. They installed five engine/generators that are fueled by this digester biogas, and these power the facility's sewage treatment process.[87]

At Jones Island, they are reducing energy needs by installing new instrumentation, control systems and power monitors. They are meeting some of the remaining energy needs through a 20 kW photovoltaic solar array and methane brought through a pipeline running from the regional landfill, which fuels new turbine generators at the facility.[88]

Landfill gas, a local source of energy, is being recycled into power at Jones Island.[89] A 19-mile long pipeline transports landfill gas from the Emerald Park Landfill in Muskego, Wisconsin.[90] Three new turbines, which replaced two 40-year-old natural gas turbines, transform the landfill's methane into electricity.[91] Through this conversion process, the Milwaukee facility will be able to produce a significant amount of the energy Jones Island needs, saving wastewater treatment customers tens of millions of dollars over a 20-year period.[92] The Milwaukee facility's 10-year contract with Veolia Water Milwaukee for the operation and maintenance of the sewers and reclamation facilities is expected to save customers US$35 million dollars.[93]

---

[87] Milwaukee Metropolitan Sewerage District, *Request for Proposal: Energy Plan A-5 – A-6* (2013), available at https://mmsd.diversitycompliance.com/FrontEnd/ProposalSearchPublicDetail.asp?XID=4343&TN=mmsd&PID=C18D60773FD2C225380C6B931D05A861C794F79FD6413E77.

[88] Ibid.

[89] Milwaukee Metropolitan Sewerage District, *Landfill Gas*, above n. 1.

[90] Ibid.

[91] Ibid.

[92] Ibid.

[93] Ibid.

(iv) Sewage treatment and digester gas production process

The Milwaukee facility implements a four-stage wastewater treatment process: screening, primary clarification, biological treatment and disinfection. First, during the screening stage, large and small objects are screened out and removed.[94] Next, during the primary clarification stage, grease and oil float to the top of large settling tanks, and organic solids sink to the bottom and are collected to make energy.[95] The organic solids, called primary sludge, are then turned into a renewable energy source.[96] A higher carbon content in the sludge results in greater energy production.[97] The Milwaukee facility's six anaerobic digesters take in the sludge, which is processed and produces methane.

The sludge needs to be agitated for maximum efficiency, and the Milwaukee facility is currently testing new systems that may increase efficiency by 10–20 per cent.[98] These new agitation systems will also enable the Milwaukee facility to treat high-strength wastes, such as glycol used for de-icing airplanes, which produce more heat and gas than sewage from household sources.[99] The Milwaukee facility partnered with Marquette University researchers to conduct an industrial survey of potential high strength wastes available within a 100-mile radius. The addition of these high-strength wastes could more than double energy production, producing an equivalent of enough energy to power 2,000 homes.[100]

After the biosolids are separated out and pumped into the digesters, the wastewater is ready to be treated biologically.[101] During the biological treatment, microscopic organisms called 'bugs' break down the organic material.[102] After the 'bugs' eat the remaining waste, they die, and their bodies become the organic matter that is turned into fertilizer.[103] Finally, during the disinfection stage, disease-causing organisms are killed by

---

94 Milwaukee Metropolitan Sewerage District, *Wastewater Treatment*, available at www.mmsd.com/wastewatertreatment/treatment-process.

95 Ibid.

96 Nusser, 'A Giant of Renewable Energy', above n. 82.

97 Ibid.

98 Ibid.

99 Ibid.

100 Ibid. The researchers anticipate high-strength waste additions to increase energy production from 800,000–900,000 cubic feet per day to 2 million cubic feet per day. Ibid.

101 Ibid.

102 Milwaukee Metropolitan Sewerage District, *Wastewater Treatment*, above n. 94.

103 Nusser, 'A Giant of Renewable Energy', above n. 82.

chemicals that are then neutralized, and the water is returned to Lake Michigan.[104]

(v) Sewer-thermal energy

After setting a goal of meeting 100 per cent of its energy needs with renewable resources by 2035,[105] the Milwaukee facility hired consultants to investigate sewage heat recovery technologies and their applicability to its sustainability goals.[106] The consultants explored heat recovery strategies within the conveyance system only; but they recommended further investigation of heat recovery opportunities at the wastewater treatment facilities.[107] Sewage heat recovery is an emerging technology in the wastewater treatment sector in the United States, but a significant number of projects have been implemented in Europe.[108] The energy that is inherent in wastewater can be captured using heat-exchange technology.[109] Heat exchangers can be placed directly in sewers to harvest the energy – in the form of heat – to offset heating demands at nearby land uses.[110] The energy can also be harvested and used in water reclamation facilities with the added benefit of reducing the temperature of the water before it is returned to a natural water body.[111]

A companion technology to a heat exchanger is a heat pump, which 'converts the low-temperature heat recovered from the sewer into high-temperature heat that can be used in building heating or hot water

---

[104] Milwaukee Metropolitan Sewerage District, *Wastewater Treatment*, above n. 94.

[105] Milwaukee Metropolitan Sewerage District, *Request for Proposal: Energy Plan at A-1. Assessment of Sewage Heat Recovery Technology and Applicability to the Milwaukee Metropolitan Sewerage District* (2013), available at www.mmsd.com/-/media/MMSD/Documents/Sustainability/Sewer%20Heat%20 Recovery.pdf.

[106] Ibid. 1.

[107] Ibid. 18. The consultants' recommendation of further analysis of the facilities was based on: (i) Wastewater treatment facilities receive wastewater with a more consistent base flow and temperature than the collection system, likely resulting in a more robust heat recovery system. (ii) Heat exchangers could be incorporated at the wastewater treatment facility influent or effluent. (iii) There are usually higher heating loads at the wastewater treatment facilities that would directly utilize recovered heat. Ibid.

[108] Ibid. 1. In the United States, Philadelphia is implementing a project, and Seattle plans to launch a project in 2015. Ibid.

[109] Milwaukee Metropolitan Sewerage District, *Sustainable Water Reclamation*, above n. 6, at 43.

[110] Ibid. 1.

[111] Ibid. 43.

systems'.[112] Recovered sewer heat can be used directly for building heat or hot water, or to preheat a boiler or a domestic hot water system.[113]

The consultants could not provide a payback for the evaluated technologies as applied to the sewage conveyance system because implementation under current conditions will not save money, due in part to the relatively low cost of natural gas.[114] However, they noted that for in-sewer heat exchangers, there could be an opportunity to install this technology as part of the overall cost of otherwise required sewer replacement in discrete parts of the system.[115]

(vi) Future efforts

The Milwaukee facility continues to explore and develop existing and new sources of renewable energy, including wind, solar, sewer-thermal and algae biofuels.[116] Algae can be cultivated, harvested and refined as biofuel.[117] Algae needs sunlight, water and nutrients to grow, and using wastewater to grow algae and create biofuel can reduce waste and help the facility meet its permit limits on nutrients.[118] The Milwaukee facility hopes to remain involved with this research.[119] The Milwaukee facility also plans to continue to evaluate ways to use all the waste heat generated by the solids drying process, the boiler system and the landfill gas-powered turbines; and plans to continue pursuing new sources of high-strength waste and the mixing and staging of waste.[120] This case study adds an example from a facility that is treating at least 20 times more waste per day than the Strass and Sheboygan facilities. It shows the power of setting goals for sustainability and experimenting with different aspects of the system to make progress toward that goal.

---

[112] Milwaukee Metropolitan Sewerage District, *Request for Proposal*, above n. 105, at 16.

[113] Ibid. Recovered sewer heat can be used for building heat if flows are generally greater than 150 gpm. Ibid. 17.

[114] Ibid. 13.

[115] Ibid. 13. A 20-year payback is required for this technology to be considered based on economics. Ibid.

[116] Milwaukee Metropolitan Sewerage District, *Sustainable Water Reclamation*, above n. 6, at 42.

[117] Ibid.

[118] Ibid.

[119] Ibid.

[120] Ibid.

IV CONCLUSION

The United Nations Intergovernmental Panel on Climate Change reported that 'the world is dangerously close to no longer being able to limit global warming to 2C over pre-industrial times'.[121] At this time when all countries need to be focused on a rapid transition to reduce reliance on fossil fuels, redesigning municipal sewage treatment to become net energy producers of renewable energy can be a critical part of progress.

Importantly, cities do not need to wait until they are building a *new* treatment system. The three case studies in this chapter demonstrate that existing sewage treatment facilities can be redesigned to be more energy efficient and to recapture for use or sale the energy contained in the sewage they are processing. The case studies involve different sizes of facilities providing a proof of concept for facilities that process the waste produced by as few as 68,000 people to as many as more than 1 million people. The case studies highlight several key drivers for this transition:

- the importance of thought leaders within the facility management;
- benchmarking across the sector on both costs and energy usage to encourage competition between facilities to be the most efficient;
- economic savings from energy efficiency and greater reliance on renewable sewage power;
- utilizing lifecycle analysis and energy costs when determining how to invest in new equipment;
- grants for energy efficiency to offset the initial up front costs; and
- partnering with a local energy utility to fund the renewable energy investments.

Several additional opportunities exist that could be drivers forward in this transition to renewable sewage power. These are beyond the scope of this chapter so will only be briefly outlined, but each may deserve analysis for municipal systems considering this transition:

- count energy generated by sewage toward meeting Renewable Portfolio Standards (RPSs);[122]

---

[121] Trinh Theresa Do, 'UN Climate Summit: 4 things to know about the talks', *CBC News*, 23 September 2014, available at www.cbc.ca/news/world/un-climate-summit-4-things-to-know-about-the-talks-1.2774110.

[122] A Renewable Portfolio Standard in the United States is 'A state or federal level policy that requires that a minimum amount (usually a percentage) of electricity supply provided by each supply company is to come from renewable

- allow sewage power to create tradable Renewable Energy Credits or Certificates (RECs) to meet RPS goals or to be sold to others that must meet such goals;
- use supplemental environmental projects in consent decrees with municipal wastewater treatment facilities to require investments in energy efficiency and use of renewable sewage power at those facilities; and
- require future government investments in sewage treatment infrastructure to assess lifecycle and energy costs.

If municipal wastewater treatment facilities could sell the renewable attribute of their excess renewable energy produced by sewage as a REC, it would generate an additional stream of financing to justify the investment in energy efficiency and renewables at these facilities. 'Purchasers of RECs are buying the renewable attributes of those specific units of renewable energy, which helps offset conventional electricity generation in the region where the renewable generator is located.'[123] That 'offset' can be used to meet either voluntary or mandatory efforts to shift electric generation away from conventional fossil fuel combustion. Underlying the concept of RECs is the assumption, verified at a system-wide level, that the sewage facility's efficiency gains or generation output will replace or 'offset' greenhouse gas (GHG) emissions from conventional power plants that would otherwise have needed to burn fossil fuels to generate power. Whether sewage power counts as renewable for purposes of selling the attribute as a REC varies by programme, mostly on the basis of whether the regional electric grid accepts as factual the assumption that that offset will occur.[124]

The market value of RECs turns on whether buyers have voluntary or mandatory reasons to purchase credits for those GHG reductions. As an

---

energy'. Green-e, *Dictionary*, available at www.green-e.org/learn_dictionary.shtml#rec. Around the late 1990s, US States started adopting renewable energy targets (RPS) for their public utilities. When a utility purchases renewable electricity along with the Renewable Energy Certificate (REC) associated with it, the utility can use that to meet the Renewable Portfolio Standard requirements. Environmental Tracking Network of North America, *REC Questions and Answers,* available at www.etnna.org/images/PDFs/ETNNA-REC-QandA.pdf. Whether sewage-based energy qualifies as renewable for these purposes is based on individual state laws.

[123] Green-e, *Dictionary*, above n. 122. Green-e is an entity that certifies RECs.

[124] Environmental Tracking Network of North America, *REC Questions and Answers*, above n. 122.

example of the voluntary market for RECs, federal agencies, such as the US Environmental Protection Agency, and companies that wish to procure renewables but lack the ability to produce all the renewable energy they need, could purchase RECs from sewage-based energy generation. As an example of the compliance market for RECs, public utilities could purchase the sewage-based RECs when bundled together with the sewage-based renewable electricity to meet their state-required Renewable Portfolio Standards.[125] The price for RECs varies by market, so in states with a higher demand for renewables and a lower supply, municipal wastewater treatment facilities would get a higher price for the RECs they sell.[126]

Related to the last item, in the United States, Congress created a federal system for underwriting the cost of municipal wastewater treatment facilities when it passed the Clean Water Act. 'For a 20-year period, starting in 1972, the federal government paid up to 75 percent of the cost of building sewage treatment plants.'[127] Now many of those sewage treatment facilities are in need of major upgrades. A primary mechanism to deliver this financing is the Clean Water State Revolving Fund (CWSRF). Since its inception over two and half decades ago, the CWSRFs have provided over US$100 billion in funding for water infrastructure in the United States, primarily through low interest loans.[128] This program is essentially an infrastructure bank where the repayment on the loans gets funneled back into the government to be used for future funding of infrastructure. Governmental funding for this wastewater treatment infrastructure could require lifecycle analysis and energy cost analysis. If so, it could provide an incentive for a more rapid transition from fossil fuels to renewable sewage power.

In 2009, the American Recovery Act created the Green Project Reserve as a subset of money allocated through the CWSRF; this funds energy

---

[125] Ibid.

[126] Ibid.

[127] Brad Plumer, 'Our Cities' Water Systems are Becoming Obsolete: What will Replace Them?', *Vox*, 6 October 2014, available at www.vox.com/2014/10/6/6900959/water-systems-pollution-drinking-water-desalination.

[128] US Environmental Protection Agency (EPA), *Clean Water State Revolving Fund*, available at http://water.epa.gov/grants_funding/cwsrf/cwsrf_index.cfm. Congress created the CWSRF with the 1987 amendments to the Clean Water Act. 'Through the CWSRF program, each state and Puerto Rico maintain revolving loan funds to provide independent and permanent sources of low-cost financing for a wide range of water quality infrastructure projects', see http://water.epa.gov/grants_funding/cwsrf/basics.cfm.

efficiency projects specifically.[129] In fact, one municipal wastewater facility in Ohio used this funding source to pay for a project to capture excess methane gas and use it to meet 60–70 per cent of the facility's energy demands and save US$300,000 annually in energy costs.[130] In other words, it has both conceptual and field experience to demonstrate its feasibility. However, to date only a very small portion of the total expenditures from the CWSRF are used for these types of projects.[131] The US government could accelerate the transition to renewable sewage power if it dedicated more of these revolving loan funds for sustainable energy projects at wastewater treatment plants.

In sum, the climate imperative is clear, the technology exists for energy efficiency and renewable sewage power, and the financial incentives are beginning to emerge. Now we need to remove roadblocks and bolster support for the drivers to make this a reality at municipal wastewater treatment plants across the United States and throughout the world.

---

[129] US Environmental Protection Agency (EPA), *Green Project Reserve*, available at http://water.epa.gov/grants_funding/cwsrf/Green-Project-Reserve.cfm.

[130] US EPA, *Green Project Reserve, Case Study: Struthers Water Pollution Control Facility Powers Up with Methane Gas,* EPA-832-F-12-019 (2012), available at http://water.epa.gov/grants_funding/cwsrf/upload/Struthers-Water-Pollution-Control-Facility-Case-Study-FINAL.pdf.

[131] The US EPA reports that, 'For FY 2010 and FY 2011, each state was directed to allocate 20% of its CWSRF capitalization grant to eligible [Green Project Reserve] GPR projects. For FY 2012, the GPR amount was reduced to 10% of each state's capitalization grant', see http://water.epa.gov/grants_funding/cwsrf/Green-Project-Reserve.cfm.

PART III

Governance gaps

13. Environmentally displaced persons in the Niger Delta: challenges and prospects

Eloamaka Carol Okonkwo

I INTRODUCTION

It is a well-established fact that Nigeria is one of the world's largest producers of petroleum.[1] It is also a well-established fact that the oil industry is a source of huge revenue. For Nigeria, oil has been the main source of revenue since 1974.[2] Currently, oil accounts for more than 80 per cent of the government's budgetary revenue, and more than 90 per cent of exports.[3] Sadly, the exploitation of the oil and gas carries with it serious human and environmental degradation caused by oil spills, gas flaring, habitat destruction, air and water pollution and land degradation.[4] Degradation often results in serial damage to health, environment and socio-economic activities that sometimes lead to displacement. Over the years, much attention has been given to the environmental and health impacts. This chapter transcends the level of environmental and health

[1] Figures show that production of oil has dropped in recent years. See the information provided by US Energy Information Administration, available at www.eia.gov/countries/cab.cfm?fips=NI.

[2] The period of the oil boom.

[3] International Monetary Fund, *Country Report No. 13/116* (2013) estimates that oil and natural gas export revenue accounted for over 95 per cent of Nigerian total export revenue in 2012, see www.imf.org/external/pubs/ft/scr/2013/cr13116.pdf.

[4] According to Amnesty International more than 2,000 sites were identified by National Oil Spill Detection and Response Agency (NOSDRA) as needing remediation in April 2008, and this was affecting fishing, forest's products and bathing and drinking water for the people. See Amnesty International, *Oil Industry has Brought Poverty and Pollution to Niger Delta* (2009), available at www.amnesty.org/en/news-and-updates/news/oil-industry-has-brought-poverty-and-pollution-to-niger-delta-20090630.

impacts to focus on the socio-economic impacts because this issue has not received as much attention from scholars and because of its importance to the study of environmental displacement.

This chapter aims to evaluate the position of Niger Deltans who relocate because of the impacts of oil pollution. Specifically, it addresses the issues of the socio-economic impacts of oil-related pollution, how they affect environmentally-displaced persons and the challenges to securing justice for them. It starts with the conceptual framework of environmental displacement and environmentally and internally displaced persons and moves on to the socio-economic consequences of oil-related pollution. It also considers whether Niger Deltans are environmentally displaced and the role of socio-economic impacts of pollution in displacing Niger Deltans, if any. Further, it considers the legal frameworks that attempt to protect the environmentally-displaced Niger Deltans and concludes with recommendations.

II CONCEPTUAL FRAMEWORK OF ENVIRONMENTAL DISPLACEMENT, ENVIRONMENTALLY AND INTERNALLY DISPLACED PERSONS

Attempts towards establishing a theoretical concept of displacement started in the mid-1980s.[5] Since then, many theoretical approaches and attempts at classification have emerged, including the concepts of conflict-induced, development-induced, disaster-induced and environmentally-induced displacement; this chapter is concerned with environmentally-induced displacement. It is important to note that earlier studies of environmentally-induced displacement focused on the concept of 'environmental refugees'.[6] This is restrictive, as environmental refugees do not

---

[5] Essam El-Hinnawi, *Environmental Refugees* (United Nations Environmental Programme, 1985).

[6] Ibid. Richard Black, *Refugees, Environment, and Development* (Addison Wesley Longman Singapore, 1998); Richard Black and Mohammed Sessay, 'Forced Migration, Environmental Change, and Wood Fuel Issues in the Senegal River Valley' (1997) 24 *Environmental Conservation* 251; Greame Hugo, 'Environmental Concerns and International Migration' (1996) 30 *International Migration Review* 105; Ogenga Otunnu, 'Environmental Refugees in Sub-Saharan Africa: Causes and Effects' (1992) *Refuge* 12, available at http://pi.library.yorku.ca/ojs/index.php/refuge/article/viewFile/21640/20313; Arthur H. Westing, 'Population, Desertification, and Migration' (1994) 21 *Environmental*

include people who relocate within the same country, who therefore could not appropriately be described as environmentally-displaced persons.

What then is the appropriate definition of an environmentally displaced person (EDP)? This is not an easy question. El-Hinnawi about 29 years ago referred to EDPs as environmental refugees and stated that they were:

> those people who have been forced to leave their traditional habitat, temporarily or permanently, because of a marked environmental disruption (natural and/or triggered by people) that jeopardi[s]ed their existence and/or seriously affected the quality of their life.[7]

Myers and Kent defined EDPs as:

> Persons who can no longer gain a secure livelihood in their traditional homelands because of environmental factors ... In face of these environmental threats, people feel they have no alternative but to seek sustenance elsewhere, whether within their own countries or beyond and whether on a semi-permanent or permanent basis.[8]

Kibreab defined EDPs as follows:

> [P]ersons who has [*sic*] been forced or obliged to flee or to leave their homes or places of habitual residence in particular as a result of, or in order to avoid the effects of, armed conflict, situations of generalized violence, violations of human rights or natural or human-made disasters, and who have not crossed an internationally recognized state border.[9]

The three definitions highlighted above show the difficulty of defining EDPs. There are many similarities and differences within these definitions, but it is important to note that the three scholars above defined EDPs from different perspectives. El-Hinnawi's definition comes from the refugee's point of view, Kibreab restricts the definition to internal movement, while Myers and Kent encompass both internal and external movement. The major similarity that appears in all three is the phrase

---

Conservation 110; Norman Myers and Jennifer Kent, *Environmental Exodus: An Emergent Crisis in the Global Arena* (Climate Institute, 1995); Astri Suhrke, 'Environmental Degradation and Population Flows' (1994) 47(2) *International Affairs* 473; and many more.

[7] El-Hinnawi, *Environmental Refugees*, above n. 5.

[8] Myers and Kent, *Environmental Exodus*, above n. 6, at 18–19.

[9] Gaim Kibreab, 'Climate Change and Human Migration: A Tenuous Relationship' (2009) 20 *Fordham Environmental Law Review* 395.

'traditional habitat, traditional homeland, habitual residence'. In all the definitions the element of force, life and quality of life is either expressly stated or implied. Despite the identified similarities, it appears to me that Kibreab's definition is fundamentally different to the author's view of EDP, because even though he used the phrase 'forced or obliged to migrate', he referred to avoiding the effects of 'armed conflict, situations of generalized violence, violations of human rights or natural or human-made disasters within same country'. It is only the idea of 'natural or human-made disasters' that relates to core EDP. El-Hinnawi's and Myers and Kent's definitions are closely related, because they both used the concept of 'semi-permanent or permanent movement'. However, it is significant to clarify the use of the phrases 'environmental disruption' by El-Hinnawi and 'environmental factors' by Myers and Kent. Environmental disruption or disturbance means any event or series of events that disrupt the ecosystem, community or population structure and alters the physical environment,[10] and environmental factors are an identifiable element in the physical, cultural, demographic, economic, political, regulatory or technological environment that affects the survival, operations and growth of an organization.[11] This implies that the concept of environmental factors used by Myers and Kent is wider.

El-Hinnawi further described three major types of environmental refugees: those temporarily displaced due to disasters; those permanently displaced due to drastic environmental changes; and those who migrate based on the gradual deterioration of environmental conditions.[12] Bates[13] criticized El-Hinnawi's description as being too broad, and gave a more detailed categorization of the different situations that fit El-Hinnawi's broad description of disasters, expropriations and deterioration. Disaster refugees originate in acute events that are not designed to produce migration; expropriation refugees result from acute anthropogenic disruptions in the environment that intentionally dislocate target populations; and deterioration refugees migrate as a result of gradual, anthropogenic

---

[10] See Mimi Environment, 'Terms of the environment', available at http://en.mimi.hu/environment/disturbance.html.

[11] *Business Dictionary*, see www.businessdictionary.com/definition/environmental-factors.html#ixzz3QCsfZuXm.

[12] El-Hinnawi, *Environmental Refugees*, above n. 5, but his study was about environmental refugees.

[13] Diane C. Bates 'Environmental Refugees: Classifying Human Migrations Caused by Environmental Change' (2002) 23(5) *Population and Environment* 465, available at http://pubfin.nccu.edu.tw/faculty/calin/doc/environmental_refugees.pdf.

changes in their environment to a point where people cannot survive on the local resource base. For Bates, the classification provides clear criteria for identifying distinct types of migrants motivated by environmental changes and which distinguishes those EDPs who are refugees from those who voluntarily migrate because of environmental problems. On her part, Cudiamat[14] opined that EDPs should be described as 'displaced persons', not refugees as used by El-Hinnawi,[15] because refugees move outside their countries. For Cudiamat, 'displaced persons' includes externally and internally displaced persons (IDPs) and therefore will effectively encompass all people who have been displaced by environmental causes. They could be refugees or IDPs. Cudiamat[16] thus proposed the following definition of EDP to:

> apply to any person who, as a result of a natural disaster, gradual environmental changes, and/or human-induced environmental stressor that threatens his life or physical integrity, is forced to relocate elsewhere because of the incident, and is unable to seek aid from the country where he has relocated to, or the country of his nationality, if the relocation is internal.

Cudiamat's definition appears more in-depth because it encompasses most of the descriptions given in the three earlier definitions. It included 'gradual environmental changes' as classified by El-Hinnawi and this is at the core of this chapter because many times, oil-related pollution increases gradually. It also includes 'natural disaster, and/or human-induced environmental factors or disruptions' as contained in El-Hinnawi's and Myers and Kent's definitions. It also contains 'forced relocation or threats to life' as contained in other definitions above. A major advancement in Cudiamat's definition is the inclusion of 'environmental stressor' which seems to the author to be wider because it includes problems caused by environmental issues and its consequences. According to the *Business Dictionary*, environmental stress is pressure on the environment caused by human activities such as pollution or by natural events.[17] On the other hand, this proposed definition appears vague when adding 'and is unable to seek aid from the country where he

---

[14] Nicole Angeline Cudiamat, 'Displacement Disparity: Filling the Gap of Protection for the Environmentally Displaced Person' (2012) 46 *Valparaiso University Law Review* 891, available at http://scholar.valpo.edu/vulr/vol46/iss3/7.

[15] El-Hinnawi, *Environmental Refugees*, above n. 5.

[16] Cudiamat, 'Displacement Disparit', above n. 14.

[17] *Business Dictionary*, see www.businessdictionary.com/definition/environmental-stress.html#ixzz3QCt1Pddt.

has relocated to, or the country of his nationality, if the relocation is internal'. In my opinion, the ability to seek aid should not be part of the definition of EDP, as being able to seek aid will not remove the fact that the person is environmentally displaced.

I will therefore adopt Cudiamat's proposed definition in part. I will say that EDP applies to any person who, as a result of a natural disaster, gradual environmental changes, and/or human-induced environmental stressor that threatens his life or physical integrity, is forced to relocate elsewhere.

Having looked at the meaning of EDP, the next question is: do Niger Deltans relocate because of the socio-economic impacts of pollution and, if they do, are they actually displaced? At this point, it is noteworthy that environmental factors are closely linked to socio-economic factors. As observed by Boano, environmental factors seem to be closely linked to economic, social and political factors therefore it is difficult to isolate displacement through purely environmental means.[18] As Boano observed, socio-economic factors caused by pollution are linked to the environment, therefore displacement can be caused by a combination of both.

Coming to the question of whether Niger Deltans are actually displaced, I will analyze this using El-Hinnawi's and Bates' classifications. Their classifications, as discussed earlier, show that environmental degradation can cause either voluntary or involuntary migration. Voluntary migrants mainly migrate because of social, economic or environmental problems, especially on recognizing that their local situation will deteriorate,[19] while involuntary migrants are forced to relocate. To El-Hinnawi, those permanently displaced due to drastic environmental changes are involuntary migrants and those who migrate based on the gradual deterioration of environmental conditions are voluntary. My argument is that gradual environmental deterioration can cause involuntary migration. To Bates,[20] migration is conceptualized as a continuum, with people who have absolutely no control over their relocation representing the right-hand end, labelled involuntary, and people with control

---

[18] For further discussion, see Camillo Boano, Roger Zetter and Tim Morris, *Environmentally Displaced People: Understanding the Linkages Between Environmental Change, Livelihoods and Forced Migration*, Forced Migration Policy Briefing 1 (2008), available at www.rsc.ox.ac.uk/files/publications/policy-briefing-series/pb1-environmentally-displaced-people-2008.pdf.

[19] E.F. Kunz, 'The Refugee in Flight: Kinetic Models and Forms of Displacement' (1973) 7 *International Migration Review* 124.

[20] Bates, 'Environmental Refugees', above n. 13.

over the decision to migrate to the left, labelled voluntary. Hugo[21] placed relocation from environmental disasters at the involuntary end of the continuum, and relocation as a result of the gradual deterioration of the environment at the voluntary end. Hugo, however, argued that there is no major difference between voluntary and involuntary movement, as even voluntary migration often occurs where the migrant actually has little or no choice.[22]

The third element of the continuum are people with more control over the decision to migrate, which is closely related to what King argued to be voluntary-forced continuum[23] because they are vulnerable with limited time and few resources.[24] Voluntary-forced continuum is further described as being either proactive or reactive. Proactive movement[25] is anticipatory migration based on the recognition of deteriorating conditions, while reactive movement is acute and unplanned, as migration is to ensure survival. Proactive movement mainly involves migrants and reactive movement involves displaced persons, but there are situations where this distinction is difficult to make, according to King.[26] Environmental degradation is a good example, as on many occasions it starts slowly, but may lead to both proactive and reactive responses. It is proactive when people migrate to safer or more productive locations because of decreasing quality of life, and reactive when others are forced to leave when the degradation reaches a threshold at which the damage becomes irreversible or the environment can no longer support them.[27]

The perspective which I adopt is that of King,[28] who concluded that slow onset problems create environmental migrants, and both slow and acute onset problems create EDPs. With that in mind, I will delve into the factual situation in the Niger Delta to determine if the Niger Deltans are environmental migrants or EDPs.

---

[21] Hugo, 'Environmental Concerns and International Migration', above n. 6.

[22] Ibid. 106.

[23] Tracey King, 'Environmental Displacement: Coordinating Efforts to Find Solutions' (2006) 18 *Georgetown International Environmental Law Review* 559.

[24] Ibid.

[25] What Suhrke calls response to both 'push' and 'pull' factors. See Suhrke, 'Environmental Degradation and Population Flows', above n. 6.

[26] See King, 'Environmental Displacement', above n. 23.

[27] Suhrke, 'Environmental Degradation and Population Flows', above n. 6, at 485.

[28] King, 'Environmental Displacement', above n. 23, at 556.

III NIGER DELTA SITUATION

A wide literature has drawn a distinction between environmental migrants, environmental refugees, IDPs and EDPs.[29] The question is: are relocated Niger Deltans migrants, environmental refugees, IDPs or EDPs? To answer this question, I will look at the situation in the Niger Delta. It will be discussed under two sub-headings: oil-related pollution in the Niger Delta and the socio-economic and societal impacts of pollution.

(1) Oil-related Pollution in the Niger Delta

The aim here is to establish the presence of oil-related pollution in the Niger Delta without an in-depth analysis, which is not the focus of this chapter. Oil-related pollution in Nigeria is mainly caused by spills; flares and effluent discharge with spills being the major cause. Frequent spills occur every year in the Niger Delta,[30] with figures varying depending on sources.[31] These spills are mainly caused by sabotage, equipment failure and operational failure/human error, with sabotage spills[32] being widely claimed to cause most spills.[33] On equipment failure, the Nigerian Oil Pipelines Act, 1969, and the Environmental Guidelines and Standards for the Petroleum Industry in Nigeria 2002 (EGASPIN) require companies to

---

[29] Kunz, 'The Refugee in Flight', above n. 19; Bates, 'Environmental Refugees', above n. 13; Hugo, 'Environmental Concerns and International Migration', above n. 6.

[30] Shell alone reported an average of 220 spills in 2008–2009, and an average of 201 between 2011 and 2013. See Shell Petroleum Development Company, 'Oil Spills in the Niger Delta', available at www.shell.com.ng/environment-society/environment-tpkg/oil-spills/monthly-data.html. From January to August 2014, Shell also recorded 120 spills in the Niger Delta: Shell Petroleum Development Company, 'Oil Spills in the Niger Delta', available at www.shell.com.ng/environment-society/environment-tpkg/oil-spills/monthly-data.html.

[31] For instance NNPC, DPR, SPDC all have different figures.

[32] Ibaba Samuel Ibaba and John C. Olumati, 'Sabotage Induced Oil Spillages and Human Rights Violation in Nigeria's Niger Delta' (2009) 11(4) *Journal of Sustainable Development in Africa* 51, available at http://jsd-africa.com/Jsda/V12NO2_Winter2009_B/Pdf/Sabotage%20Spillages%20and%20Human%20Rights%20-%20reviewed.pdf.

[33] Shell Petroleum Development Corporation, for instance, blamed 40 per cent of oil spills resulting from its operations in 2000 on sabotage: see Shell Petroleum Development Company, *People and the Environment, Annual Report 2000*; see also Shell oil spill data 2011–2014; 'How We Respond to Spills',

check and maintain oil infrastructure, with a requirement for monthly inspection of pipelines.[34] But according to Steiner's research,[35] the state of the pipelines of SPDC in particular is poor. Also Essential Action stated:

> In addition to the grave problems associated with gas flares, on-site oil leaks and ruptured pipelines are a serious problem in the Niger Delta. Decrepit pipelines, some reportedly over 40 years old, criss-cross villages and land, some of them above the ground. These pipes are rusty and in obvious need of repair.[36]

In some cases, spills are not cleaned up, therefore increasing pollution and economic problems.[37] Apart from spills, Nigeria flares about 14.6 per cent of produced gas, the second highest amount in the world after

---

available at www.shell.com.ng/environment-society/environment-tpkg/oil-spills.html, or www.shell.com.ng/environment-society/environment-tpkg/oil-spills/data-2015/monthly-data.html. See also 'Oil giant blames thieves and militants for the spilling of nearly 14,000 tons of crude oil into the Niger Delta last year', *Guardian*, 5 May 2010, available at www.theguardian.com/environment/2010/may/05/shell-oil-spill-niger-delta; Rowena Mason, 'Nigeria oil spill payouts would encourage terrorism, Shell claims', *Daily Telegraph*, 26 January 2011, available at www.telegraph.co.uk/finance/newsbysector/energy/oilandgas/8284806/Nigeria-oil-spill-payouts-would-encourage-terrorism-Shell-claims.html.

[34] Amnesty International also requested copies of SPDC monthly inspection reports between January 2008 and May 2011 without success.

[35] Richard Steiner, *Double Standard: Shell Practices in Nigeria Compared with International Standards to Prevent and Control Pipeline Oil Spills and the Deepwater Horizon Oil Spill 11* (2010), available at www.milieudefensie.nl/publicaties/rapporten/double-standard.

[36] Henry Clark *et al.*, *Oil for Nothing: Multinational Corporations, Environmental Destruction, Death and Impunity in the Niger Delta* (Essential Actions and Global Exchange Trip Delegation Report, 1999), available at www.essentialaction.org/shell/Final_Report.pdf.

[37] SPDC official in 2001 alleged saboteur paid Shell-employed guards to abandon their posts, causing serious spill in Ughelli Delta State in 2001. See Centre for Energy Economics, *Environmental Catch-22 in Nigeria* (Case study report, Austin, TX), available at www.beg.utexas.edu/energyecon/new-era/case_studies/Environmental_Catch_22_in_Nigeria.pdf; Robyn Dixon, 'Nigeria oil spills have created ecological disaster', *Los Angeles Times*, 5 August 2011, available at http://articles.latimes.com/2011/aug/05/world/la-fg-nigeria-oil-20110805; Shell, 'We Won't Pay Compensation for Oil Spill Caused by Sabotage', *Vanguard Newspaper*, 27 January 2011, available at www.vanguardngr.com/2011/01/we-wont-pay-compensation-for-oil-spill-caused-by-sabotage-shell/.

Russia.[38] World Bank and UNDP 2004 Report shows that Nigeria loses about US$2.5 billion annually to gas flaring.[39] This has socio-economic and health implications,[40] however, this chapter focuses on the socio-economic implications and these will be discussed next.

(2) Socio-economic Impacts of Pollution and Situation of Violence in the Niger Delta

The socio-economic impacts of oil-related pollution include destruction of tourism facilities and reduction in hospitality industries; destruction of cultural areas; conflicts;[41] violent clashes with police; forced evictions and displacements;[42] and even deaths,[43] among other social problems. It has impacted on the traditional respect for elders, because constant polluting activities brought about a closeness between oil companies and elders, sometimes resulting in clean-up contracts which caused conflict between the elders and the youth, ending in disintegration of customs, traditions and social values. Pollution has also led to conflicts between communities and individuals and the oil companies.[44] Also, pollution has

---

[38] For figures, see http://web.worldbank.org/WBSITE/EXTERNAL/TOPICS/EXTOGMC/EXTGGFR/0,,contentMDK:22137498~pagePK:64168445~piPK:64168309~theSitePK:578069,00.html.

[39] Joint UNDP/World Bank Energy Sector Management Assistance Programme, *Strategic Gas Plan for Nigeria* (2004), available at www.esmap.org/sites/esmap.org/files/Rpt_27904_Nigeria_GasPlan.pdf.

[40] Environmental Rights Action estimated that in one Niger Delta region alone, flaring is statistically likely to cause 49 premature deaths, 5,000 respiratory illnesses among children, 120,000 asthma attacks and eight additional causes of cancer each year. See Environmental Rights Action and Friends of the Earth Nigeria, *Gas Flaring in Nigeria: A Human Right Environmental and Economic Monstrosity* (ERA/FOE Reports, June 2005), available at www.foe.co.uk/sites/default/files/downloads/gas_flaring_nigeria.pdf.

[41] The conflicts are between different segments: within and between communities, conflict between the communities and the oil companies, and conflict between armed groups and the oil companies and Nigerian security forces.

[42] Cyril Obi, 'Oil Extraction, Dispossession, Resistance, and Conflict in Nigeria's Oil-Rich Niger Delta' (2010) *Canadian Journal of Development Studies* 30.

[43] The hanging of Ken Saro-Wiwa with eight other MOSOP members is a problem indirectly caused by pollution.

[44] In 1990, the Etche people demonstrated against Shell at the village of Umuechem because they had seen Shell continually exploit their land without adequate compensation. The Mobile Police Force was called and they massacred 80 people and destroyed 495 houses, vehicles and motor-cycles, and killed and

given rise to occupational disorientation of host communities, increased poverty, and eventually aggression amongst community members, therefore causing more conflict. Furthermore, hardship caused by oil pollution has given rise to prostitution.[45] It had also caused the destruction of cultural areas and spirituality, especially with slow responses to spills.[46] Medicinal plants[47] and herbs had been killed, with fishing and farming culture destroyed.[48]

In addition, agricultural and farm lands had been damaged, which affects the quality of crops;[49] and fishery and wildlife have also been damaged, destroying the Niger Deltans means of livelihood. The damage caused to fishery and agriculture also affects incomes, because many people are commercial fishermen and farmers. With pollution, profits and business subsistence are lost as farming and trading in agricultural and other goods to sustain families becomes almost impossible. Grace Ekanem, a women's group leader in Eket, Akwa Ibom State, said that since farms are failing, palm trees not bearing fruit and fish washed-out, women can no longer feed their families and cannot earn enough money to send their children to school, or to afford medical treatment for them.[50] Amnesty International also found that several Bodo people could not sustain their families after spills in 2008 and 2009. According to their report on Bodo, one commercial fisherman said:

---

ate all the livestock of the villagers. See also the Chevron Nigeria Ltd and United Ufuoma Fish Farmers Association conflict as reported by Emma Amaize, 'Nigeria: pollution in Niger Delta: oil firm, fish farmers fight', *Vanguard Newspaper*, 8 August 2010, available at http://allafrica.com/stories/201008090688.html.

[45] Essential Actions and Global Exchange, *Oil for Nothing,* above n. 36, at 10.

[46] Bodo spill of 2008 and 2009 is a clear example. According to Amnesty International's report, an investigation visit was not conducted until after at least ten weeks. When Amnesty International conducted its research in May 2011, Bodo people were still asking for a clean-up. See Amnesty International, *The True Tragedy: Delays and Failures in Tackling Oil Spills in the Niger Delta* (2011), available at www.amnesty.cz/zakazdoucenu/doc/Niger-Delta-True-Tragedy-Report.pdf.

[47] These medicinal plants are symbols of traditional medicine and spirituality with strong spiritual significance to most communities.

[48] Amnesty International, *The True Tragedy*, above n. 46, at 18.

[49] Ibid.

[50] Essential Actions and Global Exchange, *Oil for Nothing*, above n. 36, at 10.

> my youngest daughter is supposed to be at school ... but because we are not able to, she is now here with us. Most of our children are not at school because their fathers were perpetual fishermen. [T]here are no other jobs here, because there is no industry in Ogoniland where people can get a job. All the fish, all the sea is polluted so you can't go fishing.[51]

Also, with the destruction of biodiversity, the agricultural sector, which is the largest employer of labour in the Niger Delta, is being destroyed, therefore most people are jobless, cannot afford nutritious food or cannot afford food at all. The ultimate result is food shortage, forcing Niger Deltans to buy their food and fish at high prices or relocate if they cannot afford to buy. Given that locals are disadvantaged when compared with the purchasing power of salaried oil company employees, who are paid comparatively well by Nigerian standards, many could be forced to go without food.

With hunger and starvation, unemployment, dwindling economy, frustration and many other problems, and with little or no social security in place in Nigeria,[52] living conditions worsen by the day for the Niger Deltans. With questionable access to justice, Niger Deltans started forming groups to protest against this degradation and this moved from non-violent to violent movements. One major group is the Movement for the Survival of the Ogoni People (MOSOP) which was formed by Ogoni people in 1990 to campaign in a non-violent manner.[53] The dimension changed from peaceful to violent protest, which saw the establishment of groups like the Ijaw National Congress, Kaiama declaration, Niger Delta People's Volunteer Force (NDPVF) and Movement for the Emancipation of the Niger Delta (MEND), and many more. With all these troubles, the quality of life of average Niger Deltans continues to diminish. The consequences of all this have been uprisings and heightened insecurity. The death tolls that usually follow most of these uprisings have been appalling. Part of the reason why the Odi Community was destroyed on the instructions of the then Nigerian President was their quest to stop environmental degradation.[54] One Ogoni community held a peaceful

---

[51] Amnesty International, *The True Tragedy*, above n. 46, at 16.

[52] No free education, no free health services and many other issues.

[53] Movement for the Survival of the Ogoni People, 'About MOSOP', available at www.mosop.org/about_us.html. This movement led to the death of Ken Saro-Wiwa with eight other MOSOP members.

[54] Environmental Rights Action and Friends of the Earth Nigeria, *A Blanket of Silence: Images of Odi Massacre* (2002), available at www.eraction.org/publications/silence.pdf. Also, 27 villages were raided in Ogoni, Bayelsa State, resulting in the death of around 2,000 people and the displacement of

demonstration and the Mobile Police Force were sent, which resulted in two deaths and destruction of around 40 houses, rendering around 350 people homeless.[55]

Apart from the organized movements and groups, young people discovered other means supposedly capable of delivering a meaningful livelihood, which have caused more problems. Some young people turned to the ills of kidnap, militancy, vandalism and associated vices. This was more especially the case given the perceived unfortunate attitude of both the multinational oil companies and the Nigerian government. Youths began scooping[56] from spilled oil and found it an easier way of ensuring survival. From scooping fuel, other activities developed, such as pipeline vandalism and the siphoning of petroleum products. Vandalism increased steadily: according to Onuoha,[57] a special committee on the review of petroleum product supply and distribution in 2000 reported that there were only seven reported cases in 1995, about 909 in 2000, and this had increased to 2,258 in 2005. From vandalism, some people moved on to oil bunkering, which is a more sophisticated way of getting and selling petroleum products. Amnesty International's research on the Bodo Community,[58] revealed that the youths had taken to illegal activities to earn a living, including stealing crude oil and even illegally refining oil after the 2008 oil spill. Because of the breakdown of traditional respect for elders, their attempts to dissuade the young fell on deaf ears.[59] With all these activities, there is now unimaginable levels of pollution.

80,000–100,000, with more than 2,000 Ogoni people being forced to escape to neighbouring states.

[55] Environmental Rights Action, *Shell in Iko: The Story of Double Standards* (1995), A. Rowell, *Green Backlash, Global Subversion of the Environment Movement* (Routledge, 1996), p. 294. See also Andy Rowell, James Marriott and Lorne Stockman, *The Next Gulf: London, Washington and the Oil Conflict in Nigeria* (Constable and Robinson, 2005).

[56] Fuel scooping arose during the military rule, initially involving unemployed youths mostly in remote areas where spills occur. They were even somewhat advantaged during the era of fuel scarcity as there were ready buyers in the Nigerian market.

[57] Freedom Onuoha, 'Oil Pipeline Sabotage in Nigeria: Dimensions, Actors and Implications for National Security' (2008) 17(3) *African Security Review*, available at www.issafrica.org/topics/environmental-security-and-climate-change/01-sep-2008-oil-pipeline-sabotage-in-nigeria-dimensions-actors-and-implications-for-national-security-99-freedom-c-onuoha.

[58] Amnesty International, *The True Tragedy*, above n. 46, at 18.

[59] Ibid.

Following on vandalism, scooping and bunkering, kidnapping started to occur. Kidnapping was initially aimed at disturbing oil exploration activities, but over time, it assumed a dangerous and criminal dimension. This remains one of the most threatening criminal problems in Nigeria today. Commenting on the trend of kidnap in *Sola Odunfa*'s editorial, Onyeka Chibuife said:

> We Nigerians have built the very bomb that is exploding in our eye, when men like Ken Saro Wiwa were protesting diplomatically about the danger these corrupt oil firms constituted. [sic] We crossed our legs, sat at home and watched on television and still in the mist of all this we forget that it's this oil firm that are giving birth to these problems.[60]

From kidnapping, the youths moved on to militancy and terrorism. The militancy has led to the spate of bombings that started with the bombing of oil facilities, but progressed to bombing of arenas of public gathering. The first major bombing of a public place was the Independence Day bombing in Eagle Square, Abuja on 1 October 2010, for which Henry Okah was charged in a South African court and was convicted earlier in 2013.[61] This raised an important point: Henry Okah was one of the leaders of the militant groups[62] that started up as a result of oil-related pollution. Considering the whole problem, Okonkwo concluded:

> After few years of struggle for 'environmental justice' as defined by the global North and faced with the political realities on the ground that led to the death of Ken Saro-Wiwa, the Odi massacre and other acts of brutality, the game plan moved back to economic survival. As a result the present acts of kidnapping and armed militancy.[63]

Hon. Justice Inko-Tariah said:

> Their streams get polluted … rendering the river void of fishes … their farm crops planted on the remaining areas of farmland get damaged by oil pollution; their economic trees are hewed down; their economic situation bites

---

[60] 'Viewpoint: Is kidnapping easy money?', *BBC News Africa*, 20 July 2010, available at www.bbc.co.uk/news/world-africa-10684541.

[61] Henry Okah, 'Nigerian oil militant jailed for 24 years', *BBC News Africa*, 26 March 2013, available at <www.bbc.co.uk/news/world-africa-21937985.

[62] Movement for the Emancipation of the Niger Delta.

[63] Churchill Okonkwo, *The Preconditions for Environmental Justice and Peace in Niger Delta, Nigeria* (Nigeria Village Square, March 2009), available at www.nigeriavillagesquare.com/articles/churchill-okonkwo/the-preconditions-for-environmental-justice-and-peace-in-niger-delta-nigeria.html.

and there is no help for them. These deprivations without any compensatory benefits cause frustration … The compensations paid for these deprivations are just pittance, meagre pittance, on which people cannot subsist for even six months and they become frustrated with life.[64]

The ultimate result of the impacts is community destruction, displacements, migration and the rise of EDPs. On many occasions, youths and sometimes other able-bodied adults have been cut down in their prime while engaging in violent crime or scooping fuel from highly inflammable oil pipelines.[65] With the foregoing analysis, I agree with Opukri and Ibaba[66] when they argued that environmental degradation is responsible for many displacements in the Niger Delta communities. They pointed out, and I agree, that the collapse of local economies, induced by pollution, has displaced many people from their occupations, without providing viable alternatives.[67] And according to Pyagbara, many migrate to cities to become environmental refugees.[68] The dangerous consequence is that due to their poor economic status, they take up accommodation in shanties, slums and waterfronts, with their attendant risks. Some are then even rendered homeless, as the government demolishes these shanties.[69] With constant spills, poor response and clean-up, recovery takes much longer; some Niger Deltans therefore perpetually live in a polluted environment, and by extension with perpetual shortages, which has triggered social problems, which have in turn resulted in

---

64 *Commission of Inquiry to the Causes and Circumstances of the Disturbances that Occurred at Umuechem in the Etche Local Government Area of Rivers State Nigeria* (1990).

65 Pipeline explosion in Ilado, Lagos in May 2006 led to more than 200 people incinerated in the pipeline fire; 1998 Jesse pipeline fire killed around 1,200 villagers; and in the recent PPMC fire incident in Ogun state at least 30 people died. '30 Nigerians killed in fresh oil pipeline fire', *PM News*, 12 January 2013, available at http://pmnewsnigeria.com/2013/01/12/30-nigerians-killed-in-fresh-oil-pipeline-fire/.

66 C.O. Opukri and Ibaba Samuel Ibaba, 'Oil Induced Environmental Degradation and Internal Population Displacement in Nigeria's Niger Delta' (2008) 10(1) *Journal of Sustainable Development in Africa* 173, available at www.jsd-africa.com/Jsda/V10N1_Spring2008/PDF/OilInducedEnvDegr.pdf.

67 See also Amnesty International, *The True Tragedy*, above n. 46, at 18. With few local job opportunities, many have been forced to look for work in Port Harcourt, the state capital.

68 Legborsi Pyagbara, *Minority Rights, Development and Migration: The Case of the Ogoni People* (2004).

69 Integrated Regional Information Networks, *Nigeria: Demolition Plans Bring New Ethnic Twist to Port Harcourt Conflict* (28 August 2007).

proactive or reactive movements (using Suhrke's[70] analysis) or in the voluntary-forced continuum (using that of King).[71] Thus, a steady increase of problems caused either pollution or its effects. Some people endured to some extent and moved proactively, others could no longer endure and moved reactively. A good example of reactive movement was an explosion from the Total gas plant in 2012 that forced people to move. According to Environmental Rights Action's report, one victim of Obite Community said:

> My wife and children were here when I traveled but when I returned they had relocated to stay elsewhere ... because of the gas leakages around us.[72]

Given the facts described above and some earlier researches,[73] it is safe to conclude that oil-related pollution in the Niger Delta has caused environmental displacement. The next question is: are the Niger Deltans displaced as refugees or IDPs?

According to the 1951 United Nations Convention on Refugees and its 1967 amendment, refugees are defined as people with 'a well-founded fear of being persecuted for reasons of race, religion, nationality, membership of a particular social group or political opinion'. This is not the case of Niger Deltans and in my opinion cannot apply. IDPs on the other hand is defined by the United Nations Guiding Principles as:

> persons or groups of persons who have been forced or obliged to flee or to leave their homes or places of habitual residence, in particular as a result of or in order to avoid the effects of armed conflict, situations of generalized violence, violations of human rights or natural or human-made disasters, and who have not crossed an internationally recognized State border.[74]

---

70 Suhrke, 'Environmental Degradation and Population Flows', above n. 6, at 485.

71 King, 'Environmental Displacement', above n. 23.

72 Caposud, *Nigeria: Total/Elf's Facility Causes Multiple Gas Eruptions in Egiland* (3 May 2012), available at http://caposud.wordpress.com/2012/05/03/nigeria-totalelfs-facility-causes-multiple-gas-eruptions-in-egiland/.

73 See Amnesty International, *The True Tragedy*, above n. 46, and UNEP Report on Ogoniland, available at http://postconflict.unep.ch/publications/OEA/UNEP_OEA_ES.pdf, and many other works on continued deterioration.

74 See www.ifrc.org/Docs/idrl/I266EN.pdf.

Although the definition has been criticized,[75] it appears closer to EDPs as it relies on involuntary migration. Opukri and Ibaba[76] observed that the central element in the description of IDP is involuntary migration, however they argued that voluntary migration in search of means of livelihood or economic survival due to occupation displacement/losses can also qualify as internal displacement.[77] This reinforces the voluntary-forced continuum earlier discussed.[78] My interpretation is that people may migrate internally or externally, but once it is environmentally induced, they will qualify as EDPs. In the case of Niger Deltans, they migrate either because of pollution, stressors of pollution or environmental factors caused by pollution. The facts described above also showed that some displaced persons are subjected to threats to their physical health and are deprived of basic subsistence when they live in shanties which are sometimes demolished. This is a denial of their fundamental human rights to life, subsistence, healthy environment, and many other things. Having established that the Niger Deltans' fundamental human rights are affected, we then ask if they are legally protected and if so how?

IV PROTECTION OF THE ENVIRONMENTAL DISPLACED VERSUS THE RIGHTS OF THE DISPLACED NIGER DELTANS

By virtue of several legal frameworks[79] regulating the Nigerian oil industry, one would be inclined to believe that degradation should be at

---

[75] Kalin said that it offers 'a descriptive identification of the category of persons whose needs are the concern of the Guiding Principles; therefore non-exhaustive'. See W. Kalin, 'Guiding Principles on Internal Displacement Annotations' (2000) *Studies in Transnational Legal Policy* 32. See also UN Office for the Coordination of Humanitarian Affairs, *Guiding Principles on Internal Displacement*, UN Doc. E/CN.4/1998/53/Add.2 (1998); M. Vincent, 'IDPs: Rights and Status' (2000) *Forced Migration Review* 30.

[76] Opukri and Ibaba, 'Oil Induced Environmental Degradation', above n. 66.

[77] Ibid.

[78] King, 'Environmental Displacement', above n. 23.

[79] They include the Petroleum Act, 1969, and the Regulations made under it: Mineral Oil Safety Regulation, 1962; Oil Pipeline Act, 1965; Hydrocarbon Oil Refineries Act, 1965; Oil in Navigable Waters Act, 1968; Oil Terminal Dues Act 1969; Associated Gas (Reinjection) Act, 1979; Environmental Guidelines and Standards for the Petroleum Industry in Nigeria 2002; National Oil Spill

its lowest ebb.[80] However, existing researches and evidence shows heavy environmental degradation in the Niger Delta[81] now causing environmental displacement. Despite the fact that Niger Deltans are environmentally displaced, it is not clear how they are protected. This work neither shows any specific Nigerian legislation nor any international norms/principles or guidelines that deal specifically with EDPs. More important to note is that displaced persons do not form a juridical category either in international or domestic law. This might explain why they are only described in the UN Guiding Principles, though they have been included in the mandate of United Nations High Commissioner for Refugees (UNHCR) since 1975.[82] Having no juridical category creates a protection gap for the EDPs. Some scholars have attempted to fill in the gap for recognized displaced persons. King suggests the creation of an international body to specifically address EDPs, including existing organizations like UNEP, the UNDP, the International Office of Migration, UNHCR and the UN Office for the Coordination of Humanitarian Affairs.[83] McCue[84] and Prieur[85] have both argued for a separate Convention. McCue discusses the adoption of an international convention from an international environmental law standpoint to outline the duties of countries to prevent environmental disasters; minimize the damage; provide information prior to an impending environmental disaster; and compensate for injuries sustained.[86] The proposed Convention has been criticized for not addressing the issues of people who are forced to migrate because of environmental stressors.[87] Prieur's draft Convention

---

Detection and Response (Establishment) Act, 2006; and Petroleum Industry Bill 2012 (still with the National Assembly).

80 It is doubtfully the case.

81 There are several research studies which have exposed a high level of oil-pollution incidents. Among them are: UNEP, *Environmental Assessment of Ogoniland Report* (2012), available at www.unep.org/disastersandconflicts/CountryOperations/Nigeria/EnvironmentalAssessmentofOgonilandreport/tabid/54419/Default.aspx; Amnesty International, *The True Tragedy*, above n. 46; Essential Actions and Global Exchange, *Oil for Nothing*, above n. 36.

82 See www.unhcr.org.

83 King, 'Environmental Displacement', above n. 23, at 559–64.

84 Gregory S. McCue, 'Environmental Refugees: Applying International Environmental Law to Involuntary Migration' (1993–94) 151 *Georgetown International Environmental Law Review* 179.

85 Michael Prieur, 'Draft Convention on the International Status of Environmentally-Displaced Persons' (2011) 42–43 *Urb. Law* 250.

86 McCue, 'Environmental Refugees', above n. 84.

87 Cudiamat, 'Displacement Disparity', above n. 14, at 928.

itemizes EDPs' rights, requiring states to develop domestic law procedures that recognize the official legal status of the EDPs, and Prieur calls for the creation of a world agency to address the EDP issues and the implementation of the draft Convention.[88] This has also been criticized for being too advanced a beginning of protection of EDPs for the international community to accept.[89] At the moment there thus appears to be no viable legal principle to really protect EDPs. So what next?

With no acceptable legal principle in force, one asks the fate of the Niger Deltans. My research has brought to the fore a few legal principles, laws and regulations which could be used to protect the EDPs. The first is the 1999 Constitution of Nigeria that deals with the fundamental rights of every citizen.[90] Also, the African Union Convention for the protection and assistance of IDPs in Africa (Kampala Convention) 2009,[91] which entered into force on 6 December 2012, could be useful. It was the first legally binding regional instrument that imposed obligations on states to protect IDPs. However, the strongest clause for the protection of displaced people due to pollution is Article 10 on displacement induced by projects. Although it was ratified by Nigeria on 17 April 2012, it is yet to be domesticated, and therefore is not binding.

Apart from the Kampala Convention, the 1998 UN Guiding Principles on Internal Displacement may be applicable. These deal with persons or groups of persons who have been forced or obliged to flee or to leave their homes for reasons including natural or human-made disasters and violations of human rights within their state.[92] The challenges faced by these Guiding Principles include the fact that under their own wording they are not legally binding, and with a lack of political will or resources, their implementation has not been very successful. They also do not specifically deal with environmental displacement.

With no adequate legal frameworks, international or regional conventions which are clearly applicable, there is a protection gap for the Niger Delta EDPs. Signed instruments have not been domesticated, international laws do not adequately protect the EDPS, and successive Nigerian governments have not shown any real interest in improving protection for EDPs. There is urgent need for adequate legal protection

---

88 Prieur, 'Draft Convention on the International Status of Environmentally-Displaced Persons', above n. 85.

89 Cudiamat, 'Displacement Disparity', above n. 14, at 929.

90 Chapter 4, s. 33 deals with right to life.

91 Refworld, see www.refworld.org/docid/4ae572d82.html.

92 UN Guiding Principles on Internal Displacement, available at www.brookings.edu/~/media/Projects/idp/GPEnglish.pdf.

for the EDPs, but as Cudiamat has argued, EDPs cannot be protected unless they are legally identified.[93] This is because current definitions appear merely an appendage to the refugee protection.

How then can adequate protection for Niger Delta EDPs be secured? Protecting EDPs can start with protection of their rights, especially human rights, such as right to life, clean and healthy environment,[94] social and economic life. Right to life is very important; it has been adjudged the most fundamental right and has been widely interpreted to mean more than mere physical existence, including the right to a healthy environment. Principle 1 of the Stockholm Declaration 1972 established a foundation for linking human rights, health and environmental protection to life when it stated that: 'Man has the fundamental right [to] adequate conditions of life, in an environment of a quality that permits a life of dignity and well-being'. Also confirming this relationship, Judge Weeramantry of the International Court of Justice in 1997 said:

> The protection of the environment is … a vital part of contemporary human rights doctrine, for it is a sine qua non for numerous human rights such as the right to health and the right to life itself. It is scarcely necessary to elaborate on this, as damage to the environment can impair and undermine all the human rights spoken of in the Universal Declaration and other human rights instruments.[95]

It has also been interpreted as relying on a risk that is actual or imminent[96] and this includes displacement caused by environmental

---

[93] Cudiamat, 'Displacement Disparity', above n. 14, at 933.

[94] Human rights instruments particularly relevant to this work are the Universal Declaration of Human Rights (UDHR) 1948, Art. 3 which is the model for many human rights instruments; International Covenant on Civil and Political Rights (ICCPR) 1966; International Covenant on Economic, Social and Cultural Rights 1966; Convention on the Elimination of All Forms of Discrimination Against Women 1981; Convention on the Rights of the Child 1989; African Charter of Human and Peoples' Rights 1981; International Labour Organization's Convention No. 169 on the Rights of Indigenous People 1991; and UN Declaration on the Rights of Indigenous Peoples 2007.

[95] The Asia Pacific Forum of National Human Rights Institutions, Human Rights and the Environment, *Background Paper Prepared for the Consideration of the Advisory Council of Jurists APF* (2007), p. 55, available at www.mcmillan.ca/Files/SOCarroll_HumanRightsandtheEnvironment.pdf.

[96] Ibid. See also S. Glazebrook, 'Human Rights and the Environment' (2009) *Victoria University Wellington Law Review* 40.

problems. This is also recognized as a principle of customary international law and in many international treaties,[97] therefore should be protected even by the state.[98] Regarding right to life and EDPs, Cudiamat said that it is a central tenet of international law and is of particular concern to refugees, internally and environmentally displaced persons.[99] Niger Deltans' quality of life is affected by displacement and their land rights are also affected, leading to social and economic marginalization[100] breach of their human rights. Therefore Niger Deltans can challenge the infringement under the Universal Declaration of Human Rights and African Charter on Peoples and Human Rights 1981. They can also challenge the destruction of their subsistence lifestyle through the International Covenant on Economic, Social and Cultural Rights,[101] the 1999 Constitution of the Federal Republic of Nigeria, and many more.

V CONCLUSION AND RECOMMENDATIONS

Following the discussion herein, there is an urgent need to protect the EDPs caused by oil pollution in Nigeria.

First, there is a need for a new framework to be built on internationally agreed principles that will be legally enforceable. The framework should establish the rights that must be protected and the obligations of states parties. The Guiding Principles on Internal Displacement could be developed to include environmental damage that forces people to migrate, which in essence includes oil-related pollution.

There is also a need to adopt and implement the Guiding Principles by strengthening the international machinery which makes countries accountable, through compliance monitoring and reporting to international agencies such as the UN High Commissioner for Refugees, UN

---

[97] See the UDHR, Art. 3, and the ICCPR, Art. 6(1).

[98] See *Oneryildiz* v. *Turkey*, Application No. 48939/99, European Court of Human Rights (2004).

[99] Cudiamat, 'Displacement Disparity', above n. 14.

[100] M.M. Cernea, 'Understanding and Preventing Impoverishment from Displacement: Reflections on the State of Knowledge' (1995) 8(3) *Journal of Refugee Studies* 33.

[101] UN General Assembly Resolution 2200A (XXI), Supp. 16, Art. 15(1)(a). See *SERAC/CESR* v. *FGN*, Judgment of the African Commission on Communication 155/96, para, 66, where the African Commission held that the Nigerian government violated the fundamental human rights of the Ogoni by allowing private oil companies to destroy food sources, see www.cesr.org/nigeria.

High Commission on Human Rights and International Committee of the Red Cross.

There is also a need to strengthen policies by integrating government plans and strategies and enhancing coordination between national government ministries.

Establishment of non-governmental organizations aimed at defending the interests of the EDPs because of oil pollution production should also be encouraged.

Nigeria should develop protection norms and legal instruments for people displaced by environmental pollution, both the national and international government should be involved. Priority should be given to developing policies and norms for their protection, ensuring their needs are met using the 1998 Guiding Principles on Internal Displacement as the foundation.

There is also the need to implement regional and international instruments which provide for normative protection for displaced people, including the African Charter. Moreover, it is necessary to explore ways of developing applicable guidelines, policies and frameworks for protection measures, as well as development of professional expertise both legal and operational in human rights protection and environmental rights.

In the interim, Niger Deltans should consider challenging the oil companies for infringing their fundamental human rights, including their right to life, healthy environment, cultural rights, destruction of their subsistence, and many more. They could also challenge the Nigerian government for failing to protect their rights by directly or indirectly encouraging infringement of their rights by the oil companies leading to their displacement. Such an interim proposed solution would hopefully be successful pending enactment of suitable laws and implementation of my other recommendations.

14. Agriculture, energy and development: an uneasy relationship*

Cristiane Derani

'Civilization is the economy of power'

Justus von Liebig[1]

I AGRICULTURAL AND ENERGY PRODUCTION

The structure and dynamics of agriculture and food production in the world economy change in accordance with the modification of global production and distribution of market shares and capabilities among countries and regions. As a source of food and energy and as the basis for human life, agricultural production has adjusted its development and organization according to the migratory movements into urban areas that occurred in the nineteenth century. Furthermore, it assumes specific features in order to satisfy the demand of the urban-industrialized market of the second half of the nineteenth century. Today, agricultural production has come to be oriented by the conversion of the economy into an instrument of financial investment, something which has occurred with all economic activities.[2]

Due to this delicate correlation between agricultural modes of production and social and economic organizational structures, this chapter argues that any discourse of the right to energy sustainability in agriculture has to reflect the reorganization of global market relations that

* I would like to thank professor Eckard Rehbinder from J.W. Goethe Universität Frankfurt am Main for his valuable insights on the present chapter. I also extend my gratitude to him for the willingness to proofread my writings.

1 Kenneth M. Stokes, *Paradigm Lost: Cultural and Systems Theoretical Critique of Political Economy* (M.E. Sharpe, 1995), p. 131.

2 Eric J. Hobsbawm, *The Age of Capital: 1848–1875* (Weidenfelt and Nicolson, 1975).

condition food and timber production, and thus consider how to handle the contention for land between food and so-called biofuels.

This chapter starts by showing how the history of food production follows transformations in international commercial relationships, incorporating technologies and changing preferences until it links to the financial market and follows its dynamics. Fast but profound changes in a span of less than a century were followed by a substantial increase in energy consumption. This did not go unnoticed by the General Assembly of United Nations, who approved Resolution A/67/314, which states that there is a necessary interconnection between energy consumption and economic relationships between countries; and that contemporary agriculture has a high-energy consumption and needs to change, to ensure energy sustainability. Furthermore, the above-mentioned Resolution underlines that the relationship between food security and energy is of fundamental importance. Links between energy and food security are now stronger than ever. The food sector accounts for approximately 30 per cent of the world's total energy consumption, with the agro-food chain emitting approximately 20 per cent of total greenhouse gas emissions (point 45).

The next section brings in a very realistic perspective from the economist Georgescu-Roegen, who had the sensibility, still in the middle of the twentieth century, to understand how production can be summed up as a continuous and irreversible consumption of energy. Based on the statements of this economist, we can establish the foundations for a juridical way of thinking which will result in a agricultural production of low-energy consumption, at a local and global level. Once the theory of Georgescu-Roegen is understood, we are forced to reconsider the meaning of 'renewable energy', since all human activity is a unique and inevitable process of energy consumption, which has as one of its products the unrecoverable dissipation of energy. To achieve a society of less entropy, in other words with less energy dissipation, it is essential that the matter of energy sustainability be approached within the commercial dynamics strengthened at the end of the twentieth century.

Within the phenomenon known as globalization, world trade has created a web of economic interdependence, making the whole world sensitive to any change in the commercial processes in any of its parts. This connection is at the same time what limits the autonomy of countries to decide their own economic policies and what allows for economic changes to spread so easily. By understanding the economic process as an energy flux of consumption and dispersal, the search for a more sustainable agriculture implies changes to the global commercial logic, to be built by normative directives.

Sustainability is not built through the choice of energy sources, but through the investigation of the flow of such energy: where it moves, for what it is used, which goods are generated and which waste is produced, who takes advantage of such flows, what is its real contribution to improving life relations.

The last section of the chapter focuses, therefore, on the thesis that energy sustainability requires changes in the international juridical system/framework of trade. International law is in this sense indispensable to change economic structures which are highly energy-dissipative. The energy issue is an environmental and economic problem which should be dealt with under a common juridical system/framework. This understanding is essential in the direction of international relations, as well as in the economic-environmental policies to be developed internally by countries.

II MARKET AND AGRICULTURE

Agriculture is rather sensitive to the development of changes in human relations. It is a support to cultural expressions, facilitates adjustments to working time and structure, to mobility and housing, and even favours equalization of preferences and habits, helping to improve relations of production and consumption. It is possible to trace changes of agriculture during human changes in the formation of the industrialization process.

During the industrialization process, there was an increase of crop fields around emerging cities. The industrialization of food production was especially clear after the so-called second Industrial Revolution, when the trade of food expanded throughout the world. Pushed by the Second World War, the twentieth century witnessed the emergence of entirely new ways of producing food and distributing it all around the world; however, this has brought up new concerns regarding rural workers, subsistence agriculture, and their conflicts with farmers practising industrialized commercial agriculture. All of them struggled for subsidies and free trade. Trade flows brought a new format to the agricultural industry.

The second half of the twentieth century after the Second World War saw a great change in the structure of agricultural production, especially in countries where agriculture is one of the major sources of exports. An attempt was made to increase mechanization and so reap benefits from the economies of scale seen in industry, namely, the cost per unit decreasing as production increases; however, even though the little employment generated by the heavy infrastructure of large land holdings is low paid, there are costly diseconomies of scale, which in turn generally requires state subsidies.[3]

More extensive crops aimed at supplying the growing urban population replace peasant agriculture. Large agricultural belts are established near big cities. The urban population was previously dissatisfied with the rewards offered by peasant agriculture, which was subject to weather instabilities and seasonal limitations. The increase in coal-powered and later oil-powered transportation opened wide access to food. The goods on offer increased and the quality improved. At this point, agricultural activity started to require a high quantity of energy for transportation and crop conservation. It is in the post-war period that the new agricultural revolution occurred on the basis of extensive mechanization and intense industrialization accompanied by the application of chemical fertilizers, pesticides and preservatives.[4]

In order to increase the scale, agriculture is concentrated in the hands of business owners who offer their harvest as agricultural commodities for the valuation of their enterprises by the financial markets. From that stage on, agricultural activity is ready to be an arm of financial activity, which then guides production, location, cultivation methods and the development of the markets, including, of course, the prices for agricultural commodities. This is how economic globalization presents itself in the field of agriculture.[5]

---

[3] The development mechanisms of the second agricultural revolution, in an agriculture governed by prices, appear to be particularly effective. Nevertheless, this type of development is neither easy nor harmonious nor entirely positive. It encounters many difficulties, gives rise to disadvantages and excesses of all sorts and can even lead to actual failures: disequilibria of markets and fluctuations in prices; inequalities between farms and between regions; unequal development of some farms, crisis, poverty, and elimination for others; massive exodus, abandonment of whole regions and unemployment; attacks on the environment and on the quality of products; genetic degeneration of some domestic species and reduction in the biological diversity of ecosystems, etc. That is why, throughout this vast transformation that has generally been encouraged by the governments of the developed countries, these same governments have also implemented diverse policies aimed at removing the difficulties, limiting the disadvantages, and avoiding or correcting the excesses and failures. Marcel Mazoyer and Laurence Roudart, *A History of World Agriculture* (Earthscan, 2006), pp. 422–3.

[4] Ibid. Rachel Carson, *Silent Spring* (Houghton Mifflin Harcourt, 2002).

[5] So-called neoliberal policies, which have been dominant in the world since the end of the 1970s, only worsen the general crisis. In developing countries, these policies are expressed by the abandonment of auto-centered development strategies, based on public investments aimed at satisfying the internal market by the production of import-substitution goods, and by the

The agricultural face of globalization shows a spatial concentration of food, feed and biomass production areas, which requires a complex web of transportation and distribution. Increasing urbanization, decreasing fertility of soils, climate change with extremes of droughts and heavy rain, are causes and effects of the movement that leads to the spatial concentration in agricultural production. The impoverishment of the varieties of agricultural plant species is a result of the homogeneity of crops that result from stimulating production initiatives by the prices of commodities.[6] Developing countries are especially sensitive to this transformation, as the strength of their trade balance rests on agricultural production.

The form of production thus implemented is necessarily one of high consumption of energy and material. There is a massive energy input, from the beginning of production, in the raw material industries, to the consumer's table. The consumption of raw materials is also high and these are dissipated in the production process, exhausting the capacity to recover. The extinction of biodiversity, depletion of soils and acidification

---

adoption of external-oriented development strategies, based on private investments from many sources, attracted by low wages and focused on exports. These new strategies, encouraged by the World Bank and other development institutions, widen the field for relocations, although they do not increase world demand. In developed countries, policies for full employment and maintenance of high levels of public and private demand were abandoned and replaced by policies of generalized deregulation and denationalization, which widen the possibilities for capital to move and profitably invest without proportionately expanding global demand for consumer goods. These neoliberal policies favoured the explosion of speculation in financial markets, derivative markets, and currency exchange markets. In the mid-1990s, it is estimated that 90 per cent of the transactions on the exchange markets were speculative in nature. And, since there no longer exists an international system for regulating exchange rates and financial flows, each country is constrained to adopt policies that aim to maintain the parity of its currency and attract or retain capital, which is henceforth mobile and sensitive to the least risk and the least variation in the rates of return on capital. To do that, it is advisable to limit inflation and reduce deficits, both the public deficit and the deficit in the balance of payments current account. That explains the convergence of economic policies in the developed countries and the conformism of the thinking that justifies those policies. Mazoyer and Roudart, *A History of World Agriculture*, above n. 3, at 481.

[6] According to the FAO, 95 per cent of human food needs are satisfied by only 30 cultivated species, four of which (rice, wheat, maize and potato) are responsible for more than 60 per cent of our energy intake. See FAO, *Biodiversity for a World Without Hunger: Plants* (2011), available at www.fao.org/biodiversity/components/ plants/en/.

of oceans causes high entropy, which amounts to the destruction of structures of wealth that can no longer be restored. Matter is dissipated into lost energy, giving rise to a world that has a smaller energy potential.[7]

Agribusiness is a heavy structure with a high demand for resources and energy in both production and distribution. It starts at the farm and continues through all the phases that make the food edible and accessible to consumers worldwide. Similar processes occur with respect to feed and biomass production. The use of energy and the externalities are not expressed directly in the costs of the present production, they are shifted into the future. The next crops will have to deal with the additional costs incurred in the search for new energy sources, soil reconstruction and management of water scarcity.

While traditional forms of agricultural production continue to exist, partly due to the needs of small regions and direct food supply necessities, the overwhelming majority of arable land assumes the appearance and logic of big industries. Globalized economies require concentration of capital and specialization of production. In the field of agriculture, the increased demand for food, animal feed and biomass has required industrialized regions to get their crops from far away, developing a web of business relationships far beyond their territory. This would not be a bad deal if two essential elements are not left aside, one economic and the other ecological, which are liable to make the apparently comfortable commercial exchange structure implode.

From the economic perspective, looking at comparative advantages, any gains a country has through the concentration of its exports of raw materials such as grain and other agricultural commodities will *ab initio* be lost if the country in turn needs to acquire the bulk of industrialized products from abroad. Furthermore, it will be necessary to continuously increase production in order to mitigate the negative effect on the trade balance. Other burdens include continuous governmental support in the form of subsidies and concentration of credits on infrastructure such as roads, ports and electricity. As biomass for energy production is an essential component of the expansion of modern agriculture, countries with more available land and a weak industrial or services sector will definitively be tempted to embrace this system of agribusiness, especially because a large share of the invested capital are public goods, a gift of mother nature which can be consumed for private profit. Agricultural

---

[7] See Nicolas Georgescu-Roegen, *The Entropy Law and the Economic Process* (Harvard University Press, 1971).

goods built mostly by natural capital have no value until they become commercial goods, those so-called commodities that are priced without taking nature into account. This free appropriation of essential raw material for food and biomass production revokes the beliefs of free trade as a place for price adjustment and fair competition as a consequence of it.

Considering these facts, the ecological perspective gains prominence. Excessive appropriation of so-called public goods has resulted in the decrease of fertile soils, loss of biodiversity and climate change with extremes of drought and rain.[8] The concentration of food, feed and biomass production for distribution all over the world is an energy-intensive process. Despite the economic disadvantages and intensive use of ecological systems, this global web of food, feed and biomass production and commerce is in itself completely inefficient in terms of energy use – the main point of this chapter.

III ENERGY POLICY, MARKET AND AGRICULTURE

The United Nations proclaimed 2012 as the international year of sustainable energy for all, recognizing that sustainable development is not possible without sustainable energy.[9] The UN Secretary-General's *Report on International Year of Sustainable Energy for All* (A/67/314), presented at the General Assembly of the United Nations on 16 August 2012, was aimed at creating an appropriate environment at all levels for the promotion of universal access and more efficient use of energy, as well as to generate an increasing use of renewable energy.

The text brings important messages about strategies to be developed. Referring to UN Resolution AG/65/151, it sums up the demands that supported the declaration of the International Year of Sustainable Energy for All, of which the following are worthy of mention: modern energy services for all; access to affordable energy; energy efficiency; and the

---

[8] IPPC, *Special Report of the Intergovernmental Panel on Climate Change* (2012), available at www.ipcc.ch/pdf/special-reports/srex/SREX_FD_SPM_final.pdf.

[9] The Secretary-General, in his speech, defined three major objectives of the United Nations regarding the energy issue, to be reached by 2030: (i) ensuring universal access to modern energy services; (ii) doubling the global rate of improvement in energy efficiency; and (iii) doubling the share of renewable energy in the global energy mix (*Sustainable Energy for All: A Global Action Agenda, Pathways for Concerted Action Towards Sustainable Energy for All*, A/67/175), available at www.un.org/depts/dhl/deplib/docs/ITP/A67-PARTI.pdf.

sustainability of energy sources and use, for the achievement of the internationally agreed development goals, including the Sustainable Development Goals,[10] sustainable development and the protection of the global climate, and to promote action at local, national, regional and international levels.

In promoting new renewable energy sources, the Resolution warns that UN member states should deal both with the sustainability of energy sources and its use for development and climate protection. Although subtle, the Resolution is clear in stating that sustainability is not achieved only through the search for renewable energy sources, but that it is important to seek sustainability in conservation, energy efficiency and above all in the use of the energy generated.

The pathway towards energy sustainability requires the development of systems that support the optimal use of energy resources in an equitable and socially inclusive manner while minimizing environmental impacts. Integrated national and regional infrastructures for energy supply, efficient transmission and distribution systems, and demand programmes that emphasize energy efficiency are necessary for sustainable energy systems (point 7). According to Resolution A/67/314, what is needed is a transformation of the world's energy systems to address these interconnected challenges and thus benefit all countries (point 10).[11]

Equally important is the following statement in the above-mentioned Resolution: the Food and Agriculture Organization (FAO) seeks to address the challenges related to a food sector that accounts for approximately 30 per cent of the world's total energy consumption and is responsible for 20 per cent of total greenhouse gas emissions, by improving energy efficiency at all stages of the agro-food chain, increasing the use of renewable energy, and improving access to modern energy services through integrated food and energy production. The FAO is also leading the development of an international community of practice in this area as well as a facility for the improved coordination of efforts at the national and international levels (point 46).

At the current stage of development of agricultural practices due to urban and industrial demands, a remarkable facet is the high-energy expenditure of agriculture, which can be attributed to the application of industry's 'economies of scale' rationale to agricultural production. This

---

[10] Open Working Group, *Proposal for Sustainable Development Goals*, 'Goal 7, Ensure access to affordable, reliable, sustainable and modern energy for all', available at https://sustainabledevelopment.un.org/content/documents/1579SDGs%20Proposal.pdf.

[11] UN General Assembly Resolution, A/67/314 (16 August 2012).

results in the increase of cultivated areas, high mechanization and search for increased productivity per cultivated area, and the insertion of inputs from the chemical industry.[12] This gain in units produced allows increased food exports, permeating the globe, freeing humans from seasonality and climate constraints on food supply.

Agriculture is only one aspect of a highly energy-demanding production web. Alternative energy sources, mainly those derived from cultivated biomass, are sought and start to compete with cultivated soil for food, hazarding the purpose of expanding food production. In the 1980s, food agriculture was predominant in agro-business, especially in countries with extensive arable land, with the aim of generating the most units of food at the lowest cost and reaching a larger consumer market. Twenty years' later, food agriculture finds its limits in the competition for space for biomass production that is often heavily subsidized by states eager to improve their energy base.[13]

The desirable sustainability of energy in this production structure should be based on both the inflow of energy for the construction and maintenance of the system, and the entire flow of energy in the form of water, nutrients, light, ranging from production to agricultural products for food, feed and power generation. This energy flow for moving the factors of production and generating the product is consumed during the process and needs to be regenerated to prove sustainable. Also essential are the considerations about the purpose of what is produced. According to the document of the United Nations Conference on Sustainable Development, entitled 'the future we want', it is the goal of sustainable development to end hunger and achieve food security, promoting sustainable agriculture. This goal highlights the aspects of productivity, developing agricultural food systems and resilient agricultural practices, respectively.[14] If this primary aim is not earnestly encompassed in the national and regional policies for the production of biomass for energy

---

[12] See Mazoyer and Roudart, *A History of World Agriculture*, above n. 3; and Carson, *Silent Spring*, above n. 4.

[13] See *Biomass and Agriculture Sustainability, Markets and Policies* (OECD, 2004), available at www.oecd-ilibrary.org/agriculture-and-food/biomass-and-agriculture_9789264105546-en; *Analysis of the Scope of Energy Subsidies and Suggestions for the G-20 Initiative* (OECD, 2014), available at www.oecd.org/env/45575666.pdf.

[14] 'We acknowledge that food security and nutrition has become a pressing global challenge and, in this regard, we further reaffirm our commitment to enhancing food security and access to adequate, safe and nutritious food for present and future generations' (at 108). UN General Assembly Resolution 66/288 (27 July 2012).

generation or for any other destination of arable land, it will be lost in the black hole of beautiful statements without any concrete application.

With this preliminary understanding, one must broaden the view beyond exploited territorial strata and seek sustainable energy at a biosphere scale beyond the purely local one. What may seem sustainable locally, on a broader scale may demonstrate a shift towards unsustainability, when, for example, the product is viewed separately from material waste generated by its production and use, and energy consumed by its production and movement. Sustainable development as a political and normative concept demands putting together the understanding of energy sources and use, food security, biodiversity conservation – notably all measures relating to the consequences of climate change – in order to encompass its complex task. Through practical considerations of this kind, it is possible to speak of energy efficiency in a complex manner beyond the reductionism of a merely quantitative perspective. In the global market, energy efficiency must find a balance between the idea of complete liberalization of markets and the initiation of a process and products with a high level of entropy.

The regulatory architecture works as the balancing point for decisions on different practices of production, trade and consumption. Requirements based on the complete framework of material and energy flow of a productive process, its outcome in the form of products and energy dispersion associated with destruction of matter, may establish a perspective of sustainability of energy.

IV PRODUCTION THROUGHPUT

Understanding environmental problems, even at a simple level, requires some appreciation of the concepts and methods employed by disciplines other than law. In turn, law is shaped by the results of research in these different fields, with legal regulation and legal activities (for example, standard setting, enforcement, prosecution) supported and legitimized by the work of biologists, chemists, economists and engineers. Most importantly, environmental law is also underpinned by cultural assumptions, the sources of which – philosophies, popular culture, ecological theories – are diverse and sometimes obscure, but arguably no less influential than those from the more traditional scientific domains.[15]

---

[15] Jane Holder and Maria Lee, *Environmental Protection, Law and Policy* (2nd edn, Cambridge University Press, 2007).

To this effect, we depart from the understanding of the process of construction of the current production system and trade in agricultural commodities and move on to visualizing the energy flow within the productive process. The reflection about the flows of energy sources relies on an unwavering assumption that there is a need for concrete consideration about what is effectively offered and the consequences of appropriation of the elements offered. Even at a time when techno-science is the king colonizing the mental spaces, human beings do not stray away from the basic truths of their existence: sources of life are appropriated and not produced.

On the basis of this assessment, one must recognize the fact that human societies are given the possibility of appropriation of nature. This appropriation is carried out in a manner that is shaped culturally and historically by every society. It is not a production activity, in the sense of inaugural creation. It is a reproduction, based on the taking of resources and their employment in society's project for the production of assets, which can be qualified as more or less efficient, as long as such sources of reproduction will remain available to the society with the best use and the least social, ecological and economical cost.

Energy is at the foundation of human organization. The way in which humans acquire it and make use of it characterizes every social organization, especially its mode of economic production. Thus, any structural change made to energy sources, to the destination of energy, its conservation, dissipation or reuse, will impact on the structures of economic, cultural and social organization.

Human beings do not produce, rather, they appropriate and direct material and energy towards specific ends. In this process of transformation, what enters the economy consists of natural value resources and what is rejected consists of waste without value. This qualitative difference is assessed by economist Georgescu-Roegen from the view of thermodynamics. From the standpoint of thermodynamics, the energy or matter that is absorbed by the economic process occurs in a state of low entropy (appropriate free energy), and comes out in a state of high entropy (energy held in non-reusable chaotic disorder).[16]

According to the second law of thermodynamics, entropy (in other words, the quantity of bound energy) of a closed system increases constantly. In other words, the order of this system is continuously transformed into disorder. From such a perspective, the cost of every

---

[16] Georgescu-Roegen, *The Entropy Law and the Economic Process*, above n. 7.

biological or economic enterprise is always larger than the product created. Therefore, there is no way of talking about energy balance or homeostatic flow of energy and matter. In terms of entropy, the economic activities are necessarily conducted at a deficit.[17]

No energy insertion process is renewable, inasmuch as once used energy cannot be rearranged for reuse as it is dissipated. Likewise, matter used in the production process cannot be restored to its primeval form. The minerals that make up the machines and the means of transportation, the converted forests, the eliminated species, the organic matter disaggregated by the removal of protection, contamination or overuse of soil, can no longer be rearranged. Whatever may be recycled will require more energy, which will be dissipated from its source and will irreversibly change the environment.[18]

Therefore, the sustainability of productive activity should be sought in influencing the quality and quantity of the deficit generated: that is, considering that no activity is possible without definitive implications of changes in the environment, one must check what changes are better absorbed and how much change can be tolerated. Such considerations are important in order to avoid the word 'sustainability' from misleading people to believe that it is a zero sum game. This belief would be remote from the comprehension of the real movement of energy and matter, the simple mechanical rationale of inputs and outputs, with arithmetic calculations of how much would be possible to be transformed and how much of waste generation would be possible to be generated and assimilated without harming the environment. By the same token, the expression 'renewable energy' is misleading because from the perspective of thermodynamics there is no energy renewal because once dissipated, energy does not reorganize itself.[19]

The expression 'renewable energy' suggests that the energy source can be used for longer and more times because the process of dissipation does not lead directly to the depletion of its sources, as happens to oil as a source of fuel. For this reason, solar and wind energy are classic examples of renewable energy because their sources are inexhaustible. However, the fundamental question arises of whether the generated

---

[17] Nicholas Georgescu-Roegen, *O Decrescimento: Entropia-Ecologia-Economia* [in English: *The Degrowth: Entropy, Ecology, Economy*] (Senac, 2013), p. 60.

[18] See Elmar Altvater, *The Price of Welfare* (Verlag Westälisches Dampfboot, 1992).

[19] Georgescu-Roegen, *The Entropy Law and the Economic Process*, above n. 16 and *O Decrescimento*, above n. 17.

energy would be renewable, that is, capable of being indefinitely reproduced. The answer to this question is a negative one. Even if the use of solar and wind energy is optimized, its use for increasing disposable products, insertion of chemicals in the soil, water, food and indirectly humans hampers the renewal of previous states, substantially diminishing the idea of sustainability. Therefore, the sustainability of energy must be sought in its use, beyond the consideration of the energy source.[20]

The modern economy was built over two centuries, based on a mechanistic thought of movement of resources and products. The underlying idea was that these movements would be reversible. However, with no past, no future, no historical, geographic, cultural or ecological boundaries and in a complete abstraction from the concrete movement of matter and energy, the economic production formed inconsiderate and irreversible processes. It expropriated the future of access to matter and energy, reshaped the environment available, impoverished it and relegated to allegorical reminiscence the strength of diversity and availability of matter and energy that will never equate with the matter and energy provided by the previously existing environment. The qualitative changes promoted by the economic process have a direction in time and are irreversible. The production system transforms the raw material into goods that are valued by society, the use of which generates some type of waste which does not go back into the production chain.

There is no society without production of means of life. Similarly, there is no production without energy consumption. Our society is highly energy-intensive, which drives us to seek energy sources that bring continued enjoyment of the necessities created by an energy-hungry lifestyle. It becomes clear that during this search, the energy that is more intensively used in the reproduction of the economic process and for contemporary conveniences is a high producer of externalities that are the source, among other adverse impacts, of the climate change phenomenon. Fossil fuel energy sources release greenhouse gases into the atmosphere capable of preventing the return of solar radiation back into space.

---

[20] Speaking at the World Day to Combat Desertification (17 June 2014), Secretary-General Ban Ki-moon stated: 'The world is losing 24 billion tons of soil due to erosion, while 2 billion hectares of land are degraded, undermining efforts to increase food production and combat hunger, which affects 842 million people. That is while we waste 1.3 billion tons of food, which would be enough to feed 2 billion people and whose production in crops generates greenhouse gas emissions that adversely affect the climate, which are a major cause of erosion and desertification'.

With this framework, even considering the existing alternatives associated with lower impacts, namely, wind, solar and biomass sources, there is a clear need for drastic change in the patterns of energy consumption. Sustainability is not built through the choice of energy sources, but through the investigation of the flow of such energy. In short, it is important to consider energy sustainability from its flow in the economic process. The more complex understanding of what supposedly are energy efficiency and sustainability is implied in considering Georgescu-Roegen's assertion, presented nearly half a century ago. According to the economist, it is no longer possible to talk about 'sustainable growth', even 'zero growth' or 'steady state'. In order to ensure humanity's sustainable survival in the biosphere of our planet Earth, 'de-growth is unavoidable'.[21]

Based on this statement, law, by guiding the choice of alternatives for the use of energy in the process of reproduction of human life and in the building of values, has in principle the task to present ways and means that reflect an orientation of a radically different economic development. The construction of a legal framework for energy use must go beyond efficiency and redirection towards cleaner sources. An energy policy for the people has to reflect the framework conditions of the biosphere of the planet to which humans as a cooperative species of the living world belong.[22]

V TOWARD AN ENERGY-ORIENTED MARKET

Economic theory collects a variety of myths. One of them and arguably the strongest in the international politics of trade relations is that the most liberalism will generate the highest benefits for states because it generates higher profitability for companies. In the pursuit of achieving this ideal, traces of negative externalities are being left in the form of exclusion of competitors, isolation of productive sectors, waiving manual labour and pressure on natural resources. To mitigate these consequences other myths are created: the myth that humans can always find new sources of energy and resources, and new ways of harnessing them for their benefit.[23]

---

[21] José Eli da Veiga, 'A Condição biofísica do desenvolvimento' [in English: 'The Biophysical Condition of the Development'] in Georgescu-Roegen, *O Decrescimento*, above n. 17, at 16.

[22] Georgescu-Roegen, *O Decrescimento*, above n. 17, at 45.

[23] Ibid.

These myths are supported by another myth, that of the '*homo economicus*', which is believed to be driven by the pursuit of maximizing advantage and inspired by the possibility of continual economic gains in its activities. The human interest in profits is undoubtedly one aspect of a multifaceted and complex reality, however, it is important to accept the limitation of one-dimensional thinking so that policies and standards will not be based solely on these conceptions.

The apparent soundness of such myths is explained by history. The inter-war years showed how nationalism coupled with protectionism can destroy the world economy and fuel armed conflict. The reaction to nationalist authoritarianism was the equally authoritarian theory of liberalism. Both orchestrate the disqualification of divergent ideas and disregard the less radical alternatives. However, virtue still 'lies somewhere in the middle' and still constitutes an ethical assumption and a more balanced recipe for the composition of coexistence between humans. There is a contradiction between the assumptions of motivation and action in a globalized world. Such a fact reveals a belief that the individual will pursue several selfish interests to motivate his or her actions, that is, a plurality of interdependent collective relationships and complex considerations that are not just confined to the exchange of *property rights*.[24] One should not forget that the market environment is also an integrator of societies: cultures, countries and the decisions of investments and production must be compatible with the responsibility regarding this cosmopolitan aptitude. The market environment is much more than a simple framework for the exchange of individual interests.

The market is a social space and any changes that are designed to alter it require a collective commitment. In this broader understanding, myths should be dropped and actions that go beyond the liberal dogma should be taken.[25] The choice of a path for the maintenance of life, with the preservation of the common goods and the assumption of a true global concern for humankind in relation to energy depletion and environmental deterioration, requires a market considerate of all the processes of production of goods beyond the simple plurality of products for choice.

---

[24] See Ronald Coase, 'The Price of Social Costs' (1960) 1 *Journal of Law and Economics* 44.

[25] Herman Daly in his farewell speech from the World Bank (14 January 1994) stated: 'Move away from the ideology of global economic integration by free trade, free capital mobility and export-led growth, and toward a *more nationalist orientation* that seeks to develop *domestic production for internal markets* as the first option, having recourse to international trade only when clearly much more efficient' (original emphasis).

Though seemingly distant, the considerations about the liberal idea of building both world markets and energy sustainability are not only interconnected, but interdependent.[26]

Solving the energy problem and searching for the sustainability of energy use in food production require rewriting economics and commerce in the globalized world, focusing on substantial rules and logic of international commerce and the financial world. As energy is the metabolism of society, all the processes of appropriation, transformation, distribution and consumption of goods must be substantially affected. That said, a normative reconstruction, aiming at a more efficient energy balance in the global market must be built that balances the ideal of complete liberalization of markets with restrictions on, and a modification of, production processes entailing the generation of a high level of energy expenditure. In this sense, the trade-off in the energy mix, the form of production and the technology employed requires compositional structures, international cooperation and regulation at national, regional and international levels.

At the *national level*, countries should adopt mobilizing goals coupled with legally binding emission limits. Some of the following policies may need to be undertaken:

- achieving more sustainable energy production by incentives and taxing, taking credits and fiscal instruments as a legal-economic levelling of market decisions;
- elimination of subsidies for the production of biofuels derived from the crops competing with food crops;
- organization of consumer markets responsive to an energy footprint certification regarding the energy consumption of machines and other equipment, which, thereby, affords the consumer the power to direct the most efficient energy production both in spending and in the energy sources employed;
- more coercive measures, such as regulating the use of energy, for example by introducing emission limits; and
- incentives for food supply that exert less pressure on energy consumption (in other words, food coming from a supply chain with a lower energy throughput).

---

[26] Also from the World Bank Group comes the statement: 'Ending poverty and ensuring sustainability are the defining challenges of our time. Energy is central to both of them'. World Bank, *Sustainable Energy for All: Setting a Vision in Motion* (September 2011), available at www.se4all.org/about-us.

Still at the national level, but also for regional agreements, it is important to think about a way of regulating energy flows in order to direct the production process to a greater energy efficiency.

At the *regional level*, it is extremely important that trade agreements be vectors of joint productive transformations. Regional agreements may entail the following concepts:

- contemplate minimum requirements relating to the use of energy as well as the energy mix for efficiency in the production of goods;
- contain provisions on transfer of more efficient technologies that are associated with less energy expenditure, as well as on transfer of intellectual property rights;
- agree upon an energy mix that is more favourable to the climate and the environment as a whole, reducing the climate pressure on agriculture and industrial processes; and
- introduce a standardization of eco-labels that clearly reflect the pressure on natural resources associated with products and services including the energy mix used, not only based on quantitative and qualitative indicators, but also describing the source and origin of energy source, whether fossil, hydro, biomass or nuclear (what and from where).

At the *international level*, it is important to consider two axes: investment and trade.

Investment agreements are required in order to restrict activities demanding large amounts of energy and requiring the application of the best available technology for an activity.[27] It is important that considerations and regulations related to food safety contemplate requirements regarding the replacement of food crop areas for production of biomass for energy generation. In this sense, aids for development, credit and technology transfer are important guiding instruments of agricultural activity in developing countries.

---

[27] Although some progress related to environmental protection can be found in the North Amercian Free Trade Agreement, Jorge Viñuales concludes: 'The growing role assigned to the private sector in global environmental strategies – particularly in the context of the transition to a green economy – is, to a limited extent, mirrored by the growing space left for environmental considerations in investment and free trade agreements (IIAs). Concretly, however, the synergies between foreign investment and environmental protection are only now starting to be seriously explored'. See Jorge Viñuales, *Foreign Investment and the Environment in International Law* (Cambridge University Press, 2012), p. 391.

With specific regard to trade and its regulation, the dogma that dominates the rules and interpretations of the GATT-WTO system has already been stated. Nevertheless, even in the GATT tailor-made system for free trade, arrangements have been made under special international trade treaties: examples include the SPS (Sanitary and Phytosanitary Measures) and TBT (Technical Barriers to Trade) Agreements to allow restrictions based on phytosanitary measures and technical requirements, provided that they do not create unnecessary hurdles to international trade. Other trade agreements relating to the labelling and denominations of origin also put oxygen into the orthodoxy in order to identify qualitative differences in like products. In order to achieve high quality for products and process, free trade is not inconsistent with strong regulation. This regulation inside the WTO demonstrates a positive trend toward a general regulation, highlighting intrinsic differences among products whose likeness are merely superficial.

Based on the already created dynamics of the rule and exception dichotomy of prohibitions of restrictions to free access to the market based on the various agreements within the GATT-WTO system, it is possible to imagine a tendency for a reinterpretation of the notion of like products. One could conceive that a product made with low-carbon emission and employing an energy-efficient method is not alike to the one produced with a high-energy throughput. If consumers are convinced of this intrinsic difference, the doctrine of like products could consider that difference as well. In this perspective, products are not alike in spite of apparently being equal, aiming at the same function or utilization, if they are produced employing different energy sources showing different degrees of efficiency.

A parallel alternative would be to encourage mutual agreements to establish standards related to the technology, the management of natural and energy resources, the demonstration or labelling of the amount of energy used, as well as the sources used throughout the production chain (lifecycle analysis).

We adopt Alex Kiss's observation that trade rules aim to eliminate protectionism and promote free and globalized trade, while environmental measures seek to facilitate conservation or protection of the environment and its basic components. Therefore, the goals of the international trade and environment regimes have clashed in many aspects.[28]

---

[28] Alex Kiss and Dinah L. Shelton, *Guide to International Environmental Law* (Martinus Nijhoff Publishers, 2007), p. 777.

Nevertheless, we are also convinced that without proper adjustment of the environmental protection and international trade regimes, there is no hope for human life on earth in the not-so-distant future. The communication between these systems, the integrated consideration of economic production, development and the environment is the matrix of sustainability.[29] Rules and policies that maintain this isolation are empty representations incapable of influencing behaviours or of changing attitudes.

VI CONCLUSION

Sustainability does not summarize itself in the choices of the energy mix, which would be a challenge in their own. Making only adequate inputs of energy and matter during the entire production process and defining results in terms of energy and matter used and waste generated per product unit should be part of international policy. The instruments required to ensure energy is wisely used must be directed at the search for better allocation of resources and technologies for proper development. This is an ambitious but unavoidable task that demands concerted action by the international community, which must set rules to protect natural resources, ensure technology transfer, achieve fair trade practices, promote foreign investment and specify the principles of common but differentiated responsibility that is inherent in the principle of common concern of mankind and the sovereignty over natural resources.[30]

At the current stage of consumption of natural resources and in all spheres of economic activity, with their constant increase of energy input into the productive processes, pathways of sustainability must be found both in national and international law. Policies and law must take clear

---

[29] See the International Court of Justice (ICJ) decision on the Gabcikovo-Nagymaros Project, *Hungary* v. *Slovakia* (1997), Separate Opinion of Vice-President Weeramantry, para. 88: 'The components of the principle [of sustainable development] come from well-established areas of international law – human rights, State responsibility, environmental law, neighbourliness – to mention a few … It offers an important principle for the resolution of tensions between two established rights. It reaffirms in the arena of international law that there must be both development and environmental protection, and that neither of these rights can be neglected'.

[30] See Sand's and Peel's consideration of whether or not the common concern of mankind is a principle. Philippe Sands and Jacqueline Peel, *Principles of International Environmental Law* (3rd edn, Cambridge University Press, 2012), p. 234.

options for sustainable energy throughput even if apparently they are not, strictly speaking, consistent with international law. Nevertheless, the adoption of new international law norms considering international practice is important where necessary to clarify 'grey areas'. For international law development and effectiveness, a certain 'creative unilateralism' will help to push for a new and important action for an international 'legislative' process. According to Birnie, Boyle and Redgwell, a theoretical justification for 'creative' unilateral action might be a unilateral act which can be *de lege ferenda*, new state practice that may mature into 'opposable' custom under accepted norms of international law. The doctrine of opposability may be a creative agent of change and an important part of the international 'legislative' process.[31]

International environmental law has, since 1972, with the UN Declaration on Human Environment, been prodigious in building guiding principles for human activities that result in a more harmonious coexistence between humankind and the environment. However, the consolidation of these principles into action norms binding countries is not an easy task, even if the problems are urgent and demand an immediate solution, which is the case of the UN Framework Convention on Climate Change. Action founded on the principles of international law and based on the discussions that took place within the international institutions and in Conferences of the Parties should be taken in order to mobilize states toward introducing best environmental policies and rules, even including unilateral internal regulatory measures that have an adverse effect on international trade.[32]

The individual responsibility of every state to take action has been recognized since the Declaration of the United Nations at the Conference on Human Environment in Stockholm. This Declaration also contains the duty to adjust development to the potential offered by the planet without depleting it, but rather saving it for the future.[33] Given the certainty that

[31] Patricia Birnie, Alan Boyle and Catherine Redgwell, *International Law and the Environment* (3rd edn, Oxford University Press, 2009), p. 777.

[32] See the Norwegian Fisheries Case, ICJ, *United Kingdom* v. *Norway* (1949), Individual Opinion of Judge Alvárez, para. 37:'The starting point is the fact that, for the traditional *individualistic* regime on which social life has hitherto been founded, there is being substituted more and more a new regime, a regime of *interdependence,* and that, consequently, the *law of social interdependence* is taking the place of the old individualistic law' (original emphasis).

[33] Principle 4: 'Man has a special responsibility to safeguard and wisely manage the heritage of wildlife and its habitat, which are now gravely imperiled by a combination of adverse factors. Nature conservation, including wildlife,

a set of rules is required to bring about direct changes in the movement of production and circulation of goods, international law with its solid legal structure should establish clear rules that govern the relationship between global commons – global concern of humankind – and international trade, for instance determining the legitimacy of formal discrimination of import of products even in relation to process and production methods. This set of rules has the task to implement changes at the national, regional and international levels described above.

According to Leal-Arcas, a potential synergy between trade and environmental law with particular regard to climate change lies in the principle of common concern of humankind. The concept of common concern was introduced to foster international cooperation and shared responsibility in combating the challenges of climate change and, eventually, other environmental challenges. It refers to a shift in focus from interests of national sovereignty over natural resources towards joint responsibility for specific resources.[34]

Just as climate change has become a common concern of humankind, the energy crisis possesses the same universality, especially because of the high economic interdependence among nations that is caused by intensive international commercial exchange and financial investment. Although national solutions are important, it is equally important to promote a global reorientation of the way humankind solves its energy mix and the intensity of energy consumption during the productive process and consumption. International decisions are often inspired by national or regional matters. Therefore, the exchange of national policies and regulation is substantially important in order to build global regimes, since the ultimate aim is to pursue a common concern.

Underlying decisions about the use of energy is an axiological assumption that every decision regarding energy use today eliminates the use of energy by future generations. According to Georgescu-Roegen:

---

must therefore receive importance in planning for economic development'. Principle 11: 'The environmental policies of all States should enhance and not adversely affect the present or future development potential of developing countries, nor should they hamper the attainment of better living conditions for all, and appropriate steps should be taken by States and international organizations with a view to reaching agreement on meeting the possible national and international economic consequences resulting from the application of environmental measures'.

[34] Rafael Leal-Arcas, *Climate Change and International Trade* (Edward Elgar, 2013), pp. 82–3.

> [o]ne of the major ecological problems of humanity is that of the relationship between the quality of life of one generation and that of another, and more particularly, the distribution of the dowry of humanity among all generations.[35]

Furthermore:

> [t]he only way to protect future generations is by re-educating ourselves so as to feel some sympathy for our future fellow humans in the same way in which we care about the well-being of our contemporary 'neighbours'.[36]

According to the author, this requires an ethical reorientation.

Even conceding the difficulty of setting clear guiding rules for a production process that integrates energy in a less dissipative and more efficient way, national, regional and international actions must be sought in conformity with a common understanding of the need and legitimacy of rules that respect and promote the interdependence and the sustainable coexistence between peoples.

Rules that govern the use of common goods and respect the common concern of humankind should be conceived and respected for their integrative spirit and respect for collective values such as morality, respect for life, equity, solidarity and coexistence. One should even assert the *jus cogens* nature of these principles due to the absolute values that underlie them. Following this rationale, one can advocate more frequent and extensive political action for corrective devices and market adjustment to the new energy reality. The legal grounds that allow this interference in the free market are found in the values of the people in times of global environmental change, which, being a part of the set of rules that ensure respect for life, may expect their future recognition in international law. To reflect upon energy in production and rearrange its flows in an efficient way so as to decrease its use and maximize its material benefits requires a strengthening of the idea of interdependence among peoples and recognition of necessity at all levels of normative construction.

Human conduct must be founded on the key principles for the solution of increasingly more common problems, especially the principle of shared responsibility and the principle of common concern of humankind. The compliance with these principles must be the real aim of improving energy efficiency. This is a concept of intergenerational

---

35 Georgescu-Roegen, *O Decrescimento*, above n. 17, at 125.

36 Ibid. 130.

efficiency based on the understanding of the crucial importance of the energy flow in the productive process. It aims at the non-depletion of resources and energy sources, and thereby at a more balanced and equitable development of economic production – an economic outlook where the compass points towards an overall happier society, discarding the obscure pathway of production of material goods for unlimited satisfaction.

Index